MW00578900

Production and Operations Management

00/01

First Edition

EDITOR

P. K. Shukla
Chapman University

Dr. P. K. Shukla is associate professor of management at Chapman University. He received his bachelor's degree from California State University, Long Beach, his master's degree from the University of Southern California, and his doctorate from the University of California at Los Angeles. He is certified in Production and Inventory Management by APICS—The Educational Society for Resource Management. His research and consulting interests include operational and strategic planning. Dr. Shukla resides in Villa Park, California, with his wife and children.

Dushkin/McGraw-Hill
Sluice Dock, Guilford, Connecticut 06437

Visit us on the Internet
http://www.dushkin.com/annualeditions/

Credits

1. Performance Improvement
Unit photo—courtesy of TRW, Inc.
2. Quality
Unit photo—courtesy of TRW, Inc.
3. Human Resource Management for Productivity
Unit photo—courtesy of General Motors/Buick Motor Division.
4. Forecasting and Product Design
Unit photo—courtesy of NIST Center for Manufacturing Engineering.
5. Capacity, Location, Logistics, and Layout Planning
Unit photo—courtesy Saab-Scania of America.
6. Inventory and Supply-Chain Management
Unit photo—courtesy of TRW, Inc.
7. Emerging Trends in Operations and Production Management
Unit photo—courtesy Motorola Corp.

Copyright

Cataloging in Publication Data
Main entry under title: Annual Editions: Production and operations management. 2000/2001.
   1. Operations research. 2. Production scheduling. 3. Management science. I. Shukla, P. K., *comp.*
II. Title: Production and operations management.
ISBN 0–07–233373–1   658'.4034   ISSN 1525–3627

© 2000 by Dushkin/McGraw-Hill, Guilford, CT 06437, A Division of The McGraw-Hill Companies.

Copyright law prohibits the reproduction, storage, or transmission in any form by any means of any portion of this publication without the express written permission of Dushkin/McGraw-Hill, and of the copyright holder (if different) of the part of the publication to be reproduced. The Guidelines for Classroom Copying endorsed by Congress explicitly state that unauthorized copying may not be used to create, to replace, or to substitute for anthologies, compilations, or collective works.

Annual Editions® is a Registered Trademark of Dushkin/McGraw-Hill, A Division of The McGraw-Hill Companies.

First Edition

Cover image © 1999 PhotoDisc, Inc.

Printed in the United States of America   1234567890BAHBAH543210   Printed on Recycled Paper

Members of the Advisory Board are instrumental in the final selection of articles for each edition of ANNUAL EDITIONS. Their review of articles for content, level, currentness, and appropriateness provides critical direction to the editor and staff. We think that you will find their careful consideration well reflected in this volume.

Editors/Advisory Board

EDITOR

P. K. Shukla
Chapman University

ADVISORY BOARD

Mohammad Ala
California State University, Los Angeles

Neal Bengtson
Barton College

Thomas Callarman
Arizona State University Tempe

Cem Canel
University of North Carolina Wilmington

Richard B. Chase
University of Southern California

Phillip Chong
California State University Long Beach

Leonard Gaffga
Mercer University

Deborah Gibbons
Georgia State University

Edward M. Knod
Western Illinois University

Bill Lightfoot
North Carolina Wesleyan College

Russell Radford
University of Manitoba

Marc Schniederjans
University of Nebraska Lincoln

Sridhar Seshadri
New York University

Staff

EDITORIAL STAFF

Ian A. Nielsen, Publisher
Roberta Monaco, Senior Developmental Editor
Dorothy Fink, Associate Developmental Editor
Addie Raucci, Senior Administrative Editor
Cheryl Greenleaf, Permissions Editor
Joseph Offredi, Permissions/Editorial Assistant
Diane Barker, Proofreader
Lisa Holmes-Doebrick, Program Coordinator

PRODUCTION STAFF

Brenda S. Filley, Production Manager
Charles Vitelli, Designer
Lara M. Johnson, Design/Advertising Coordinator
Laura Levine, Graphics
Mike Campbell, Graphics
Tom Goddard, Graphics
Eldis Lima, Graphics
Juliana Arbo, Typesetting Supervisor
Jane Jaegersen, Typesetter
Marie Lazauskas, Typesetter
Kathleen D'Amico, Typesetter
Larry Killian, Copier Coordinator

To the Reader

In publishing ANNUAL EDITIONS we recognize the enormous role played by the magazines, newspapers, and journals of the public press in providing current, first-rate educational information in a broad spectrum of interest areas. Many of these articles are appropriate for students, researchers, and professionals seeking accurate, current material to help bridge the gap between principles and theories and the real world. These articles, however, become more useful for study when those of lasting value are carefully collected, organized, indexed, and reproduced in a low-cost format, which provides easy and permanent access when the material is needed. That is the role played by ANNUAL EDITIONS.

New to ANNUAL EDITIONS is the inclusion of related World Wide Web sites. These sites have been selected by our editorial staff to represent some of the best resources found on the World Wide Web today. Through our carefully developed topic guide, we have linked these Web resources to the articles covered in this ANNUAL EDITIONS reader. We think that you will find this volume useful, and we hope that you will take a moment to visit us on the Web at **http://www.dushkin.com** to tell us what you think.

Organizations today are faced with challenges to improve performance and to increase customer service. Firms must provide greater quality and faster delivery than ever before and simultaneously reduce costs. Important decisions are required in forecasting demand accurately, human resources management, capacity, location, logistics, and layout planning. Supply-chain management has emerged as a major area of importance for all firms. These challenges are dealt with by the utilization of operations and production management concepts.

The field of production management has its roots in scientific management principles from the early 1900s that were developed when the United States economy was primarily manufacturing-based. As the economy shifted to more service-based and information-based sectors, the focus shifted away from production management to operations management within service organizations. As we see greater globalization, firms must now ensure that they are world class to remain competitive. With the dynamic environment in the field, managers need to keep up with these new developments. This first edition of *Annual Editions: Production and Operations Management* is designed to provide students and managers with a concise review of recent developments in theory and company illustrations of practice.

This publication contains a number of features designed to be useful for managers and students interested in production and operations management. These features include a *topic guide* for locating articles on a specific subject and a *table of contents* with abstracts that summarize each article, highlighting key ideas in bold italics. Also, there are selected *World Wide Web sites* that can be used to further explore the topics. These sites are cross-referenced by number to the topic guide.

This volume is organized into seven units, each dealing with specific interrelated topics in production and operations management. The seven units cover performance improvement; quality; human resources management for productivity; forecasting and product design; capacity, location, logistics, and layout planning; inventory and supply-chain management; and emerging trends in operations and production management. These seven units cover the major decision areas and considerations faced by managers in the field. The units are interrelated and cumulatively provide the reader with concepts of management within both manufacturing and service environments. Each unit begins with an overview that provides the necessary background information and basic core concepts. These unit overviews allow the reader to place the selections in the context of the book. Important topics are emphasized, and challenge questions address major themes.

This is the first edition of *Annual Editions: Production and Operations Management* and it is designed to provide the reader with the most complete and current selection of readings available on the subject. We would like to know what you think. Please take a few minutes to complete and return the postage-paid article rating form at the back of the volume. Any book can be improved, and we need your help to improve *Annual Editions: Production and Operations Management*.

P. K. Shukla
Editor

Contents

UNIT 1

Performance Improvement

Six articles in this section examine
some of the elements in improving
the process of business operations:
reengineering the supply chain,
benchmarking, job design, and
the management of services.

The concepts in bold italics are developed in the article. For further expansion please refer to the Topic Guide and the Index.

UNIT 2

Quality

Seven selections consider job design, tracking quality, effective service strategies, and improving the various job processes.

The concepts in bold italics are developed in the article. For further expansion please refer to the Topic Guide and the Index.

UNIT 3

Human Resources Management for Productivity

Six articles in this section discuss the various challenges faced by human resources when targeting productivity. Some of the topics considered are: job design, product design, supply chain management, and information technology.

The concepts in bold italics are developed in the article. For further expansion please refer to the Topic Guide and the Index.

vii

UNIT 4

Forecasting and Product Design

Four articles in this section assess the importance of new product development, the impact of effective management on the project, the role of forecasting, and the need for improving the necessary processes.

UNIT 5

Capacity, Location, Logistics, and Layout Planning

Seven selections in this section discuss the importance of creating the proper atmosphere for a productive manufacturing company.

The concepts in bold italics are developed in the article. For further expansion please refer to the Topic Guide and the Index.

UNIT 6

Inventory and Supply-Chain Management

Eight articles in this section consider the importance of proper and effective inventory control, the value of Just-in-Time manufacturing, and the general need for a well-designed supply chain system.

The concepts in bold italics are developed in the article. For further expansion please refer to the Topic Guide and the Index.

ix

The concepts in bold italics are developed in the article. For further expansion please refer to the Topic Guide and the Index.

UNIT 7

Emerging Trends in Operations and Production Management

Seven articles in this section look at some of the challenges facing an effective production management system.

Topic Guide

This topic guide suggests how the selections and World Wide Web sites found in the next section of this book relate to topics of traditional concern to production and operations management students and professionals. It is useful for locating interrelated articles and Web sites for reading and research. The guide is arranged alphabetically according to topic.

The relevant Web sites, which are numbered and annotated on pages 4 and 5, are easily identified by the Web icon (◉) under the topic articles. By linking the articles and the Web sites by topic, this ANNUAL EDITIONS reader becomes a powerful learning and research tool.

TOPIC AREA	TREATED IN	TOPIC AREA	TREATED IN
Decisions/ Capacity, Location, Logistics, Layout	23. Airlines May Be Flying in the Face of Reality 24. Is It the Sunshine? 25. No Fizz in the Profits 26. Pulling Customers Closer through Logistics Service 27. Improving Shop Floor Operations through Production Sequencing 28. Changes in Performance Measures on the Factory Floor 29. Using Queueing Network Models 30. Checking in under Marriott's First Ten Program 39. GM: Modular Plants Won't Be a Snap ◉ **4, 5, 6, 9, 19, 27, 28, 29**		42. Digital Denim ◉ **3, 32, 33, 34, 35, 36**
		Job Design	1. Empirical Assessment of the Production/Operations Manager's Job 4. Putting Commitment to Work through Short-Cycle Kaizen 5. Rally of the Dolls 7. Evolution of the Quality Profession 9. Conversation with Joseph Juran 10. One More Time: Eight Things You Should Remember about Quality 12. Whatever Happened to TQM? 13. Critical Implementation Issues in Total Quality Management 15. Million-Dollar Suggestion Box 16. Tellers Who Hustle 17. How Mirage Resorts Sifted 75,000 Applicants 18. Legal Limitations of Self-Directed Work Teams 19. How Great Machines Are Born 30. Checking in under Marriott's First Ten Program ◉ **1, 2, 3, 5, 6, 9, 11, 12, 13, 21, 22, 23**
Forecasting	6. Fly, Damn It, Fly 22. Seven Keys to Better Forecasting 23. Airlines May Be Flying in the Face of Reality 44. Global Six 45. First: The Automakers: More Mergers. Dumb Idea ◉ **6, 7, 8, 24, 25, 26**		
Global Issues	1. Empirical Assessment of the Production/Operations Manager's Job 6. Fly, Damn It, Fly 7. Evolution of the Quality Profession 9. Conversation with Joseph Juran 11. ISO 9000 Myth and Reality 39. GM: Modular Plants Won't Be a Snap 43. Three Decades of Progress 44. Global Six 45. First: The Automakers: More Mergers. Dumb Idea. ◉ **16, 34, 35, 36**	**Managing Services**	7. Evolution of the Quality Profession 16. Tellers Who Hustle 17. How Mirage Resorts Sifted 75,000 Applicants 30. Checking in under Marriott's First Ten Program ◉ **29**
Information Technology	2. Reengineer or Perish 17. How Mirage Resorts Sifted 75,000 Applicants 19. How Great Machines Are Born 40. Electronics Manufacturing: A Well-Integrated IT Approach 41. Are You Ready for the E-Supply Chain?	**Process Improvement**	1. Empirical Assessment of the Production/Operations Manager's Job 2. Reengineer or Perish 3. Perceived Impact of the Benchmarking Process on Organizational Effectiveness 5. Rally of the Dolls 6. Fly, Damn It, Fly 9. Conversation with Joseph Juran

2

⬤ AE: Production and Operations Management

The following World Wide Web sites have been carefully researched and selected to support the articles found in this reader. If you are interested in learning more about specific topics found in this book, these Web sites are a good place to start. The sites are cross-referenced by number and appear in the topic guide on the previous two pages. Also, you can link to these Web sites through our DUSHKIN ONLINE support site at *http://www.dushkin.com/online/*.

The following sites were available at the time of publication. Visit our Web site—we update DUSHKIN ONLINE regularly to reflect any changes.

General Sources

1. American National Standards Institute [ANSI]
http://web.ansi.org/default.htm
ANSI Online is designed to provide convenient access to timely information on the ANSI Federation and the latest national and international standards-related activities.

2. APICS Online
http://www.apics.org
APICS is the Educational Society for Resource Management. The *Performance Advantage* magazine is located here as well as a link to certification testing information.

3. Data Interchange Standards Association [DISA]
http://www.disa.org
DISA is a not-for-profit organization that supports the development of EDI standards in electronic commerce.

4. Introduction to Operations Management
http://members.tripod.com/~wwwtomi/whatis.html
Here is an excellent starting place for understanding the basics of operations management. This TOMI site uses interesting examples on the Web to illustrate its points.

Performance Improvement

5. Agile Manufacturing Project at MIT
http://web.mit.edu/ctpid/www/agile/atlanta.html
This interesting paper describes the research plan, methods, and early progress of two coordinated Agile Pathfinders focused on the aircraft and automobile industry respectively. The paper's working hypothesis is that a network of companies can improve its performance if participants take proactive steps during early product design.

6. American Productivity and Quality Center [APQC]
http://www.apqc.org
APQC is a nonprofit education and research organization. Its Web site shows how benchmarking and best practices can help an organization improve its processes and performance.

7. Business Forecasting
http://forecasting.cwru.edu
Use this page to access the thinking of business researchers who, using statistics, economics, psychology, and related disciplines, attempt to predict the future.

8. Demystifying Supply Chain Management
http://www.manufacturing.net/magazine/logistic/archives/1998/scmr/myst.htm
Peter J. Metz shows that SCM is, in fact, a logical development of lasting value, and not just a buzzword.

9. Design for Competitive Advantage TOC
http://dfca.larc.nasa.gov/dfc/toc.html
The table of contents of Ed Dean's book *Design for Competitive Advantage* leads to chapters on technologies of business, quality, cost, and others.

10. Galaxy: Manufacturing and Processing
http://galaxy.einet.net/GJ/mnfg.html
Billed as "the professional's guide to a world of information," Galaxy is a rich source of links to engineering and technology (cryogenics, quality control and more).

11. Kaizen
http://akao.larc.nasa.gov/dfc/kai.html
This selection explains Kaizen and its relationship to Total Quality Control.

12. Voice of the Shuttle: Postindustrial Business Theory Page
http://humanitas.ucsb.edu/shuttle/commerce.html
Subjects covered at this Web page include the team concept, the quality movement, outsourcing, diversity management, restructuring, reengineering, downsizing, knowledge work, knowledge management, and learning organizations.

13. WARIA, the Workflow and Reengineering International Association
http://www.waria.com
This nonprofit organization tries to make sense of what is happening at the intersection of business process reengineering, workflow, and electronic commerce.

Quality

14. American Society for Quality [ASQ]
http://www.asqc.org/index.html
Subtitled "Your Quality Resource," ASQ covers the field. The site includes a glossary, quality-related sites, and a quality forum, as well as standards and certification.

15. Concept Corner
http://members.tripod.com/~wwwtomi/concepts.html
Concept Corner provides an introduction to Internet sites that help explain concepts, tools, and techniques that may be applied within the subject of operations management.

16. International Organization for Standardization [ISO]
http://www.iso.ch/welcome.html
Through ISO's home page find out everything you need to know about ISO, ISO 9000, and ISO 14000.

17. John Grout's Poka-Yoke Page
http://www.campbell.berry.edu/faculty/jgrout/pokayoke.shtml
Find out about mistake-proofing, zero defect quality (ZDQ), and failsafing here. Choose from 20 selections, including Poka-Yoke Resources, Bad Designs, and Quality Links.

18. Plan-Do-Check-Act
http://www.inform.umd.edu/CampusInfor/Departments/cqi/Outlook/Tech/pdca.html
This article offers a clear explanation of PDCA as well as an example of how to put this concept of Continuous Quality Improvement (CQI) to work.

Human Resources Management for Productivity

19. Business Environments: Corporate Office Design, WorkSpace Resources
http://www.workspace-resources.com/business/busi02.htm
The Work Place offers information about the societal changes that have been made in the commercial office over the past 50 years. Ergonomics, the use of color, the impact of technology, workplace safety, and other issues are discussed.

20. Just-in-Time Manufacturing
http://rolf.ece.curtin.edu.au/~clive/jit/jit.htm
Curtin University of Technology offers this introduction to the basic concepts of a JIT manufacturing system.

21. Quality Circles
http://www.nw.com.au/~jingde/homepa6.htm
This interesting Web page from Australia is all about the behavioral science technique called quality circles.

22. SDWT: Self-Directed Work Teams
http://users.ids.net/~brim/sdwtt.html
This very complete site links to discussions of the what and why of SDWT, skills and steps needed for success, examples of teams, work teams in public, and related resources.

23. TQM: Total Quality Management Diagnostics
http://www.skyenet.net/~leg/tqm.htm
Offered at this Web site is a simplified TQM diagnostic model, designed for leaders who want to improve already-existing TQM initiatives or who want o become internal consultants to their company's TQM system.

Forecasting and Product Design

24. New Product Development: Practice and Research
http://www.eas.asu.edu/~kdooley/nsfnpd/practices.html
These are the results of a research project that surveyed over 40 New Product Development programs. From this page link to a description of the theory behind this work.

25. Project Management Institute [PMI]
http://www.pmi.org
PMI aims to build professionalism into project management and this Web site is part of that endeavor. Download *A Guide to the Project Management Body of Knowledge* here. The site also contains links to other organizations.

26. STORES June 1998: Editor's Choice
http://www.stores.org/archives/jun98edch.html
This article on sales forecasting, "Retailers, Suppliers Push Joint Sales Forecasting" by Ginger Koloszyyc, introduces the concept of information sharing known as collaborative planning, forecasting, and replenishing (CPFR), and is being pioneered by the retail giant Wal-Mart.

Capacity, Location, Logistics, and Layout Planning

27. Manufacturers Information Net
http://mfginfo.com/newhome2.htm
A complete source of information for industry and services related to manufacturing is provided at the site. Visit What's New, Online Manufacturing Discussion Groups, Industry Resources, Manufacturing Articles, and the search engine.

28. Operations Management Group, Warwick Business School
http://www.wbs.warwick.ac.uk/omgroup/index.html

Visit this page for some downloadable research papers. See also Focus on Research for topics on operations strategy, capacity management, supply chain management, service quality and design, and performance measurement.

29. TWIGG's Operations Management Index [TOMI]
http://members.tripod.com/~wwwtomi/index.html
This Index is an entry point to operations management resources on the Web, providing information on topics such as purchasing, product development, manufacturing strategy, inventory control, quality, and service operations.

Inventory and Supply-Chain Management

30. JBA System 21 Master Production Scheduling
http://jbaworld.com/solutions/infosheets/masterprodsched.htm
This description of JBA System 21 manufacturing is an example of using the computer in a manufacturing environment.

31. MAGI: Master Production Scheduling
http://www.magimfg.com/Master_Production_Scheduler.htm
MAGI, the Manufacturing Action Group Inc. opens windows and shows you the screens it uses in setting up this Web program of master production scheduling.

32. Informs: Institute for Operations Research and the Management Sciences
http://www.informs.org
From the home page of Informs you can link to research on operations research and management science (OR/MS) and also explore articles that have appeared in the press.

Emerging Trends in Production and Operations Management

33. Centre for Intelligent Machines
http://www.cim.mcgill.ca/index_nf.html
CIM's mission is to excel in the field of intelligent machines, stressing basic research, technology development, and education. Domains such as robotics, automation, artificial intelligence and computer vision systems are explored.

34. International Center for Research on the Management of Technology [ICRMOT]
http://web.mit.edu/icrmot/www/
ICRMOT will show you its scope at this site. Specific research themes include managing complex global projects, capturing the value of technological innovation, and creating and delivering technology-based services.

35. Information Technology Association of America
http://www.itaa.org
An interesting article at this Web site is one about global information technology spending. The ITAA provides information about the IT industry and links to other sites.

36. KPMG United States
http://www.us.kpmg.com/cm/article-archives/actual-articles/global.html
KPMG, knowledge management experts, offers this article, "Tips for Improving Global Supply Chains," at their United States Web site.

We highly recommend that you review our Web site for expanded information and our other product lines. We are continually updating and adding links to our Web site in order to offer you the most usable and useful information that will support and expand the value of your Annual Editions. You can reach us at: http://www.dushkin.com/annualeditions/.

www.dushkin.com/online/

Unit Selections

1. **An Empirical Assessment of the Production/Operations Manager's Job,** Brian D'Netto, Amrik S. Sohal, and John Trevillyan
2. **Reengineer or Perish,** G. Berton Latamore
3. **The Perceived Impact of the Benchmarking Process on Organizational Effectiveness,** Dean Elmuti
4. **Putting Commitment to Work through Short-Cycle Kaizen,** Ed Heard
5. **Rally of the Dolls: It Worked for Toyota. Can It Work for Toys?** Alex Taylor III
6. **Fly, Damn It, Fly,** Business Week

Key Points to Consider

❖ What forces within the United States and globally have pressured firms to seek performance improvement?

❖ What are the similarities and differences in the performance improvement approaches presented in this unit?

❖ The firms cited in this unit have been successful in implementing performance improvement initiatives. Why do you think that other firms resist implementing these approaches?

 **Links**   **www.dushkin.com/online/**

5. **Agile Manufacturing Project at MIT** *http://web.mit.edu/ctpid/www/agile/atlanta.html*
6. **American Productivity and Quality Center (APQC)** *http://www.apqc.org*
7. **Business Forecasting** *http://forecasting.cwru.edu*
8. **Demystifying Supply Chain Management** *http://www.manufacturing.net/magazine/logistic/archives/1998/scmr/myst.htm*
9. **Design for Competitive Advantage TOC** *http://dfca.larc.nasa.gov/dfc/toc.html*
10. **Galaxy: Manufacturing and Processing** *http://galaxy.einet.net/GJ/mnfg.html*
11. **Kaizen** *http://akao.larc.nasa.gov/dfc/kai.html*
12. **Voice of the Shuttle: Postindustrial Business Theory Page** *http://humanitas.ucsb.edu/shuttle/commerce.html*
13. **WARIA** *http://www.waria.com*

These sites are annotated on pages 4 and 5.

Given the increased challenges facing managers and firms today, a greater emphasis is placed upon production and operations management. Organizations today are faced with the need to improve performance and to increase customer service. Firms must provide greater quality, faster delivery, and simultaneously reduce costs. Firms recognize that they can not ensure their survival by maintaining the status quo. Performance improvement is necessary and the operations area of a firm plays a vital role in securing this improvement. This unit examines the job of a production/operations manager, reviews approaches for performance improvement, and presents case illustrations from firms.

The job of a production/operations manager is of great importance today. In the first article of unit 1, Brian D'Netto et al. provide an empirical ass- essment of the activities of a production/operations manager. The article contrasts the reality of the job in practice with the traditional profile of a production manager.

Various approaches have been proposed over the last two decades to increase performance improvement. This unit presents articles that review approaches such as reengineering, benchmarking, and kaizen. These newer approaches focus upon critical examination of existing processes, com- parison of a firm's performance to that of leading firms, and a focus upon continuous improvement. The newer approaches toward performance improvement recognize that slow, gradual change will not meet the demands of a competitive marketplace. Major changes are often necessary in firms and these changes need to be implemented quickly and

carefully. The articles in this unit emphasize how the operations and production area of a firm is central to attempts at change. Although these newer approaches involve commitments of time, effort, and capital, the long-term gains can be substantial.

The final articles in the unit present illustrations of firms that have succeeded at or that are in the process of improving performance. The approaches developed for performance improvement should be equally adaptable to service firms as they are to manufacturing firms.

Performance Improvement

AN EMPIRICAL ASSESSMENT OF THE PRODUCTION/OPERATIONS MANAGER'S JOB

BRIAN D'NETTO, PHD
AMRIK S. SOHAL, PHD
Department of Management, Monash University, Victoria 3145, Australia

JOHN TREVILLYAN
Monash Mt. Eliza Business School, Monash University, Victoria 3145, Australia

Past assessments of the production manager's job have been very unfavorable. Two earlier studies of the British manufacturing industry have found that the malaise of the manufacturing industry was undoubtedly due, in part, to a marked lack of well-qualified and ambitious people in production management [3, 6]. These studies also indicated that when compared to other managers in the organization, production/operations managers see their job as less glamorous, with less pleasant working conditions, poor career prospects and low pay. In a study on Australian manufacturing managers, Sohal and Marriott [8] had indicated that manufacturing managers are ill-prepared for managing the major changes taking place in technology and work practices. These authors argue that some explanation for poor performance lies in the human resource development function of manufacturing organizations.

Studies on the changing nature of the production manager's job have indicated that the modern production manager is a vastly different individual from the traditional profile of a production manager, i.e., the old-fashioned autocrat that worked himself up from the shop floor [6]. Today, a production manager must have technical knowledge relevant to his/her industry, highly developed interpersonal skills, knowledge of advanced manufacturing technology, knowledge of other functional areas within the organization and an ability to accept and guide change. Gone are the days when the production manager could concern himself/herself only with getting the product out. He/she now needs to produce continually changing products on time, more cheaply and with increasingly better quality. The continuous improvement of the manufacturing operation is an essential part of any production manager's responsibilities.

The nature of the production manager's job has changed from a traditional department-centered approach to cross-functional linkages with marketing, engineering, human resources, finance and accounting. Cross-functional linkages represent the latest challenge in current market needs; the need for more new products faster, with fewer modifications and a shorter product life cycle [1]. Production managers must have expertise in the use of new technologies and philosophies such as programmable automation (PA), Just-in-Time (JIT), computer-integrated manufacturing (CIM), statistical process control (SPC),

From *Production and Inventory Management Journal*, First Quarter 1998, pp. 57-61. © 1998 by APICS, the American Production and Inventory Control Society. Reprinted by permission.

and total quality management (TQM). Entry-level jobs in manufacturing management are being replaced by jobs in the areas of quality planning and control and purchasing management. In view of the dynamic nature of the environment, an individual must be ready to change jobs and even functional areas several times in a career lifetime. With the increase in cross-functional integration, production managers need to constantly update their knowledge and skills base, particularly along the chain of product development through product distribution [4]. Manufacturing professionals must relate not only to people in other functional areas, but also to other organizations including vendors, customers, government institutions and regulatory bodies. Thus, the ability to communicate effectively, motivate other people, manage projects and work on multidisciplinary teams are essential attributes for effective performance [2, 7].

While several authors have documented changes in the production function, there has been very little empirical research to assess the current job of the production manager. In the present study, we sought to make an empirical assessment of the job of the production/operations manager. Specifically, the study focused on the educational qualifications, career progression, job content, and reward perceptions of production/operations managers in Australia.

CHARACTERISTICS OF THE SAMPLE

The total sample in this study consisted of 600 large, medium and small organizations in Australia. A modified version of the questionnaire used in a previous study [6] was mailed to the production/operations managers in the organizations included in the sample. From the 600 mailed, 254 completed and useable questionnaires were received, yielding an overall response rate of 42.3%. Pertinent facts included: 68.1% of the respondents represented manufacturing organizations, while 31.9% represented non-manufacturing; 25 different industries were included in the sample; and 64.6% of the companies were Australian owned. As to size, 30.3% of the organizations had under 100 employees, 40.9% had between 101 and 400 employees, while 28.8% employed over 400 people. These findings indicate that small, medium and large organizations were included in the survey.

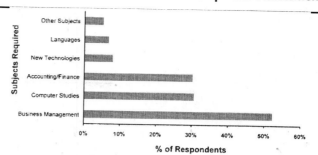

FIGURE 1: Subjects required for present job but not studied earlier

ASSESSMENT OF EDUCATIONAL QUALIFICATIONS AND CAREER STRUCTURES

The findings of the study indicated that Australian production/operations managers are well-qualified, with 78.8% of them having completed a diploma or higher degree. Given that over one-half of the respondents began their careers when they were younger than 19 years old, it appears that a large proportion of the respondents subsequently completed their tertiary education on a part-time basis. Over the past decade, both employees and organizations in Australia have realized the value and importance of higher education. Several companies have provided "study time allowances" and have also agreed to pay for the education of their employees. This could explain the high level of qualifications that production/operations managers possess.

Respondents were asked to identify subjects they felt were required for their present job, but were not studied earlier. The most important subjects identified were business management, computer studies and accounting/finance (see Figure 1). In fact, additional training in business management was also identified as the most important area for future career success.

With respect to career structures, early career mobility appears to be very high, with respondents having worked in several other functions before entering the production/operations function. However, once respondents joined the production/operations management function, they tended to remain in the same functional area; 76.3% of the respondents had been working in production/operations management for over ten years. This considerably long tenure in the same function, together with high levels of job satisfaction, indicates that production/operations managers in Australia do not find the job distasteful

TABLE 1: Control of Different Functions

Control of Functions	% of Respondents		
	Total	Partial	None
Direct Production/Operations	67.8	25.2	7.0
Quality	48.1	47.2	4.7
Planning	44.5	52.4	3.1
Maintenance	40.6	41.3	18.1
Work Study	36.6	49.6	13.8
Costing (routine)	32.3	52.7	15.0
Purchasing and Supply	26.0	59.0	15.0
Personnel/HRM	24.8	64.9	10.3
Costing (new product/services)	24.0	61.8	14.2
Systems Design (product/information)	19.7	64.9	15.4
Development of New Product Services	16.1	69.7	14.2

as indicated in the earlier British studies. These findings are strengthened by the fact that 45.8% of the respondents entered the production function when they were quite young (less than 25 years old).

ASSESSMENT OF THE JOB CONTENT

An examination of the job content indicated that 67.8% of the respondents had total control of production/operations (see Table 1). However, less than one-half of the sample indicated that they had total control over quality, planning and maintenance.

The most important areas in which respondents believed their control should be increased were planning, systems design, human resources management (HRM) and quality (see Table 2).

Satisfaction with their relationship with other functions and with their jobs was expressed by 70% of the respondents. The greatest job satisfaction was derived from the key tasks of improving productivity, solving managerial problems, opportunities for personal initiative and opportunities for innovation (see Figure 2).

The current organizational restructuring and downsizing has increased the span of control, with 75.2% of the respondents supervising ten or more employees. Besides, with the increasing focus on the bottom line, the most important areas in which managers were responsible for making improvements were cost reduction, productivity and organization

of work and people. Nearly three-fourths of the respondents had defined targets for improvements and specific programs aimed at achieving these targets. However, only 45.7% of the respondents had staff allocated exclusively to the improvement program, while 92.9% of the respondents indicated that their department had its own budget.

ASSESSMENT OF SALARY LEVELS AND SATISFACTION WITH REWARDS

Annual salaries of the respondents varied considerably, from below $60,00 per annum to over $150,000 per annum. However, an interesting finding is that only 9% of the respondents had annual salaries of below $60,000. The results indicate that production/operations managers receive relatively high salaries, with 61.5% of the respondents earning over $90,000 per annum.

Respondents were asked to rate their level of satisfaction with 12 different rewards for their job, compared to the rewards for managers in other functions in the organization (see Table 3).

It is interesting to note that respondents had very positive perceptions of the rewards for their job. In fact, compensation (salary) for the job was perceived as being better than in other functional areas. Intrinsic rewards such as work variety, work importance, authority, control and autonomy appear to be very high. According to Herzberg [5], while extrinsic rewards such as compensation remove dissatis-

TABLE 2: Functions Requiring Change of Control

Change of Control Required	% of Respondents	
	Increased	No Change
Planning	53.2	46.8
Systems Design (product/information)	42.5	57.5
Personnel/HRM	41.3	58.7
Quality	40.2	59.8
Development of New Product Services	37.8	62.2
Direct Production/Operations	33.1	66.9
Costing (new product/services)	29.9	70.1
Work Study	29.2	70.8
Purchasing and Supply	28.0	72.0
Maintenance	24.8	75.2
Costing (routine)	22.4	77.6

faction, intrinsic rewards which flow from the work itself motivate individuals. Given that compensation is good, and intrinsic rewards are high, it is possible that production/operations managers are highly motivated. The results indicated that rewards that need some improvement are benefits, work load, feedback and advancement opportunities. While perceived inequities of benefits with other functions need to be investigated further, problems with the other three rewards could be due to the increasing pressure placed on the production/operations function during streamlining operations in which most Australian organizations are currently engaged. With the pressure to be more competitive, work load has increased. Lack of time can result in performance appraisals and feedback being largely ignored. Flatter organizational structures reduce advancement opportunities, especially if the incumbent does not possess adequate managerial skills and cannot move out of the production/operations management function.

AREAS FOR IMPROVEMENT

There were several areas identified by respondents which require improvement. First, only 4.3% of the respondents were female. It is sad to note that in spite of equal employment opportunity and affirmative action legislation, women have not been able to make inroads into this traditionally male-dominated profession. Second, while 78.8% of the respondents were well-qualified, nearly one-half of the sample were not members of any profes-

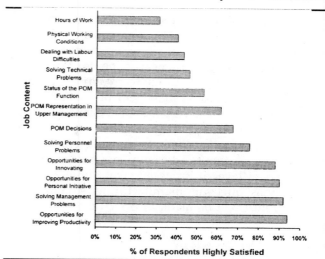

FIGURE 2: Level of job satisfaction

sional institution. Professional institutions play a significant role in providing current information and discussing recent changes in the field. This low rate of membership could be an indication of the failure of production/operations managers to keep up with current trends in the field. This could be due to paucity of time, as respondents indicated that their work load was too high. Failure to keep abreast of current changes could explain why respondents indicated that solving technical problems was one of the areas which yielded the lowest job satisfaction. Third, while tertiary education appears to have provided technical skills, there is clearly a need for more skills in business management, computers, finance and accounting. Flatter organizational structures and increasing spans of control have made it necessary for managers to possess these skills. Over one-half of the respondents indicated that they required additional business management skills for their current and future jobs. The lack of management skills that production/operations managers possess could be the reason dealing with labor is one of the areas which yields the lowest job satisfaction. Besides, 18.9% of the managers indicated that they required foreign language skills. This could be a result of the high proportion of work force diversity in Australia. Fourth, while nearly three-fourths of the respondents had targets and programs for improvements, less than 50% had staff allocated exclusively to the improvement program. Improvement programs will not be successful unless adequate time and resources are devoted to them. In addition, managers

TABLE 3: Perceptions of Rewards (Percentages)

Rewards	Below Average	Average	Above Average
Compensation	17.7	32.7	49.6
Benefits	36.7	41.7	21.6
Social Interaction	18.9	24.4	56.7
Job Security	21.2	22.8	56.0
Status/Recognition	20.5	23.2	56.3
Work Variety	15.0	10.6	74.4
Work Importance	7.5	12.2	80.3
Work Load	33.9	20.5	45.6
Autonomy	7.5	12.2	80.3
Advancement Opportunities	25.5	31.1	43.4
Feedback	30.8	31.5	37.7
Working Conditions	19.7	31.5	48.8

indicated that they require control over planning, systems design, human resource management and quality in order to enhance their performance. Fifth, nearly one-third of the organizations did not have any written production/operations management policy. Over one-half of the respondents believed that the board of directors did not have knowledge of the production/operations management function. Without adequate knowledge at the board level, it is possible that important decisions affecting manufacturing strategy and policy will be made incorrectly.

CONCLUSION

The findings of this study indicate that there have been significant positive changes to both the individual and the job in the production/operations management function in Australia. The most important finding is that, overall, production/operations managers are well-qualified, have positive perceptions of their jobs and are generally satisfied with the rewards. Also, perceived intrinsic rewards from the job appear to be high. The job of the production manager in the future is likely to be very exciting. The rapid increase of technology, and the advent of the knowledge worker, is likely to require highly qualified individuals with outstanding managerial skills to effectively manage the production function. The importance of the production management function in organizations is likely to increase, and outstanding production managers will be required to create and maintain a sustainable competitive advantage.

REFERENCES

1. Bandyopadhyay, J. K. "Redesigning the POM Major to Prepare Manufacturing Managers of the 1990s." *Production and Inventory Management Journal* 35, no. 1 (1994): 16–30.
2. Calvacca, L. "Managing Change: What Production Executives Need to Know." *Folio: The Magazine for Magazine Management* 23, no. 19 (1995): 200–201.
3. Gill, R. W. T., and K. G. Lockyer. "The Career Development of the Production Manager in British Industry." London: *British Institute of Management*, 1978.
4. Gordon, J., and J. Wiseman. "Thriving on Competition." *Business Quarterly* (Spring 1995): 79–84.
5. Herzberg, F. *Motivation to Work.* New York: John Wiley, 1959.
6. Oakland, J. S., and A. Sohal. "The Education, Training, and Career of Production Managers in British Industry." *International Journal of Operations and Production Management* 9, no. 8 (1989): 63–90.
7. Rao, A. R. "Manufacturing Professionals of the 1990s: How Should They Be Prepared." *Report of the APICS Academic/Practitioner Liaison Committee,* 1989.
8. Sohal, A. S., and F. Marriott. "Manufacturing Management in Australia: The Human Resource Management Implications." *International Journal of Manpower* 14, no. 9 (1993): 41–55.

About the Authors—

BRIAN D'NETTO, PhD, is a lecturer in human resource management at Monash University. Prior to joining the university, he completed his PhD in human resource management at the State University of New York at Buffalo. He has worked in the field of human resource management in industry for seven years. Dr. D'Netto's current research interests include recruitment and selection, training and development, compensation and managing work-force diversity.

AMRIK S. SOHAL, PhD, leads the operations management group in the Department of Management at Monash University, where he is professor and Director of the Quality Management Research Unit. Dr. Sohal's previous academic appointments were with the Graduate School of Management at the University of Melbourne (Australia) and with the University of Bradford (UK). His current interests are in manufacturing/operations strategy, quality management, Just-in-Time systems and technology management. He has received research grants from the state and commonwealth governments and the Australian Research Council.

JOHN TREVILLYAN is the director of the Workplace Management Centre, Monash Mt. Eliza Business School. Mr. Trevillyan has directed programs in Australia, Papua New Guinea, Fiji, Indonesia and New Zealand for various groups and companies. He has also undertaken a number of consultancies for organizations in the areas of organizational culture, performance management, best practice management techniques and was a board member of a metropolitan public hospital. Mr. Tevillyan's areas of research include learning technologies, performance management and operations management.

Reengineer or Perish

By G. Berton Latamore

Emerging factors, such as shorter product cycles and the rise of the super customer, put increasing pressure on companies to reengineer business practices, says management guru Dr. Michael Hammer. Those companies experiencing success have reengineered the supply chain to speed cycle times, cut costs, improve asset use, and add more value to the customer.

THE IDEAS OF DR. MICHAEL HAMMER, one of the world's foremost business thinkers and the originator of both reengineering and process-centering, have transformed the modern business world. In 1992, *Business Week* named him one of the four preeminent management thinkers of the 1990s, and in 1996 *Time* magazine named him to its first list of America's 25 most influential individuals.

A former professor of computer science at the Massachusetts Institute of Technology, Hammer is the founder and director of several high-tech companies. He serves as an advisor to leaders of the world's most progressive companies and his public seminars are attended by thousands of people annually. He is the author of *Reengineering the Corporation: A Manifesto for Business Revolution* (with James Champy) (HarperBusiness, 1993); *The Reengineering Revolution: A Handbook* (HarperBusiness, 1995); and *Beyond Reengineering: How the Process-Centered Organization is Changing Our Work and Our Lives* (HarperBusiness, 1996).

In this exclusive interview with *APICS—The Performance Advantage*, Hammer discusses how reengineering the supply chain is the key to manufacturing success in the new millennium.

APICS—The Performance Advantage: **When you wrote** *Reengineering the Corporation,* **the U.S. economy was in recession. The first chapter focuses on why U.S. businesses were failing. Today, despite the economic problems of much of the rest of the world, the U.S. economy seems to be continuing near-record growth. Does this change your view of U.S. businesses?**
Hammer: The economic boom does not change my view. In fact, in some sectors of our economy, companies' reengineering of business practices in the last five years is the main reason for success. This is particularly true in key areas of manufacturing such as automotive.

Some companies may be doing well without making those changes, but that is not going to last. A new set of factors are creating new business problems that are putting a lot of pressure on companies. For example, we are seeing the rise of the super customer as many companies see the number of customers go down and the size of their remaining customers increase. The service and price demands of these more powerful customers are much more exigent. Manufacturers also face shorter product life cycles. There is the relentless drive of innovation among competitors. So even if a company has squeaked by until now, that doesn't mean it will be able to continue.

So I think some of the business pressures we talked about five years ago are still there and others have changed, but the name of the game remains improving performance.

you have to assume the worst and *stockpile* supplies

From *APICS—The Performance Advantage,* January 1999, pp. 44-48. © 1998 by APICS, the American Production and Inventory Control Society. Reprinted by permission.

APICS: **You advocate reengineering of the supply chain as an important step for U.S. manufacturers. But the term supply chain means different things to different people. What is your definition of the main components of the supply chain for the purposes of reengineering?**

Hammer: To some companies, a supply chain is nothing but a euphemism for procurement and logistics, but I think that misses the point. To me supply chain really means everything that happens to fill the demands of the ultimate customer. That means all the work that is done by everybody who is contributing to the product and service that leads to the final customer. One of my favorite definitions is from a company in the tissues business that defines the supply chain as "from stump to rump."

Over the last five years we have made a lot of progress on the *intra*company order fulfillment process. The problem is the system breaks down. What makes supply chain a very different kind of process is that it does not exist within the walls of a single company. By its nature, supply chain is an *inter*company endeavor. It does not end with supplying the manufacturer's customer. It extends to the customer's customer and goes back to the supplier's suppliers.

It is a set of activities that are performed by a number of companies. They need to perform those activities coherently. Right now, different parts of the supply chain are done by different companies at arm's length from each other. We need everyone to work in synchrony. The goal is virtual integration. Companies should work together with no more overhead or difficulty than if they were part of the same enterprise. It should be no more difficult to get something from a supplier than from your own warehouse.

APICS: **Why should manufacturers reengineer their supply chains?**

Hammer: One reason is to improve financial performance by lowering costs. If you work synchronously with your customers and suppliers, you can eliminate a lot of redundant work to save money. But the more important reason is that you reduce asset utilization—raw materials, work in process, and finished goods in storage. And you can get better use of your production assets. If you do not know your supplier's schedule, you have to assume the worst and stockpile supplies in a warehouse. If your supplier does not know your production schedule, he has to assume the worst and stockpile supplies in his warehouse. If we reengineer to work together, we can eliminate most of that inventory and eliminate a great deal of waste and cost. That is probably the main reason companies reengineer their supply chains.

The second reason for reengineering the supply chain is to make it easier for customers to do business with you. In a world of increasing commoditization, how easy you are for your customers to do business with and how little overhead you add to your customers' costs can be critical differentiators.

In the long term, the most important reason for supply chain reengineering is to add more value to customers. If you really rethink your supply chain, you can end up adding more value to customers and even extending the nature of your product to deliver product bundled with service. This means you are doing more for the customer, which entitles you to higher margins and gives you greater market differentiation.

All of these goals are very important. Achieving them demands looking at the supply chain process from end to end and finding opportunities for eliminating redundancies and improving asset utilization throughout the process.

APICS: **What are some specific examples of how manufacturers achieved these goals through supply chain reengineering?**

Hammer: One example that is very current is IBM's answer to Dell Computer's new manufacturing model that allowed it to build PCs to order direct from the customer, with a short time to delivery. This gave Dell a major advantage over IBM in the PC marketplace. At the time, IBM had 12 weeks of PC inventory in the supply chain to its distributors. Twelve weeks of inventory in a system where product life is 12 to 18 months is a recipe for disaster.

IBM had to do something. But instead of just looking at its internal processes, it examined the entire fulfillment process from the time the customer places an order with the distributor until it is filled. [The reengineering team] asked themselves who should do each step of the process. One thing they found was that often distributors had to disassemble the PCs they received to modify them to meet the customer's requirements. So IBM started delivering components rather than assembled PCs to its distributors, saving both IBM and the distributors time and money. The assembly work IBM was doing is now being done by the distributor.

inventory is a *substitute* for information

On the other hand, the team discovered IBM was better at managing the distributor's inventory of components than the distributors were. Today, IBM manages its distributors' inventories.

So IBM does some of the work the distributor used to do, and the distributor does some work that IBM used to do. IBM and its distributors went from 12 weeks to two weeks of inventory in the system and eliminated a lot of errors, redundancies, and duplications. It is now cost competitive with Dell's direct build-to-order model.

APICS: **One major change that is often part of supply chain reengineering is choosing a single supplier for key raw materials or components. How does the manufac-**

turer ensure he doesn't end up paying inflated prices for those components once competition in the supply chain has been eliminated?

Hammer: The consolidation of suppliers is, in fact, a common aspect of supply chain reengineering. In theory, there is risk in being captive to that supplier, but that risk is more theoretical than real. The supplier with a single-source contract with a customer has a lot riding on that customer's success. Often, the supplier will succeed or fail depending on the success of that customer. If the supplier abuses that customer, the customer will terminate the relationship. So we have not seen that as a problem. I sometimes say this reminds me of mutually assured destruction. The two organizations are so dependent on each other that if either harms the other they end up killing both.

APICS: **Another major change is the much closer relationship between manufacturer and suppliers in many reengineered supply chains. Often this includes sharing sensitive information, such as designs for new products. Is the sharing information necessary for success of a reengineered supply chain?**

Hammer: Yes. Often, inventory is a substitute for information. If you are a customer, and I don't know what your demands will be, I have to assume the worst and pile up inventory. If you are the supplier and do not know my production plans, you have to assume the worst and pile up inventory. If you do not know my plans for a new product, you often will end up holding inventory that no longer has any value when the product changes. If we share with each other, we can both win.

Product life cycles are getting much shorter. If I share my new product plans with my suppliers, they can help design those products so they can produce higher quality components at lower cost. They can design and implement their component manufacturing processes in parallel with mine. As a result, when I am ready to start production of the new product, they're ready to provide the materials and components I need, eliminating huge amounts of delay and, often, redesign of products.

APICS: **How do manufacturers ensure that sensitive business information is adequately protected when shared with other companies in the supply chain who may have multiple commitments and divided loyalties?**

Hammer: Obviously, you have to put procedures in place to protect sensitive information, but it is in everybody's best interest to maintain that confidentiality. Any immediate benefit a supplier might realize from divulging secret information about a customer in a reengineered relationship would be far outweighed by what it would suffer through the termination of that relationship.

APICS: **How have manufacturers benefited from the creation of this close relationship?**

Hammer: We are really talking about the virtual enterprise or what Chrysler calls the "extended enterprise." Some industries, such as automotive, have adopted this concept already, and Chrysler has been a leader.

Chrysler and its suppliers try to work as one company. Chrysler realizes it needs to focus on product design and development, and on marketing. That means it must simplify manufacturing. The auto industry uses the concept of the "multi-tier supply chain." Some suppliers are designated as tier one, which means they produce whole subsystems like automobile seats. They deal with tier-two suppliers who provide springs, fabric, etc., for those seats. They, in turn, deal with tier-three suppliers who provide the raw materials. The tier one suppliers have the responsibility of bringing the supply chain together to deliver finished seats to the right Chrysler factory, ready to install, rather than springs, bolts, and fabric. The result is that the tier one suppliers concentrate on what they do best—producing specific car subsystems, freeing Chrysler to do what it most needs to do—design and sell cars.

APICS: **What part does information technology (IT) play in supply chain reengineering?**

Hammer: Information technology is the enabler for reengineering. The key to allowing companies to integrate across boundaries is sharing information, which is achieved by IT. Electronic Data Interchange (EDI) has been the primary mechanism for information sharing between partners in the supply chain until now, but we are starting to move past EDI. For example, as we speak, the automotive industry is going live with the Automotive Network Exchange (ANX) to allow sharing of a lot of information on the Internet along the entire manufacturing process.

APICS: **It's often advised that manufacturers should change their business practices first and then automate the new methods. However, IT often creates the opportunity to reengineer in ways that are impossible with paper-based methods. Which should come first—the installation of IT tools or reengineering?**

Hammer: You don't install the technology first, but you do have to understand it first. You cannot design your new business processes without a knowledge of what technology can allow you to do. Learning that spurs your imagination to design the process, and then you use technology to implement the design.

APICS: **You have said that a successful reengineering process needs a leader, a process owner, a reengineering team, and a steering committee. Who are the best candidates for leader and process owner for supply chain reengineering projects that, by their nature, involve two or more companies?**

Hammer: You really need a pair of people on each role because you are crossing enterprise boundaries. Typically, you need an executive leader and a process owner at both the customer and supplier. The leaders, in particular, need

How Reengineering Changes Jobs

Supply chain reengineering enormously affects the jobs of individuals within companies and their relationships with their counterparts among the company's suppliers and customers, says Hammer. As with internal reengineering efforts, supply chain reengineering shifts the focus of individual employee efforts from following the rules and pleasing the boss to improving corporate efficiency and meeting or exceeding customer expectations.

"Jobs become much bigger and broader," Hammer says. Responsibility moves down the corporate organization toward the people actually doing the work. As a result, people have much larger responsibilities for major chunks of the whole process rather than being confined to single tasks.

"Workers are expected to make their own decisions about the best way to accomplish complex pieces of the process as opposed to following orders and referring all issues up the chain of command," he points out.

To meet this responsibility, they need a greater understanding of customer requirements and customer operations. They need the authority to make the decisions that are now their responsibility and see those decisions carried through. "So we have moved from the narrow specialized jobs to big, broad and responsible jobs."

For instance, Hammer says, one manufacturing company he works with used to have a central group that created the production schedules everyone followed. The problem with this approach was its inflexibility, and the company could not respond quickly to customer requests.

To gain competitive advantage, it wanted to move to a build-to-order model with short production times between customer order and product delivery. To do this, it reorganized its manufacturing effort into production teams, each linked closely to customers. Every day, each team decided what it would build that day based on the customer orders it needed to fill and the raw materials available.

"The important concept for this model is the team," Hammer says. "The workers on the manufacturing floor work together as a team to decide not just how to produce the product but what to produce and when. So much more authority is pushed down to the front lines.

"Information about customer needs and the raw materials available are what lets these teams take on this broader authority," he says. By harnessing IT to provide direct links between the teams on its factory floor and its customers, it cuts through the normal chain of information from customer manufacturing engineers to customer supply managers to the manufacturer's sales force and through that to manufacturing schedulers and finally to the manufacturing floor.

Instead, the people who do the work hear directly and instantly from the key people in the customer's organization and can respond quickly to satisfy customer needs. The result is a major reduction both in the time it takes to deliver products and in the inevitable errors that happen as complex information on customer requirements are passed from hand to hand through the old information chain. —B.L.

to be reasonably senior people because you are expecting massive behavioral change in the organization, which never comes easily or lightly. You are asking people to change their attitudes and share information with other companies, which is very counter cultural.

Most important, they must be willing to share the benefits of reengineering with the other organization. A company that wants to hog all the benefits of reengineering will get slaughtered because no one will be willing to play with it. Everyone has to benefit for everyone to be willing to make the massive changes in operations that reengineering demands.

These are radical changes in traditional modes of operation. Unless someone at the very top is driving the process, these changes tend to be lost in the resistance of the organization to massive change, and the reengineering effort will fail.

Similarly, the process owner needs to be highly visible and respected person to demonstrate that reengineering is being taken seriously. A token person does not make a statement that the company is serious about cross-boundary change.

APICS: **Should the reengineering team include representatives of other organizations in the supply chain?**
Hammer: Yes, very much. Your suppliers and customers tell you what to do. Chrysler, for instance, has a program called Score in which their people work with suppliers to help the suppliers figure out better ways to do business.

APICS: **Do the people involved in reengineering have a personal stake in its success—what happens to those who succeed in reengineering their companies?**
Hammer: Success in reengineering can be a big career boost for the key people involved in it. At Texas Instruments (TI), for example, the process owner for one of the first reengineering efforts was Tom Engibous. At the time, he was vice president and general manager of a TI business unit. He had the authority and clout to drive fundamental change that lead to enormous improvement. Now, six years later, he is CEO of the company.

APICS: **In general, what advice do you have for manufacturers who are considering supply chain reengineering?**
Hammer: First, if you haven't already started, you're behind. Second, you must push the envelope. Merely replicating in 1999 what your competition did in 1996 will not get you far enough. You must go beyond, look for new ways to speed cycle times, cut costs, improve asset use, and add more value to the customer.

Bert Latamore is a freelance writer in Alexandria, Va.

THE PERCEIVED IMPACT OF THE BENCHMARKING PROCESS ON ORGANIZATIONAL EFFECTIVENESS

DEAN ELMUTI, PHD
Lumpkin College of Business and Applied Sciences, Eastern Illinois University, Charleston, IL 61920

In a 1995 survey of *The Benchmarking Exchange* [5] members, benchmarking was in the top five most popular business processes on which there is current focus. More than 70% of *Fortune* 500 companies use benchmarking on a regular basis, including AT&T, Eastman Kodak, Ford Motor, GM, IBM, Weyerhaeuser, and Xerox [9]. The essence of benchmarking is the process of identifying the highest standards of excellence for products, services, or processes, and then making the improvements necessary to reach those standards, commonly called "best practices." The justification lies partly in the question: "Why reinvent the wheel if I can learn from someone who has already done it?" C. Jackson Grayson, Jr., chairman of the Houston-based American Productivity and Quality Center, which offers training in benchmarking and consulting services, reports an incredible amount of interest in benchmarking [21].

Robert C. Camp headed up the now-famous study at Xerox in which the buzzword "benchmarking" was coined in late 1980. When asked whether the best work practices necessarily improve the bottom line, he replied: "The full definition of benchmarking is finding and implementing best practices in our business; practices that meet customer requirements. So the flywheel on finding the very best is 'does this meet customer requirements?' There is a cost of quality that exceeds customer requirements. The basic objective is satisfying the customer, so that is the limiter. [11]"

Benchmarking has been gaining popularity, especially in the last few years. The process of benchmarking is more than just a means of gathering data on how well a company performs against others. Benchmarking can be used in a variety of industries—both services and manufacturing. It is also a method of identifying new ideas and new ways of improving processes [17].

Sprint Corporation believes benchmarking should be used as a tool within strategic business process improvement and reengineering. According to Jeff Amen, benchmarking manager at Sprint, it's the process of understanding what the organization does and what the critical components are. The underlying question is: who does it and what can we do to become or remain the best of the best [19]?

As stated by McNair and Leibfried in *Benchmarking, A Tool for Continuous Improvement* [15], "To benchmark is to shrug off history and to embrace the future. There are many defining features that are a part of the benchmarking process. Benchmarking must be: purposive, externally focused, measurement based, information intensive, objective, and action-generating. It shouldn't be done merely for the image of the organization. All practices performed must be sincere and with good intention. Benchmarking is often used to meet, or exceed expectations." According to Anthony Rainey, administrator of benchmarks and strategic planning for the city of

From *Production and Inventory Management Journal*, Third Quarter 1998, pp. 6-11. © 1998 by APICS, the American Production and Inventory Control Society. Reprinted by permission.

Gresham, Oregon, "Benchmark may cause and effect relationships visibly by aligning goals with the external environment, employees with key objectives, and measurement activities with organizational goals [20]."

Benchmarking is increasing in popularity as a tool for continuous improvement. Organizations that faithfully use benchmarking strategies achieve a cost savings of 30% to 40% or more. Benchmarking establishes methods of measuring each area in terms of units of output as well as cost. In addition, benchmarking can support the process of budgeting, strategic planning, and capital planning [12]. There are many companies who have used the benchmarking process: Avon products, Exxon Chemical, Microsoft, Ford, AT&T, IBM, General Motors, and Anderson Windows [7, 8, 9, 13]. Successful implementation of benchmarking has been credited with helping to improve quality, cut cost of manufacturing and development time, increase productivity, and improve organizational effectiveness [1, 2, 3, 4, 8, 15, 19]. However, concepts as powerful and ubiquitous as those put forward by the benchmarking movement in business tend to evoke scepticism. Muschter [16], a leading researcher on benchmarking, argues that the main problem with benchmarking is the focus on data as opposed to the processes used to result in that data. Benchmarking should be used as a guide, not for statistical precision. According to Pat Jones, corporate controller at Intel Corporation in Portland, Oregon, their benchmarking efforts were not a success because they had the problem of clarity on where the data originated [8]. Furthermore, Arun Maua, vice president at Arthur D. Little, mentions that you can't just impose a best practice. It has to be adapted to your own company's style [13]." This points out the assumption made by some proponents of the benchmarking concept that all processes work for all companies.

The claims by proponents of the benchmarking concept and findings from organizational behavior knowledge suggest five research questions to guide an investigation of the relationships between benchmarking programs and organizational effectiveness:

1. To what extent does the degree of familiarity and utilization of the benchmarking process vary across a variety of settings?
2. Does the benchmarking process seem to contribute in any measurable extent to perceptions of higher levels of organizational productivity and performance?
3. Does the benchmarking process achieve its stated objectives of improving quality of products and services?
4. Does the benchmarking process achieve its stated objectives of influencing and enhancing employees' job satisfaction?
5. Does the benchmarking process lose its momentum and its positive contribution to organizational effectiveness after a short period of time of its implementation (one to three years) as claimed by critics of the benchmarking process?

MEASURES

A survey was used to assess the status and effectiveness of benchmarking techniques across a variety of settings throughout the United States. A questionnaire was designed to assess benchmarking concept familiarity, duration of the program, and the effectiveness of benchmarking technique(s) among several types of industries across a variety of settings.

The questionnaire was mailed to 1,000 organizations throughout the United States. The names of the firms were generated randomly from a computer database known as "Compact Disclosure" in 1997. These firms were selected among several types of industries and across a variety of settings. Survey respondents were presidents, vice presidents, general managers, project managers (in charge of benchmarking activities), functional managers, and supervisors in these selected organizations. A total of 292 questionnaires were returned for a response rate of 29%. Forty questionnaires were not acceptably completed, thus reducing the response rate to 25%. The remaining 252 were usable questionnaires and these responses were analyzed in this study.

To measure organizational effectiveness, Likert's profile of organization characteristics [10] was used because, unlike other potential measures, it allowed additions to be made to the questionnaire in order to assess overall effectiveness with specific new programs or initiative.

Several variables were identified as significant for the purpose of this study. First, there were the elements used to measure the independent variables—the benchmarking process with measures derived from Ross [21] and Matter and Evans [14]. The benchmarking technique or process is an external focus on internal activities, functions, or operations in order to achieve continuous improvement. Functions, activities, and processes can be measured in terms of specific output measures of operations and performance. In general, these measures fall into four broad categories: cost and productivity, cycle time, quality and differentiation, and business processes. These functions or performance indicators were used to measure the independent variables in this study as defined in the questionnaire; in other words, the results and corrective actions of comparing a company's strategy, products and processes with those of world leaders, best in class organizations, and the effects of these results on organization effectiveness. The second variable focused on the elements used to measure the dependent variables—organization effectiveness—which included productivity, quality, satisfaction, and performance [8, 10, 14, 21].

RESULTS

About 40% of the respondents (100 organizations) reported that they did not have an existing benchmarking program. Of the remaining 152 organizations (60%), 40 indicated that they have had a benchmarking program for less than one year, 64 have had a benchmarking program for less than three years, and only 48 organizations have had a benchmarking program for over three years. These organizations have adopted benchmarking programs either in whole to include the entire organizational activities or in part to include only the areas of human resources activities, information systems, and customer process. At the same time, about 88% of the organizations surveyed reported that they were familiar with the benchmarking concept. However, less than 12% of the respondents reported that they were not at all familiar with such a concept.

Why Are Benchmarking Projects Undertaken?

Why do organizations take the risk of benchmarking? To examine this question, data was collected in three areas: (1) the reason benchmarking was initiated; (2) the process or activities the organizations benchmarked; and (3) the specific goal of the benchmarking project. First benchmarking projects are undertaken for several reasons. The top reasons identified in the survey results were: to reduce costs, to improve productivity, to improve

quality, to improve profitability, to improve customer service, to improve a certain operation process, to protect market share, to get a jump on competitors, to open up an opportunity for growth, and to enhance job satisfaction. An ingredient in any total quality management or reengineering effort, a benchmarking concept has been advocated by very well-known organizations. This suggests that benchmarking is undertaken for purposes that have a large impact on the organization's bottom line, although a more distant purpose such as strategy, competitive advantage, and competitor actions may have been the rationale for the more direct reasons. Table 1 shows the results of this inquiry.

TABLE 1: Reasons for Benchmarking

Rank	Why Benchmark? N = 152*	Respondents (%)
1	Reduce cost	78
2	Improve productivity	76
3	Improve quality—continuous improvement	75
4	Improve profitability	74
5	Improve customer service	68
6	Improve a certain operation process	61
7	Protect market share	52
8	To get a jump on competitors	46
9	To gain competitive advantage	44
10	Opens up an opportunity for growth	38
11	To enhance job satisfaction	32
12	An ingredient in TQM and/or reengineering efforts	30
13	Advocated by well-known individuals and firms	22

* N = 152 respondents; those who indicated they had a benchmarking program.

Second, benchmarking projects target specific types of processes or activities. Organizations were asked to identify the types of processes they benchmarked or were attempting to benchmark. The top processes identified were human resources, information systems, customer process (service and satisfaction), quality, purchasing function, and supplier management. This coincides with a 1995 survey of *The Benchmarking Exchange* members' findings that human resources, information systems, and quality management were among the top processes targeted for improvement by many organizations [5].

Finally, benchmarking a process should have a specific goal. Organizations were asked to identify their most specific goal in benchmarking a process. The survey choices were: performance, quality, productivity, cycle time, customer service, market share, and improve key business processes, which were suggested by several authors [6, 14, 18]. Table 2 shows the results of this inquiry and the number of respondents who indicated that they achieved some improvement in attaining the primary goals.

The Degree of Success or Failure of Benchmarking Process

Another primary intent of this study was to examine the degree of success or failure of the benchmarking process among organizations who indicated that they did have a benchmarking program in their establishments. About 40% (60 firms) of the 152 organizations who reported they did have a benchmarking program in their organizations reported that their benchmarking programs had failed to achieve their stated objectives of influencing and enhancing organizational effectiveness, productivity, quality, satisfaction, and performance. However, 92 of the 152 firms (60%) who indicated that they have a benchmarking program in their organizations reported that benchmarking programs were making a great contribution to organizational effectiveness. They indicated that the dollar savings and indirect benefits generated by the benchmarking programs were greater than the costs of implementing these programs. Benchmarking principles were believed to help improve performance, enhance responsiveness to customer needs, contribute to organizational goals of increased efficiency, reduce costs, reduce cycle time, improve the quality of the goods and services in their organizations, enhance job satisfaction through employee empowerment and improve key business processes.

Further evaluation of the relationships between benchmarking programs and organizational effectiveness was done with the use of multiple regression analysis to evaluate the dependence of measures of organizational effectiveness on benchmarking techniques. This analysis determines the proportion of variance

TABLE 2: Primary Goals for Benchmarking Processes

Number of Respondents	Primary Goals	Attained Goals
45	Performance (e.g., profit margins, return on investment, sales per employee, and cost per unit of product or service)	30
30	Quality (e.g., percentage of defects and defect rates)	16
22	Productivity (e.g., efficiency rate, percentage of hours spent on production, and output produced divided by input used)	12
18	Cycle time (e.g., cycle time/asset turnover)	11
16	Customer service (e.g., customer satisfaction rates, repeat purchase, and retention rates)	10
11	Market share (e.g., compared to past years and to competitors)	7
10	Business processes (e.g., key functions, waste delays, empowerment, and job satisfaction)	6
152		92

in organizational effectiveness scores explained by benchmarking technique scores. Multiple regression analysis was also used in this study to determine the strength of the dependency relationship between the benchmarking technique and organizational effectiveness. Table 3 presents the results of this analysis, which indicates a positive relationship between measures of the benchmarking process and effectiveness as reflected in the multiple regression ratios. The results show that 32% of the variation in productivity, 28% of the variation in quality, 24% of the variation in satisfaction, and 35% of the variation in performance is explained by linear regression on the benchmarking process dimensions. The F-ratios indicate that these linear associations are positive and statistically significant at $P<.05$. Furthermore, statistical analysis was found to indicate that involvement in benchmarking programs was positively related to perceived changes in organizational effectiveness among employees in more than half of the surveyed firms.

What Factors Are Associated with the Success or Failure of Benchmarking Programs?

To examine risk factors that are associated with the success or failure of benchmarking projects, the questionnaire listed several factors and asked respondents to check all applicable answers and specify any other factors that might be considered appropriate. To further enhance the analysis, factors were analyzed independently for successful and unsuccessful firms. The responses are shown in Tables 4 and 5.

Success Factors Affecting Benchmarking Projects

Table 4 lists 20 factors which may have affected the success of benchmarking projects among the majority of the respondents of the 92 firms who reported that their benchmarking projects were successful in their organizations. It can clearly be seen that the most important aspects of effective implementation of benchmarking projects are adequate planning, training, and open interdepartmental communication, and these factors are ranked among all the critical success factors for benchmarking projects.

The following three factors are a strong strategic focus: flexibility in achieving the goals set forth by management and sponsorships, interest, and support by senior management. This coincides with many academicians' claims that senior management must sponsor benchmarking projects because their impact is so broad that only senior management can sanction it [2].

Factors Affecting Benchmarking Projects Failure

Table 5 lists 14 factors which may have contributed to failure of benchmarking projects among the majority of the respondents of the 60 firms who reported that their benchmarking projects had failed to achieve the stated objectives of enhancing organizational effectiveness.

It can be clearly seen that unclear and inadequately understood objectives and goals of benchmarking projects is ranked first among all the critical factors for benchmarking projects failure. The following two factors are the lack

TABLE 3: Multiple Regression Analysis

Dependent Variable (Effectiveness)	Multiple Regression	Regression Square (R^2)	F-Ratio
Productivity (1)	0.38	0.32	9.30
Quality (2)	0.30	0.28	7.26
Satisfaction (3)	0.29	0.24	5.50
Performance (4)	0.43	0.35	4.11
Effectiveness (1 + 2 + 3 + 4)	0.40	0.30	8.40

All $p < .05$.

TABLE 4: Factors Affecting Benchmarking Success

Rank	Success Factors	Respondents (%)
1	Adequate planning	78
2	Adequate training	76
3	Effective implementation	74
4	Open interdepartmental communication	73
5	Strong strategic focus	70
6	Flexibility in achieving goals	68
7	Senior management interest and support	65
8	Adequate resources and information	63
9	Clear understanding of methodologies	60
10	Effective cross-functional teams	58
11	Solid understanding of own operations	56
12	Openness to change and new ideas	54
13	Willingness to share information with benchmarking partners	52
14	Dedication to ongoing benchmarking efforts	50
15	Focus on the customers and employees	49
16	Know how performance will be measured	46
17	Focus on the process not just the data	44
18	Clarity on where the data originated	42
19	Feedback and participation in all levels of the organization	41
20	Benchmarking must provide added value to the user	40

of effective methodology to implement benchmarking projects and the lack of support of senior management for benchmarking effort.

Other factors or serious impediments to successful benchmarking efforts identified include: lack of effective communication, poor team communication, fear of change, inadequate training, focus on the numbers not the process, and loss of focus on the customers and the employees.

SUMMARY

Several significant findings emerged as a result of this study. The attitudinal result presented in this article provides support for the claims of benchmarking proponents that the technique improves participants' productivity, quality, satisfaction and performance, and appears to be effective. The influence of participation in benchmarking techniques on organizational effectiveness was tested statistically for directionality and magnitude as well as for dependency. Statistical analysis was found to indicate that involvement in benchmarking programs was positively related to perceived changes in performance, quality, productivity, cycle time, customer service, job satisfaction, and business processes among employees in more than half (60%) of the surveyed organizations. At the same time, almost 40% of the surveyed respondents who implemented benchmarking techniques indicated that their benchmarking programs had failed to achieve their stated objectives of influencing and enhancing organizational effectiveness. One way to explain this finding is by suggesting that the stated objectives were too high, i.e., too much was expected from benchmarking projects. Hence, stated objectives were not met or the implementation of benchmarking was ineffective.

Additionally, the results presented in this study showed that there were several significant factors which may have contributed to benchmarking project success among more than half of the surveyed firms who had implemented benchmarking programs. Among these factors were the following: adequate planning, training, open interdepartmental communication, support and commitment by senior management, detailed implementation plans to perform benchmarking projects, cross-functional teams, and focus on customers and employees.

The results of this study also indicated that benchmarking was a huge job and a complex task, and must have a dedication to ongoing effort. These findings coincide with the claims of many academicians that success in benchmarking projects requires managers to know how to organize, inspire, deploy, motivate, enable, measure, and reward the value-adding operational work [19].

TABLE 5: Factors Affecting Benchmarking Failure

Rank	Failure Factors	Respondents (%)
1	Unclear goals and objectives	84
2	Lack of effective methodology to implement benchmarking	82
3	Lack of senior management support and participation	80
4	Lack of effective communication and feedback	76
5	Poor team communication	70
6	Fear of change and new ideas	65
7	Not enough training on measurement of data	62
8	Focusing on the numbers not the process	58
9	Lack clarity on where the data originated	52
10	Losing focus on the customers	50
11	Losing focus on the employees	46
12	Resistance by some staff	38
13	Legal and ethical issues	30
14	Lacking employee participation	28

Another finding emerging from this study showed that more than half (58%) of the surveyed respondents disagreed with the statement which indicates that the benchmarking program loses its momentum and its positive contribution to organizational effectiveness after a short period of time of its implementation. At the same time, almost 42% of the surveyed respondents who implemented benchmarking techniques indicated that their benchmarking programs had less significant contributions to their organizational effectiveness after one or two years of their implementation because of the lack of executive leadership support and participation.

CONCLUSION

Benchmarking has been prescribed as an important tool for attaining and maintaining competitive advantage. It also supports the organization's budgeting, strategic, and capital planning. Companies must be aware of ethical and legal issues. These issues serve as guidelines for both benchmarking partners to ensure mutual achievement of objectives.

Benchmarking makes it easy to identify the gap between where the organization would like to be and where it actually is. The gap analysis provides a measure of the improvement an organization would like to make. It is an effective tool because it involves everyone, management and workers. The drawback to this process is that mistakes are inevitable. However, senseless mistakes can be avoided by setting goals and following the rules to get there. By having top-level commitment, and by developing an effective project team with all the right components, managers can view benchmarking as an effective tool to attain competitiveness.

REFERENCES

1. Bateman, G. "Benchmarking Management Education, Teaching, and Curriculum." In *Benchmarking: the Search for Industry Best Practices that Lead to Superior Performance*, by Robert Camp. White Plains, NY: Quality Resources, 1994: 6.
2. *Benchmarking Action Plans and Legal Issues*. New York: Bureau of Business Practices, Paramount Publishing Business Technical and Professional Group, 1996.
3. Brookhart, S. "Benchmarking Networking." http://www.benchnet.com:80/bcode.txt. (March 10, 1997).
4. Certo, S. C. *Modern Management*. Boston, MA: Allyn and Bacon, 1994: 73–74.
5. Dolan, T. "Benchmarking Past, Present and Future/." *The Benchmarking Exchange*. http://www.benchet.com/bppf.htm (1997): 2.
6. Feltus, A. "Benchmarking Best Practices." http://ieiris.cc.boun.edu.tr/assist/akyuz/BENCH1.txt. (April 14, 1997).
7. Finch, B. J., and R. L. Luebbe. *Operations Management*. Ft. Worth, TX: The Dryden Press, 1995: 112–115.
8. Fuller, S. "Tools for Quality." http://www.abo.fi/sfuller/Ab-Van593.html (April 15, 1997).
9. Greengard, S. "Discover Best Practices Through Benchmarking." *Personnel Journal* 74, no. 1 (November 1995): 62(10).
10. Likert, R. "Human Resource Accounting Buildings and Assessing Productive Organizations." *Personnel* 2, no. 8 (May/June 1973): 8–24.
11. Linsenmeyer, A. "Fad or Fundamental?" *Financial World* (September 17, 1991): 34.
12. Lyonnais, P. "Why Benchmarking?" http://www.tbs-sct.gc.ca/tb/iqe/bmrkg e/benchme.html (April 15, 1997).
13. Martin, J. "Are You as Good as You Think You Are?" *Fortune* (September 30, 1996): 142–150.
14. Matters, M., and A. Evans "The Nuts and Bolts of Benchmarking." http://www.ozemail.com.au/~benchmark/nuts.bolts.html (February 18, 1997).
15. McNair, C. J., and K. H. J. Leibfried. *Benchmarking: A Tool for Continuous Improvement*. Essex Junction, VT: Oliver Wright Publications, 1992.
16. Muschter, S. "Research in Benchmarking." http://www.iwi.unisg.chi...m/ researchsmu/ index.html (March 10, 1997).
17. Omachonu, V. K., and J. R. Ross. *Principles of Total Quality*. Delray Beach, FL: St. Lucie Press, 1994: 137–154.
18. Pattison, D. D. "The Benchmarking Management Guide." *Accounting Review* 69 (April 1994): 42.
19. Power, J. V. "Sprint Corp: Blending in Benchmarking with Quality." *Continuous Journey*. American Productivity and Quality Center, 1995.
20. Rainey, H. A. "Benchmarking to Become Best in Class: Guiding Principles in Gresham, Oregon." *Government Finance Review* (February 1997): 5–9.
21. Ross, J. E. *Total Quality Management*. Delray Beach, FL: St. Lucie Press, 1995: 230–235;

About the Author—

DEAN ELMUTI, PhD, is a professor in the Department of Management and Marketing in the Lumpkin College of Business at Eastern Illinois University. Previously, he was employed for seven years by multinational corporations in the United States and the Middle East and was in charge of computer information systems for Toyota Motor Company in Saudi Arabia.

PUTTING COMMITMENT TO WORK THROUGH SHORT-CYCLE KAIZEN

Continuous improvement is all the rage in the world of manufacturing. A few programs get incremental results so fast that improvement looks continuous. Others, however, yield little because they put systems and people under a constant state of tension, demanding ever-better results without providing improvement tools or education. Successful programs rely on repeated, rapid but very systematic, methodology-based, crossfunctional attacks on bite-size plant floor targets. When the goal is continuous improvement, short-cycle kaizen is the gift that keeps on giving, but it is not free. Its price is measured not in dollars, but in the self-discipline it takes to conquer old habits, learn new methodologies, and rigorously adhere to new improvement protocols. Forget your old kaizen paradigm. This is a whole new ball game, and it's played by different rules.

by Ed Heard

Theory of Provided Conditions:
If you want to create a certain result,
you must first create the conditions that will
absolutely force that result to occur.

—Kazuma Tateisi

When kaizen first burst onto the American scene in 1986, initial reactions were varied. While many senior managers, told that it meant continuous improvement, welcomed it with open arms, others, already overwhelmed by intermittent but never-ending demands for better results, responded much less enthusiastically.

Traditionally, senior management relies on periodic operating unit performance reviews to identify and communicate the need for incremental improvement. After each review, the plant manager, in turn, translates senior man-

Ed Heard, DBA, president of Ed Heard & Associates, Inc., Brentwood, Tennessee, is a manufacturing management innovator, educator, and consultant who helps his wide variety of clients use kaizen and other time-based strategies to take time and money out of their processes while adding quality and value to them. Previously, he worked in manufacturing and electronics before becoming a professor at the University of South Carolina.

agement's feedback into instructions to each function or department. Such instructions leave little doubt as to which issues are hot and which are not.

Charged with getting better scores on one or more hot measures, each function or department responds predictably. First, each increases the volume settings for its hot issue activities. Second, each redirects its people resources to support higher volumes of hot issue activities. Third, each allows its cold issue activity volumes to decrease to the levels that the remaining resources will support.

To those who have experienced the phenomenon just described, the result is obvious. Borrowing resources from this period's cold issues creates the list of hot issues for the next period. Meanwhile, since no one addresses the waste and variation in the existing processes, cycle times are just as long, operating costs are just as high, and the defect rate is just as great as ever.

No doubt, adopting the term "continuous improvement" made it easier for senior managers to communicate their expectations more clearly. Yet, for some of their subordinates, it was catastrophic. As they quickly learned, improving performance on one or a few measures while letting others degenerate is one thing. Scoring better on one or a few measures without allowing others to worsen is quite another.

From *National Productivity Review*, Summer 1998, pp. 75-79. © 1998 by John Wiley and Sons, Inc. Reprinted by permission.

THE ADVENT OF THE LEAN THINKING ERA

Although continuous improvement took root and is still with us, kaizen gradually faded from the collective awareness of the industrial world. There it might well have remained except for a revolution in American manufacturing practices that began nearly 20 years ago. Originally introduced as the Toyota Production System, the new thinking was periodically reincarnated as just-in-time production, short-cycle manufacturing, world-class manufacturing, lean manufacturing, demand-flow technology, and most recently as lean thinking.

Although these incarnations clearly differ in small details, all question not just how well a manufacturer does what it does, but whether it does the right things. That difference shifts the focus from individual outcomes, results, or measures—dependent variables one and all—to independent variables—the actions, choices, and processes that govern manufacturing performance. Likewise, that difference clearly puts the improvement ball in management's court because no single function or department controls the collective set of things a manufacturer does.

As with every revolution, there were winners and losers. Some fell into the big-bang trap—trying to implement major changes across whole plants overnight. The winners appear to have been those who proceeded in the same way you would eat an elephant—one bite at a time.

Many got lost in a seemingly endless search for the one best answer, the optimal combination of several factors, or the best solution to a single issue like plant layout, just one of many issues that needed rethinking. Some reeducated everybody at once and hoped fruitlessly for a miracle. By contrast, those who put together crossfunctional SWAT-type teams for quick all-out assaults on bite-size

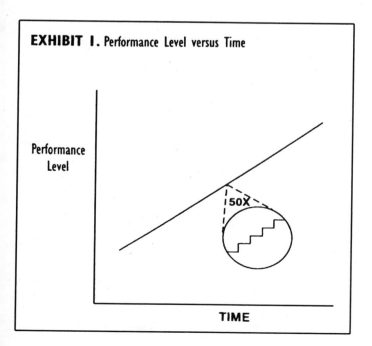

EXHIBIT I. Performance Level versus Time

Performance Level

50X

TIME

product/process combinations were well represented among the winners (see **Exhibit 1**).

The abilities to focus on small targets and rapidly mobilize crossfunctional resources are clearly two keys to successful improvement, but there is yet a third. The real winners of the American manufacturing revolution were those few that searched for and found not only the principles-based methodologies that identified the changes that needed to be made, but also a proven methodology-based, time-compressed, crossfunctional improvement process—short-cycle kaizen (SCK).

IMPROVEMENT IS NOT OPTIONAL

With few exceptions, this year's successful performance level is next year's failure threshold, regardless of arena or issue. Improve or stagnate. Stagnate and die. Improvement truly is not optional.

In the absence of continually escalating returns, owners get restless. After all, they supply the equity capital that fuels the engines of individual enterprises, large and small. When returns remain constant, or diminish, other capital pastures start to take on particularly attractive shades of green. There is no doubt that every enterprise needs to keep its owners happy, but what about its customers? In many respects customers are harder to keep happy than owners.

Although owners tend to demand higher levels of financial performance from quarter to quarter, customer demands are much more complex. Not only do they require ever-higher levels of performance on the current measures of supplier performance, they also add new measures from time to time. Delivery is a case in point. It used to be enough to deliver on time, but not any more. Now you've got to have short lead times and, once you've promised, deliver neither too early nor too late.

Competitors, of course, are behind much of the improvement pressure that customers put on enterprises. Customers reason that if your competitor can perform at a certain level on an accepted measure of performance in your market, then so should you. Likewise, if your competitor finds and exploits a brand new customer-sensitive product or service variable, then you must quickly match that capability just to stay even.

Historically, management decided what needed to be improved and engineering figured out how to get it done—until the sixties. Since then, information technologists have shared the improvement load with engineering.

Plant managers often complain that they have too much to do and too little time in which to do it. Perhaps that is because managers, engineers and information technologists typically share a common strength—or failing, depending on your point of view. All are predisposed by education and experience to think big. Consequently, the typical response to a genuine improvement need is a proposed project that will require big capital bucks and take 6 to 18 months to implement.

Launching new projects with several already in process guarantees that each one individually will take longer, cost more, and yield less. Too bad so few realize that excess projects in process affect project cost and completion times the same way that excess work-in-process affects manufacturing overhead and cycle times. Couple long project completion times with a few simultaneous externally driven changes in the plant, and the net result is often a very expensive solution to a problem that no longer exists in its original form.

As described earlier, the plant manager typically translates senior management's operating unit performance review feedback into instructions to each function or department. Unfortunately, such instructions typically address symptoms rather than causes. Then, functions or departments redirect resources to alleviate the symptoms. Unfortunately, the net effect is new symptoms elsewhere, a situation that is not likely to change until senior and plant managers understand the difference between symptom-based and methodology-based approaches to improvement.

The real problem is that every manufacturing entity is a system governed by simultaneous equations. Some relate activity volumes to various measures of performance, others relate activity volumes to resource constraints. In such systems, interaction among the resource constraints and the performance measurement equations ensures that gains in one or two measures are likely to be offset by losses in others. By contrast, methodology-based improvements modify the contribution and rate of usage coefficients of the performance measurement and resource consumption equations, respectively.

SUPPORT FROM THE FIELD FOR A ROBUST NEW TECHNOLOGY

In 1986, Masaaki Imai's book *Kaizen* launched the continuous improvement movement in North America. Yet a clear distinction between the ends approach to continuous improvement, described earlier, and the means approach, SCK, did not begin to emerge until the mid-nineties. Even now, the distinction is not widely appreciated.

In 1996, *Lean Thinking*, by James P. Womack and Daniel T. Jones, highlighted the schism in the continuous improvement movement. Specifically, the authors used detailed case histories to report very impressive means-based SCK improvements at Lantech, Wiremold, Pratt & Whitney, Porsche, and Showa. Examples include tenfold quality and throughput time improvements, four- to fivefold inventory turns improvements, and a halving of space and labor costs.

The importance of the means-based approach to improvement was underscored a year later, in 1997, when Imai's *Gemba Kaizen* appeared. Although the book is primarily about the application of nuts and bolts SCK methods in the workplace (gemba), it also incorporates several case histories. Because this collection of case histories also includes Wiremold, it is reassuring that the reported ac-

EXHIBIT 2. Heard's 14 Kaizen Points

1.	Dedicate	commit resources
2.	Measure	take before & after
3.	Focus	on bite-size chunks
4.	Train	teach recipes & tools
5.	Mix	functions/levels/sexes
6.	Empower	team to apply training
7.	Compress	limit start to finish time
8.	Authorize	priority & queue bypass
9.	Repeat	attack same target again
10.	Urge	do it before time runs out
11.	Reinforce	recognize and praise results
12.	Involve	combine veterans and virgins
13.	Proliferate	repeat kaizen elsewhere soon
14.	Perpetuate	require post-kaizen adherence

complishments are very much consistent with those described in *Lean Thinking*.

The outcomes of several SCK projects facilitated since 1994 suggest that the accomplishments reported in *Lean Thinking* and *Gemba Kaizen* are no flukes. Even more reassuring is the fact that results for plants with significantly different processes and products can be verified. Specific examples include plants that fabricate, assemble, and finish furniture; fabricate and assemble excavator buckets and articulated logging equipment; fabricate microchip wafers; hand-finish automotive trim; and cast and finish turbine blades and other small parts. The 14 points in **Exhibit 2** summarize what these organizations have learned about maximizing kaizen effectiveness.

Short-cycle kaizen is not about putting people and systems under a constant stress in hopes of continuous improvement. Instead, SCK is a methodology-based improvement process that can be used to generate changes for the better so fast that, seen from the distance of accounting numbers, improvement looks continuous.

Friction losses occur when individuals, functions and departments have the discretion to support or take a pass on supporting an individual improvement project. The discretion in question typically exists when an individual, function, or department is obligated to support multiple improvement projects simultaneously. Likewise, the longer the duration of the individual projects, the greater the probability that such discretion will be exercised. SCK incorporates a time-compressed format and 100 percent dedicated crossfunctional teams to avoid friction losses.

The cost justification trap prevents the implementation of many apparently sound improvement proposals. One problem is that some benefits are particularly hard to quantify. Another problem is that while first-order impacts are easy to spot, second-, third-, and higher-order effects are not; SCK uses improvement methodologies that are not capital intensive and simple physical before-and-after measurements to avoid the cost justification trap.

Concentrating resources on a particular portion of the opponent's defense is the key to winning in activities as diverse as politics, football, and warfare. But bringing in hired guns and throwing them at a small problem is hardly an efficient way to address the need for continuous improvement. SCK provides a way to concentrate small groups of people resources on bite-size chunks of the plant floor for short periods of time. The results are typically dramatic—quick step-function improvements.

Each kaizen, or, SCK project, progresses through three distinct stages (see **Exhibit 3**). Preparation, the first stage, starts with the selection of a concentrated plant floor target, continues with the definition of the project's objectives, and ends when resource needs have been identified and filled. Ideally, the preparation phase generates several outputs:

- **Team mandate**—specifies the objectives of the kaizen team, the people who will be members of the team, and what the team is and is not authorized to do.
- **Kaizen schedule**—specifies when the kaizen will occur and how that time will be split between education, analysis, reporting, planning, and implementing.
- **Results scorecard**—defines how the impact of the changes will be measured.
- **Participant manual**—provides tools and templates, as well as the necessary target-specific conceptual background.
- **Resources checklist**—designates general and specific support needs.

The keys to the success of the second phase, execution, are:

- **Educate**—a facilitator introduces the SCK process and a lean production vision, shows how the team's mandate relates to that vision, and provides the tools and templates the team will need to carry out its mandate.
- **Harness**—a facilitator helps the team understand and fill leadership positions, and internalize how its results scorecard and tools and templates relate to its mandate.
- **Attack**—the team, assisted by the facilitator, uses its tools and templates to analyze current conditions and to design and implement changes for the better in its target area.

Done correctly, the perpetuation phase produces at least the following:

- **Work standards**—detailed sequential descriptions of the individual actions and times that take place during an iteration of a worker's cycle time.
- **Immediate training needs**—workers who will need to be trained to conform to the new work standards, by shift and name.
- **Adherence control plan**—a list of what must be checked, when or how often it must be checked, where it must be checked, who must check it, and how they must check it to ensure the changes for the better become part of the daily routine.
- **Documentation impact checklist**—a reminder to the formal organization that certain documentation may need updating to support the changes for the better.
- **Transaction impact checklist**—a way to inform the information technology group of any impact that the changes for the better may have on transactions.
- **30-day follow-up checklist**—a way to spot areas where improvement actions have been abandoned and to identify appropriate remedial actions.

TEACHING OLD MANAGERS NEW TRICKS

Although SCK is very attractive, it is still just one weapon in the improvement war. What about formal engineering programs, ongoing continuous improvement teams, and individual suggestion systems? When it comes to improvement, one size definitely does not fit all. Each of the above approaches has its own strengths and weaknesses, just as SCK does. It takes all four to cover all of an organization's improvement bases.

Like everything else, SCK has its price. Yet unlike engineering-driven improvements, that price can't be measured in dollars. Instead, its price is measured in the self-discipline it takes to conquer old habits, learn new methodologies, and rigorously adhere to new improvement protocols.

The management commitment requirements, for example, are unprecedented. It is one thing to publicly commit to ever-better results, quite another to commit to a never-

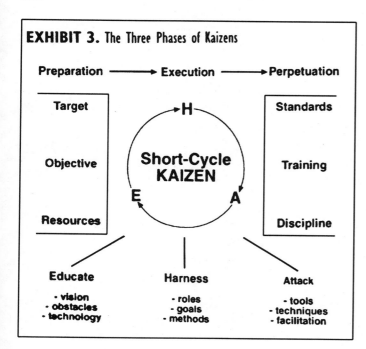

EXHIBIT 3. The Three Phases of Kaizens

ending series of methodology-based changes for the better. Yet, that's the level of commitment that SCK requires.

Committing to SCK implies willingness to accept and rely on the two basic process improvement principles: waste elimination and variance reduction. Still further, it implies willingness to redirect much of the discretionary energy and resources at plants to support the applications of improvement methodologies based on those two principles.

One of the most effective ways for top management to signal its commitment is to set up SCK promotion offices at corporate headquarters and at each individual plant, then to assign each office dual missions: first, to coordinate and promote kaizens; second, to transfer the SCK technology from external sources to local operations.

Plants that embrace SCK and weave it into the fabric of everyday life receive a gift that keeps on giving. Each project reveals at least two or three clear improvement opportunities beyond the scope of the current one. These opportunities combine with a steady stream of suggestions and requests to ensure a perpetual backlog of improvement opportunities. Inevitably, some of these opportunities are in areas that were targets of previous projects.

If you find yourself wondering why the former team or teams didn't do it right the first time, you're probably suffering from optimitis—the belief prevalent among traditional managers and engineers that one is, or should be, smart enough to anticipate and avoid all possible future negative outcomes of current choices.

By contrast, consider the changes for the better that are implemented during kaizens. Each change is incorporated into one or more work standards to perpetuate the changes for the better. In turn, the work standards act as "watch-dogs" in the continuous improvement ratchet to prevent performance from degenerating to its former level. Each subsequent visit to the same target area results in another turn of the ratchet—that is, still higher performance. Counterintuitive as it may seem to traditionalists, each turn of the ratchet also reveals clear obstacles to the next higher level of performance, obstacles that simply can't be addressed during the time frame of the current project.

Plant managers can signal their commitment to continuous improvement by appointing a credible full-time professional head of the SCK promotion office. Fulfilling the responsibilities of that position requires Toyota Production System expertise, evangelical zeal, persistence, persuasiveness, diplomacy, and administrative competence. Finding all those skills in one person is unusual. Typically you have to settle for someone who meets two or three of these requirements, and has the potential and drive to pick up the remaining skills on the fly. Clearly it is not a job for the fainthearted or someone just marking time until retirement.

What about the technology handoff issue? How do you acquire the necessary kaizen methodology, tools, templates, and expertise to get started? You can make it, buy it, or rent it. Each has its drawbacks, but choosing the rental option for a limited startup period is the shortest route to early benefits and a well-developed internal capability.

As the intervals between kaizens become shorter, the lines on performance measurement graphs smooth out and bend in the desired direction. If continuous improvement is your goal, a never-ending series of rapid, repeated, crossfunctional, methodology-based attacks (kaizens) on contained plant floor targets is your only viable alternative.

RALLY OF THE DOLLS

It Worked for Toyota. Can It Work for Toys?

FOR THREE-QUARTERS OF A CENtury, little girls have been unwrapping Madame Alexander dolls at Christmas. The collectible dolls, which cost from $40 to $600 apiece, are modeled on figures both fictional (Cinderella) and real (Elizabeth Taylor); with their hand-painted faces and elaborate costumes, they're charming artifacts of an age before Nintendos and Furbies. But the company that makes them has had to struggle to stay alive for its 75th Christmas. That the dolls are still around is due to an unusual group of manufacturing experts, who have adapted their experience in streamlining the assembly of fenders and crankshafts to the task of turning out wigs, shoes, and all the other tiny bits that go into a doll.

Alexander Doll Co. was founded in 1923 by "Madame" Beatrice Alexander, a daughter of Russian immigrants who was raised over her father's doll hospital in New York City. Her business prospered, and in the 1950s she moved it to a six-story building in Harlem. But after it was sold to two local investors for $20 million, the company faltered. It was headed into bankruptcy in 1995 when it was bought for $17.5 million by an investment group formed by TBM Consulting.

The partners of TBM, a North Carolina–based firm of manufacturing specialists, had studied Toyota's

SUZANNE OPTON (3)

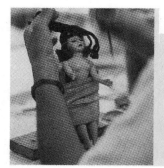

At Alexander Doll Co. new managers have overhauled the factory in Harlem using Toyota techniques.

Reprinted from the January 11, 1999, issue of *Fortune*, p. 36, by special permission. © 1999 by Time, Inc.

lean production system in Japan and had taught it to dozens of American manufacturers. TBM had assembled a buyout fund and was looking for underperforming companies where they could put their know-how to work. "We have a contrarian strategy," says TBM vice president Bill Schwartz. "Instead of moving production somewhere else, we want to make it lean and efficient at its current location."

Making dolls is easier than making, say, Lexus LS400s, but not as easy as you'd think. The costumes alone contain 20 or more separate items, which have to go through as many as 30 production steps. Accurate planning is essential because doll fabric is bought in tiny quantities that can't be reordered, and 75% of the styles change every year. As if that weren't difficult enough, before TBM arrived the factory was using archaic methods: It was organized according to old-fashioned princi-

ples of batch manufacturing, so boxes of costume material and vinyl doll parts were stacked to the ceiling. Since nothing was built to order, more than 90,000 dolls were stored in partly finished condition, and customers waited up to 16 weeks for delivery.

That began to change in August 1996 when TBM installed a new CEO: Herbert Brown, an earnest, fast-talking manufacturing expert who had run operations for Black & Decker and Johnson & Johnson. When Brown tried to fill a customer order for 300 dolls, only 117 could be completed because so many pieces were missing. So he went to work reorganizing the factory and, in true Toyota fashion, enlisted the aid of the 470 workers, mostly Dominican immigrants who speak limited English.

Instead of individually producing parts, the workers were organized in seven- or eight-person teams, each

of which is responsible for completing about 300 doll or wardrobe assemblies a day. The amount of work in progress has been cut by 96%, and orders can now be filled in one or two weeks instead of two months. TBM also hired Bain & Co., a consulting firm, to help expand sales to collector doll shops and to create new marketing programs for home-shopping channels on cable television.

Gradually Alexander Doll is returning to health. Sales have risen from $23.8 million in 1995 to an estimated $32 million for 1998, though the company isn't expected to turn a profit until next year But the workers of Alexander Doll have a vivid incentive to apply Toyota's techniques, because the building itself is a constant reminder of what happens to companies that don't adapt to changing times. The doll factory's first occupant? Studebaker.

—*Alex Taylor III*

STRATEGIES

FLY, DAMN IT, FLY

A new Boeing crew tries to navigate a turnaround

Since Alan R. Mulally was named president of Boeing Co.'s commercial airplane unit on Sept. 1, he has conferred with his top 14 managers every Thursday morning for four hours. The meetings move from one Puget Sound plant to another, but the agenda remains the same: fixing Boeing. These managers aren't jawboning about airy vision statements. They're poring over production numbers and cost reports, trying to drive operating margins for Boeing's largest business from near zero back up to 8% or more. Mulally recites the same mantra at each meeting: "The data will set us free."

That focus on numbers is a novel and long overdue change in Boeing's hidebound culture. Underlying its well-publicized travails—staggering production snafus and cost over-runs that led to big losses despite a record boom in orders—are much deeper problems. In an era when price and efficiency are king, the company is saddled with bureaucracy, redundant processes, and antiquated information technology. "Boeing has not changed very much since World War II," says Bill Whitlow, investment manager for SAFECO Northwest Fund, holder of $2.7 million in Boeing stock. Adds Paul H. Nisbet, president of aerospace analyst JSA Research Inc.: "Boeing needs a thorough scrubbing of its operations from top to bottom."

Now, after a management shakeup at its August board meeting, the scrubbing has begun in earnest. The reorganization came in the wake of $4.45 billion in writedowns over the past 18 months and net profits of only $308 million—or less than 1.2%—on first-half 1998 revenues of $26.3 billion. Boeing was split into three units—commercial, defense, and space—and the former head of commercial aircraft was forced out. New executives are now in charge of the units, including two who aren't Boeing lifers. That's almost unprecedented, and reflects how far Chief Executive Philip M. Condit, 57, and Chief Operating Officer Harry C. Stonecipher, 62, are willing to go.

They don't have much choice: Their own jobs are on the line if they can't end Boeing's seemingly endless litany of troubles. One Boeing director says privately that the pair still has board support. But Peter L. Aseritis, an analyst with Credit Suisse First Boston Corp., figures the

BACK TO THE HANGAR

Boeing execs says they have production woes under control, but more steps are needed to assure long-term health

FIX PRODUCTION FOR GOOD Boeing has unkinked the snarls that plagued its Seattle factories for the past year. But computer systems that were supposed to streamline purchasing and production still aren't in place, and costs remain above historic levels. Fixing those problems is Job No. 1 for new management.

MAKE UP WITH SUPPLIERS During its ramp-up, Boeing stretched suppliers with extravagant demands for parts and raw materials—and then lured away many of their workers. Now, it is trying to treat those companies more like partners, including them on decisions and signing long-term contracts.

PUSH BACK DELIVERIES Given the state of the world economy, Boeing needs to take a reality check on its goal of making 620 jets next year. If Boeing can persuade customers to delay deliveries, it will gain some breathing room and hold on to the orders until 2001, when annual deliveries drop to 476.

DEAL WITH UNNEEDED ASSETS By 2001, all commercial McDonnell Douglas lines will have been shut down in Long Beach, Calif. The 100-seat 717 won't generate enough volume to carry the facility. Boeing needs to pare away or redeploy excess personnel and facilities like Long Beach that it acquired through mergers.

Reprinted with special permission from *Business Week*, November 9, 1998, pp. 150-156. © 1998 by The McGraw-Hill Companies, Inc.

board will give Condit a nine-month grace period before "taking him by the scruff of the neck and throwing him out the door."

Those nine months will go by fast. Condit and team say they are on the verge of fixing the bottlenecks that have slowed airplane deliveries and hammered profits. Facing enormous pressure to deliver airplanes on time, Boeing execs say they have to focus first on getting products out the door. "We have to get productivity back to the levels we've had before, and then redesign the process to take more cost out," Condit says. But beyond that, the plan Condit has spelled out is a course of incrementalism. And so far, it's lacking in details. The broad outlines: complete stalled plans to modernize the computer systems used to produce planes, trim tens of thousands of jobs, and remake relationships with Boeing's enormous supply chain.

Will it be enough? As long as Boeing continues to beat profit estimates, as it did for the third quarter, Wall Street seems to be regaining patience. Boeing's turmoil battered its stock by 50%, from 60½ in July 1997 to 30⅜ last August. But since the reorganization, it has recovered 16%, to around 35. "They've bought themselves some time," says investor Robert Finch, whose Aeltus Investment Management in Hartford, Conn., holds $4.6 million in Boeing shares. The reorganization, he says, shows the company is "paying attention to the bottom line."

Certainly the changes come none too soon. A redesign actually has been under way for five years, but it was seriously sidetracked by Boeing's production push. The process began in the early 1990s, during the trough of the last business cycle, when Boeing unveiled an ambitious plan to streamline aircraft assembly. But when business took off in 1995, Boeing focused on grabbing as many orders as it could. Management had been shocked the year before when its arch-rival, the European government-subsidized Airbus Industrie consortium, outsold it for the first

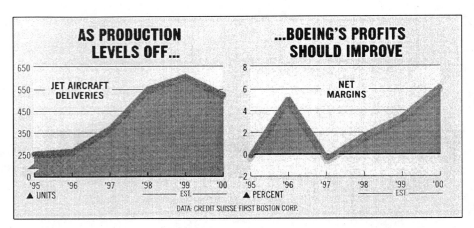

AS PRODUCTION LEVELS OFF...

JET AIRCRAFT DELIVERIES

650 550 450 350 250 0

'95 '96 '97 '98 '99 '00

▲ UNITS — EST. —

...BOEING'S PROFITS SHOULD IMPROVE

NET MARGINS

8 6 4 2 0 -2

'95 '96 '97 '98 '99 '00

▲ PERCENT — EST. —

DATA: CREDIT SUISSE FIRST BOSTON CORP.

CHART BY ERIC HOFFMANN/BW

time. To protect share, Boeing launched an all-out war, with discounts as high as 25%, analysts say.

Boeing won the battle, but ended up with a bulging order book of low-balled planes. Scaling up production to build all those planes sent costs soaring. That's why analysts expect the commercial airplane group, which lost $1.8 billion after charges in 1997, to end this year some $61 million in the red. "I'm convinced it was one of the most dysfunctional maneuvers in the history of American business," says Richard Aboulafia, director of aviation consulting for Teal Group Corp.

HOMELESS PLANES. Boeing is still digging out. Its anemic net margins, which are expected to be 1.7% this year, will creep up to 3.4% in 1999, analysts predict. Even customers are feeling the cost-cutting push; Boeing, for example, now makes them pay for nonstandard features on planes. In early October, both United Airlines Inc. and United Parcel Service Inc. complained to Boeing that it was balking at making minor fixes to planes they had ordered. After a heated meeting on Oct. 8, however, United went away satisfied. "I am very, very positive about the steps they are taking," says Andrew P. Studdert, a senior vice-president for United parent UAL Corp.

Customers and investors are pinning their hopes especially on Stonecipher. The hard-nosed former CEO of McDonnell Douglas Corp., who arrived in 1997 with Boeing's

$16.3 billion acquisition, has already instilled a more by-the-numbers approach. He pressed Boeing, for the first time, to provide earnings guidance to Wall Street. And he supported Mulally's plan to push profit and loss responsibility down to individual plants, another first.

Still, any fixes could be swamped by worldwide economic problems. As America's largest exporter, Boeing is especially vulnerable to turmoil in Asia, where it sells a third of its commercial planes. Even as it gets production back on track, 34 finished aircraft are parked in the Arizona desert, unclaimed by strapped airlines such as Garuda Indonesia and Philippine Airlines. Condit himself now admits that earlier estimates of Asia's impact on orders may have been too low.

Those undelivered planes weigh heavily on the balance sheet, and Boeing can't turn off its production spigot quickly. Indeed, the company is still planning to raise output to a record 51 planes a month in the first quarter of 1999 because it has to meet longstanding delivery commitments. Yet it told analysts on Oct. 22 that up to 15% of its output for the next five quarters, or more than 120 planes, may go homeless, pending new financing deals or resales to other airlines.

Longer term, Condit must take a cold look at demand for aircraft. He still holds to forecasts that the global market will demand new planes at an average annual rate of 8% of the world's fleet for the next 20 years—

5% growth and 3% replacement. But analysts and customers say that may be high. "Boeing is like a huge freight train that takes a couple of miles to slow down," says John Plueger, co-chief operating officer of International Lease Finance. "They have to talk to their customers now about deferrals." On Oct. 20, Malaysian Airlines became the latest Asian carrier to back out, delaying 12 planes worth $2 billion.

Boeing's challenges aren't borne solely by the commercial-airplane unit, which accounts for 64% of revenues. In the defense arena, executives must figure out how to hike revenues while military budgets shrink. Indeed, some production lines could shut down in two years if new orders don't appear from the U.S. or abroad. And in the fast-developing space and communications business, a run of bad luck and heavy research spending are holding margins to less than 4% (see box, "A Space Venture That's Sputtering").

The new management team has a healthy dose of non-Boeing blood. The commercial airplane group, based near Seattle, is now under Mulally, 52, who previously headed Boeing's Information, Space & Defense Systems group. That group is now split in two: Michael M. Sears, 51, a veteran McDonnell Douglas exec, runs the defense operation out of McDonnell's old St. Louis home. And James F. Albaugh, 48, who came to Boeing when it bought Rockwell International Corp.'s space business in 1996 for $3.1 billion, heads space and communications in Southern California.

All three need to boost profit margins, but Mulally faces the toughest job. So far, though, his plans are short on specifics. Clearly, first priority is to finish cleaning up Boeing's production woes. Once parts are all arriving on time and workers are better trained, he'll focus on cutting costs. "We have another year to go before we get back to efficiency levels we had before we traumatized the whole system," he concedes.

Aside from tweaking the production flow, the only ways he can lower costs now are automation and layoffs. Both are already under way. Boeing has said it aims to cut total payroll, now at 235,000, to as low as 210,000 by the end of 1999. For a change, much of the pain could fall to white-collar workers, not to the factory staff Boeing needs to get planes out the door. Pink slips have already gone out to 1,100 employees. But analyst Nicholas P. Heymann of Prudential Securities Inc. thinks Boeing might have to cut as many as 70,000 people.

The automation problem is even more nagging. Boeing is one of the world's largest users of information technology, but it hosts a bewildering array of 400 systems. Data are so diffused that Boeing can't centralize procurement of the millions of parts used across its product line: An identical part may be manufactured in-house for one airplane and outsourced for another. Boeing is putting in place a new $1 billion system that ties together all its old computers, but it has ballooned in complex-

ity and now won't be fully operational until after 2000.

PROCUREMENT OVERHAUL. With good systems in place, Mulally should eventually be able to better track inventory and forecast demand for parts. Even so, Boeing is years behind Airbus in electronically managing its supplier relations, a crucial step that saves costs on both sides. And software alone won't make partners of suppliers, many of whom felt burned by Boeing's extravagant demands for parts and raw materials during the production surge. For that, Boeing is overhauling procurement, forging long-term deals like the 10-year, $4.3 billion contract it announced Aug. 31 to buy aluminum from just five firms instead of the previous 50. Top suppliers invited to a two-day Boeing schmoozefest in early October say they were impressed by the company's new focus.

Still, Boeing has to prove it can keep that focus, even as boom times come to an end. But the economic crisis could have a silver lining: Order deferrals from carriers could help Boeing smooth the peaks and valleys of the cycle. "Just about the time we need another good kick, [Asian carriers] are going to be ready to go again," says Condit. "That'll help us carry on long-term." Assuming that by the time orders pick up again, Boeing has learned how to build planes for a profit.

By Andy Reinhardt in San Mateo and Seanna Browder in Seattle, with bureau reports

Unit 2

Unit Selections

Key Points to Consider

❖ How would you define and measure quality for a manufacturer? How would you define and measure quality for a service firm?

❖ What are the basic beliefs and principles of Total Quality Management (TQM)?

❖ Some critics believe that TQM is just a management fad, whereas others see it as a permanent fixture in management. What is your belief and why?

 **Links** **www.dushkin.com/online/**

These sites are annotated on pages 4 and 5.

Over the last two decades greater emphasis has been placed upon quality and TQM: Total Quality Management. After World War II, American manufacturing firms had little significant foreign competition. European and Japanese factories were destroyed to a great extent during the war. American firms were able to increase their volume of exports to the world and labor enjoyed requesting and receiving higher wages. By the 1970s, American firms recognized growing production capabilities abroad. Clearly, by the 1980s, American firms faced greater challenges from foreign competitors. The growing United States trade deficit provided evidence of increased imports into the United States and evidence of greater difficulty in exporting American products.

By the 1980s, American firms recognized that they could no longer compete in a global market on the basis of lowest cost per unit. With lower wages abroad, foreign competitors had an advantage in competing on low cost. Some American manufacturers sought to deal with this situation by pressuring labor unions to accept minimal wage gains in negotiations and others relocated production overseas. Even with these efforts, American firms continued to face a trade challenge.

One solution that emerged in the 1980s was for American firms to compete globally on the basis of quality. The late Dr. W. Edwards Deming, a pioneer in the quality movement, had taught Japanese firms how they could improve quality. His approach to quality improvement relied upon statistical process control and a focus upon manufacturing principles that emphasized continuous improvement. The growth of exports from Japanese firms after the 1950s provided

Quality

evidence that total quality management was a desirable approach for company success.

The articles in this unit examine the evolution of quality and attempts by firms to implement TQM. A conversation with Joseph Juran reviews the beliefs of one of the pioneers in quality control. With ISO 9000 quality system standards required in Europe, firms see the necessity of improving and documenting quality systems.

The final articles review some difficulties that firms have encountered in implementing TQM. Through proper care in implementing TQM, including both top management support and lower-level employee buy-in, most firms should see favorable results.

Evolution of the quality profession

Navin Shamji Dedhia
5080 Bougainvillea Drive, San Jose, CA 95111, USA

Abstract *The quality profession evolved from quality control to quality engineering to quality system in the twentieth century. The future of the quality profession is bright, but challenging and demanding, and provides many more opportunities.*

Introduction

No other profession has seen as many changes as the quality profession. The quality profession grew from simple control to engineering to systems engineering. Quality control activities were predominant in the 1940s, 1950s and 1960s. The 1970s were an era of quality engineering; the 1990s show quality systems as an emerging field. Quality systems require global thinking in many facets. These days one-sided views have been replaced by many-sided views for assessing and deciding the course of actions.

In the past, people in the quality field needed to be proficient in statistics, statistical control charts, regression analysis, sampling plans and other techniques. Over the years, many software packages have been developed and the quality professionals can use these as aids in making intelligent decisions. ISO element 4.20 requires the use of statistical techniques to establish control, and verify process capability and product characteristics.

Quality professional recognition came in the late 1960s with the introduction of Certified Quality Engineer (CQE)

From *Total Quality Management*, Vol. 8, No. 6, 1997, pp. 391-393. © 1997 by Carfax Publishing Ltd. Reprinted by permission.

examinations by the American Society for Quality Control (ASQC). Since then, other certification examinations, such as Certified Reliability Engineer (CRE), Certified Quality Auditor (CQA), Certified Quality Manager (CQM), Certified Quality Technician (CQT) and Certified Mechanical Inspector (CMI) examinations have been introduced by ASQC.

The state of California was the first to introduce Professional Engineer in Quality recognition through examination in the late 1970s. Lead assessors and auditors gained recognition with the acceptance of ISO 9000 standards worldwide.

New advantages were found in using proven tools and techniques such as teamwork, reengineering, benchmarking, total quality management and six sigma. These buzz words were not in the quality dictionary a few years ago.

Universities and community colleges started offering degrees and certificates in the quality science field. Short courses were offered by some universities and colleges to those who did not have the time to pursue degree courses. Training courses and tutorials, from the basics to advanced material, are available from many sources. Books, magazines, periodicals, audio/video tapes and CD-ROM devices provide study tools to enable progress at one's own pace. The explosion of information on electronic highway media (the Internet) has created much more interest in the quality field. Productivity and efficiency increases have been realized with the evolution of personal computers, electronic communication and the Internet.

The quality profession came into the limelight with an increase in global competition, the loss of market share, national quality award schemes and the ISO 9000 standards. From layman to the top executive, everyone became familiar with the quality profession. The quality profession field became popular in the 1980s and 1990s.

Quality roles

They are called quality engineer, process quality engineer, procurement quality engineer, quality manager, reliability engineer, quality auditor or some other title, but their job is to satisfy internal and ultimate customers by taking appropriate course of actions. Manufacturing floor responsibility was of prime importance to quality professionals in the 1940s and 1950s. With the increase in liability lawsuits, quality professionals became more involved in product usage by customers. As manufacturers started buying products from more and more suppliers, auditors' role increased considerably. As customers and consumers placed a heavy emphasis on quality of the product, quality organizations grew. The words quality and the quality profession attracted everyone. The quality profession became an attractive career for many.

Environment

Then came stiff competition and global marketing approach. The need was to decrease cost and increase profitability. Companies started to look at ways to reduce the cost. Quality organization has always been viewed by outsiders as a non-value added function. As a result, quality professionals became the target of lay-offs. At the same time, companies started to re-engineer the processes. Business process analysis showed new ways of running the processes. Work simplification, automation, re-engineered processes and other approaches demanded fewer and fewer quality professionals. Quality organizations have been reduced owing to cost-cutting measures, down-sizing and right-sizing. The maker of the product is responsible for the quality of the product.

Prevention, appraisal and failure cost data analysis showed where to keep the emphasis. Appraisal and failure costs were high compared to prevention costs. Appraisal and failure costs were reduced with the preventive approach. Initially, prevention costs increased, but with time they decreased considerably.

Quality organization in big corporations reduced to less than 20% of what it was a few years ago. Quality organization remains mainly for auditing or monitoring purposes. Fewer and fewer inspectors are left on the manufacturing floor as the inspection work has been reduced by automation, rigid design and an emphasis on training and education of the assembly workers. In many organizations only a skeleton crew of quality professionals are left in advising and consulting roles. Many organizations hire outside quality consultants on a temporary basis instead of hiring permanently. As a result, quality consulting companies and independent quality consultants grew in number and size.

The future

With few quality professionals left in any one organization, they will play key roles in the company's operation. Quality professionals will be like consultants or advisors. Their advice and views will be sought for critical decisions. Keen global competition and quality consciousness will not reduce the importance of the quality professionals. Systems and global thinking will play key roles. Quality professionals will be required to be masters of all trades. Specialization will be replaced by generalization with an overall view of the business operation.

More opportunities are waiting for the quality professionals in service industries and small companies. Health care, educational institutions and governments have started taking a keen interest in the quality science field.

Conclusions

The role played by the quality professional in the twenty-first century will be quite different from the role played in the twentieth. The quality profession will require systems thinking, a strategic approach and team playing. The quality profession will not be part of the individual contributor, but will be a team contributor. Working smarter rather than working harder will be a norm for the quality profession. Knowledge of human psychology, software applications and teamwork concepts will be an asset, besides statistical knowledge.

It will not be an easy path for quality professionals. There will be a constant fight for survival. The demanding and challenging future will not accept a bureaucratic approach. A flexible approach based on sound judgement and ethical principles will be accepted wholeheartedly. An efficient and effective approach will be required in all actions undertaken.

Don't read this article unless you want to add the term "poka-yoke" to your vocabulary. In the hands of Richard Chase, the Japanese term for "foolproof" becomes the means to do all of the tantalizingly simple actions necessary to do it right the first time.

fool

PO•KA YO•KE

PROOF SERVICE

BY RICHARD B. CHASE The Justin Dart Term Professor of Operations Management and Director of the Center for Operations Management Education and Research & DOUGLAS M. STEWART PhD '95

We know of no book on quality that does not advocate the "first principle of quality"—Do It Right the First Time—in chapter one. Likewise, we know of no book that provides any detailed theory or specific actions for doing this for services. There remains, therefore, the monumental challenge of quality assurance where the goal is to achieve zero defects in the day-to-day provision of services. While we are in favor of creating quality cultures, continuous improvement processes, quality training in statistics and the like, managers are missing a good bet by not starting fail-safing early in parallel with traditional quality initiatives.

Mr. Improvement

The idea of fail-safing is to prevent the inevitable mistake from turning into a defect. This basic precept was articulated by the late Shigeo Shingo (known as "Mr. Improvement" in Japan). In his many writings, Shingo showed examples of how manufacturing companies have set up their equipment in manual processes to prevent errors, particularly where full-scale automation is too costly or is otherwise impractical.

Central to Shingo's approach is inspection and "poka-yoke." A poka-yoke is a simple, built-in step in a process which must be performed before the next stage can be performed. In a manufacturing context, this may mean that someone running a brick-cutting machine would be forced to push a button with each hand simultaneously

before the blade will come down, assuring that there are no hands left to be injured in the machine. Service poka-yokes function in exactly the same manner, assuring that some important step is performed so that the server is literally forced to perform the service well.

Task Poka-Yokes

Errors in the service task are errors in the functional aspects of the service, such as doing the work incorrectly, doing work not requested, doing work in the wrong order or doing work too slowly. There are many examples of poka-yoke devices for the detection and avoidance of task errors, including computer prompts to aid in technical discussions, strategically placed microphones to assure server's and customer's voices are audible, placing bills on a tray on top of the cash register to avoid making errors in change and use of the appropriate types of measuring and weighing tools. The french-fry scoopers at McDonald's are a perfect example of such a measuring tool. Sewell Cadillac and other like facilities use color-coded tags or icons on the tops of cars to help identify customers who belong to a specific service adviser and to show the order of arrival; the adviser can then look out across the sea of cars and find the next car he or she should deal with.

Due to the extreme costs of errors, hospitals are heavy users of poka-yokes in their medical processes. Trays used to hold surgical instruments have indentations for each instrument, and all of the instruments needed for a given

From *USC Business*, Spring 1994, pp. 33-35. © 1994 by the University of Southern California. Reprinted by permission.

operation will be nested in the tray. In this manner, it is clearly evident if all instruments have not been removed from the patient before the incision is closed.

Treatment Poka-Yokes

Treatment errors by the server are errors in interpersonal contact between the server and the customer, such as failure to acknowledge to the customer, failure to listen to the customer and failure to treat appropriately. Standard treatment poka-yokes include signals such as eye-contact to acknowledge the customer's presence in a restaurant and the sound of bells from the shop door.

A novel poka-yoke is used by a major hotel chain to fail-safe recognition and timely acknowledgment of a guest's repeat business. The way it works is that when the bellman greets the arriving guest to bring his luggage, he asks if it is her first visit. If the guest says she has been there before, the bellman will discreetly tug on his own ear to indicate this fact to the front desk. The clerk at the desk will then greet the guest with a hearty "Welcome back!"

Many service companies train their service personnel to read negative non-verbal clues given by the customer early in the service encounter. This inspection activity allows the employee to take timely action to prevent any communication mistake. One poka-yoke for this is used at a bank to ensure eye contact with the customer: tellers are required to check-off the customer's eye color on a checklist as they start the transaction. In a similar vein, some companies place mirrors next to customer-service reps phones to fail-safe a "smiling voice" to their unseen customers.

A fast-food restaurant listed "friendliness" as one aspect of front-line employee behavior they wished to fail-safe. Rather than mandating that employees smile all the time, the mentors provided four specific cues as to when to smile. These were: when greeting the customer, when taking the order, when telling the customer about the dessert special and when giving the customer change. Employees were encouraged to observe whether the customers smiled back—a natural reinforcer for smiling. While it is tempting to disparage such behavioral management as simply Skinnerian manipulation, the fact is that when properly executed, the approach has been shown to lead to positive results for both the server and the served.

Tangible Poka-Yokes

Tangible errors made by the server are errors in the physical elements involved in the service, such as dirty waiting rooms and incorrect or unclear bills. There are many examples of poka-yokes to prevent tangible errors. One action is to position a mirror so that the worker can auto-

> **A *poka-yoke* is a simple, built-in step in a process which must be performed before the next stage can be performed.**

matically check his or her appearance before greeting the customer. The paper strips that are wrapped around towels in many hotels serve as a poke-yoke to the housekeeping staff. The strips identify the clean linen and show which towels should be replaced. Most software programs have built-in checks for spelling and arithmetic errors, some of which even prompt the user to use before printing. W. M. Mercer Inc., a leading consulting firm in benefits and healthcare, engages in "peer review"—systematic preauditing by pairs of its associates—of all consulting reports. And Motorola's legal department performs a similar double checking with its two lawyer rule: all aspects of the legal work, memorandums, oral presentations, contract drafts and so on are reviewed by a second lawyer.

The Customer Is Always Right

While "the customer is always right," he also is frequently error-prone. In fact, research done by TARP, a service research firm, indicates that one-third of all customer complaints are caused by the customers themselves. Because of the customers' integral part in the service, their actions must therefore be fail-safed in all three phases of a service encounter: the preparation, the encounter itself and the resolution to the encounter.

Preparation Poka-Yokes

Specific examples of preparation error include failure to bring necessary materials to the encounter, failure to understand and anticipate their role in the service transaction and failure to engage the correct service. Preparation poka-yokes we have all encountered are "dress code" requests on invitations, reminder calls about dental appointments and the use of bracelets inscribed with the wearer's special medical condition. Many doctors and dentists give patients a card with information about a follow-up appointment rather than trusting them to note it themselves.

Encounter Poka-Yokes

Customer errors during the encounter can be due to inattention, misunderstanding or simply a memory lapse. Such errors include failure to remember steps in the service process, failure to specify desires sufficiently and failure to follow instructions.

Examples of the poka-yoke devices and procedures to warn and control customer actions include chains to configure waiting lines, locks on airline lavatory doors which must be turned to switch on lights (and at the same time activate the "occupied" sign), height bars at amusement rides to assure that riders do not exceed size limitations, frames in airport check-in for passengers to gauge the allowable size of carry-on luggage and beepers to signal customers to remove their cards form the ATM. Even symbols worn by employees can be warning devices: trainee buttons, badges, and gold braids are standard signaling methods to shape expectations about service before any actions are taken.

One example consistent with the low-cost solution philosophy underlying fail-safing is the use of pagers at the 300-seat Cove Restaurant in Deerfield Beach, FL. Since there is often a 45-minute wait for a table, the maitre-d' provides customers with small pagers that vibrate when activated from the master seating control board at the host stand. This has the advantage over a passive take-a-number system since it allows guests to roam outside without missing their table call. The system cost about $5,000. A dentist, whose office is in a mall, loans parents a similar pager so that they can shop while their child receives dental attention.

Many service encounters take place over the phone. The most common mistake facing cable-TV companies in their telephone troubleshooting occurs when people report a supposed reception problem when in fact they have inadvertently changed the channel setting on their TV. However, if a service representative asks the customer if his or her TV is "on the correct channel," the customer will often feel embarrassed or will automatically say "yes." A multi-step fail-safing process employed by one company is to instruct the customer to "turn the channel selector from channel 3 (the correct setting) to channel 5 and then back to 3." This assures that the check is performed, while preventing the customer from feeling inept.

Resolution Poka-Yokes

Customers may also make errors in the resolution stage of the service encounter. Following the encounter, the customer typically evaluates the experience, modifies expectations for subsequent encounters and, ideally, provides feedback to the service provider. A range of errors can occur in this process, including failure to signal dissatisfaction with the service, failure to learn from experience, failure to adjust expectations appropriately and failure to execute appropriate post-encounter actions.

As an example of a follow-up poka-yoke at hotel checkout, management may include a comment card plus a certificate for a small gift in the bill envelope to encourage the guest to spend the time to provide feedback. Childcare centers use such resolution poka-yokes as toy outlines on walls and floors to show where toys should be placed after use. (In fact, a childcare consultant advocates placing

> **One *poka-yoke* is used at a bank to ensure eye contact with the customer: tellers are required to check-off the customer's eye color on a checklist as they start the transaction.**

photographs by the door to show kids what a "clean room" looks like.) In fast-food restaurants, strategically located tray return stands and trash receptacles act as reminders for customers to bus their trays at the end of their meal.

A clever resolution poka-yoke of historical interest is found in the bathrooms at L'Hotel Louis XIV in Quebec. Because the bathrooms were shared by two rooms, problems would arise when a guest forgot to unlock the door leading to another's room. The hotel installed a poka-yoke to take the place of the locks on the bathroom doors. Since the doors, on opposite sides of the bathroom, opened out into the guest rooms, a leather strap was connected to the handles on each door. When a guest was in the bathroom, the straps would be hooked together, thus holding both doors shut. It would be impossible for the guest to leave the bathroom without unhooking the strap and "unlocking" both doors.

Your Own Poka-Yokes

While this article relied on examples or anecdotes, they are meant to provide the imagery for you to begin to design your own poka-yokes. Some of the examples herein may be directly applicable to your business; hopefully others will trigger solutions by inspiration.

Admittedly, coming up with poka-yokes is part science and part art. You have probably been performing dozens of self-imposed and subconscious poka-yokes for years, such as placing your keys in a certain dish in your room so they can always be found. The science comes in sharing and systematizing the actions to turn them from a trick to a technique.

—Adapted from "Make Your Service Failsafe," *Sloan Management Review,* Spring 1994.

About the Authors

Richard B. Chase, The Justin Dart Term Professor of Operations Management, serves as Director of the Center for Operations Management Education and Research (COMER). He is a specialist in the design of service systems and manufacturing management. He recently gained attention for offering a money-back guarantee of satisfaction for his course on service. He received his BS, MBA and PhD from UCLA.

Douglas M. Stewart is pursuing his PhD at USC. He received his BS and MS from the University of North Carolina.

TOWARD THE CENTURY OF QUALITY

A Conversation With Joseph Juran

BY THOMAS A. STEWART • *Joseph M. Juran turned 94 on Christmas Eve. He is now exactly twice the age he was when he published his* Quality Control Handbook, *as much a classic in its field as Paul Samuelson's* Economics *is in his. A few weeks before his birthday, Juran came to New York City to talk up the Juran Center for Leadership in Quality at the Carlson School of Management at the University of Minnesota. We talked in a meeting room at the Warwick Hotel; next door two score police officers were attending a seminar on interrogation techniques. Compared with the beefy cops, some with pistols strapped to their hips, Juran seemed slight and frail, his voice soft. But there was nothing soft about his thinking or frail in his energy level; our conversation, scheduled for an hour, went half again as long, and Juran was going strong at the end. We started by chatting about the other nonagenarian guru, Peter F. Drucker, then turned to the past, present, and future of the quality movement.*

I got interested in Drucker when I read *The Concept of the Corporation*, which I thought was wonderful stuff—a little wordy, but wonderful. I remember contacting Drucker on the way to visit my boys at summer camp. He was a professor at Bennington College in Vermont, which in those days was a girls' school. I asked him, "What in the world are you doing here?" He moved to Montclair, N.J., and made contact with the business school at NYU. Our paths continued to cross, and we've become good friends. Of course, he moved to Claremont, Calif. From Montclair to Claremont—no imagination, you see.

On why quality matters: Historians will define our century, as far as economics is concerned, as the Century of Productivity. One of its biggest events was Japan emerging as an economic superpower. That came about primarily because of the Japanese quality revolution. While our consumers loved Japanese imports, our manufacturers did not. We exported God knows how many millions of jobs; our trade balance was shattered. We were forced to undertake a counterrevolution. Competition in quality intensified enormously.

The next century has to be the Century of Quality. We've got a situation where we have locked ourselves in with the technological revolution. We have put ourselves at its mercy. I've given a name to that: "life behind the quality dikes." We are in a situation that resembles that of the Dutch, who have gained a great deal economically by pushing the sea back behind enormous walls. But there's a price: They have to maintain those dikes forever. In the same way we put ourselves at risk with our communications system, transport system, and other systems. They're wonderful while they

work. Just-in-time manufacturing is wonderful while it works. But if something isn't delivered on time, the factory stops.

We've made dependence on the quality of our technology a part of life. When I was a child, I lived in an Eastern European village. We never had power failures—because we never had power! Washing machines never failed; we had no washing machines. A satellite went down six weeks ago; my Visa card suddenly wouldn't work in the gas pump. You've got a satellite, satellite manufacturer, the communications company that manages it, Visa, and the gas company, all of whom have to deliver in order for me to pump gas. The interlocking is such that any part of it that fails may shut down the whole system. Why are we so afraid of Y2K? Massive quality failure.

On why quality takes so long: Our effort is going to occupy us for decades to come. It started up in the 1980s. A huge number of companies undertook initiatives in quality, but only a tiny number of them succeeded and became quality leaders. We know what they did. How they did it provides us the lessons to scale up.

It's a slow process. One of the limitations is cultural resistance. There are all kinds of ways of dragging one's feet. It's so universal, each language has its own expression for it. Invariably each industry says, "Our business is different." Within

  Reprinted from the January 11, 1999, issue of *Fortune*, pp. 168, 170, by special permission. © 1999 by Time, Inc.

the industry each company says, "We're different." And in each company managers are different. Of course there are real differences, but with respect to management and quality, they're identical. They don't know that; some of us who have worked in a lot of different industries and companies do know that.

Department heads in a company don't march forward simultaneously. They march in single file, the most adventuresome at the head. You've always got one or two willing to have their departments become test sites. So the thing takes time, because the test site may take a couple of years before results are achieved and demonstrated and propagated. Those results become the means of convincing neighbors. And then it starts to spread. The companies that ended up as role models, like Motorola and Xerox—both were clients of mine—none of them got there in less than six years.

On the cost of quality: There's a lot of confusion as to whether quality costs money or whether it saves money. In one sense, quality means the features of some product or service that make people willing to buy it. So it's income-oriented—has an effect on income. Now to produce features, ordinarily you have to invest money. In that sense, higher quality costs more. Quality also means freedom from trouble, freedom from failure. This is cost-oriented. If things fail internally, it costs the company. If they fail externally, it also costs the customer. In these cases, quality costs less.

I had a look around Xerox before I got to talk to David Kearns [then CEO] on grand strategy. I was just dismayed. The top guys had no scoreboard relevant to quality. I started talking with people who had field reports. I wanted a list of the ten most frequent field failures, because this was killing Xerox. Their field-failure rate was ever so

"WE'RE AT THE MERCY OF TECHNOLOGY. WHY ARE WE AFRAID OF Y2K? MASSIVE QUALITY FAILURE."

much greater than that of the Japanese. Xerox was losing huge amounts of money during the warranty period.

So I get the ten top failures for the current models. I ask, Have you got the same information relative to the models preceding these? *Both lists are identical.* They knew these things were failing, and they didn't get rid of them. Well, it wasn't too difficult when I did sit with Kearns to point out to him, "You're putting out models you know are going to fail."

On control vs. creativity: Take this example: In finance we set a budget. The actual expenditure, month by month, varies—we bought enough stationery for three months, and that's going to be a miniblip in the figures. Now, the statistician goes a step further and says, "How do you know whether it's just a miniblip or there's a real change here?" The statistician says, "I'll draw you a pair of lines here. These lines are such that 95% of the time, you're going to get variations within them."

Now suppose something happens that's clearly outside the lines. The odds are something's amok. Ordinarily this is the result of something local, because the system is such that it operates in control. So su-

pervision converges on the scene to restore the status quo.

Notice the distinction between what's chronic and what's sporadic. Sporadic events we handle by the control mechanism. Ordinarily sporadic problems are delegable because the origin and remedy are local. Changing something chronic requires creativity, because the purpose is to get rid of the status quo—to get rid of waste. Dealing with the chronic requires structured change, which has to originate pretty much with the top. You've got two totally different processes that have to work here: the control process, to maintain the status quo, and the improvement process, to get rid of it. You need both, and good managers engage in both.

On perfection: Bob Galvin of Motorola has come out over and over again with a big finding of his—"perfection is possible." Back in the '20s when I first came out of engineering school, nobody in industry would have said that. We had what we call "tolerable percent defective"—stuff that's one or two or several percent defective. That was part of life. We've developed quite a few means of achieving perfection when it comes to very critical things, like airplanes. You have redundancies, backups; you deliberately understress materials; you keep people's hands off to limit human error.

We have to dig deeper into the approach to perfection now, given that we're pushing the use of information technology so that we depend on it for transmission and communication and financial systems. I'm not sure where to dig. I can say that those of us who have been around a long time have never seen a limit to human ingenuity. Toyota makes over a million improvements a year. Human beings have no limit to their creativity. The problem is to make it possible for them to use that creativity.

One More Time: Eight Things You Should Remember About Quality

by John P. Mello Jr.

HOW DOES AN organization maintain its dedication to quality? Quality encompasses more than goals and numbers—it embraces the emotions as well. Once quality standards are in place and an organization has an intellectual commitment to quality, how does it turn that commitment into conviction? The experts and in particular two consultants, Patrick L. Townsend and Joan E. Gebhardt, authors of *Quality in Action,* have a few suggestions. Here are eight of them.

1
Nothing pumps up conviction like increased profits.

Surveys by the American Society for Quality Control (ASQC) show that consumers are willing to pay more for an item if it is guaranteed to meet their expectations when they buy it. In the ASQC study conducted in 1988 by the Gallup Organization,

when the item was a $12,000 automobile, 82% of the consumers surveyed said that they were willing to pay more for a quality automobile. How much more? On average, $2,518. Townsend and Gebhardt note, "People are willing to spend more in the hope that the extra money spent will bring them the peace of mind that comes with services and products that are trustworthy."

On the flip side, poor quality results in repair work, rework and scrap costs, returned goods, warranty costs, inspection costs, and lost sales—all told, some 30–35% of gross sales for most companies.

The executives in a company producing quality products are in a very attractive strategic position. If they cut prices, quality improvements will enable them to maintain their profit margins, while their lower prices will enable them to garner a larger market share. And once the company's reputation for quality spreads, it can cash in

on that reputation by raising prices and increasing profit margins.

2
Avoid future problems by aggressively seeking out customer opinions.

The adage "The squeaky wheel gets the grease" is anathema to the quality-conscious company, which strives to anticipate which wheels need greasing before they start to squeak. Townsend and Gebhardt cite the cautionary tale of the Tennant Company, a maker of floor-finishing equipment in Minneapolis, Minnesota. Soon after entering the Japanese market, Tennant began to receive complaints that their machines leaked. Managers were mystified—they had never heard this complaint from their American customers. The company really began to worry when it learned that Toyota was considering entering the market, so it started interviewing its American

Reprinted by permission of *Harvard Management Update,* May 1998, pp. 8-9. © 1998 by the President and Fellows of Harvard College; all rights reserved.

customers in earnest. Sure enough, the machines did leak. But the American customers didn't "squeak": they just wiped up the leak, silently suffering and waiting for a competitor to enter the market so they could shift their business to it. Tennant eventually fixed the problem, and Toyota never entered the market. But had it not been for the squeaky wheels in Japan, Tennant might not have found out about its quality problems until it was too late.

3
Guarantees + deep customer knowledge = 1 potent combination.

Anyone who has ever gagged on cafeteria food can appreciate the guarantee made by Daka, Inc., the food service contractor at Clark University in Worcester, Massachusetts: if you don't like the food, we'll give you your money back. The guarantee certainly pleased the customers, but the managers had a larger goal—a quality goal—in mind. They wanted to get past the general whining that comes with the territory and obtain specific criticisms that could be used to improve their operations. In addition to the guarantee, Daka stations a manager in each of the two campus dining halls every Wednesday to discuss food issues with students. A record of those discussions, in the form of questions and answers, is posted every week for the benefit of all.

During the first year of the program, only 28 refunds were made, but many more meals were adjusted to assuage students. Those adjustments could be thought of as part of the Daka's "service recovery plan"—originated by Ron Zemke, a well-known writer on quality issues. Such plans, says Zemke, are part of an intentional strategy for returning an aggrieved customer to a state of satisfaction after a service or product has failed to live up to expectations. When Daka launched the program, there was a flurry of activity, but by the end of the first year, that activity

had dwindled to the point that now the guarantee is invoked only once every two weeks or so.

4
Cast a net that catches both big and little ideas.

It's difficult for a culture weaned on the belief that size matters to accept the importance of small ideas. But as Masaaki Imai reveals in his seminal work *Kaizen: The Key to Japan's Competitive Success,* when trying to improve quality, the weight of the catch is more important than the size of the fish. Toyota has spent two decades building up a suggestion system that now produces 2.6 million ideas a year, or about 60 ideas per employee. What's even more amazing is the fact that 95% of them are implemented. Most of those ideas are small, but when they're taken together, their impact is huge.

Some companies offer their workers a cut of the savings that result from an idea. But this dampens idea generation because it encourages workers to look for the "big fish" so they can get the big payoff. By contrast, a company that encourages small ideas is playing the percentages. It's easier to find 100 people who can improve a process by 1% than it is to find a single wizard who can improve a process by 100%. When the wizard has a bad day, the process improves 0%; if 10 of the 100 workers have a bad day, the process still improves 90%.

5
In a quality shop, everybody has customers.

A commitment to continuous quality improvement requires that all workers know who their customers are. A customer can be the person into whose "In" box you dump your "Out" box— or just about anyone to whom you provide a product, service, or information. This maxim applies especially to top managers, whose customers include the people and organizations who

buy the company's services and products as well as the people who work for it. If the latter group isn't happy, there's a good chance the former won't be happy either. As Townsend and Gebhardt note, "To simply exhort employees to provide worry-free products and services without providing a worry-free work environment is folly."

6
Beware the disciples of complexity.

How can workers be responsible for the quality of their work if they're told the measurement of it is too complicated for them to understand? Firms should be wary of quality-control specialists who act as if their discipline is beyond the ken of mere mortals. If you want an effective quality-control program, design it so employees at every level can implement it. Having everyone participate in the design ensures that it will be implemented across your organization.

7
"Look out, Jim, that joke could rip a man in half!"

Humor helps create a sense of proportion in a shop. Without it, everything becomes a molar-gnashing crisis. With it, the management of a company that wants its workers to commit to quality can humanize itself and the quality process.

When the Mutual of Omaha Companies launched their 100% employee participation quality process in 1991, they had Jim Fowler, the host of the company-sponsored TV show "Wild Kingdom," introduce the process. Fowler brought along a 20-foot boa constrictor and, in an impromptu moment, invited company president Jack Weekly—known for his no-nonsense, bottom-line bent—to handle the snake. Gales of laughter erupted from the audience as Weekly tried to keep the snake from crawling into his trousers. What's an employee to think after watching that spectacle? Perhaps this: if the president of the company is willing to get off his high horse for this quality thing, maybe management's commitment to quality is as deep as it says it is.

Either that or: if Fowler had only brought a hamster instead, now that would have been funny.

8
If there are reasons to celebrate, do it. If not, look for them.

Companies large and small have found that appreciating employees through celebration helps build solidarity and loyalty—two qualities essential to the quality process. Fluoroware, Inc., in Chaska, Minnesota, celebrated ZD-Day (Zero Defects Day) by giving each employee a cooler with the label "Jazzed On Quality." Inside each cooler was an assortment of novelties carrying the same message. A recognition luncheon followed the giveaway.

Celebration of quality doesn't have to be an exclusively annual event. It works best if a company has recognition celebrations throughout the year. Indeed, without continuous recognition, annual awards can divide the company into the winning few and the many who finished last. At Paul Revere Insurance Group in Worcester, Massachusetts, the top managers recognize team efforts throughout the year. In the first four and a half years of its quality program, Paul Revere held more than 1,500 ceremonies. And when the Baldrige Award examiners were scheduled to pay a visit, the company kitchen baked 1,400 cookies in the shape of a Q, which were given out to workers by executives trailing the company snack cart when it made its morning run.

Paul Revere won a Baldrige Award that year.

If you want to learn more . . .

Commit to Quality by Patrick L. Townsend and Joan E. Gebhardt (1990, John Wiley & Sons. Inc., 208 pp., $12.95, Tel. 800-CALL-WILEY or 212-850-6000)

Gemba Kaizen: A Commonsense, Low-Cost Approach to Management by Masaaki Imai (1997, McGraw-Hill, 354 pp., $24.95, Tel. 800-722-4726 or 212-512-2000)

Kaizen: The Key to Japan's Competitive Success by Masaaki Imai (1986, McGraw-Hill, 259 pp., $43.12, Tel. 800-722-4726 or 212-512-2000)

Quality in Action: 93 Lessons in Leadership, Participation, and Measurement by Patrick L. Townsend and Joan E. Gebhardt (1992, John Wiley & Sons, Inc., 262 pp., $16.95, Tel. 800-CALL-WILEY or 212-850-6000)

Why TQM Fails and What to Do About It by Mark G. Brown and others (1994, Business One Irwin, 252 pp., $30.00, Tel. 630-789-4000)

ISO 9000 MYTH and REALITY: A Reasonable Approach to ISO 9000

Frank C. Barnes, *The Belk College of Business Administration, The University of North Carolina at Charlotte*

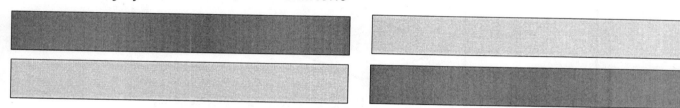

Is ISO 9000 just another imposing title on consultants' brochures or is it a system you must adopt to survive?

ISO 9000 quality systems standards have undoubtedly become more prevalent over the last decade. More than 90 countries have adopted the ISO 9000 series or its equivalent as national standards. Adherence to ISO 9000 standards has become mandatory for companies wanting to sell medical devices or telecommunications equipment in Europe, where more than 20,000 companies are registered. In the U.S., suppliers to the electrical, chemical, and nuclear industries are expecting certification to become mandatory. The number of ISO 9000 registrations is doubling every nine to 12 months in the U.S., from 100 in 1990 to 4000 in 1994.[1]

As more companies have gained first-hand knowledge, myths are giving way to reality. Success with ISO certification has not guaranteed success in business. The focus is often on paperwork, which may not directly benefit the firm. Registration can be expensive and has unfortunately become a vehicle to increase consulting revenues. Studies show that the majority of installations come from customer demands, maybe just a vendor qualification checklist, instead of from internal needs to improve quality. As a result, several groups around the world are reexamining the nature and role of ISO 9000 and certification.

What should a company do about ISO certification? We believe most companies should open up a moderate project on ISO 9000 but not give implementation any more time or money than is clearly justified. After providing a very brief overview of ISO 9000, we will examine more deeply the costs and benefits, the industries and size of companies where it is more relevant, the complaints about registration, and where ISO appears to be going. In the end, we will suggest a proactive but prudent course of action for any company.

ISO Background

ISO 9000 is "a series of international standards dealing with quality systems that can be used for external quality assurances purposes," according to the original 1987 bulletin from the International Organization for Standardization.[2] This group, founded in 1946, has become the focus of efforts to develop international quality standards to facilitate worldwide trade. The organization is a coordinating, consensual group with member bodies from more than 90 countries. The U.S. representative is the American National Standards Institute.

ISO 9000 sets standards for systems and paperwork, not products. It provides companies with a series of guidelines on how to establish systems for managing quality products or services. ISO 9000 requires organizations to document practices that affect the quality of their products or services. Organizations are then expected to follow these procedures to gain and maintain certification. Proponents see the key to quality as the creation of an internal auditing system whereby all company functions are constantly monitored.[3]

Reprinted with permission from *SAM Advanced Management Journal*, Spring 1998, pp. 23-30. © 1998 by the Society for Advancement of Management, Texas A&M University–Corpus Christi, College of Business, 6300 Ocean Drive, FC111, Corpus Christi, TX 78412.

Exhibit 1
"ISO 9000" systems

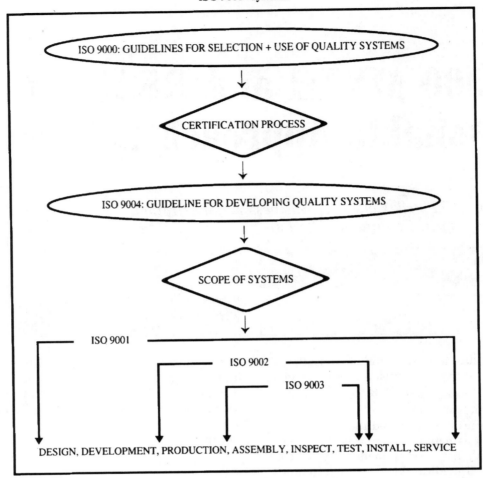

What is referred to as ISO 9000 is actually made up of five different subsets (Exhibit 1). ISO 9000 is the general guide to the others. ISO 9001 is the most comprehensive, covering research, design, building, shipping, and installing. ISO 9002 is for companies that only produce and supply existing products; ISO 9003 is for companies which do even less, such as assembly. ISO 9004 is a document to guide further internal quality development, and ISO 14000 is a new standard to address environmental issues.

Certification rests on an audit by an independent "registrar" after all the systems are in place. The original ISO technical committee envisioned a simpler system than what has developed. It saw ISO 9000 as a guide mainly for self-certification or certification by customer companies and did not anticipate the profusion of outside groups offering to guide, audit, and register companies.

Why do companies seek ISO certification? Well, why do people go after C.P.A., CPIM, or P.E. certification? External goals are first: customer expectations, market advantage, and competition are the major reasons half the companies seek certification. Reduced

costs and quality improvement were the reasons for less than a quarter of the companies. One in 10 was driven by international issues.[4] So, having the "ISO 9000 Certified" sticker on the box is an important driving force for ISO 9000.

Benefits

What benefits are reported? A survey by Lloyd's "Register of Quality Assurance" indicated that ISO 9000 increased net profit.[5] Some companies saw cost reduction of 5% to 30%.[6] A joint study by Deloitte-Touche and Quality Systems Update reported that companies claimed average annual savings of $175,000 from registration.[7] Another Deloitte-Touche survey reported that the costs of registration were recovered in three years.[8] But, in fact, ISO registration is a cost, and any savings are indirect, the result of using the ISO work to improve a company's practices.

Access to markets is the one possible direct ISO impact. While ISO 9000 is not a requirement for doing business in the United States, it can be one in other countries. The European Council of Ministers now requires certification for the producers of certain types of products, including commercial scales, construction products, gas appliances, industrial safety equipment, medical devices, and telecommunications terminal equipment.[9] In the European Community, any type of product that is potentially hazardous or involves personal safety is a candidate for ISO 9000 requirements.

However, most ISO requirements are not government mandated. Large certified corporations, mainly in Europe, are requiring ISO 9000 certification of their suppliers. ISO 9000 requires that certified companies qualify their vendors, and many companies fulfill this requirement by mandating that their suppliers become certified as well.

It is frequently stated that ISO 9000 certification will improve company standings in the important European Community. On January 1, 1993, the EC became the second most powerful economy in the world and the largest trading partner of the U.S.[10] The U.S. exports more than $100 billion to the EC annually. More than half of this amount is affected by ISO 9000 standards. In Europe, more than 70,000 sites are registered for the series, so ISO 9000 certificates are becoming like passports and visas.[11] Therefore, to international companies, certification provides the opportunity to do more business in Europe. Some other reasons include EC regulations requiring ISO 9000 compliance, EC companies preferring ISO 9000 standards, or suppliers voluntarily adopting ISO 9000 as a way to be more competitive.

Because ISO 9000 standards are intended to be uniform throughout the world, corporations should have the assurance that a certified company has had to demonstrate and document proper quality systems. Certification also provides credibility. It gives assurance to a corporation that its potential suppliers can provide products of a consistent quality. And ISO 9000 certification tends to cut down on the number of audits performed by customers on their suppliers.[12] If the supplier base, including first-, second-, and third-tier suppliers are ISO certified, then the final products, which may consist of thousands of parts and components from registered suppliers, should have superior quality, performance, and reliability. Also, ISO 9000 certification may allow the company to control risks and exposures associated with defective products. With extensive quality systems in place and operating properly, future failures and possibilities for defective product litigation should be minimized.[13]

• *Improved Communication*

Zuckerman claims that ISO 9000 serves not only as a quality tool but as a communication system. If implemented correctly, the ISO 9000 system:

• Builds communication between managers and employees.
• Helps resolve political conflicts, work procedure inconsistencies and conflict between formal and informal communication flows.
• Trains management and employees in communication skills, such as interviewing, writing and editing.
• Creates a documentation system and a system for disseminating information company-wide and to all customers.
• Provides the basis for a networked communications system.
• Lays a foundation for using employees as sophisticated information gatherers and sorters.[14]

• *Good Business Sense*

The system standards in the ISO 9000 series provide a comprehensive model for a quality management system that should make any company more competitive. The standards offer a solid foundation for establishing a total quality management philosophy and help companies establish the discipline, procedures, and methods to assure that all areas in the company are aligned with the principles set forth in the company's quality policy statement. So we see there are many potential benefits from the ISO 9000 program.

• *The ISO 9000 Process*

The ISO 9000 program is somewhat complex and has a number of requirements. Many books, such as Johnson's[15] and Zuckerman's[16] as well as articles suggest a step by step process to achieve certification. The Autumn 1995 issue of *SAM Advanced Management Journal* provided a "manager's guide" to understanding and implementing ISO 9000.[17] They all suggest the following five steps in some form:

1. *ISO 9000 Assessment.* The initial assessment is a detailed review of the company's quality systems and procedures compared with ISO 9000 requirements. This process defines the scope of the ISO 9000 project. It might take two or three days to complete.

2. *Quality Assurance Manual.* While ISO 9000 standards do not require a quality assurance and policy manual, they do require the company to document everything it does and every system that affects the quality of the finished product. The quality manual is often used because it is a good way to get all the necessary documentation together in one place.

3. *Training.* Everyone, from top to bottom, needs training in two areas. First, they need an overall understanding of ISO 9000 vocabulary, requirements, role of the quality manual, and benefits that will be derived from the system. Second, they need to be aware of the actual day-to-day process of upgrading and improving procedures.

4. *Documentation of work instructions.* Processes that have been improved will need new documentation. Once completed, this manual should outline every process a company undertakes that affects the quality of a finished product.

5. *Registration Audit.* The final step in the ISO 9000 program is an audit by a company-chosen registrar to see that the system is working as described in the quality manual and that the system meets ISO 9000 requirements. But, as we'll soon see, certification is now subject to some criticism.

• *Certification*

The length of the registration effort depends on many factors, including the firm's size and complexity, current level of quality, extent of current documentation, and the degree of management commitment. (See Table 2) Typically, a 6 to 12-month training and preparation period is followed by an intensive year-long effort to adapt one's procedures to the ISO standard. In 1992, about 35% of companies failed the assessment the first time around, but the success rate has now risen to more than 70%. About half of the failures are due to a lack of documentation.[18] A registered organization faces follow-up visits by auditors every six months to make sure the company follows its quality procedures. After three years, the organization must undergo another full assessment.

Cost

ISO 9000 certification can be expensive. "Quality Systems Update" reported that the average total cost was $245,200.[20] The factors influencing the cost are the size of the company, the number and type of products, and the existing state of the quality control system.

In a 1994 survey of equipment manufacturers, large corporations reported spending more than $1 million for certification, whereas smaller companies with about $25 million in annual sales spent an average of $250,000 plus annual maintenance costs of more than $70,000. These costs include set registration fees of about $35,000 for a three-year cycle, employee time and, in some cases, additional employees.[21] See Table 3.

The level of documentation prior to implementing ISO 9000 is also a factor in the cost picture. In a survey conducted by Microwaves & R-F, companies that had already received ISO 9000 certification reported on average that they invested nearly $100,000 to prepare and achieve certification. In the same industry, Maxim Integrated Products spent only $25,000 because many systems were already in place.[23] Bethlehem Steel required about eight months to achieve certification in one of its plants, while a similar-sized company with no prior quality program took two and a half years.[24]

Colorado State University found 58% of ISO registered companies indicated that they did not keep track of costs, many because the decision to seek registration was strategic, customer-driven, or in the long-term business interest of the company. Ninety-three percent reported that they did not attempt to justify the cost of the ISO 9000 registration process.[25] Table 4 shows the breakdown of ISO costs.

Training for a single site may cost $4,000 to $5,000. A core group, consisting of the ISO coordinator, senior managers, and team leaders would receive a formal overview through a one-day introductory class typically costing under $500 per person. The coordinator should take about two advanced seminars, which take two days and cost about $1,000.[26] A major expense is the internal costs of preparing documents, document control, and retraining of employees.

Consultants are available to assist with any part of the process. For a fee ranging from $700 to $1,500 a day, consultants can provide a package to take a company from start to finish, promising quick, easy passing of the ISO audit.[27]

We believe this is an area for solid business decision-making. Each cost should be subject to cost-bene-

Table 2	Relevant Time Requirements
Time Frame	**Existing Condition of Organization**
3 to 6 months	Company in full compliance to a military or nuclear standard.
6 to 10 months	Company has fairly current procedures, job descriptions, and a working quality organization.
10 to 16 months	Company has only sketchy procedures and its records are haphazard. The quality organization is still responsible for final inspection, and still takes the blame for the substandard product shipped if plant is very large.
16 to 24 months	Company has no commitment from senior management.

TABLE 3	Cost and Savings by Company Size	
Sales Volume of Companies	**Avg. Annual Savings**	**Avg. Cost per Company(*)**
Less than $11 million	$25,000	$62,300
$11 million–$25 million	$77,000	$131,000
$25 million–$50 million	$69,900	$149,700
$50 million–$100 million	$130,000	$180,800
$100 million–$200 million	$195,000	$208,700
$200 million–$500 million	$227,000	$321,700

(22)*

fit analysis. Some suggested activities are so logical they should have already been done. Some have no benefit except getting certified. A company should clearly understand where each proposal fits between these extremes. As we'll see, it may not be necessary, or desirable, to buy into the whole program.

• *Registration Fees*

In a survey of ISO 9000 registrars in North America, the National ISO 9000 Support Group tried to clarify the costs of assessment by asking a sample of registrars to submit a quote for a 250 employee automotive supplier with a single manufacturing site. The average estimate for registration fees was $11,300, ranging from $4,000 to $20,000. Half of the registrars said they had special pricing packages for businesses with fewer than 75 employees.[28] The fee for a large business site could reach $40,000. Surveillance costs over the three-year period can run another $3,000 to $4,000, plus travel. Bibby reported the base costs of registration may run over $50,000. However, fees paid to consultants, employee time, and documentation can drive costs over $200,000.[29] Gallagher suggested additional costs from ongoing biannual audits range from $5,000 to $10,000.[30] Doing business in Europe will cost more. Britain's BSI charges a 15-person facility about $25,000 for a three-year certification process.[31]

• *Problems With Certification*

The last step, registration or certification, is becoming the subject of a good deal of criticism. Many experts believe that ISO 9000 has become a pursuit of quality certificates rather than a pursuit of quality.[32] Jacques McMillan, chief of the senior standards group for Directorate-General III, Industry, a major force behind European standardization, stated "we just need to be sure that certification is used when it's necessary and isn't overused ... to put certification back into perspective."[33]

ISO left the regulation and implementation of the standards up to the participating countries' standards organizations, which select the organizations that are qualified to issue ISO 9000 certificates. Once registrars become accredited, there is no single set of operating guidelines for them to follow, and the amount of work a company is required to perform varies according to the registrar. Therefore, not all companies or countries will acknowledge certification from all registrars. Perry Johnson referred to the international scene as a "bureaucratic Byzantium."[34] Furthermore, many companies in Europe only accept certification from European registrars. To eliminate this problem, the national standards organizations are in the process of creating operating guidelines. The U.S.'s Registrar Accreditation Board has signed Memorandums of Understanding with the Netherlands, U.K., Italy, Japan, and Australia to move these countries toward mutual Recognition of registrars.[35]

TABLE 4 Source of ISO Costs

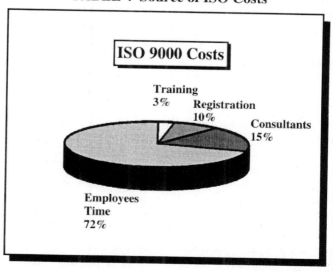

• *Compliance Versus Registration*

The ISO 9000 documents were written as two-party documents between buyers and sellers and did not address certification, which has largely been a commercial response to legal mandates in Europe and the competitive push to sell outside the US.

Brown, in *Machine Design*, stated, "While rooted in good intentions, once dissected, it is painfully obvious that ISO certifications are merely more expensive and elaborate schemes that promise high quality and a competitive edge . . . namely, certification costs are astronomical and growing, and an ISO registration in the U.S. means little in Europe. When the smoke clears, the only organizations guaranteed to profit from this experience will be those deemed qualified to do the audits and issue the certificates."[36] The Chicago Metal Working Consortium considers ISO 9000 a "cash cow" for consultants and the service sector.[37]

Computer giant, Hewlett-Packard, along with Motorola, Novell, Microsoft, and others, is leading a self-certification movement. This option provides greater flexibility to meet business objectives, reduce costs, and increase customer understanding the quality management systems.[38] Likewise, the National Tooling & Machining Association is asking its 3,000 members to conform with ISO 9000 rather than pursue actual certification. Self-paced compliance is clearly an option for domestic U.S. companies, and industry-specific programs have merit.

There is no law requiring ISO 9000 compliance for all products sold in Europe. Some now say that ISO 9000 is overrated, even counter productive. The Senior Officials Group for Standardization Policy of the EC's Directorate-General III for Industry, concerned that ISO 9000 has turned into a pursuit of certificates rather than quality, called for the creation of a Europe-wide quality program that could include a European quality award, like the Deming or Baldrige Awards.[39]

The ISO 9000 certification process requires a mountain of paperwork. Opponents claim that it is only for documentation, but proponents believe that if a company has documented its quality systems as it should, then most of the paperwork has already been completed.

Some say ISO 9000 discourages free thinking and employee empowerment. They claim that the ISO 9000 program is so structured that companies lose their power to develop creative solutions to problems or to think of new, better ways of doing things.

• *Other Problems*

It is charged that ISO 9000 focuses too much on the company involved and not enough on its customers. ISO 9000 is not directly connected to product quality but to the company systems. Many opponents believe that the program focuses on product consistency at the expense of product quality. (There is the often repeated claim, "One can manufacture cement life-preservers and still receive ISO 9000 certification").[40]

ISO 9000 is not industry-specific. Opponents claim ISO 9000 is too general and fails to address the problems and issues inherent in particular industries.

ISO is strongest worldwide in the transportation, oil, chemicals, electronics and computer industries. Tool manufacturers, automakers, steelmakers, and woodwork machine manufacturers are among those who tend to say that ISO 9000 is a program created by consultants primarily to benefit consultants.

The Big Three auto manufacturers have chosen their own system, QS-9000, which includes ISO 9000 as a baseline. Auto industry leaders say ISO 9000 is too immature to impose on their suppliers and they hope to save their suppliers the expense of ISO registration. QS 9000 "was created to reach beyond the limits of ISO 9000 by incorporating the powerful components of continuous improvement, a parts approval process, and manufacturing capabilities."[41] European officials are not pleased with this development, which they see as unnecessary duplication and fragmentation.[42]

There is not much enthusiasm for ISO 9000 in the steel industry, where leaders view ISO certification as a marketing tool. But Bethlehem Steel, the first integrated mill to be registered, views ISO 9000 as a means of cutting down on customer audits.

On the other hand, the chemical processing industry, which faces tough international competition, has openly embraced ISO 9000. In fact, DuPont has created its own ISO 9000 consulting service for use both inside and outside the chemical industry.

Although ISO 9000 certification is prevalent in the electronics industry, Motorola's quality chief dismisses the standard. AMP's director of supplier programs and performance comments that "We would not arbitrarily impose the additional costs on our suppliers."[43]

Recommendations

Over the years we've observed a pattern with new business practices; can we say "fad?" There is the period of euphoria and wild overpromise. It appears ISO 9000 is emerging from this phase and good business sense will be reinstated. Several trends are apparent. There will be a continued growth in U.S. firms registered, but there will be more attention to industry-specific standards, such as auto's QS-9000 or Motorola's self-certification. There will be reform. An editorial in *Quality Progress* called ISO 9000 Europe's "revenge" for years of American management fads.[44] Registrars will be subject to more regulations. Effort will be made to streamline the process and increase the effectiveness of registration in assuring quality products and services. There will be some deemphasis of ISO 9000 registration. The European Council is likely to back a proposal to deemphasize ISO 9000 registration and promote a European quality award like the Baldrige Award. There is a push for EC approval of a Europe-wide quality policy that will recommend ISO 9000 as only one quality tool that companies can use on the path to improvement.[45]

We recommend that a company use its own sales department and top management to determine clearly the role of ISO certification in its industry and markets. Is certification important to the marketing plans of the company?

We recommend that the company use the ISO 9000 model as a benchmark to assess the adequacy of its quality program. Those responsible for the quality function should become thoroughly familiar with ISO 9000. This might be a one-month or a 12-month goal, depending on company needs. During the ongoing operation of the quality function there should be routine and regular opportunities and advantages from aligning the company's systems with the ISO model. This should contribute to the systematic improvement of quality and profit. If it becomes important in your markets to have certification, the company could take that step with little disruption or costs. Good business sense is your guide to confronting ISO 9000.

_____

With over 20 years of teaching experience and 10 in professional positions with leading corporations, Dr. Barnes has developed extensive expertise in problem solving and systems design to improve managerial and operational success, and has contributed case studies of successful corporations to a number of textbooks.

NOTES

1. Gallagher, M. (1995, April) ISO Expands; Most large companies have adopted ISO 9000 and new the standard is moving down all levels. *Chemical Marketing Reporter,* 247, 12.
2. International Standard (1987) Quality systems model for quality assurance in production installation.
3. Zuckerman, A. (1994, July). The Basics of ISO 9000. *Industrial Engineering,* 26, 13–14.
4. Rabbit, J.T., & Bergh, P.A. (1993). *The ISO 9000 book: A global competitor's guide to compliance & certification.* New York: Quality Resources.
5. Study finds that gains with ISO 9000 registration increase over time. (1994, May). *Quality Progress* 27, (5) 18.
6. Zanetti, R. (1993, January). ISO 9000: The benefits are boundless. *Chemical Engineering.*
7. Johns, V.H. (1994). Beyond the myths: The ISO 9000 certification process is still hampered by a number of misunderstandings. *Chemical Marketing Reporter,* 245 (15), 8–10
8. Murphy, P. (1996, March). Essay by Invitation. *LD+A* 19.
9. Johnson, P. (1997). *ISO 9000: Meeting the new international standards.* New York; McHill, Inc. 2nd Edition.
10. Craig, R.J. (1994). *The no-nonsense guide to achieving ISO 9000 registration.* New York; ASME Press.
11. Vasilash, G.S. (1995, August). Tooling up for better quality. *Production,* 107, 54–57.
12. Avery, S. (1994). ISO 9000 certification: Does it help or hinder? *Purchasing,* 116 (1), 102.
13. Hutchins, G. (1993). *ISO 9000: A comprehensive guide to registration. Audit guidelines and successful certification.* Vermont: Oliver Wright.
14. Zuckerman, A. (1996, July). How companies miss the boat on ISO 9000. *Quality Progress,* 23–24.
15. Johnson, Op. Sit.
16. Zuckerman, A. (1995). *ISO 9000 made easy: A Cost saving guide,* Amacon.
17. Hormozi, A.M. (1995). Understanding and implementing ISO 9000: A manager's guide. *SAM Advanced Management Journal,* 4–11.
18. Wingo, W. (1994, September 26). ISO 9000 certification snowball. *Design News,* 90–97.
19. Rabbit, & Bergh, Op. Sit.
20. Weston, F.C. (1995, October). What do managers really think of the ISO 9000 registration process? *Quality Progress,* 67–73.
21. Zuckerman, A. (1994). The high price of admission. *Appliance Manufacturer* 42(5), 8.
22. *Quality Systems Update.* (1997). Deloitte-Touche, Fairfax, VA.
23. Schneiderman, R. (1994, Jan.). ISO 9000 generates debate among industry companies. *Microwaves & R-F,* 42–46.
24. Zuckerman, A. (1994, Oct.). Second thoughts about ISO 9000. *Across the Board,* 51.
25. Weston, Op. Sit., pp 67–73.
26. Mancine, B.J. (1994, February). Succeed at ISO 9000 registration. *Chemical Engineering Progress,* 55–59.
27. Brown, R. (1994, June 6). Does America need ISO 9000? *Machine Design* 70–74.
28. Rubach, L. (1995, January). First-time ISO 9000 registration tops 70%. *Quality Progress.*
29. Bibby, T. (1995, July). ISO 9000, not a total quality solution, but a catalyst for continuous improvement. *Rubber World,* 212, 15–17.
30. Gallagher, M. (1995, April). ISO Expands: Most large companies have adopted ISO 9000 and new the standard is moving down all levels. *Chemical Marketing Reporter,* 247, 12.
31. Wingo, Op. Sit., p. 90–97.
32. Zuckerman, Op. Sit., p. 51.
33. Avery, S. (1996, Oct. 17). What's going on overseas could impact quality here. *Purchasing,* 50.
34. Johnson, Op. Sit., p. 137.
35. Murkami, R. (1994, March). How to implement TSO 9000. *CMA Magazine,* 18–21.
36. Brown, Op. Sit., p. 70–74.
37. Avery, S. (1994). What's wrong with ISO 9000? *Purchasing,* 116 (3), 49–52.
38. Morrow, M. (1994). Gauging the importance of ISO 9000. *Chemical Week,* (24) 38, 155.
39. Zuckerman, Op. Sit., p. 51.
40. Zuckerman, Op. Sit., p. 52.
41. Brown, J. (1997, Jan.). Achieving peak to peak performance using QS 9000. *IIE Solutions,* 34.
42. European officials have their say about QS 9000. (1996, Oct. 17) *Purchasing,* 52.
43. Avery, S. Op. Sit., p. 101–105.
44. O'Conner, P. (1995, March). ISO 9000 is Europe's revenge. *Quality Progress,* 8–10.
45. Zuckerman, A. (1996, September). European standards officials push reform of ISO 9000 and QS-9000 registration. *Quality Progress,* 131–134.

WHATEVER HAPPENED TO TQM? OR, HOW A GOOD STRATEGY GOT A BAD REPUTATION

Why has TQM seemingly become a dirty word among business leaders? As this article explains, many of the organizations that have failed with TQM did so because they relied too heavily on the ideas that leadership must be 100 percent committed to the change strategy and that employees must be empowered fully. Here the author gives practical tips and real-life examples of how to bring about substantial organizational improvement with TQM-like strategies, even if an organization cannot obtain full leadership commitment and employee empowerment right away.

by George Bohan

Many of us in the business of helping our own or other organizations continuously improve operations are trying busily to think of words other than "total quality management" to describe our approach. (And of course, we don't dare use the term "reengineering"; that one went out the window as soon as it became a euphemism for laying off middle managers.) And it's a shame, too; TQM was such a handy term. Most managers didn't really know what it meant, but we all used it anyway because it seemed to make conversations about organizational change go a lot more smoothly than they had in the past. Those who wanted to improve didn't really have to articulate why or specifically where they wanted to see improvement. Those of us helping the organizations improve didn't have to articulate what we had in mind or how our models would work. A good number of consulting contracts probably were signed with no more conversation than the following:

Potential Client: "I would like to implement total quality management within my firm. Can you help me?"

Eager Consultant: "Why, total quality management is exactly what we do best. Of course we can help you."

Why has TQM become a term that those of us who still believe in its efficacy use almost apologetically? In spite of some bad press, it's fairly easy to show that TQM worked well in organizations that implemented it correctly. It's also easy to show that the strategy is relatively robust—that is, successful implementation can be achieved in many ways as long as a few core principles are attended to. So, what happened to total quality management?

A number of things happened, but most important is this: Many of us who espoused and taught total quality management to others by virtue of our positions as internal or external change agents did a bad job of it. In particular, we did not do a good job of presenting TQM in terms that were meaningful to managers who had to show up at their offices and shop floors for work on Monday morning and get work done. In communicating and teaching

George Bohan is director of advisory services for WINOC in Cleveland, Ohio. With more than 20 years of experience in manufacturing, health care, and the public sector, he is a recognized authority on the design and implementation of quality and productivity improvement processes. He has served as an advisor to Avery Dennison, Eaton Corporation, Mt. Sinai Medical Center, Stouffers Hotels and Resorts, and many other organizations.

From *National Productivity Review,* Autumn 1998, pp. 13-16. © 1998 by John Wiley and Sons, Inc. Reprinted by permission.

TQM to others, several mistakes were made. Some of the most serious were

1. Referring to total quality management as a philosophy and failing to emphasize that it is also a specific strategy for improving operations
2. Continually referring to the need for leadership commitment to the process while giving leaders little clue as to how that commitment should manifest itself.
3. Emphasizing empowerment without:
   a. Distinguishing between empowerment and other forms of participation;
   b. Clarifying why empowerment is useful; and
   c. Explaining how to establish empowerment.

IT'S A STRATEGY, NOT A PHILOSOPHY

Total quality management isn't easy to implement, but it may not be as difficult as we change agents make it seem. In particular, we seem to work hard to convey the idea that TQM is more mysterious than it is. While it's not altogether incorrect to refer to TQM as a philosophy, it's not very helpful to managers and their associates to do so. After all, how do you implement a philosophy?

In general, change agents are much too vague when telling others about change efforts. To help others improve, we need to do a better job of telling them what they need to do differently rather than what they are doing now.

When talking about total quality management as a philosophy, change agents are usually trying to convey the idea that changes of the heart and habit, changes in "worldview," are needed if the organization is to implement total quality leadership successfully.

Although it's true that total quality management requires a change in culture, it's more helpful to convey a new TQM as a concrete *strategy* for improving operations. We need to have fewer discussions about "change in culture" and "raising awareness" and more talk about reducing cycle times and improving margins.

It could readily be argued that total quality is much more than simply moving work. It does represent an entirely different approach to doing work. Nonetheless, managers and their associates *are* required to move work out the door. This is as true for the CEO as it is for the purchasing clerk. We change agents often fail to dig deeply enough into the work to show managers and then associates how to do it differently. We don't dig deeply enough into existing procedures, processes, and systems to show clients how they must change if they are to support the behavior we espouse. Managers would be helped more by change agents who taught them the tools they need (e.g., how to reduce the cycle time of hiring new employees and how to get them fully productive) than they would by change agents who tell them what their Myers-Briggs profile is.

SCAPEGOATING LEADERSHIP

We change agents have pulled a bait and switch on organizations' leaders who turned to us for help in implementing total quality management. We tell everyone that the sine qua non of TQM is leadership commitment. We tell the stories of W. Edwards Deming's refusal to teach some class or other of middle managers at Ford until their bosses showed up. We quote leaders of other organizations who have led successful improvement strategies saying that it was their own commitment and involvement that made everything possible. We drill this into our listeners' heads: Unless leadership is 100 percent committed and involved, successful change isn't possible. Then, when the program fails, we say, of course, that leadership wasn't 100 percent committed and involved. No wonder many leaders have a hard time showing much affection for change agents.

There are two important problems with this insistence that leadership commitment is a requisite for any successful change process:

1. Change agents do a rotten job of telling leaders how to demonstrate that commitment.
2. It's not altogether true that 100 percent commitment from all senior leaders is necessary to achieve good results from a TQM process.

It is not enough to tell leaders, "Get committed." As a matter of integrity, we must tell them what commitment means and what they should do come Monday morning to exhibit it. If it means giving them a checklist to get them started, so be it.

I've gotten into some healthy debates over this point with others who don't believe we should be "telling managers what to do." In their view, we should spend our time facilitating discovery on the part of managers. I don't disagree, but I've always wondered why we are reluctant to put our abstractions in concrete terms.

What sorts of things do truly committed leaders do? They write a column for the newsletter every month, and they talk about the importance of quality. They hold meetings in which the new goals for change and improvement are first on the agenda. They walk up and down the halls talking with people about the changes taking place. They teach classes. They visit customers to find out what their company could do better for them. They visit operations in the field to recognize behavior and performance consistent with the quality vision. They make lists of what they are doing differently and what they need to do differently.

I think we're not inclined to give leaders such checklists because, inevitably, they are incomplete. Some will say, "You can write all the newsletter columns and give internal quality awards and wear out the soles of your shoes doing the managing-by-walking-around routine, but it won't ensure the success of TQM or any other plan for change." Commitment to change is more than a collection of new activities meant to fulfill a "to do" list." But commitment starts with these sorts of behaviors, and we are unfair to leaders when we don't give them a clear picture of what we expect them to do. We have to be of more help than simply telling them that their support of the strategy is important. They already know that.

As for the second point, above, although it's undoubtedly true that little positive value can be obtained from a change effort that receives no support from senior leadership, improvement has occurred in organizations in which senior leadership was only moderately involved in the change effort. In most of these cases, senior leaders gave permission to others in the organization to carry out the tactics of total quality management (conducting training, creating teams, and redesigning work with employee input).

This is not to say that positive change can occur with no support or involvement on the part of leadership. Successful change requires that somebody in a leadership position get excited about the possibilities. It also requires that leaders provide the necessary resources. But change agents have nearly convinced their audiences that total commitment and involvement on the part of the most senior individual and his or her direct reports must exist before anything of value can be achieved. This can lead to long periods of inactivity (apart from lots of steering committee meetings) when nothing much gets done.

Leadership commitment is best achieved by finding out what leaders want to accomplish, then helping them do that. Set some goals, develop some yardsticks for those goals, and get moving. The leadership culture will change as leaders see how the new paradigm works . . . or it won't change at all.

If you wanted your daughter to have an abiding appreciation of and the requisite skills for the game of baseball, you would not insist that she read a book on the history of baseball, another on baseball skills, and a third on the sociology of sport in our culture. You would take her out back with the ball and glove and tell her to turn the opposite shoulder toward you when she throws. Change agents need to take a similar approach with senior leaders; mix the commitment building with skills building and direct action.

THE WRONG TALK ABOUT EMPOWERMENT

Does anyone know a manager who isn't fed up with hearing the word empowerment? We change agents have taken a perfectly good concept (and practice) and turned it into a curse word because:

- We didn't make distinctions between involvement and empowerment. (Many of us may not have known there were such distinctions.)
- We made the same mistake with empowerment as we did with leadership commitment: We told managers that the only way to success was to have a lot of it. (Again, if the program failed, it wasn't our fault;

it was leadership's fault for not empowering employees enough.)

In any organization, lots of problems need to be solved, decisions made, projects undertaken, and systems improved. It's true that the more we push this work to the people who have to implement and live with the consequences of this change, the more successful the organization will be. On the other hand, we don't need to rely on empowerment to accomplish all these things.

Empowerment means just what it says. Presidents, vice presidents, and directors are empowered because they get to make budgets, spend money, tell other people what to do, and make it stick. Most employees aren't so empowered, no matter what the vision statements of their organizations say, because they can't do these things. Empowerment doesn't mean (merely) that employees can make suggestions, offer advice, provide input, communicate information, supply data, and help carry out actions. All this is involvement, and it's a good and vital part of any change effort. Empowerment means employees get to do powerful things, like decide who gets hired, who gets promoted, what gets bought, how much money gets spent, which suppliers are kept, and which are told to go find somebody else to sell to.

The overuse of the word empowerment has caused too many of us to forget that the concept and practice of empowerment is a big deal. Successful empowerment is achieved only with the commitment of time, energy, and money. The benefits are real, and so are the costs. Often, though, all we need is a bit of good, old-fashioned involvement and participation. Managers need those suggestions, ideas, data, bits of information, and other forms of input to help them make decisions.

The overuse of the word empowerment also has caused too many of us to forget the practical value of involvement. Involvement, it's true, doesn't have nearly the panache of empowerment, so change agents don't talk about it much. Many employees would like to be a little more involved with their organizations, never mind empowered. Increased involvement on the part of workers and staff can obtain a large part (though not all) of the benefits of full-blown empowerment, with less stress and strain on the organization.

The following example illustrates the distinction between empowerment and involvement. An organization, known by its customers for its high-quality product and good workforce, formed several teams whose mission was to look into the problem of inadequate tools. The teams were taught a basic problem-solving model that they were to use to identify the worst tool problems and gather data on the cost of not having that tool or fixture. Some of the teams simply prepared lists of desired tools to hand over to management. They were told that merely handing over a wish list wasn't enough. They were going to be involved in the entire process of identifying the needed tools, justifying their acquisition, making the purchase, and providing the means for keeping the tools in good shape once they were in the shop.

Occasionally, a team didn't understand this explanation. Wouldn't it be easier and more efficient to acquire the tools that everyone knew were needed? The response stressed that the mere purchase of tools was only part of the objective, the team's involvement in the process was essential. The team members were told, "You may not always like it, but you're always going to be involved." The team members were not told that they had been empowered because, indeed, they hadn't been.

But wouldn't it have been better to have empowered the employees to purchase those tools themselves? Eventually, that will be the way things are done in this operation, and at that point, empowerment will work well because the employees will have learned how to effectively manage the tools' acquisition and utilization function through increased involvement. Going straight from where the plant started (management purchases tools when it is good and ready) to full and complete empowerment would not have worked. And yet, too many change agents imply that just such a tactic is the only effective one.

Some of the practices that get employees more involved in the business and create the foundation for full empowerment are:

- Regular communications of company, department, and work group performance indicators;

- High visibility of senior leadership;
- Multiple, associate-friendly channels for the voice of the worker/staff to be heard by senior management;
- Frequent feedback and recognition regarding work group performance;
- Getting those who must apply or adhere to policies and standard operating practices to develop them when possible; and
- Regular communications regarding how and why senior management makes the decisions it does.

These admittedly prosaic practices are often given lip service when they are not completely ignored by change agents and managers alike. They seem too elemental; it's too easy to convince oneself, even in the face of evidence to the contrary, that the organization is already adequately undertaking these practices. But organizations that systematically, consistently, and regularly (not to say frequently) carry out these simple practices find that they get results. Further, these practices lead directly to successful efforts to truly empower employees and staff.

Total quality management, or whatever name it takes today, can be beneficial for many companies if it is used as a strategy. If change agents bend just a little bit on their strict rule that leadership's commitment to the strategy must be complete, and if they don't insist that employees jump over involvement into empowerment right away, then positive change will occur slowly, and TQM will not fail.

Critical Implementation Issues in Total Quality Management

Dooyoung Shin, *Professor of Management and Chairperson, Department of Management, Mankato State University*

Jon G. Kalinowski, *Professor of Management, Mankato State University*

Gaber Abou El-Enein, *Dean, College of Business, Mankato State University*

Recently, many business magazines, newspapers, and academic journals that have praised TQM as a critical source of sustainable competitive advantage have begun to publish reports on its failure (Fuchsberg (1992), Brown (1993), Jacob (1993), Harari (1993). While many companies have demonstrated improvement in achieving high quality and business performance, others have either abandoned or reduced their efforts toward TQM programs. Frustrated by the lack of visible improvements, unconvincing results, and the reports of unsuccessful TQM efforts, some organizations have begun to question the value of TQM or view it as a distracting management fad (Ackoff (1993), Becker (1993), Bemowski (1993), Jacob (1993), Wilkinson *et al.* (1994).

Is the TQM age over? Is it indeed a passing management fad? Or, is it a revolutionary concept making fundamental contributions to the improvement of quality and business performance? Despite the potential benefits of TQM articulated by quality gurus and consultants, and despite anecdotal success stories, the high failure rates (60%–67%) quoted in the literature have made many companies believe that TQM has not been delivering on its promises.

Why then has TQM been failing? Even though some critics argue that TQM is a faddish concept created on a flimsy footing, many published reports proved otherwise. It is generally accepted that when TQM has failed, it is not because there was a basic flaw in the principles of TQM, but because an effective system was not created to execute TQM principles properly. Nevertheless, since the implementation of TQM requires unwavering organizational commitment, substantial time and effort, and drastic changes

in the organizational culture and business practices, it is important for companies to clearly understand what it takes to succeed and achieve high performance. The purpose of this paper is to examine possible answers to the questions raised here, and to provide managers with guidelines for the successful implementation of TQM.

Key TQM Principles

There have been numerous studies examining what constitutes TQM, what quality activities most directly affect business performance, what the common barriers to TQM implementation are, and what factors are critical for the success of TQM (Saraph *et al.* (1989), GAO (1991), Easton (1993), DDI (1993), Ernst and Young (1993), Mann and Kehoe (1994), Plimpton *et al.* (1996), Black and Porter (1996). Many of these studies are based on surveys of CEOs, middle managers, employees, quality specialists, and the Baldrige winners, and reflect a fairly common and pragmatic view of TQM. Although these studies have provided slightly different results, some key threads run through them. In an effort to determine if quality improves organizational performance and to identify factors critical to the success of TQM, these studies have identified a common set of principles considered essential to the success of the overall TQM program.

As frequently discussed in the TQM literature, the following have been deemed critical for successful TQM implementation: strong top management leadership and commitment, customer focus, employee involvement and empowerment, a focus on continuous

Reprinted with permission from *SAM Advanced Management Journal*, Winter 1998, pp. 10-14. © 1998 by the Society for Advancement of Management, Texas A&M University–Corpus Christi, College of Business, 6300 Ocean Drive, FC111, Corpus Christi, TX 78412.

improvement, supplier partnerships, and the recognition of quality as a strategic issue in business planning. The use of SPC and statistical tools, product and service quality in design, performance measures focusing on quality, actions based on facts, and the new role of a quality department and quality specialists are also considered critical. These underlying TQM principles are commonly applicable to any organization and compose a set of key determinants for a successful TQM program. Although these principles prevail in most quality improvement programs, simply adopting them will not guarantee success. It may create confusion unless they are properly implemented. While these principles appear obvious, many organizations have found them very difficult to execute. This is reportedly due to the fact that the implementation is cumbersome, time-consuming, and frequently lacking in focus. Some TQM critics report that the principles are too theoretical and broad to be practical. It is noteworthy that no single approach contains all of the keys to quality, and no cookbook can be equally applied to all company situations and cultures. A combination of many different factors, such as an organizational culture conducive to total quality, the proper quality infrastructure, and system readiness, also contribute to the success or failure of TQM programs.

We do not want to revisit issues related to the definition of TQM and its key principles in this paper because numerous studies have already focused on them. Instead, we focus on implementation issues that have not been discussed but are critical for TQM success. We want to provide managers with additional guidance when considering the implementation or review of a quality program. The lessons described in the following sections are identified through a review of the TQM literature. We believe that lessons can be learned from failures as well as successes, and these lessons can be valuable for the successful implementation of TQM.

Lessons for Successful TQM Implementation

Lesson 1: Know thyself. Above all things, it is very important for companies to clearly understand what TQM really means for them before they start a TQM journey. Many do not have a coherent view of what TQM really means except at the most basic level. Raising the following questions will often help companies identify their needs and wants, concerns and capabilities, and help determine focus. What is TQM? Why is TQM necessary? What are the key areas in need of significant improvement? How should we use TQM tools, techniques and practices, and when should we use them? How do we define "success"? On what measures is "success" based? What are the target performance levels in the areas of financial performance, customer satisfaction, employee satisfaction, and quality performance? Are these numerical targets concrete, realistic, and achievable? Often, delusional measurement of success results in failure. Performance should be measured against the company's own, concrete TQM goals, and continual feedback should be used to monitor the progress of the plan.

Knowing who you are, what you do, how you compete, and where you stand in the quality journey would help companies measure the organization's awareness of the need for change, its readiness for planned improvement, and help identify action programs for mobilizing company resources. In light of this, conducting a self-audit or a self-assessment could help identify organizational weaknesses and strengths and identify areas on which efforts and resources should be focused. For this purpose, the criteria and guidelines of the Baldrige Award and ISO 9000 can be used in evaluating a company's current status and designing a company-specific total quality system.

Lesson 2: Create a culture that is conducive to and supportive of TQM implementation. The cultural barrier has been one of the frequently mentioned obstacles faced by organizations attempting to implement TQM. Many organizations do an excellent job of committing to total quality by adopting the aforementioned TQM principles, but neglect to create culture conducive to the establishment and continual improvement of quality. It should be recognized that the organization culture interweaves key TQM principles and allows the organization's energies to move in the same direction toward the achievement of total quality. Bounds *et al.* (1994) suggest that the following principles be considered for a supportive quality culture:

- The importance of determining what customers value as opposed to what management thinks they need.
- A customer versus an organizational focus.
- A focus on optimizing organizational performance rather than maximizing functional end results.
- The importance of experimentation for knowledge and openness to new information.
- Acceptance of mistakes that lead to organizational learning.
- Recognition of the importance of continuous improvement versus working to specification or adherence to the status quo.
- Recognition that performance improvement comes from process/system improvement and not just improving people.
- Willingness by managers to seek out root causes of problems.
- Understanding that continuous improvement is demanded at every level of the organization.

Lesson 3: TQM implementation should be clearly aligned with the company's strategic priorities, competitive environment, and goals. One of the frequently mentioned problems associated with TQM implementation is the fear that it can be counterproductive when combined with other management techniques such as Management By Objectives (MBO). Salegna and Fazel (1995) argue that the success of TQM depends on the organization's implementation plan and the congruency that exists between the TQM plan and the organization's goals and culture. They suggest that a careful plan is, therefore, required to integrate TQM into the organization's core values, and the implementation process be approached from an integrated system viewpoint and not piecemeal. To this end, it is recommended that everyone in the organization be informed not only of the strategic direction of the business but also of the current imperatives and current performance. Everyone should also understand where they fit in working toward those imperatives and achieving those goals.

Lesson 4: Understand the necessary time and effort. Management should set realistic, achievable, and concrete goals rather than trying to encompass too many elements at the same time. Quality action programs should be allowed sufficient time to adapt and assimilate, and a strong resource base is also required. The development of planning through an integrated flowchart often helps identify teams and departments responsible for certain activities, projected completion time, and efforts required for each activity. A pre-implementation plan also helps develop the right attitude and the level of awareness crucial to achieving success in a quality improvement program.

Lesson 5: TQM implementation should be unique to each company. The success of TQM is a function of many variables (both controllable and uncontrollable), and many of them are unique to the company situation. It should be noted that there is no "one-size-fits-all" approach for TQM. Certain quality activities may be more appropriate for some organizations than for others. When establishing quality programs, companies should look for a fit between their current situation and the environment in which they compete, rather than relying on an off-the-shelf TQM package. No single prepackaged quality program or approach can be installed intact in any organization. Each company should custom-make its own program to fit its culture, current practices, and policies (Ernst and Young (1993)). For example, the study by Ernst and Young (1993) recommends that lower-performing companies focus on the development of people, customer interaction, process improvement and cost reduction rather than trying to do too much, too soon. Medium performing companies should focus on vendor quality, employee training, cycle time analysis, and process simplification. This study also suggests that the widely touted

practices of benchmarking and employee empowerment only had beneficial results for higher-performing companies. As companies progressed from one level of performance to the next, the focus of their quality programs need to expand. Usually, practices were cumulative, with each level building on the one before. Customer input and employee training were key at all levels of performance.

Lesson 6: Take a "holistic" approach. TQM is neither a canned program nor a simple sum of quality tools, techniques, and practices. It requires an effective system to implement target plans. Since the boundary of TQM is so broad and encompasses many disciplines and functional areas, a holistic approach that can integrate many activities is recommended. Interactions between and among departments, functional disciplines, and people at different levels should be recognized and managed to generate a synergistic effect. In light of this, a cross functional systems approach that integrates activities throughout the organization toward strategic objectives and breaks down barriers between departments and levels is often recommended (Bounds *et al.* (1994). This approach will raise everyone's attention to a higher level, above functional concerns, toward a holistic view of the organization with the purpose of serving customers. Larson and Sinha (1995) provide evidence that the cooperation between people and departments ignites a chain reaction leading to increasing customer and employee satisfaction while improving quality and productivity.

Lesson 7: Remember the key word. The term "Total Quality Management" conveys the comprehensive nature of quality improvement activities with emphasis on the word "total" and a broad definition of "quality." This "total" view of quality includes all activities at all levels in all areas, integrating them into a comprehensive approach to continuous improvement. It also necessitates total participation, total commitment, and total responsibility of everyone in an organization (top management, employees, suppliers and customers). While the concept of "totality" is essential to the success of TQM, this somewhat unbounded and ambiguous view has also created confusion among managers as to where to start, how to mobilize organizational resources, and what areas to include. As discussed in *Lessons 2 and 5*, it is recommended that the organization fully understand its ability (strengths and weaknesses, distinctive competence, limited resources, quality infrastructure such as employees' knowledge and skill base, quality awareness, and organization-wide commitment to quality) to deal effectively with quality-related issues. A myopic view or traditional approach that relies primarily on top management and quality specialists is not recommended.

Lesson 8: Understand that TQM is not a "magic bullet" or panacea for quality. Many companies simply jump on the bandwagon without fully understanding what

TQM means for them or its possible consequences. A common misconception includes wishful thinking that TQM will fix short-term problems and quickly improve business performance—a view which is considered to be one of the biggest reasons for TQM failures. As is often said, TQM is not a destination but a journey requiring a long-term, unwavering commitment to the improvement of product or service and process quality. TQM should be considered as a means to an end rather than [an] end in itself.

Summary and Conclusion

Implemented properly, TQM can be a powerful vehicle by which companies can achieve excellence in business performance. However, despite the fact that many companies adopt an archetypical TQM framework and its key principles, some of them have not been achieving TQM's potential benefits and have begun to abandon its practices. The TQM framework and key principles should not be blamed for its failure. It is the lack of understanding of what TQM means for each unique organization and how to implement it effectively that has created skepticism on the effectiveness of TQM. In this paper, we have examined several critical issues and provided lessons that may improve the possibility for successful implementation of TQM.

As we have emphasized, the success of TQM depends on many variables, controllable and uncontrollable, many of which are specific to the company's culture, customers, capability, and infrastructure. Therefore, each company should tailor its approach to exploit its unique strengths and focus on its particular weaknesses.

Finally, TQM is not a short-term fix. It is a long-term, never-ending commitment to the improvement of quality and performance. Organizations must be willing to stick with their efforts because results are not usually immediate. Finally, organizations should carefully examine their readiness for certain quality initiatives, keeping in mind the critical stages where certain practices are more appropriate than others.

Dr. Shin's teaching and research interests include production and operations management, quality management, JIT manufacturing, and management science; he chairs the Management Department. Dr. Kalinowski, a member of the Academy of Management and Decision Science Institute, researches strategic management, quality-related initiatives, and executive succession. Dr. Elenein, who is Dean of his university's College of Business, is also a member of the Academy of Management, the Decision Sciences Institute, and the North American Case Research Association.

References

Ackoff, R. (1993, March). Beyond TQM. *Journal for Quality and Participation* 66–78.

Ahire, S. L., Golhar, D. Y. & Waller, M. A. (1996). Development and validation of TQM implementation constructs. *Decision Sciences,* 27(1), 23–56.

Barclay, C. A. (1993). Quality strategy and TQM policies: Empirical evidence. *Management International Review,* 33(2), 87–98.

Becker, S. W. (1993, May). TQM does work: Ten reasons why misguided attempts fail. *Management Review,* 30–33.

Bemowski, K. (1995, July). TQM: flimsy footing or firm foundation. *Quality Progress,* 27–28.

Black, S. A. & Porter, L. J. (1996). Identification of the critical factors of TQM. *Decision Sciences,* 27(1), 1–21.

Bound, G., Yorks, L., Adams, M. & Ranney, G. (1994). *Beyond Total Quality Management: Toward the Emerging Paradigm.* McGraw-Hill. New York, NY.

Brown, M. G. (1993). Why does total quality fail in two out of three tries? *Journal for Quality and Participation,* 16(2). 80–89.

Dean, J. W., Jr. & Bowen, D. E. (1994). Management theory and total quality: Improving research and practice through theory development. *Academy of Management Review,* 19(3), 392–418.

Development Dimensions International, Quality & Productivity Management Association and Industry Week. (1993). *TQM: Forging ahead or falling behind?* Pittsburgh: Development Dimensions International, Inc.

Easton, G. S. (1993). The 1993 state of U.S. total quality management: a Baldrige examiner's perspective. *California Management Review,* 35(3), 32–54.

Ernst & Young and the American Quality Foundation. (1993). *International quality study: Best practices report.* New York: Ernst & Young.

Fisher, T. J. (1992). The impact of quality management on productivity. *The International Journal of Quality and Reliability Management,* 9(3), 44–52.

Fuchsberg, G. (1992, May 14). Quality programs shows shoddy results. *The Wall Street Journal,* B1, B9.

General Accounting Office. (1991). *U.S. companies improve performance through quality efforts.* (NSIAD-91-190). Washington, DC: United States General Accounting Office.

Harari, O. (1993, Jan.). Ten reasons why TQM doesn't work. *Management Review,* 33–38.

Jacob, R. (1993, Oct. 18). TQM: More than a dying fad? *Fortune,* 66–72.

Larson, P. D. & Sinha, A. (1995, Spring). The TQM impact: A study of quality managers' perceptions. *Quality Management Journal,* 53–66.

Mann, R. & Kehoe, D. (1994). An evaluation of the effects of quality improvement activities on business performance. *The International Journal of Quality and Reliability Management,* 11(4), 29–44.

Nadkarni, R. A. (1995, Nov.). A not-so-secret recipe for successful TQM. *Quality progress,* 91–96.

Plimpton, A. P., Kalinowski, J. G., Abou El-Enein, G. & Shin, D. (1996, March). Assessing the impact of total quality management on performance—a recent review of literature. *The Proceedings of The 1996 Conference of The Midwest Business Administration Society,* 69–75.

Salegna, G. & Fazel, F. (1995). An integrative framework for developing and evaluating a TQM implementation plan. *Quality Management Journal,* 73–84.

Saraph, J. V., Benson, P. G. & Schroeder, R. G. (1989). An instrument for measuring the critical factors of quality management. *Decision Sciences,* 810–829.

Sitkin, S. B., Sutcliffe, K. M. & Schroeder, R. G. (1994). Distinguishing control from learning in total quality management: A contingency perspective. *Academy of Management Review,* 19(3), 537–564.

The Malcolm Baldrige National Quality Award 1995 Criteria, National Institute of Standards and Technology, Gaithersburg, MD.

Wilkinson, A., Redman, T. & Snape, E. (1995, Winter). New patterns of quality management in the United Kingdom. *Quality Management Journal,* 37–49.

Unit 3

Key Points to Consider

❖ Economists argue that jobs should be designed with job specialization to gain efficiency. Behavioral scientists argue that jobs should be designed with enrichment. What is your belief and why?

❖ Firms are moving to more technology use, automation, and replacement of workers with robotics. Given these trends, will human resources be of less importance in the future?

❖ European firms have had a longer history of having semiautonomous work units. What factors might hinder greater acceptance of semiautonomous work units in the United States?

 **Links** **www.dushkin.com/online/**

These sites are annotated on pages 4 and 5.

Production and operations management involves not just equipment, raw materials, and capital; the field also involves workers. Whereas competitors can gain access to the same equipment, hardware, software, and raw materials, the human resources of a firm can provide for a strategic advantage. For a long period of time, many firms have used the phrase, "our employees are our greatest asset" in their recruitment brochures. In the past some employees questioned the sincerity of these firms. Now it appears that many firms actually believe this claim that their employees are a critical strategic asset.

Earlier schools of management thought, such as the scientific management school, placed less emphasis upon the worker's psychological needs and more emphasis on the procedures of a job. With the behavioral school of thought and evidence from research after the 1930s, there was a recognition of how psychological factors affect worker performance and productivity. Firms and managers needed to now consider leadership style, motivation techniques, design of rewards and incentives, and performance appraisal systems. There was an agreement that human resources management practices were linked to employee morale and employee productivity.

Classical economists such as Adam Smith back in the late 1700s and the scientific managers of the early 1900s favored job designs that limited the number of tasks and jobs that were highly specialized. Although efficiency could be gained from division of labor and job specialization, boredom and low worker morale could occur. The behavioral scientists recommended a change to job rotation, job enlargement (increasing the number of tasks performed), and job enrichment (increasing the depth of the tasks and responsibility given to the worker). Many firms today are moving toward concepts such as employee empowerment, job empowerment, the inverted pyramid (where frontline workers are given more empowerment because they are closer to the customers), and semiautonomous work teams.

The articles in this unit show examples of firms that see the importance of human resources management to overall operations and production management success. Steven Abraham and Michael Spencer's article identifies legal limitations to self-directed work teams in production planning and control. The final article, by Stuart Brown, examines how user-friendly machines are developed for home and industry use. These machines are developed by utilizing human factors analysis and ergonomics (the study of workers and their work environment) analysis.

Human Resources Management for Productivity

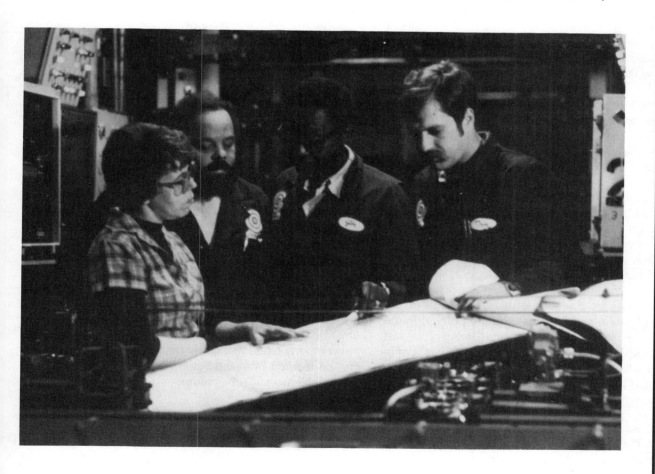

RELYING ON THE POWER OF PEOPLE AT SATURN

Since its inception, the Saturn Corporation has served as an example of what partnership, teamwork, and principle-centered leadership can accomplish in an organization that thoroughly understands and tries to apply those concepts. Dedicated to quality and productivity, the company believes that meeting the needs of people—customers, suppliers, team members, retailers, and the community—is the only route to long-term growth and profitability in a global economy. Its experiences in achieving this goal can light the way for other companies that are struggling with releasing the reins of positional power and transitioning to a team-oriented environment.

by Eleanor White

If you drive down Interstate 65 about 40 miles south of Nashville, Tennessee, you find an exit called the Saturn Parkway. Take a right turn onto the parkway and drive about five miles. Visitors must exit at this point, or they will wind up at Saturn—not the planet, but the car company. Signs direct you south onto Highway 31, where you follow a country road with a white-board fence on the right surrounding green fields of corn and soybeans. Not far down this road, you come upon a stately white Southern mansion sitting well back from the highway, with a low stone wall separating the green, free-covered grounds from the highway. The scene is a reminder of the South's pre-Civil War glory, and, more recently, home to Tennessee walking horses. Where's the multibillion-dollar manufacturing facility, the monstrous plant that builds hundreds of automobiles every day?

At the Saturn Welcome Center, still with no factory in sight, you find yourself in a horse barn. You pass multiple rooms of automotive displays. Signed banners hang from the rafters shouting messages about values, partnership, and teamwork. The interior of polished wood, plaques, and mementos exudes a feeling of warmth and pride.

After identification and badging, you are pointed in the direction of the factory. A winding road takes you past duck ponds and low-lying gray buildings more than a mile in length blending into the haze of the Tennessee landscape. A muted red stripe encircling the tops of the build-

ings complements the colors of the farms dotting the surrounding countryside.

Inside the assembly plant, a busy world of car building unfolds with hundreds of people gliding along on a "skillet" with the cars, rather than chasing them down the line, while lifting, placing, polishing, sorting, and building world-class automobiles. The car builders wave occasionally with a welcoming smile for visitors riding through the plant on tour trams. The finished product leaves the plant at the end of the line, where "Inspiration Point" is written on a placard over the door. Another Saturn is on its way to a customer.

People are asking some thought-provoking questions about Saturn's success that deserve answers. How were self-managed teams implemented so successfully when most organizations, trying to work with teams, are really struggling? Why are Saturn team members so enthusiastic? After all, building a car is very difficult work, even in the best of circumstances. What is it that makes working for this company different? Saturn speaks of mission, philosophy, principle-centered values, partnership, teamwork, and self-management as being crucial to its success. How have these concepts been applied and integrated into the day-to-day business of building cars? What mistakes has the company made that could be avoided by others? What can be learned from the Saturn experience? What are its main challenges for the future?

* * *

A member of the General Motors University organizational development staff, Eleanor White oversees the alignment of training programs with the vision, values, and competencies needed by the corporation. She is also responsible for development of strategies and processes related to measuring the impact of training and development. Before joining GM-Saturn in the early 1980s, she was a secondary school English teacher.

From *National Productivity Review*, Winter 1997, pp. 5-10. © 1997 by John Wiley and Sons, Inc. Reprinted by permission.

The answers to these questions are evolving at Saturn. As one challenge is resolved, others surface, and the challenges continue to get tougher. The company's philosophy says that meeting people's needs is paramount and that:

- Everyone has input into decisions that affect them.
- People are loyal and care about their jobs and each other.
- People take pride in themselves and their contributions.
- People want to share in the success of their efforts.

In the day-to-day worklife, this philosophy is reflected in the Saturn commitment to nurture a sense of belonging in an environment of mutual trust, respect, and dignity. Creative, motivated, responsible team members are Saturn's most important asset. Meeting the needs of people is the primary focus of the organization. If "people needs" are met effectively, the quality and quantity of product leading to profit and long-term success is assured. Therefore, the corporation has been built around meeting the needs of *all* its people—team members, customers, suppliers, retailers, and the community.

The cornerstone of this philosophy lies in the company's mission and values—and getting the workforce to understand the what, how, and why of their application. Decisions are measured against this cornerstone, and those that are not compatible are not made. Saturn's mission is: "Market vehicles developed and manufactured in the United States that are world leaders in quality, cost and customer enthusiasm through the integration of people, technology and business systems and to exchange knowledge, technology and experience throughout General Motors." The five Saturn values complete this vision:

- Customer Enthusiasm
- Teamwork
- Commitment to Excel
- Trust and Respect
- Continuous Improvement

All together, the mission, philosophy, and values are like a three-legged stool. The mission says what the organization is trying to accomplish; the philosophy states how to achieve the mission; and the values reflect team members' behaviors toward one [an]other in working toward these goals. No leg can stand alone.

This three-part vision was created as a partnership agreement between management and Local 1853 of the United Auto Workers when Saturn was formed in the mid-1980s. The partnership relationship is the primary reason that the mission, philosophy, and values are integrated into the everyday business of Saturn. The union is instrumental in ensuring that everyone has a business focus, while management is very much in tune to the idea of treating people fairly and doing the right thing, not just doing the thing right.

Nothing is more important in a team-based environment than modeling of the values by leaders. Leaders in all parts of the organization must serve as examples of what the philosophy and values mean. Values training is important for everyone, but training is no substitute for seeing the appropriate behaviors modeled by leaders, every day, five minutes at a time. People will not necessarily behave as they are trained to behave if, in their environment, they observe conflicting behaviors, especially among their leaders. Saturn believes that leadership should be distributed based on the task being faced, and that instead of imbuing the "boss" with all the power and all the responsibility, the approach should be self-organization and self-leadership. The designation of someone to sign approvals does not equate to their being the only "leader." So, interpersonal skills, vision, the ability to deal with ambiguity, the ability to delegate, and resourcefulness become ever more important for everyone.

Symbols of division are absent. Senior management promotes a culture which says that everyone in the organization is special. There are no special parking spaces or cafeterias for a select few. Senior managers' offices are open and accessible. Dress is casual; no white shirts, suits, or ties. Managers mix with the team members and validate the lack of hierarchy by asking for help and input instead of dictating how work is done. They foster an environment where ideas are solicited and welcomed.

LETTING TEAMS TAKE CHARGE

Saturn has self-managed teams with no supervisors, inspectors, time clocks, or union stewards. These teams are responsible for their business, including quality, cost, production, and people. When things go wrong, whether it is technology- or people-related, the expectation is that the team will solve the problem, if possible, since its members are closest to it. Technicians have a lot of responsibility. They seek help only when they have exhausted their ability to deal with the issue, including interpersonal conflicts.

Saturn believes that leadership should be distributed based on the task being faced, and that instead of imbuing the "boss" with all the power and all the responsibility, the approach should be self-organization and self-leadership.

The tendency in a traditional environment is to follow a predetermined process rather than to identify the most effective and efficient way to solve a problem. Jobs are strictly classified and those boundaries are not crossed. If there's a technical problem, the supervisor is responsible for solving it or for getting a technical expert who can. If a people-related issue arises, the union steward is called to work with a supervisor or manager designated to handle it. At Saturn, the team handles the majority of the problems that come up. If a team has conflict, team leaders will not get involved until the individuals confront each other and try to work it out among themselves. A more traditional approach would have the supervisor or the union steward handle interpersonal conflicts. Those job roles do not exist at Saturn. Interpersonal conflicts are the responsibility of the team members. They go to their advisors only when they are unable to handle a particular problem. Management and the union work together as team advisors. Everyone is responsible for their own behavior and their own work, with the support of a team and clear communication from leaders who provide direction, support, and resources.

Cross-functional communications are reflected in a circular organizational structure made up of decision rings. Each decision ring meets weekly. The outer ring meets on Monday. The next ring meets on Tuesday, etc. By Friday, current knowledge and information from all rings is available to the 600 work teams that produce the product, since all teams have met and transferred the information to the next ring. Team safety, quality, budget, materials, training, and maintenance champions also meet on a regular schedule to facilitate communications across rings. Each day, team members enter data into a computer on cost, production schedule, quality, and people. These data are tracked by leaders who help teams address problems before they escalate.

Nothing is more important than leader behaviors that establish and reflect the expectations of the culture. Everyone is encouraged to take the initiative to grow their skills and to demonstrate their ability to lead as well as follow.

To resolve any issues that come up, everyone is encouraged to express their views without censure. During problem-solving sessions, the opinion of the leader has no more weight than that of a team member. The goal is to look at varying alternatives and try as a team to come up with the best answer, focusing on what is the right thing to do, not necessarily the most expedient or politically correct. This approach takes time, and those used to a more traditional leadership style can become highly frustrated with the consensus process; but in the long run, it works. The best answer is always the result when all stakeholders have an opportunity to say their say, with no hidden agendas, and the one best answer as the goal.

There are no job classifications that restrict operating technicians from handling common operating problems. Safety and competence drive the troubleshooting rather than job classifications. If a problem involves complex issues, it is up to the team to contact the maintenance, engineering, or other appropriate resources.

It is very important for management to value everyone's input and ideas equally, for the company's philosophy implies that everyone is equal. Leaders must let go of the hierarchical, competitive, divisive, unequal separation of people and the "boss" mentality. Every person and every job is important and should be treated as such. Teams run the business of their team. Leaders provide training, support, direction, resources, counseling, consulting, and open communication. People are treated fairly and respected for their contribution, whether they are in production, planning, engineering, or administration. Owners and managers are servant leaders in partnership with their union counterparts. They have personal rather than positional power, which comes from giving teams support and resources when needed, helping them to do the job as needed, and pitching in to solve problems rather than criticizing when things go wrong.

LABOR AND MANAGEMENT WORKING IN TANDEM

Management and union leaders are guardians of the belief that making mistakes is acceptable. Making a mistake does not automatically lead to punishment. If an organization allows people to make mistakes in pursuit of continuous improvement, it becomes a learning organization.

Union and management leaders are also guardians of the organization's vision and direction. They hold the compass and create a path leading in that direction. Followers expect that leaders know where they are headed. Nothing is more important than leader behaviors that establish and reflect the expectations of the culture. Everyone is encouraged to take the initiative to grow their skills and to demonstrate their ability to lead as well as follow. The most powerful limitations in this environment are self-imposed. There is no intention of downsizing or laying off people, for they are a long-term capital asset. The intention is a lifetime job, which is about 30 years. Commitment works both ways. People take ownership and give their best when they feel safe, and trust the company to look after their best interests.

An annual minimum of 92 hours of training for everyone ensures continuous improvement of the company's most important asset. The achievement of organizational performance goals related to quality, production, training, teams, and profitability depends on the input of every individual to do a good job. Goals are clearly defined and performance is communicated daily. Continuous measurement is important to continuous improvement. It is to the team's advantage to help its team members be effective. Coaching in both technical and people skills is the primary method for growing individual team members. Modeling of expected behaviors is a must for leaders if the coaching is to have any lasting effect. Everyone, rather than just a few owners and managers, is concerned with company success. Everyone is an owner/manager of their work and their job. It is difficult to maintain mediocrity or the status quo when continuous improvement is the only way to survive. The goals define excellence, and they continue to move forward.

Results are measured, not people. The mission says to build a product that is a world leader in quality, cost, and customer enthusiasm. That is what is measured. People are responsible for results. They are rewarded financially and otherwise for achieving that result. A favorite saying around Saturn is, "If we always do what we have always done, we always get what we always got." We can't expect a different result if we do things the same way. Therefore, the first thing to do is to define the result wanted. Then put together a team to decide what needs to be done differently to get that result.

Factors that cannot be measured effectively, at least in quantitative terms, are trustworthiness, character, integrity, synergy, fairness, kindness, talent, and commitment; yet, these are the most important factors leading toward long-term viability in today's world. The successful achievement of these qualitative, or "soft," results is the secret that yields an extra edge. Being 90 percent right is not good enough any more in the face of increasing competition.

Good people were doing their best to erase the abuses of the past, while inadvertently creating new abuses related to abdication rather than delegation of responsibility. There were no models to follow.

Saturn's management structure is extremely fluid and flexible. The company reinvents itself every day trying to get closer to its vision. It falls back and goes forward based on new knowledge. As new people come into the organization, they must be socialized into this complex, yet so simple, business philosophy of shared vision and values where everyone is responsible and able to share in the rewards, as well as the risks.

The risk/reward program encourages and motivates team members to continuously improve their job performance. The risk portion of pay requires that 12 percent be withheld until specific organizational performance goals are met. These goals relate to 5 percent of worktime spent in training, car quality that meets the industry standard as measured by an external auditor, and team effectiveness measured in terms of specific goals, strategies, and team meetings. If the measurements show that the goals have been met, the money withheld is paid back in a quarterly lump sum.

The reward portion of compensation is paid only if the risk goals are met. The reward performance goals relate to car quality that exceeds the industry standard, production schedule attainment of 95 percent or more, and meeting the organizational financial goals for the year. The maximum reward is $12,500. The actual amount paid is determined by the relationship of the actual performance to the goal. Everyone in the organization receives the same amount, with the quality and production rewards paid quarterly and the profitability reward paid annually. Every year the goals, percentages, and dollar amounts change as necessary to ensure continuous improvement.

The company's management practices were created with an emphasis on intellectual capital and a shared vision of involvement of all stakeholders in running the business, win-win thinking, finding and doing the right thing as the only acceptable solution to problems, and partnerships with character, competence, and trustworthiness as the key values. The structure, systems, and strategies were formed to ensure support for this vision. The work teams, style, symbols, culture, skills, and management of self and one's behaviors evolved around this vision as well.

BEWARE OF DOING TOO MUCH TOO SOON

A misjudgment that Saturn made early in its history—and there was not enough information at the time to avoid it—was the delegation of too much responsibility too soon to the teams. The best course would have been to release power and responsibility to the teams as they demonstrated the competence to handle them. The problem was that the leaders did not have the competence they needed to go in that direction. There was a mission, a philosophy, and a set of values that spoke of personal rather than positional power and support rather than direction. A positive work environment was the goal, with positive interpersonal behaviors such as active listening, honoring people not present, trust, respect, and information sharing. Self-management responsibilities were given too soon with a lot of confusion thrown into the mix. Good people were doing their best to erase the abuses of the past, while inadvertently creating new abuses related to abdication rather than delegation of responsibility. There were no models to follow. A fresh trail had to be blazed for others to follow, with the blessing and the money of General Motors, one of the most successful companies in the world. Some very painful lessons were learned from some sobering challenges that raised serious questions about the future of Saturn's approach to self-management.

An early "abdication versus delegation" of responsibility problem arose when teams were given responsibility for attendance. Time clocks were never installed at Saturn. Everyone was put on salary. The teams entered exception hours, such as overtime, vacations, and emergency leaves, into a computer system. More than 90 percent of the teams handled this well, but a few took advantage of the freedom such a system allows. They came up with some very creative ways to take extra time off, including doubling up on jobs and getting the lines full as much as two hours before the end of the shift, allowing most of the team to leave with a skeleton crew left behind to take care of the unexpected. Their leaders looked the other way as long as quality and production were not affected. This created some resentment among most of the teams, which were trying to do the right thing, those that could not do this because of production constraints, or when the unavailability of a fully staffed team resulted in downtime or a lack of parts. This abuse was never widespread, but it was serious enough to cause a lot of negative interaction. The teams themselves asked for more guidance concerning attendance issues.

The leaders had to step up to this task, which was never a team issue, but always a leadership issue. In partnership, the union and management determined what was best for the people and the process. They defined some very clear attendance guidelines. The process involves six steps that walk individuals right out of the organization if their unplanned absences get them all the way through step six. Since the implementation of these guidelines, unexcused absences have dropped to less than 1 percent. A lesson from this experience is that self-managed teams need the parameters of self-management defined for them. If clear boundaries are established by leaders, the teams will cooperate, as long as the business reasons for the boundaries are clear and both union and management are saying the same thing.

The real challenge in Saturn's future is to maintain what has been achieved so far, continuously improve it, and continue to fulfill the latter part of its mission, which is to "exchange knowledge, technology, and experience throughout General Motors."

The presence of leaders must be seen and felt. Team building is a process, not an occasional event. Saturn teams have a tool kit available to them when they need to resolve specific team issues. The kit contains 14 modules that support such topics as conflict resolution, effective meetings, and decision making. The material provides guidance for the facilitator of the team activity. Occasionally, a team is given formal or informal training and counseling as needed. In addition, team members attend 100 hours or more of team training during their early months at Saturn.

Another very early trial for Saturn—which was product, not people, related—came within the first year after start of car production. It became necessary to recall over 1,800 cars that had been filled with corrosive coolant.

The company's Strategic Action Council had to decide what to do based on Saturn's values. The traditional approach would have been to send out a bulletin to the retailers and recall the cars with a few hundred miles on them for repairs of any damage to the engine, transmission, or coolant system. The cars with fewer miles would have had the coolant system flushed and then they would be watched for any future problems. But that solution could not be the answer in a principle-centered organization.

The long-term effects of corrosive coolant were not known. This specific problem had never occurred before this incident. Customer needs had to be placed above all else. The answer had to be to take back all the cars and give the customers new cars or return all the money paid, whichever the customer preferred. The company also decided to support the supplier by solving the problem with the supplier rather than resorting to mudslinging, threats, and retaliation. That's what partnerships are all about.

These actions were the only "right things to do" no matter how much other solutions might be rationalized. Every time a test comes along, and that's a frequent occurrence at Saturn, there is at least one right answer or one right thing to do. Sometimes making that decision appears on the surface to be the one that will hurt the company, at least in the short term. But principles must guide decisions—not fear, expedience, or politics.

Shortly after the coolant decision was made, which looked at the time like the death knell for Saturn, some interesting things happened. Customers came in droves, impressed with a car company that would actually do what was right for the customer. The supplier took the responsibility for the cost of the disaster. The root cause was found for the problem. The same supplier still supplies coolant to Saturn.

Important business decisions are made daily at Saturn at all levels of the organization. If political or personal agendas get in the way, someone says, "Wait! We're Saturn. What's the *right* thing to do here?" There's always at least one right thing to do. It's up to the leaders to hold that mirror up to the organization so that everyone can see more clearly what needs to happen. Decisions must be grounded on principles. Nothing less will do.

Saturn has now been building cars for seven years. The company is not, and never has been, an "experiment." The first part of the mission is being fulfilled. More than 90 percent of the Saturn product is made of American parts. The quality of a Saturn puts it at the head of its class in the small car market segment. Costs are favorable, with a competitive price that allows for long-term viability.

The main lesson that other companies, regardless of their industry, can learn from Saturn is the importance of doing the right thing by people—customers, suppliers, retailers, team members, and the community. In this modern world of global competition, you must take the short-term pain to get the long-term gain.

Some might say, "Why should we put our organization through such pain? We're doing okay, better than ever, with a traditional structure. We have no teams and a traditional hierarchy. We have bosses with employees who do what they are told. Management makes the decisions and employees carry them put. Our people are happy; we make good products; and we have satisfied customers."

Saturn sees some real challenges in global competition that have never been faced by companies in the past. How does an organization with fierce worldwide competition get that extra competitive edge? Is it by using the brains, talent, commitment, and ownership of a few people in the organization, with the rest doing the bidding of the few? Or is it by creating an environment where everyone takes ownership of company success, including the bottom line? Creating and maintaining the latter is extremely difficult and extremely rewarding at the same time. Hearts and minds have to change. Management must release the reins of positional power and recognize the greater power in servant leadership with the emphasis on support instead of direction. If unions are to survive, they must focus on supporting their people in a different way. They must continue to ensure that the company is fair and treats people right, but they must also keep the business plan close by, recognizing their responsibility in contributing to the bottom line. Work stoppages and strikes will not take you into the future. Instead, they lead to oblivion. The new game is win/win, not win/lose—or worse—lose/lose.

The real challenge in Saturn's future is to maintain what has been achieved so far, continuously improve it, and continue to fulfill the latter part of its mission, which is to "exchange knowledge, technology, and experience throughout General Motors." This is the reason GM, the parent company, created Saturn.

The technology exchange has been easy. The exchange of knowledge and experience throughout GM is the greatest challenge of all, since GM is so diverse and has been, for most of this century, the most successful company in the world. As GM goes forward, global expansion is the primary goal. Taking what is being learned at Saturn and trying to integrate it into the way GM does business is a most important future business for Saturn. That extra competitive edge comes with how a company treats its people, and Saturn has learned a lot about that, which can only enhance GM's future. Those who are the best at meeting the needs of people will win in the long run every time.

How do you get sexy returns from slag, cement and dirt?
TXI got some clever answers from its rank and file.

The million-dollar suggestion box

By Caroline Waxler

PITY ROBERT ROGERS, the 62-year-old chief executive of Texas Industries in Dallas. The business his father started in 1951 is as unglamorous as you can get: It sells $1.2 billion a year worth of cement, steel, slag and dirt. Talk about being prey to commodity cycles. The company, which does most of its sales in Texas, made good money during the early-1980s oil boom, but by calendar 1989 was in the red and laying off workers.

Confronting such ups and downs, many an executive would be tempted to diversify into something like software or movie production. Rogers stuck to his business and put out the word that he wanted ideas from his employees. He got some.

Barrett Reese, 54, then a sales manager in Houston's cement office, was staring at a pile of red clay and shale that he couldn't sell. Why not mix them and sell the stuff as a magic carpet to keep the puddles out of baseball infields? The designer dirt is now a big seller at $100 a ton delivered, which is ten times as much as the ingredients are worth.

Glenwood Rutledge Jr., 42, then the north Texas transportation manager, had the bright idea to use a $250 personal computer in a way that would allow Texas Industries to consolidate some freight car dispatching stations, at a savings of more than $100,000 a year.

Rom Young, 72, has been a cement chemist at Texas Industries since 1960. Libor Rostik, 64, was a refugee from communist Czechoslovakia who took a steel job with the company as vice president of engineering in 1985. Rogers put the two of them together and mentioned "synergy." The two guys came up with something clever that is worth $10 million a year to Texas Industries' pretax income.

The Young-Rostik invention, patented in 1995, has to do with slag, which is the scum that collects on top of molten steel. Why not throw the slag from Texas Industries' Mid-lothian steel plant into the Texas Industries cement kiln across the street?

Slag has been used as a sort of hamburger helper in cementmaking ever since 1774. But until the Texas Industries men started experimenting with the process, it was taken for granted that you had to grind the slag into a fine powder and inject it into the flame end of the cement kiln. The grinding process is energy-intensive and expensive. Few cementmakers bothered to use slag.

The new process calls for tossing 2-inch chunks of slag into the top of the cement kiln at the start of the process. This eliminates a grinding step and—because slag is chemically similar to cement and has already been heated—has the added benefit of increasing the capacity of the cement plant.

The slag that Texas Industries used to dump onto road-grading projects at $1 a ton is now worth 10 to 15 times that as a cement ingredient, according to David Lee Smith,

Reprinted by permission from *Forbes* magazine, September 7, 1998, pp. 171-172. © 1998 by Forbes, Inc.

analyst at Dain Rauscher Wessels. Texas Industries is also collecting royalties from cement companies that license the process, yet may buy their slag elsewhere. Great timing for the invention, since cementmakers in the U.S. are getting orders faster than they can fill them and will do whatever they can to boost capacity.

"Everyone else is now saying: 'Why didn't I think of this?' " says Rostik. "The idea is so simple."

Joe Smith, manager of sand and gravel operations in Austin, found himself sitting on too much inventory when his biggest customer went bust. A golf course contractor came

by, talking about mixing those ingredients with peat moss for a sod underliner to improve drainage. Smith had the inspiration that Texas Industries should do the mixing. Result: His employer now supplies "prescription sand" to 95% of the golf courses in central Texas as well as to hundreds of athletic fields. The stuff fetches $20 a ton, double the cost of the raw materials.

What do the employees get out of their new product ideas? No million-dollar royalties, although they get group bonuses that can reach 20% of salary.

For now, it's boom time in Texas for vendors of construction materi-

als. In its May 31 fiscal year Texas Industries earned $102 million, or $4.69 a share, for an enviable return on equity of 21%.

What happens in the next construction bust? The company will suffer, but not as much as it did in the late 1980s and early 1990s. The company derives 15% of its earnings from recent innovations like the slag process. Rogers wants to double that percentage within five years.

Says Rogers, "The construction recession was the best thing that ever happened to us. If we hadn't been forced to reexamine ourselves, we wouldn't have realized we had a gold mine underneath our noses."

COMPANIES Modern Bankers are doing ATMs and Internet services. Old-fashioned Kerry Killinger is sinking Washington Mutual's efforts into branches.

Tellers who hustle

By Seth Lubove

KERRY KILLINGER learned about incentive-based compensation at the University of Iowa by fixing brass instruments at a music shop for commissions instead of a fixed salary. "You just watch the productivity of someone on that deal," muses Killinger, 49, now the chairman and chief executive of Washington Mutual Inc. He made a better living repairing instruments than he did for three years in the business world as a newly minted M.B.A.

These days the soft-spoken but intense Killinger is applying those early lessons on a grand scale. After swallowing California's H. F. Ahmanson & Co.—Killinger's 20th S&L acquisition since becoming president in 1988—he runs, from modest leased offices in a Seattle high-rise, the nation's largest thrift, with $156 billion in assets. While many big banks push their retail customers to ATMs, he's going the other direction. He

likes branches, and he wants customers to talk to the tellers. Killinger may be some kind of freak in thinking that automatic teller machine usage has peaked.

Lured by a loss-leader free checking account with no minimum balance, customers come to the branch only to get the hard sell on other products. Everyone from the teller to the branch manager is earning commissions on something. Indeed, the branch managers earn 40% of their pay from overrides on their tellers.

Open a "free" checking account at one of Washington Mutual's 1,200 branches and you'll also be offered a $3-a-month add-on that includes such things as accidental death insurance, discount coupons and a travel service. Then you may get a call at home from the friendly chap at the branch who opened your account, making sure that you received your checks and that everything else

is in order. As long as he's got you on the phone, perhaps you'd be interested in a home equity line, a personal loan, a new mortgage? Bounce a check, as lower-income customers who are lured by free checking are prone to do, and you'll pay a stiff $17-to- $20 charge—but, by the way, can we help you consolidate those nagging debts? Of the thrift's free-checking customers, 77% buy other, fee-based, services.

Washington Mutual's expected 1998 return on assets of 1.11% is decent enough for the industry. But its return on equity, which Dain Rauscher Wessels analyst R. Jay Tejera projects at over 20% for 1998, beats many big banks.

Salesmanship explains why Washington Mutual, while merely the fourth-largest mortgage originator in the nation last year, ranks first in writing adjustable-rate mortgages for its own portfolio. ARMs are preferred by lenders because they elimi-

 Reprinted by permission from *Forbes* magazine, November 2, 1998, p. 56. © 1998 by Forbes, Inc.

nate much of the investment risk in home mortgages, but are feared by homeowners. Industrywide, 13% of new mortgages during the first half were ARMs; at Washington Mutual, half were.

How do you get a home buyer to sign an ARM? You look him in the eye and talk "flexibility." Since Washington Mutual can afford to hold on to a mortgage if it is adjustable, it can break some of the usual rules that apply to mortgages aimed at the resale market. Among other things, Washington Mutual can accommodate borrowers who want to occasionally pay down their mortgages faster than called for. "It takes personalization, face to face," says Craig Davis, executive vice president of mortgage banking and financial services.

And Washington Mutual knows how to get in its customers' faces. Even his grocery-store branches differ from the pint-size ATM outposts popular among commercial banks. Many of Washington Mutual's instore branches are staffed with tellers offering the full range of products.

Branch managers are given wide discretion to sell the most appropriate products for their area and develop their own marketing campaigns. At the Fountain Valley, Calif. branch, in a middle-income area rich with small businesses, manager Deborah Miekle aims at getting the owners to open up accounts. When their workers come in to cash their paychecks, her tellers try to get them to open checking accounts.

A few miles away, in Anaheim Hills, the clientele is wealthy enough to qualify for free checking anywhere. The bubbly manager, Angela Deister, trains her employees to greet the folks as they step in the door, maybe ask how junior's soccer team is doing. When the branches participate in community affairs, there's usually a practical motive—auxiliaries and the like all are potential customers.

Incentives for Killinger? He stays in Holiday Inns and flies bare-bones Southwest Airlines. But his company's stock was recently up eightfold from when he took over, and he owns $31 million of it.

How Mirage Resorts Sifted 75,000 Applicants to Hire 9,600 in 24 Weeks

BY EILEEN P. GUNN
For Las Vegas' hugest new property, the company had to reinvent the process.

A typical mass hiring goes like this: Thousands of hopefuls answer an open call, then wait hours in line to fill out applications that will get dog-eared, coffee-stained, and sometimes misfiled long before the last job is filled. It's what Mirage Resorts wanted to avoid when it had to hire 9,600 workers for Bellagio, a huge new luxury resort opening in Las Vegas in October.

So Mirage spent $1 million on a computerized process that let it screen 75,000 applicants in 12 weeks. It spent ten weeks interviewing the 26,000 finalists. The entire feat, including background checks, took 5½ months, down from nine the last time Mirage hired en masse.

Vice president Arte Nathan estimates he saved as much as $600,000 on paper, file space, and temporary help. More important was what the process itself revealed about the applicants. "If people didn't show up for their appointments, we figured they'd be no-shows at work too," he says.

Infotech Enables a New Way to Hire

1. WE'RE HIRING!
Mirage runs a newspaper ad that says it's hiring and offers a toll-free number that operates from 8 a.m. to 8 p.m. Callers make an appointment, confirmed by a reminder letter, to fill out an application.

2. THE APPOINTMENT
As many as 1,200 job seekers arrive daily. In the parking lot staffers confirm their identity and, using headsets, notify staff at the door, who greet applicants by name and assign them to a computer terminal that also knows their name.

3. THE APPLICATION
Mirage has broken down the generic job application into 165 basic questions that pop up one at a time on applicants' computer screens. Many of the jobs don't require computer skills, so helpers circulate in case anyone gets stuck.

4. THE APPLICATION REVIEW
Applicants then head to a checkout desk. HR staffers make sure everything has been properly answered and note whether appearance and behavior seem appropriate.

A staffer asks an applicant for permission to do a background check.

5. THE DATABASE SEARCH
Every department has someone who searches the database for people with the backgrounds the department is looking for. Candidates are called in for interviews.

6. THE INTERVIEW
As many as 700 people are interviewed, by 25 managers at a time, over a 12-hour day. A total of 180 interviewers have been specially trained. The results are fed into the database.

7. THE BACKGROUND CHECK
Mirage checks for criminal records and looks into the job, school, and maybe credit histories of 18,000 candidates. The 11,600 finalists must also take a drug test.

8. THE OFFER
Mirage hopes the courtesy and consideration it has shown applicants leave an impression that will last until Bellagio is ready to make an offer, which could be a few months after the interview. Only 3% of the people Mirage liked dropped out somewhere along the way.

RICK RICKMAN—MATRIX(2)
Mirage made its computers as easy to use as ATM machines.

Reprinted from the October 12, 1998, issue of *Fortune*, p. 195, by special permission. © 1998 by Time, Inc.

THE LEGAL LIMITATIONS TO SELF-DIRECTED WORK TEAMS IN PRODUCTION PLANNING AND CONTROL

STEVEN E. ABRAHAM, PHD, JD
Department of Management, State University at New York—Oswego, Oswego, NY 13126

MICHAEL S. SPENCER, PHD, CFPIM
Department of Management, University of Northern Iowa, Cedar Falls, IA 50614

During the past ten years enormous changes have been observed throughout business organizations. Change has been especially profound in the production planning and control (PP&C) activities of both manufacturers and service providers. One specific change has been the rapid incorporation of Japanese management methods, such as Just-in-Time (JIT) and total quality management (TQM). One critical component of JIT is the use of employee-driven problem-solving teams [5, 8, 22], often called quality circles.

Change has been so rapid that often something relatively new, like quality circles, becomes the expectation. Entrants into the workplace begin to assume that current practices have always been the way things were done and, therefore, must be completely legal. After all, someone at headquarters must have reviewed and approved of quality circle teams. However, production management is somewhat isolated compared to the human resource management, accounting and marketing functions with respect to the legal environment of business. This may be the case with TQM, especially with the use of self-directed work teams. The fact that a team is in place does not necessarily mean that it fits

correctly into the legal framework. In fact, the use of teams can expose the production management function to legal sanctions more rapidly than most of our other management aspects.

Most research into the implementation of TQM takes a positive stance towards, perhaps even advocating, employee empowerment [2, 23]. Personnel/human resource management problems that are discussed are usually the reward system, general supervision responsibilities, union-management relations, and overall change management [12, 21, 22]. Treatment of the legal implications of teams is found only in law journals. It is not discussed in the production management literature.

The purposes of this article are to examine the legal limitations of using employee teams in production planning and control and to provide a set of guidelines production managers can use in implementing employee teams.

BACKGROUND

Dumond [6] concluded that the use of employee teams is a key component to TQM success, finding that all companies in his study of successful companies reported using functional employee teams. Further, Tatikonda and Tatikonda concluded that "Flat organizations, empowerment, cross-disciplinary and cross-departmental efforts are essential for TQM success.... Quality improvements gained through empowered cross-functional teams can be 200% to 600% more effective than improvements obtained through functional teams." [26, pp. 7–8]. As organizations adopt the team approach, there appears to be a continuum of team structures used. The major determinant in the team structure continuum is the degree of employee empowerment [3]. Teams can range from a quality circle on one end to a self-directed work group on the other. A quality circle is defined as "[a] small group of people who normally work as a unit and meet frequently to uncover and solve problems concerning the quality of items produced, process capability, or process control [1]." A self-directed work team, on the other hand, is defined as "[g]enerally a small, independent, self-organized, and self-controlled group in which members flexibly plan, organize, determine and manage their duties and actions, as well as perform many other supportive functions. It may work without immediate supervision and can often have the authority to select, hire, promote, or discharge its members [1]."

What is clear from the definitions cited above is the blending of traditionally management-related activities with the activities assigned to the teams. Can an employee team be given the responsibility to find and solve production problems legally? What is management's reaction should the team fail? To what degree can the following common production planning and control activities be assigned legally to an employee team?

- Scheduling jobs to a specific piece of equipment
- Assigning jobs to specific employees
- Selecting or changing job priorities
- Scheduling overtime of individuals or the team
- Adding or deleting workers to the team
- Improving the process by changing methods or equipment
- Refusing additional jobs in a given time period.

The answers to the above questions are not as clear as some production managers might think. We will look first at the applicable laws and judicial findings, then establish a set of managerial guidelines.

EMPLOYEE TEAMS AND CASE LAW

One important legal pitfall for employee teams stems from the National Labor Relations Act (NLRA or the "Act"). Specifically, managers need to know that such teams might run afoul of §8(a)(2) of the Act. That section prohibits employers from "dominating, interfering with or supporting labor organizations." In a number of cases since the Act was passed in 1935, the United States Supreme Court and the National Labor Relations Board (NLRB or the "Board") have ruled that an employer violated this section by establishing a quality circle, self-directed work group, or similar program. In fact, a number of commentators have expressed the view that the current interpretation of §8(a)(2) would actually prohibit employers from establishing *any* type of employee participation program without violating the Act [15, 20, 24].

Others, however, find this interpretation to be mistaken, and argue that the NLRA does permit employers to establish teams and other employee groups without violating the Act [4, 14, 25]. Even William Gould, the current chairman of the NLRB, argues that employee teams and other employee participation programs are permissible under the NLRA [11]. Based on the relevant case law, we contend that an employer is able to establish a legitimate employee participation program without violating the NLRA, provided the employer avoids certain things likely to put the program in violation of the Act.

A potential complication with predicting what employers may and may not do stems from the fact that the Board and the courts have rendered arguably inconsistent opinions on the contours of the pertinent portions of the NLRA. Even under the most conservative approach, however, we contend that it would be possible for employers to establish employee teams without violating the Act.

Section 8(a)(2) of the NLRA states:

> (a) It shall be an unfair labor practice for an employer—(2) to dominate or interfere with the formation or administration of any labor organization or contribute financial support to it: *Provided*, ... an employer shall not be prohibited from permitting employees to confer with him during working hours without loss of time or pay (italics by authors).

"[L]abor organization" is defined by Section 2(5) as:

> any organization of any kind, or any agency or employee representation committee or plan, in which employees participate and which exists for the purpose, in whole or in part, of dealing with employers concerning grievances, labor disputes, wages, rates of pay, hours of employment or conditions of work.

Therefore, whether an employee participation program (quality circle, employee team) would violate the NLRA would depend on a two-part analysis: (1) would the team be considered a "labor organization" under §2(5) of the Act; and (2) if so, does the employer dominate that labor organization according to §8(a)(2)?

IS THE TEAM A LABOR ORGANIZATION

According to the NLRB's current interpretation, an organization will be considered a "labor organization" if the following four criteria are met: (1) employees participate, (2) the organization purports to represent others; (3) the organization exists, at least in part, for the purpose of dealing with employers, and (4) these dealings concern conditions of work or other statutory subjects such as grievances, labor disputes, wages, rates of pay, or hours of employment [13]. If any one of these elements is not met, the team will not be considered a labor organization and therefore would not violate the NLRA.

Employee Participation

It is possible that the members of a TQM team would not even be considered employees under the NLRA. The Act specifically defines the "employees" covered, and the definition of employee expressly excludes a "supervisor" from being an employee under the Act. According to section 2(11) of the Act:

> The term "supervisor" means any individual having authority, in the interest of the employer, to hire, transfer, suspend, lay off, recall, promote, discharge, assign, reward, or discipline other employees, or responsibly to direct them, or to adjust their grievances, or effectively to recommend such action, in connection with the foregoing the exercise of such authority is not of a merely routine or clerical nature, but requires the use of independent judgment.

Recent case law shows an ever-broadening view on the types of people the Supreme Court classifies as supervisors [18]. Hence, it is possible that all the members of a team would be treated as supervisors under the Act. If this were the case, §2(5) would not even apply and there would be no problem with the NLRA. Further, in [16], the Supreme Court held that "managerial" employees also were excluded from being employees under the NLRA by §2(11). Therefore, if the members of a team were treated as managers under the Act, §2(5) again would not apply and there would be no problem with the NLRA.

The Organization Purports to Represent Others

A TQM team would only be considered a labor organization if it purported to represent *other* employees (i.e., employees who were not part of the team). Hence, if all of a company's employees were organized into teams, or if there were one team with the members rotating on a regular basis, it is likely that the team would not constitute a labor organization under the Act, because it would not represent *other* employees. For example, in *General Foods* [10], the employer implemented a "job enrichment" program. All of the employees were divided into four teams, and each team: divided assignments, established rotations and scheduled overtime (among other things). Each team also periodically conferred with management on a variety of topics related to working conditions. The Board held that these teams were "nothing more nor less than work crews established by [the employer] as administrative subdivisions of the entire employee compliment." [10, p. 1234] The teams functioned as a "committee of the whole" rather than a "labor organization." The Board held that these teams were not §2(5) labor organizations. "If such a set of circumstances should give rise to the existence of a labor organization, no employer could ever have a staff conference without bringing forth a labor organization in its midst." [10, p. 1235]

Purpose of the Organization

The next question concerns whether the organization exists, at least in part, for the purpose of dealing with employers. The Supreme Court has defined the term "dealing with" in §2(5) quite broadly in *NLRB v. Cabot Carbon Co.* [17]. Anytime a group of employees discusses things with the employer, the "dealing with" re-

TABLE 1: Summary of Legal Team Actions

1. Overall Purpose
   If the purpose of using teams is to solve problems, then it is legal.
   If the purpose is to dissuade formation of a union, then it is illegal.
   If the purpose is to encourage the decertification of a union, then it is illegal.
2. Membership
   If team members are all supervisors or managers, then it is legal.
   If team members are all non-supervisors, then it is legal, subject to all points below.
   If the team is mixed then see point 5.
3. Labor Organization
   If the team is empowered to take actions rather than ask permission, then it is not a labor organization.
   If the team does not represent other employees, then it is not a labor organization.
   If the team deals with matters other than working conditions (i.e., wages, grievances, hours of employment etc.), then it is not a labor organization.
4. Specific Production Planning Activities
   If the team is empowered to:
   • Schedule jobs to a specific piece of equipment,
   • Assign jobs to specific employees,
   • Select or change job priorities,
   • Schedule overtime of individuals or the team,
   • Add or delete workers to the team,
   • Improve the process by changing methods or equipment,
   • Refuse additional jobs in a given time period
5. Team Organization
   If management takes any of the following actions:
   • Calling or scheduling the team's meeting,
   • Conducting the meeting,
   • Selecting which employees attended the meeting,
   • Setting the agenda for the meeting, then it is illegal.

quirement is likely to be satisfied. Nevertheless, there is one important exception. If the team has the authority to resolve employment-related problems on its own (i.e., without input from the employer), the "dealing with" element is likely to be absent. The critical issue appears to be: "Is the team able to take action with information provided to management, or is the team required to ask permission to take the action?" If the former is true, the team is likely *not* to be a labor organization.

Concerns of the Organization

The final issue concerns the subject matter of the TQM program. If the team deals solely with matters other than "conditions of work or other statutory subjects such as grievances, labor disputes, wages, rates of pay, or hours of employment," it is not likely to be a labor organization. While the Board and courts have found a wide variety of subjects to be encompassed by the phrase just quoted, if the team deals with matters apart from those subjects, it would not be considered a labor organization. In this regard, the Supreme Court's decision in *First National Maintenance Corp. v. NLRB* [9] would be relevant. In *First National Maintenance*, a case involving whether the employer was required by the Act to bargain over certain subjects, the Supreme Court held that subjects which "have only an indirect and attenuated impact on the employment relationship" were not considered "conditions of employment." Examples given by the Court were advertising and promotion, product type and design. Although *First National Maintenance* did not deal with the issue of labor organization status under §2(5), it is nevertheless relevant. Presumably, since an employer is not required to bargain over certain issues such as: scheduling work across machines, scheduling overtime or rearranging the job priorities in order to minimize setups, a group of employees could discuss these issues with the employer and not be considered a labor organization under §2(5).

DID THE EMPLOYER DOMINATE, INTERFERE WITH OR SUPPORT THE TEAM

Assuming the team is held to be a labor organization, the next question is whether the employer's dealings with the team are prohibited by §8(a)(2). That section has been held to prohibit the interference with or domination of the formation of a TQM team. In this regard, the following types of activities have been held to violate the section: formulating the idea for the organization, creating it, forming its structure, selecting the members, and retaining veto power over its decisions. In addition, the section has been held to prohibit the interference with or domination of the administration of a TQM team. In this regard, the following types of activities on the part of management have been held to violate the section:

- Calling or scheduling the team's meeting
- Conducting the meeting
- Selecting which employees attended the meeting
- Setting the agenda for the meeting.

According to the NLRB's most recent interpretation, "a labor organization that is the creation of management whose structure and function are essentially determined by management . . . and whose continued existence depends on the fiat of management" is unlawfully dominated [7]. In other words, the NLRB and many courts have treated §8(a)(2) as a blanket prohibition on any and all employer involvement with a group that is considered a labor organization under §2(5). In addition, it is clear that anti-union actions or a specific motive to interfere with employees' rights to organize is not necessary for a finding of unlawful domination [19]. Although several circuit courts have been less restrictive, allowing employers to establish labor organizations as long as no anti-union bias was involved, there is a potential that any employer "involvement" with an employee team that is a labor organization would be prohibited by §8(a)(2) even if there is no anti-union animus.

OBSERVATIONS AND CONCLUSIONS

Managers involved in production planning and control should be aware of the legal limitations on using quality circles or any other type of employee-driven work team presented by the various laws and cases. Some general guidelines now can be established (see Table 1).

First, the intent of the organization forming employee-driven teams is important. If the teams are formed to improve productivity or better use employee ideas, then they are likely to be legal. If, however, the teams are formed to dissuade the formation of a union or to encourage employees to decertify an existing union, the team will be illegal. Secondly, teams must not be dominated by the employer as defined in the previous section: no scheduling for the team's meetings, no establishing their agenda, no selecting specific employees to attend the meetings. It is not clear whether or not a supervisor can be part of a team if the supervisor's normal duties are management of the work group. The best approach is that, if a supervisor is on the team, he (she) should not be the team leader. Empowerment means empowerment; the team has the responsibility to make the changes by taking its own action rather than asking permission of management. The team may keep management informed of its actions, but management must not hold veto power over those actions. Finally, limit the scope of the team's responsibility to accepting the current working conditions, such as pay levels and hours of work at its inception. The conditions of work are for union negotiation, if a union exists.

Managers must also be aware that labor law is constantly evolving. While the concept of legal precedent is firmly part of our tradition, it does not guarantee that a court or the Board will interpret or apply the law to a changing business environment the same way every time, or that each situation will come out the same way. One key point is that managers must be able to prove their intent before the appropriate judicial bodies.

REFERENCES

1. *APICS Dictionary.* 8th ed. Edited by J. F. Cox III, J. H. Blackstone, and M. S. Spencer. Falls Church, VA: American Production and Inventory Control Society, 1995.
2. Baker, B. R. "The Empowered Employee in a Biotechnology Company: A Case Study." *Production and Inventory Management Journal* 34. no.1 (1993): 73–76.
3. Benson, J., S. Bruil, D. Coghill, R. H. Cleator, T. Keller, and D. Wolf. "Self-Directed Work Teams." *Production and Inventory Management Journal* 35, no. 1,(1994): 79–82.
4. Datz, H. J. "Employee Participation Programs and the NLRA—A Guide for the Perplexed." *Daily Labor Report* (BNA) No. 30 at E1 (Feb. 7, 1993).
5. Denton, D. K. "Creating High Performance Work Practices." *Production and Inventory Management Journal* 37, no. 3 (1996): 81–84.
6. Dumond, E. J. "Learning From the Quality Improvement Process: Experience From U.S. Manufacturing Firms." *Production and Inventory Management Journal* 36, no. 4 (1995): 7–13.
7. *Electromation, Inc.,* 309 N.L.R.B. 990 (1992).

8. Evans, J. R. "Quality Improvement and Creative Problem Solving." *Production and Inventory Management Journal* 31, no. 4 (1990): 29–32.

9. *First National Maintenance Corp. v. NLRB*, 452 U.S. 666 (1981).

10. *General Foods*, 231 N.L.R.B. 1232 (1977).

11. Gould, W. B. "Employee Participation and Labor Policy: Why the Team Act should be Defeated and the National Labor Relations Act Amended." *Creighton Law Review* 30 (1996): 3.

12. Hue, F. "Labor Issues in the Implementation of Group Technology Cellular Manufacturing." *Production and Inventory Management Journal* 33, no. 4 (1992): 15–19.

13. McLain, J. R. "Participative Management Under Sections 2(5) and 8(a)(2) of the National Labor Relations Act." *Michigan Law Review* 83 (1985): 1736.

14. Moberly, R. B. "The Worker Participation Conundrum: Does Prohibiting Employer-Assisted Labor Organizations Prevent Labor Management Cooperation?" *Washington University Law Review* 69 (1994): 331.

15. Moe, M. T. "Participatory Workplace Decisionmaking and the NLRA: Section 8(a)(2), Electromation and the Spector of the Company Union." *New York University Law Review* 68 (November 1993): 1127.

16. *NLRB v. Bell Aerospace Co.*, 416 U.S. 267 (1974).

17. *NLRB v. Cabot Carbon Co.*, 360 U.S. 203 (1959).

18. *NLRB v. Health Care Retirement Corp.*, 114 S. Ct. 1778 (1994).

19. *NLRB v. Newport News Shipbuilding Co.* 308 U.S. 241 (1939).

20. Price, K. "Tearing Down the Walls: The Need for Revision of NLRA §8(a)(2) to Permit Management–Labor Participation Committees to Function in the Workplace." *University of Cincinnati Law Review* 63 (Spring 1995): 1379.

21. Saraph, J. V., and R. J. Sebastain. "Human Resource Strategies for Effective Introduction of Advanced Manufacturing Technologies (AMT)." *Production and Inventory Management Journal* 33, no. 1 (1992): 64–69.

22. Sevier, A. J. "Managing Employee Resistance to JIT: Creating an Atmosphere that Facilitates Implementation." *Production and Inventory Management Journal* 33, no. 1(1992): 83–87.

23. Smith, P. A., W. D. Anderson, and S. A. Brooking. "Employee Empowerment: A Case Study." *Production and Inventory Management Journal* 34, no. 3 (1993): 45–49.

24. Stokes, M. L. "Quality Circles or Company Unions? A Look at Employee Involvement After Electromation and DuPont." *Ohio State Law Journal* 55 (Fall 1994): 897.

25. Summers, C. W. "Employee Voice and Employer Voice: A Structured Exception to Section 8(a)(2)." *Chicago Kent Law Review* 69 (1993): 129.

26. Tatikonda, L. U., and R. J. Tatikonda. "Top Ten Reasons Your TQM Effort is Failing to Improve Profit." *Production and Inventory Management Journal* 36, no. 3 (1995): 5–9.

About the Authors—

STEVEN F. ABRAHAM, PhD, JD, is an assistant professor in the Department of Management, School of Business, State University of New York—Oswego. He holds a PhD in industrial relations from the University of Wisconsin-Madison, a JD from New York University School of Law, and a BS from Cornell University. He is a member of the New York State Bar as well as the bars of the eastern and southern districts of New York. Dr. Abraham has practiced labor/employment law in New York City in two law firms and one corporation. He has also provided advice to law firms on several occasions in areas of labor/employment law.

MICHAEL S. SPENCER, PhD, CFPIM, is an assistant professor of management at the University of Northern Iowa. He received his PhD in operations management from the University of Georgia. Dr. Spencer previously held various materials management positions at the John Deere Engine Division where he implemented both MRP and JIT systems. Dr. Spencer has served on the APICS board of directors, and is currently the vice-president of the APICS Educational and Research Foundation.

HOW Great Machines ARE BORN

In the home or in industry, friendly machines based on "human factors" are a joy to use. They are more efficient too, and often safer.

BY STUART F. BROWN

THE PLEASING, "BUTTERY" FEEL OF manual shifting that motor buffs crave in an agile car. The welcoming contours of a power-tool handle. The sensuous blend of fluidity and resistance in the focusing knob on a pair of binoculars. These and more are the details of machines that are great to use because they fall naturally to hand and feel right and logical.

Devices so inviting don't just spring into existence. They result from the patient work of largely unsung specialists known as human-factors engineers. Also called ergonomists, these experts know the sizes and shapes people come in, how they can and can't move, how they acquire and digest information, and how machines can be shaped to accommodate them. Human factors traces its origins to World War II, when the U.S. and British military wanted

to figure out, among other things, how many sizes of gas masks were needed to fit the troops. Industry designers still rely on the military's "anthropometric" tables that tally human dimensions.

Smart companies have been cashing in on the latest human-factors wisdom with a wide array of machines:

• The sleek, accident-minimizing oil field equipment developed by a unit of Schlumberger.

• Forklift trucks from Crown Equipment Corp. whose comfortable, rounded shapes and lovely controls are popular with warehouse workers.

• Deere's 8000-series tractor, which gives farmers control-tower visibility and whose four-wheel-drive version turns on a dime.

• DaimlerChrysler's minivans, whose latest user-friendly features have helped the company hang on to the biggest slice of the U.S. minivan market.

• A hot-selling, easy-to-load Maytag washer that boasts the same energy efficiency as other models that are more awkward to use.

In sorry contrast to these successes are the many products whose human-factors aspects are ignored or executed badly. Think of VCRs with hard-to-understand timers. Or elevator buttons labeled with convergent and divergent arrows that many passengers can't figure out fast enough to open the door for somebody. At the extreme end of the failure spectrum are catastrophes: the reactor meltdown at Three Mile Island, caused in part by hard-to-interpret control-room displays.

Reprinted from the March 1, 1999, issue of *Fortune*, pp. 164C-164F, by special permission. © 1999 by Time, Inc.

THE NAM/FORTUNE MANUFACTURING INDEX

Breathing Easier

Because of good prospects on the domestic front, manufacturers are feeling a bit more optimistic. In a January survey of more than 500 companies by the National Association of Manufacturers and FORTUNE, 67.1% of large companies said they were very positive about the business outlook or somewhat so, up from 60.2% in December. Among small and medium-sized manufacturers—those employing fewer than 1,000—optimism held steady:

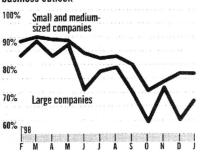

Percent of manufacturers with a positive business outlook

Pricing power remains weak. The percentage of companies expecting to increase prices over the next year has actually fallen slightly since last October. But the ranks of large companies expecting sales to rise at least 5% increased in January, to 47.2%, after having dropped for nearly a year. The sales expectations of smaller companies also improved slightly:

Over the next year, what do you expect to happen to your company's sales?	Large companies	Small and medium-sized companies
Increase more than 10%	14.3%	22.7%
Increase 5% to 10%	32.9%	24.5%
Increase up to 5%	24.3%	13.6%
Stay the same	18.6%	22.7%
Decrease up to 5%	7.1%	7.0%
Decrease 5% to 10%	2.9%	4.3%
Decrease more than 10%	—	5.2%

There are lessons in the way well-designed machines are created. One is not to rely unduly on market research, since potential customers may not know what they really want or what is possible. Another is to bring in human-factors people at the very beginning of a product-development program, when they can do the most good. In the later stages, bad ideas have often gained too much momentum to be changed, says Steve Casey, president of Ergonomic Systems Design, a consulting firm in Santa Barbara that has worked with three of the companies cited in this story.

When Casey is called in to consult on a new product, he first learns how to use existing versions. "I've been on 300 farms around the world to learn about the machines and talk to the people who use them," he says. Listening to users' gripes and praises, a human-factors engineer begins to compile what's called a function analysis, which asks every conceivable question about the purpose of the product under development. Once a product's purpose is clearly defined, the designers carry out a detailed "task analysis" charting the way people will interact with the device. Finally, different prototype components must be tested to find out which work best in the hands of users.

The happy results are products like these:

Schlumberger's new way to "complete" an oil well. Though human-factors engineering is most familiar in cars and consumer products, it is just as important in heavy machinery. The Dowell division of Schlumberger Ltd. in Sugar Land, Texas, provides services to oil and gas drilling companies around the world. Many of its jobs involve operating heavy equipment called a coil-tubing unit at well sites. A new version that Dowell has designed, called CT Express, takes a lot of the cost, complexity—and hazard—out of the work.

One job of a coil-tubing unit is to "complete" a well, as the roughnecks say. When a well is drilled, large-diameter steel casing is put in place as a liner, and cement is pumped in to fill the gap between the casing and the hole. Once this is done, a large volume of drilling "mud," the heavy fluid used to lubricate the bit and flush away cuttings, must be removed before the well can begin producing oil or gas. The coil-tubing machinery includes a 10,000-foot reel of flexible, narrow-diameter steel pipe that is stuffed down the hole by a device called an injector head. To drive the mud up and out of the hole, nitrogen gas is pumped down the pipe.

The scene at a traditional well completion has a Wild West flavor to it. Four major vehicles collectively worth nearly $3 million are involved: a truck carrying the big reel of tubing, a crane truck that suspends the five-ton injector head above the well, a liquid-nitrogen tank truck, and a pump truck. The four operators of these noisy machines and their supervisor communicate by walkie-talkie. Keeping a close watch on the injector head is critical. This mechanism has powerful hydraulically driven grippers that look like a pair of bulldozer treads facing each other. They shove the tubing into the well and pull it out when the job is done.

Setup time with Dowell's old system was three hours, and 75 hydraulic hoses had to be connected. The new system is up in half an hour.

As the tubing goes farther and farther down, the weight the injector head must support keeps increasing. If the tension is wrong and the device loses its grip, the tubing can go shrieking down the hole, and perhaps rip the reel off the truck as well. When underground pressure is high, on the other hand, the tubing can come spitting out of the hole like satanic spaghetti, spraying corrosive acid propelled by pressurized nitrogen. "If this starts to happen, and your efforts to control it don't work, it is time to run like hell," says Dowell engineer Athar Ali. He's the designated "product champion" in charge of overseeing and tweaking two prototype CT Express units that are designed to improve on this situation.

Heading the team that developed CT Express is Terry McCafferty, Dowell's section manager for coil-tubing surface equipment and an electrical engineer who makes dulcimers in his spare time. One of the first things the designers looked at was the accident history of coil-tubing units. Statistics showed that 74% of lost-time injuries occurred during rig setup and breakdown at the job site, and that 57% of these involved workers falling or having fingers crushed while working on the injector head.

"These numbers," McCafferty says, "led us to set goals of keeping the people on the ground and not having them work under something that's hanging in the air." Improved productivity was another goal. Setup time with the old system was more than three hours, as the crane pulled up near the well and hoisted the 10,000-

pound injector head, upon which workers scrambled to thread the tubing into the grippers. And 75 hydraulic hoses had to be connected between various pieces of equipment, creating an opportunity for errors.

The system McCafferty's team came up with, which could be seen in operation in western Canada in January, costs $1.5 million. It fits on two stately orange Peterbilt trailer trucks, needs only three operators, and incorporates a lot of features designed to improve safety and efficiency. The system uses a self-erecting mast on the reel truck, which brings a prethreaded injector into place above the well. No hydraulic connections need to be made.

Instead of having four operators, with each running some of the equipment, CT Express puts one person in charge of it all. Housed in a booth that is heated in winter and air-conditioned in summer, the operator sits in an ergonomically designed chair equipped with integrated keypads and fighter-plane-style control sticks. A pair of large flat-screen displays shows the functioning of various subsystems in an iconic fashion that's easy to grasp. The injector is largely controlled by sensors that automatically detect slippage by comparing pipe speed with gripper speed, making any needed correction and alerting the operator. Says McCafferty: "We want the operator to be able to focus more on the mission and not on the individual devices."

At a 5,000-foot-deep gas well in central Alberta owned by Canadian 88 Energy Resource Corp., McCafferty and Ali recently watched a small crew get a prototype CT Express unit up and ready to go to work in less than half an hour. Dowell plans to order about 25 more of the units from its equipment supplier, Hydra Rig of Fort Worth, as soon as all the feedback from early users has come in.

Cool lift trucks from Crown Equipment. The small town of New Bremen, Ohio, in farm country about 50 miles northwest of Dayton, is the sort of place a film crew would go to make a movie about the early career of the Wright Brothers. Many of the perfectly restored buildings there belong to Crown Equipment Corp., a billion-dollar, privately held maker of electric lift trucks that dominates the local economy. Used in warehouses, factories, and stores, Crown machines can raise loads weighing as much as 8,000 pounds as high as 45 feet.

At the start of a shift, it's widely said, warehouse workers sprint to be the one who gets to spend the day aboard a Crown machine instead of another make—that's how slick they are to use. The operator's perch on a Crown lift truck looks like a Milan designer's idea of the personal transportation device of the future, with soft, rounded shapes everywhere and color-keyed, contoured controls that welcome

the hand. Over the years, the Industrial Designers Society of America and other groups have heaped awards on Crown's designers.

How did a hard-boiled industrial-equipment company get so far into squishy aesthetic and human-factors considerations? It happened, well, by design. In the early '60s, when Crown was a newcomer in the mature lift-truck market, Tom Bidwell, then the company's director of engineering and manufacturing, decided that combining quality with clean lines and easy-to-understand controls was the way to stand out.

Crown attracted praise in the '70s with the introduction of a counterbalanced lift truck on which the operator stands sideways instead of facing in the direction of travel, a change since adopted by most competitors. The inspiration came from paying attention to human factors. A designer observing the machines then in use was bothered to see operators driving down narrow warehouse aisles facing forward, and then reversing the journey by turning around so they could see where they were going and working the controls behind their backs. Crown's new "side stance" layout allowed an operator to see either way by simply turning his head.

While pondering how to lay out the controls for this unorthodox machine, the designers hit upon another idea: combining functions in a joystick. The new trucks captured a 40% share of their market segment within four years of their introduction.

A Crown tradition has evolved in which designers brainstorm, sketch, and construct mockups, unmolested at first by engineers and marketing types. Design director Michael Gallagher entered this supportive environment when he left the consumer-electronics industry in 1994 to join Crown. A lanky guy who likes fast cars, Gallagher brings a perfectionist's zeal to defining and refining the trucks. The designers spend a lot of time watching videotapes of how they are used. "Real lift-truck maestros are silky smooth, and they never stop moving," Gallagher says. "They just dance with the truck."

The studio builds a lot of models to see how new ideas look and feel. Lines of sight receive particular attention, because when operators pick up something with the weight of a car and put it into a spot 30 feet up on a rack, accidents can be serious.

For its latest generation of side-stance truck, the RR 5000S, Crown devised a flip-up seat and extra foot pedals that allow the operator to relieve body fatigue during the workday by varying his posture from sitting to leaning slightly back to standing. The controls are within easy, ergonomically sound reach to keep the operator's body stable, with hands and feet firmly planted to minimize his chance of falling off while whipping around corners. As an extra safe-

guard, brake switches underneath spring-mounted floorboards prevent the trucks from moving if the operator doesn't have both feet in the proper position.

Crown puts extensive research and testing into its displays, which give the lift operator information in an uncluttered fashion. By switching to remote, electrical control of the lift's hydraulic valves, the company has been able to place switches and buttons near the operator's hands and feet. All the controls are "electroproportional" these days, which means that the farther you push, the more you get, be it travel speed, fork-raise rate, or whatever. The company has also invested a lot of development time in deciding how sensitive a control should be through its range of motion. It's akin to calibrating the response increments of a radio's volume knob.

Deere's big but nimble tractor. Deere & Co. is proud to hear farmers say they have "green blood" and won't consider buying another brand of tractor. "It's their life, working with these machines," says Bruce Newendorp, a human-factors staff engineer at Deere's product-engineering center in Waterloo, Iowa. Newendorp helped develop the powerful 8000 series of tractors that first went on sale in 1994. Built in both wheeled and tracked versions, the machines cost from $109,000 to $138,000, and you can see them working the fields wherever there are big-acre farms.

When it launched the 8000 tractor development program, Deere wanted to design in features that customers hadn't thought to ask for. At the top of the list was forward visibility from the operator's cab. "It's very valuable to be able to clearly see the front wheels and the rows of crops as you drive a tractor through a field," Newendorp explains. "So we did a lot of things, including finding other places to put the instruments that formerly narrowed the view."

Another goal was to give the four-wheel-drive versions a tight turning radius. The majority of wheeled-tractor customers these days order four-wheel drive. But the bigger wheels and fatter tires used on the front of these machines bump up against a traditional tractor frame, restricting the turning radius. Wide turns are not the farmer's friend. They can force him to leave land uncultivated at the ends of a field.

To fix the problem, Deere designers rethought the front layout of the machine. Now the tractor has a pinched waist when seen from above, which allows the front wheels to pivot under the frame during a tight turn. The company ran an ad showing its 8000 series four-wheel-drive model carving a figure eight inside a competitor's minimum turning circle.

Climbing up the steps and slipping behind the wheel of these tractors is a delight.

The glass area is immense, almost like an airport control tower. The front portion of the cab floor slopes slightly downward to increase visibility by a few degrees, and there's a cup holder on the floor atop an air-conditioner vent to keep drinks cool. Deere's engineers grouped the primary controls, which include the throttle, 16-speed shifter, and implement controls, on an extension of the right armrest called the Command Arm module.

Interiors matter most
in minivans: "It's a little cabin with a homey feeling, and the outside is just a wrapper."

That makes possible another nifty improvement. When the farmer looks over his shoulder to check a plow or other attachment through the back window, the seat of the tractor swivels and the Command Arm module moves too. Details like this mean a lot to farmers during harvest season, when they may spend 14-hour days in the driver's seat and work into the night with floodlights burning.

DaimlerChrysler's driver-friendly vehicles. A lot of human-factors thinking went into the original minivan, which when it hit the showrooms in 1983 rescued Chrysler Corp., now part of DaimlerChrysler, from looming extinction. The minivans have been through two redesigns since then, and engineers are toiling behind locked doors on a fourth generation. Though competing makes have crowded in, DaimlerChrysler has hung on to a 45% share of the U.S. market by drawing on a rich body of knowledge about drivers' preferences, as well as their dimensions, physical and cognitive capabilities, and lifestyles.

When planning was under way for the current generation, launched in 1996, Chrysler's human-factors staff reexamined critical dimensions such as the driver's seat height. "We tried different heights and found out that the one we had chosen in 1978 was truly the optimum for most people, so we left it there," says David Bostwick, director of corporate market research. "This is one of the details that makes owners feel like the vehicle was made for them, because they didn't have to climb up or plunk down into the driver's seat."

But there were changes too. Chrysler widened the vehicles, creating room for the driver to extend her or his legs straight to reach the brake and accelerator pedals. The company also added 40% more window-glass area, which improved the lines of sight through the top and bottom of the windshield, and put as many controls as possible within the driver's comfortable reach.

Access was improved. Market research had long indicated that people wanted two doors on each side of a minivan, but with past engineering methods that would have required adding excessive weight to strengthen the body. In the latest generation, computers came to the rescue. The CATIA computer-aided-design system from France's Dassault group of companies, which Chrysler has been using to develop all its vehicles, can run finite-element analyses that tell precisely where to add and delete metal to get the strongest, lightest body. The new four-door structure turned out to be stiffer than the old three-door one.

Perhaps more than on any other vehicle, the interior layout of the minivan is what can make or break a customer's purchase decision. In years of Chrysler research, exterior styling has never ranked among the top ten reasons for buying, which it almost always does with cars. Says Bostwick: "It's a little cabin that has a homey feeling to it, and the outside is just a wrapper for what's inside."

All of Chrysler's "cabins," be they for vans or sedans, are previewed and refined these days on a virtual reality system. An engineer working on an interior design sits down, straps on sensors that track his hand locations, and dons special goggles that display a virtual-interior model stored in the CATIA system. Looking around, he can check the lines of sight through the windshield, to the sides, and even out the back window. Grasping an authentic 7-Eleven Big Gulp cup, he can check the reach to a virtual cup holder. Other people in the room can see what he's seeing projected on a wall screen.

"Early in a development program," says advance vehicle engineering manager Kenric Socks, "we use virtual reality to evaluate a lot of visual and reach-oriented things. It has hugely cut down on the number of go-arounds with physical mockups."

One future product Socks is able to talk about is the 2000 model year Neon subcompact, which DaimlerChrysler has displayed in prototype on the auto show circuit. When designers of a new model like this one go to work on the interior at CAD terminals, Socks says, they are guided by anthropometric descriptions of the sizes people come in and how they sit in a vehicle. From this starting point, they can begin to block out the locations of primary controls such as the steering wheel, shifter, brakes, and throttle. Then they begin selecting the placement of secondary controls, including turn signals, light switches, radio and climate controls, and so forth.

As these decisions get firmed up through successive design reviews, what are known as the "first surfaces" of the interior become precisely defined. "The first surfaces of the interior are what you and I see as customers," says Socks. "From an ergonomic standpoint, you really want to lock them in early in a project, which is why we're a part of advance-vehicle engineering. If you want a small-car interior to feel big enough, you've got to get this stuff right. Then comes second-surface design, which is the car's structure underneath."

Some of the Neon's changes have been prompted by complaints. Shorter Neon owners groused about bumping their arms on the seat cushion while lowering the window with a manual crank. Engineers built a test jig with a movable window crank, and measured and plotted the preferences of people of widely varying stature. Now they know the crank-pivot point that will satisfy 95% of the population, which is more than two inches higher than in the current model.

Maytag's easy-loading washer. With gasoline selling for less than bottled water, it might seem that Americans no longer care about energy conservation. The strong demand for the high-efficiency Neptune clothes washer from Maytag Appliances of Newton, Iowa, indicates otherwise. The Neptune, which lists at a relatively high $1,099, was a hit from the moment it reached showrooms in June 1997. People like it because it's easy to use and can save as much as 38% on water usage and 56% on electric bills.

That combination of attributes is missing in the top-loading washers Americans have traditionally preferred. While easy to load and unload, these machines require an agitator mechanism and a relatively large amount of water to get the clothes clean. Front-loading machines, popular in Europe, have a horizontal-axis drum inside that uses gravity's natural assist to tumble away dirt while conserving water. But they're almost impossible to sell in the U.S. because people don't like bending or kneeling to reach the low door opening.

The Neptune's design is one of those happy compromises that seems obvious after someone else has thought of it. To achieve the efficiency of a front loader but improve access, the designers tilted the washer's drum axis upward 15 degrees from the horizontal. And they devised a door that runs up the machine's front and then slopes back along the top to create a large opening. The Neptune's user can load it without aggravating those creaky knees.

Government was the spark plug that ignited the $50 million Neptune development program. Back in the early '90s, the U.S. Department of Energy was making noises about issuing water- and electricity-efficiency standards, which sent appliance makers scrambling. Maytag formed a partnership with the Electric Power Research Institute, a Palo Alto utility-industry group with a mandate to help members minimize investments in the next big round of expensive generating equipment.

Maytag sequestered 30 specialists from all parts of the company in a "war room" for three weeks to hammer out a new strategy. In subsequent consumer testing, the company learned that Americans had little fondness for the high-efficiency front loaders built by Miele of Germany, which are well regarded by Europeans living in cramped quarters. Too little capacity, too long a wash cycle, and too much bending over, said the focus groups. Maytag even built several front-loading prototypes with more capacity than the Mieles, but consumer panels rejected those too. "We were slow to learn on this, and the light bulb didn't just instantly come on," admits Dave Ellingson, Maytag's director of product design engineering.

Progress began when engineers studied the Brandt washers popular in France, which have a sideways horizontal drum for efficiency but load from the top. The prototypes the engineers built required two inner drums and a total of three doors, however, which made loading too complex. Then one engineer began experimenting with tilting a horizontal drum upward a bit. Colleagues rejected the idea at first. But he stuck to his guns, performing washability tests and loading trials that proved it was a good design.

Using cardboard, a wooden dowel, and other low-tech stuff, the engineers then rigged up a variable-angle drum mockup that could be tilted from five to 40 degrees and turned a focus group loose on it. The panelists preferred a 20-degree angle, but Maytag settled on 15 degrees to meet some engineering considerations. When this type of drum was housed in a mockup with a vertical front and a door that wrapped over the top edge, Maytag was startled by the handsome price people said they'd be willing to pay for it.

Then came news that the Energy Department wasn't going to issue a washer-efficiency standard after all. But it was a no-brainer to forge ahead with what promised to be a moneymaker. One moral of the story, says Don Erickson, Maytag's manager of horizontal-axis washer design, is that "it's good to have conflict early on in design, to have people with different ideas. We want to take the time and effort to prove things right or wrong early, rather than later." The other moral, whether for Maytag washers or equipment used at lonely oil fields, is that if machines are designed around people, the customers will come.

Unit 4

Unit Selections

Key Points to Consider

❖ Why is forecasting so central to operations/production management?

❖ Given the various techniques available for sales forecasting, how should a manager go about selecting the technique to use?

❖ Give examples of when a firm would be forced to utilize qualitative techniques to sales forecasting.

 **Links**   **www.dushkin.com/online/**

These sites are annotated on pages 4 and 5.

When examining the critical decisions and stages of operations/production management, the two initial areas of concern are forecasting and product design. A firm needs to have an accurate forecast of demand that will have an impact on capacity design, production scheduling, staffing, inventory, material requirements planning, and transportation. Even for service firms, an accurate forecast of demand is necessary to determine adequate staffing levels and requirements of supplies.

Various qualitative and quantitative techniques exist for sales forecasting. The major qualitative techniques rely upon opinions and include the sales force composite, jury of executive opinion, and buyer/user expectations. The sales force composite consists of pooling the next period sales forecast opinions of the sales representatives. The jury of executive opinion pools the opinions of managers instead of sales representatives. With both of these approaches there are potential biases to underestimate (to have a lower quota/target, to look better when exceeding the low target) or to overestimate (to secure more resources, to secure a larger budget, or to ensure enough inventory on hand to avoid a customer cancellation of a sale due to stock-out). With the buyer/user expectations, care needs to be taken in unbiased sampling, getting credible responses from consumers, and recognizing that the buyer's stated intentions to buy do not always translate into actual sales in the marketplace.

There are also several quantitative techniques, such as the naive method, simple moving average, weighted moving average, exponential smoothing, simple regressions, and multiple regressions. These quantitative techniques rely upon extrapolation and analysis of historical data. The naive method assumes that sales for the next period will equal sales for the last known period. Simple and weighted moving averages involve an averaging of the last periods to forecast the next period's sales. Exponential smoothing, which is similar to a moving average, utilizes a formula involving an alpha factor (the weight placed upon the last period's sales) and smooths out prior period sales data. Regressions are causal models that assume that the dependent variable (sales) is a function of one or more of the independent variables (time, advertising, company price, interest rates, etc.).

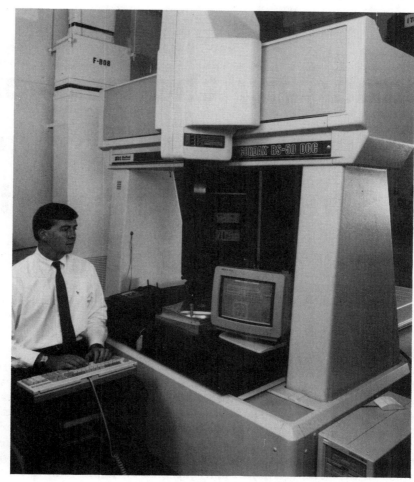

A manager can determine which sales forecasting technique is best for use by their firm by considering factors such as data required, costs involved with the forecast, accuracy required, whether the forecast time horizon is long-term or short-term, and an examination of errors. Software packages for sales forecasting are widely available to assist firms with their sales computations.

Once a sales forecast has been developed, it is important to design the product. Although the marketing department is responsible for marketing research and initial product development, the operations/production area should be involved with technical support. With the use of techniques such as project management, new product launches can be kept on schedule and within budget. Project management techniques such as PERT (Program Evaluation and Review Technique) and CPM (Critical Path Method) can aid managers in developing a product more quickly and successfully.

The articles in this unit review forecasting approaches and provide illustrations from firms. A few articles on product development/project management are presented. In their article, Mark Moon et al. review seven key focus points that help a company to improve its forecasting performance.

Forecasting and Product Design

Managing the new product development process: Strategic imperatives

Melissa A. Schilling and Charles W. L. Hill

Executive Overview

For many industries, new product development is now the single most important factor driving firm success or failure. The emphasis on new products has spurred researchers from strategic management, engineering, marketing, and other disciplines to study the new product development process. Most conclude that in order to be successful at new product development, a firm must simultaneously meet two critical objectives: maximizing the fit with customer needs, and minimizing time to market. While these objectives often pose conflicting demands on the firm, there is a growing body of evidence that the firm may employ strategies to successfully meet these objectives. Successful firms are those that articulate their strategic intent and map their R&D portfolio to find a fit between their new product development goals and their current resources and competencies. Their success also rests on how well the technology areas they enter contribute to the long term direction of the firm by helping them build new core capabilities critical to the firm's long term goals. Strategic alliances to obtain enabling technologies may shorten the development process, but partners must be chosen and monitored carefully. When firms are choosing technologies to acquire externally, they must assess the importance of the learning that would be accrued through internal development of the project, and its impact on the firm's future success. Other imperatives include using a parallel (rather than sequential) development process to both reduce cycle time and to better incorporate customer and supplier requirements in the product and process design, and using executive champions to ensure that projects gain the resources and organizational commitment necessary to their completion. Development teams should include people from a diverse range of functions and should include suppliers and customers to improve the project's chances of maximizing the fit with customer requirements while reducing cycle time and potentially reducing costs. Tools such as Stage-Gate processes, Quality Function Deployment, Design for Manufacturing, and Computer Aided Design/Computer Aided Manufacturing may be useful on different projects.

The importance of new product development (NPD) has grown dramatically over the last few decades, and is now the dominant driver of competition in many industries. In industries such as automobiles, biotechnology, consumer and industrial electronics, computer software, and pharmaceuticals, companies often depend on products introduced within the last five years for more than 50 percent of their annual sales. However, new product failure rates are still very high. Many R&D projects never result in a commercial product, and between 33 percent and 60 percent of all new products that reach the market place fail to generate an economic return.[1]

These trends have prompted a great deal of research on how to optimize the new product development pro-

From *Academy of Management Executive*, August 1998, pp. 67-81. Republished with permission of Academy of Management, P.O. Box 3020, Briar Cliff Manor, NY 10510-8020. Reproduced by permission of the publisher via Copyright Clearance Center, Inc.

cess. This research is both large and diverse, originating in disciplines as wide ranging as strategic management, engineering, and marketing. The purpose of this paper is to review the previous research on managing the NPD process, and make sense of it through a cohesive organizing framework. Through this synthesis, a number of strategic imperatives emerge for improving the management of new product development. Our focus is on how the firm may increase the likelihood of new product success, emphasizing the management of projects once the ideas have been proposed.

The strategic imperatives in this paper represent a synthesis of the best industrial practices in this area, and are the result of a high degree of consensus among various research efforts. Our objective is to provide a working guide for managers to identify opportunities for improving their NPD processes and a perceptual map for scholars to identify fruitful areas for research.

The Competitive Environment and Critical Objectives of New Product Development

The dramatic increase in emphasis on new product development as a competitive dimension can be traced back to the globalization of markets, and the fragmentation of markets into ever smaller niches.

The globalization of markets is a natural result of the steady decline in barriers to the free flow of goods, ser-

---

The dramatic increase in emphasis on new product development as a competitive dimension can be traced back to the globalization of markets, and the fragmentation of markets into ever smaller niches.

---

vices, and capital that has occurred since the end of World War II. The result has been a substantial increase in foreign competition. The more competitive a market becomes, the more difficult it is for companies to differentiate their product offerings on the basis of cost and quality. As a result, new product development has become central to achieving meaningful differentiation. Product life cycles have been shortening as the innovations of others[2] make existing products obsolete. Schumpeter's "gale of creative destruction," blowing at full force, fosters shorter product life cycles and rapid product obsolescence.

While product life cycles have compressed, markets have also fragmented into smaller niches. Lean manufacturing technologies, developed in Japan, have enabled this fragmentation. By reducing set-up times for complex

equipment, lean manufacturing makes shorter production runs economical and reduces the importance of production economies of scale.[3] As a result, it is now economical for manufacturing enterprises to customize their product offerings to the demands of fairly narrowly defined customer groups, thereby out-focusing their competitors. A prime example is Nike, which produces over 250 variants of its popular athletic shoes in twenty different sports categories, a portfolio of products that appeals to every conceivable market niche.[4] As a result, not only are product life cycles compressed, but the size of the potential market for each variant of a product declines because of the rise of niche marketing.

In order to recoup development costs and make an economic return in an environment characterized by rapid product obsolescence and market fragmentation, a company's new product development must meet two critical objectives: (1) minimize time-to-market, and (2) maximize the fit between customer requirements and product characteristics.

Minimize Time to Market

Minimizing time to market—or cycle time—is necessary for a number of reasons.[5] A company that is slow to market with a particular generation of technology is unlikely to fully amortize the costs of development before that generation becomes obsolete. This phenomenon is particularly vivid in dynamic industries such as electronics, where life cycles of personal computers and semiconductors can be twelve months. Indeed, companies that are slow to market may find that by the time they have introduced their products, market demand has already shifted to the next generation of products.

Companies with compressed cycle times are more likely to be the first to introduce products that embody new technologies. As such, they are better positioned to capture first mover advantages. The first mover in an industry can build brand loyalty,[6] reap experience curve economies ahead of potential competitors, preempt scarce assets, and create switching costs that tie consumers to the company.[7] Once achieved, first mover advantages can be the basis of a more sustained competitive advantage.

In many industries, issues of dominant design are paramount.[8] When a new technology is first introduced, competing variants of that technology are often based on different standards. Different companies will promote different technological standards, and the company that establishes its particular design as the dominant standard can reap enormous financial rewards, while those that fail may be locked out.[9] Some examples of this include Microsoft's Windows (which locked out Geowork's Ensemble 1.0, among others) and Intel's CPU platform. Companies with reduced cycle time have a greater probability of establishing their design as the dominant standard.[10]

Companies with short cycle times can continually upgrade their products, incorporating state of the art technology when it becomes available. This enables them to better serve consumer needs, outrun their slower competitors and, build brand loyalty. It also enables them to offer a wider range of new products to better serve niches.

Some researchers have pointed out problems with rushing new products to market. For example, Dhebar points out that rapid product introductions may cause adverse consumer reactions; consumers may regret past purchases and be wary of new purchases for fear of obsolescence.[11] Other researchers have suggested that speed of development may come at the expense of quality.[12] However, numerous studies have found a strong positive relationship between speed and the commercial success of new products.[13] The objective, then, is to minimize time to market by making the NPD process more efficient, without sacrificing product or service quality.

Maximize Fit with Customer Requirements

For a new product to achieve significant and rapid market penetration, it must match such customer requirements as new features, superior quality, and attractive pricing. Despite the obvious importance of this imperative, numerous studies have documented the lack of fit between new product attributes and customer requirements as a major cause of new product failure.[14] Illustrative anecdotes abound—for example, the failure of Lotus to establish Lotus 1-2-3 for Windows as the major spreadsheet for Windows, and the commensurate rise of Microsoft's Excel spreadsheet for Windows, can be attributed to the failure of Lotus 1-2-3 for Windows to satisfy customer requirements with regard to features (e.g., program speed) and quality. Similarly, Philips' CD-Interactive home entertainment system failed because of a lack of understanding of its customers' needs. The product was overly complex and expensive, and required almost an hour of training, and could not compete against the more straightforward game systems produced by Nintendo, Sega, and Sony.

Optimizing the New Product Development Process

Successful NPD requires attention to four strategic issues (see Figure 1). Strategic Issue 1 is the technology strategy, or the process by which the company constructs its new product development portfolio. Strategic Issue 2 is the organizational context within which a NPD project is embedded. Strategic Issue 3 involves the construction and use of teams, and Strategic Issue 4 addresses the use of tools for improving the NPD process.

Technology Strategy

A crucial step in optimizing the NPD process is to ensure that the company has a clear and consistent technology strategy. The purpose of technology strategy is to identify, develop, and nurture those technologies that will be crucial for the long run competitive position of the company. These technologies must have the potential to create value for customers. A coherent technological strategy, therefore, focuses explicitly on customer requirements as they are now, and as they are likely to become in the future.

Many companies lack a well-articulated technology strategy. A northwestern company that recently imple-

---

A crucial step in optimizing the NPD process is to ensure that the company has a clear and consistent technology strategy.

---

mented a project tracking system found to its dismay that there were many more projects underway than the company could support. As one engineer put it, "We never saw a problem we didn't like." Because the company was attempting to support too many projects, employees were assigned to many project teams and had little commitment to any particular project. Furthermore, because development resources were stretched too thin, projects were delayed and several had been abandoned. One major project that was expected to take nine months in development had stretched to three and half years, and by the time the product was released, it was no longer clear that a market existed.

A company can focus its development efforts on projects that will create long-term advantage by defining its strategic intent.

Strategic Imperative 1: Articulate the company's strategic intent

An ambitious strategic intent should create a gap between a company's existing resources and capabilities and those required to achieve its intent.[15] At the same time, the company's strategic intent should build on existing core competencies. Once the strategic intent has been articulated, the company is able to identify the resources and capabilities required to close the gap between intent and reality. This includes identification of any technological gap and enables the company to focus its development efforts and choose the investments necessary to develop strategic technologies and incorporate them into the company's new products.[16]

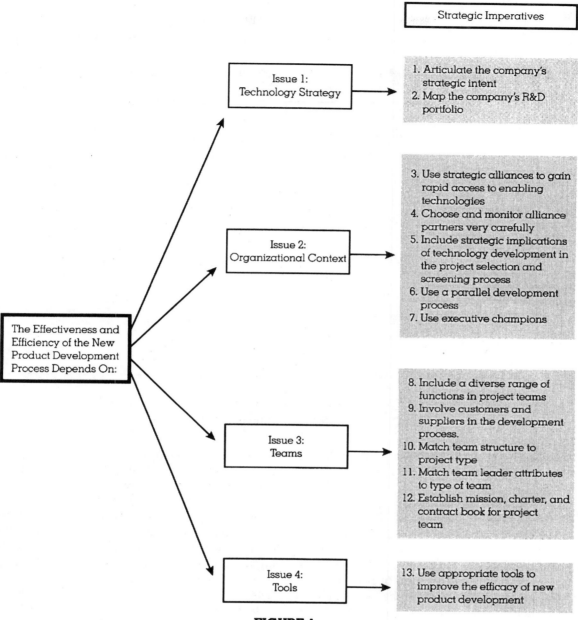

FIGURE 1
A Model of the New Product Development Process

Strategic Imperative 2: Map the company's R&D portfolio
New product development must be managed as a balanced portfolio of projects at different stages in development.[17] Companies may use a project map (similar to that depicted in Figure 2) to aid this process. Four types of development projects commonly appear on this map—pure R&D, breakthrough, platform, and derivative projects. Over time, a particular technology may migrate through these different types of projects. R&D projects are the precursor to commercial development projects and are necessary to develop cutting edge strategic technologies. Breakthrough projects involve development of products that incorporate revolutionary new product and process technologies. Platform projects typi-

cally offer fundamental improvements in the cost, quality, and performance of a technology over preceding generations. Derivative projects involve incremental changes in products and/or processes. A platform project is designed to serve a core group of consumers, whereas derivative projects represent modifications of the basic platform design to appeal to different niches within that core group.[18] Companies need to identify their desired mix of projects on a project map and then allocate resources accordingly. It is important that the mix of projects represented on such a map be consistent both with the company's resources, and with its expression of strategic intent.

Along with a coherent technology strategy, a company must establish an organizational environment that en-

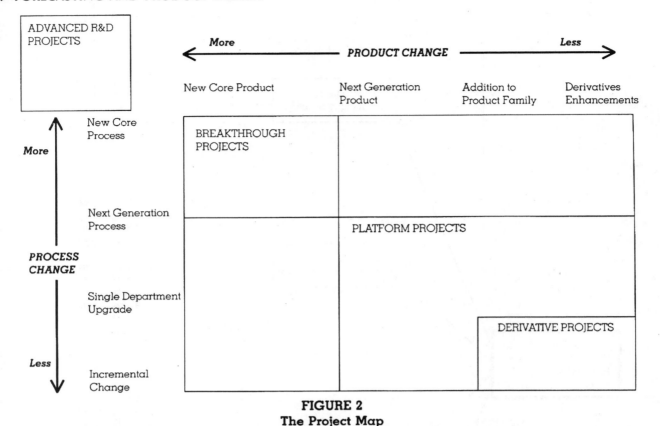

FIGURE 2
The Project Map
(adapted from Wheelwright, S. C. and Clark. K. B. 1992. *Revolutionizing Product Development*. New York: Free Press)

ables it to optimize its likelihood of new product development success.

Organizational Context

Organizational context factors important in reducing cycle time and achieving a fit between customer requirements and new product attributes are: (1) the use of strategic alliances, (2) the determination of how alliance partners are chosen and monitored, (3) the use of appropriate project valuation and screening mechanisms, (4) the development process scheme used by the firm (sequential process versus partly parallel process), and (5) the involvement of executive champions.

Strategic Imperative 3: Use strategic alliances to gain rapid access to enabling technologies

Developing new products often requires the joining together of complementary assets. Consider a company that has developed a body of technological knowledge with commercial possibilities, such as the pen-based computer company, GO Corp. To transform this knowledge into a viable product, the company had to assemble a set of assets that included complementary technological knowledge, market knowledge, manufacturing knowledge, and financial ability.[19] GO Corporation's product, a pen-based personal digital assistant (a palm-sized computer) lacked value without complementary

software, a powerful CPU, lightweight and long-lasting batteries, and adequate marketing and distribution channels. While the company was successful in developing its core product, the product did not integrate seamlessly with desktop environments because the software was not compatible. The product was also too heavy, slow, and too expensive. The company spent several years improving the product and trying to figure out the appropriate target markets, but eventually ran out of capital and failed.

It is not unusual for a company to lack some of the complementary assets required to transform a body of technological knowledge into a commercial product. The company can develop such assets internally, at the expense of cycle time. Alternatively, the company might gain rapid access to important complementary assets by entering into strategic alliances.[20] Consider Microsoft's strategic alliance with America Online (AOL). By the time Microsoft realized the importance of offering internet utilities such as a web server and a web browser, it had lost considerable ground to Netscape Communications Corp. Netscape's web browser, Netscape Navigator, beat Microsoft's Internet Explorer to market by almost a year. To rapidly deploy Internet Explorer and increase its exposure, Microsoft set up an exclusive contract with AOL, the largest online service provider in the US.[21] In this case, the asset gained was a distribution channel that encouraged rapid adoption of Microsoft's web browser. If Microsoft had taken the time to build a better online service itself, it might have never been able to catch up with the market lead attained by Netscape's Navigator.

Strategic Imperative 4: Choose and monitor alliance partners very carefully
Not all alliances for complementary technologies are beneficial.[22] It may be difficult to determine if the complementary assets provided by the alliance partner are a good fit, particularly when the asset gained through an alliance is something as difficult to assess as experience or knowledge. It is also possible that an alliance partner will exploit an alliance, expropriating knowledge while giving little in return. Furthermore, since managers can monitor and effectively manage only a limited number of alliances, the firm's effectiveness will decline with the number of alliances to which it is committed. This raises not only the possibility of diminishing returns to the number of alliances, but also negative returns as the number of alliances grows. These risks can be minimized if the company undertakes a detailed search of potential partners before entering an alliance, establishes appropriate monitoring and enforcement mechanisms to limit opportunism,[23] and limits the number of strategic alliances in which it engages.

Strategic Imperative 5: Include strategic implications of technology development in the project selection and screening process
Methods used to evaluate and choose investment projects range from informal to highly structured, and from entirely qualitative to strictly quantitative. Quantitative methods such as net present value (NPV) techniques provide concrete financial estimates that facilitate strategic planning and trade-off decisions. However, NPV may fail to capture the strategic importance of the investment decision. Failure to invest in a project that has a negative NPV may prevent a company from taking advantage of profitable future projects that build on the first development effort. For instance, NPV analysis may value platform projects or derivative projects much higher than advanced R&D or breakthrough projects (see Figure 2) because the former are more likely to result in immediate revenues from product sales. However, a firm that forgoes basic research or development of breakthrough projects may quickly find itself behind the technology frontier, unable to respond to technological change.

Some research has suggested that these problems might be addressed by treating new product development decisions as real options.[24] A venture capitalist who makes an initial investment in basic R&D or in breakthrough technologies is buying a real call option to implement that technology later should it prove to be valuable.[25] However, implicit in the value of options is the assumption that one can acquire or retain the option for a small price, and then wait for a signal to determine

if the option should be exercised.[26] In the case of a firm undertaking solo new product development, it may not be possible to secure this option at a small price, and in fact, it may require full investment in the technology before a firm can determine if the technology will be successful. Furthermore, while stock option holders can wait and exercise their option once its value is clear, a firm considering new product development may not have this luxury. By the time it becomes clear that the technology will be profitable, the firm may be locked out of the market by a competitor's dominant standard.[27]

Research has indicated that the support of an executive champion can improve a project's chances for success in a number of ways.

Although the use of option theory does not provide a problem-free solution to the development investment decision, it does provide a useful perspective for evaluating a firm's strategic alternatives. A firm may have either a project strategy of seeking direct venture gains from the immediate project at hand, or an option strategy that emphasizes development of new technologies. While these strategies are not mutually exclusive, they represent different perspectives on the opportunities available to the firm: the former emphasizes the short run gains of the project under consideration and does not consider other strategic implications of the investment; the latter seeks to evaluate and incorporate the less tangible and longer-term returns of the development project.

Strategic Imperative 6: Use a parallel development process
Until recently, most US companies used a sequential process for new product development, whereby development proceeds sequentially from one functional group to the next (see Figure 3, panel A). Embedded in the process are a number of gates, where decisions are made as to whether to proceed to the next stage, send the project back for further work, or kill the project. Typically, R&D and marketing provide input into the opportunity identification and concept development stages, R&D takes the lead in product design, and manufacturing takes the lead in process design. According to critics, one problem with such a system emerges at the product design stage, when R&D engineers fail to communicate directly with manufacturing engineers. As a result, product design proceeds without manufacturing requirements in mind. A sequential process has no early warning system to indicate that planned features are not manufacturable. Consequently, cycle time can lengthen as the project it-

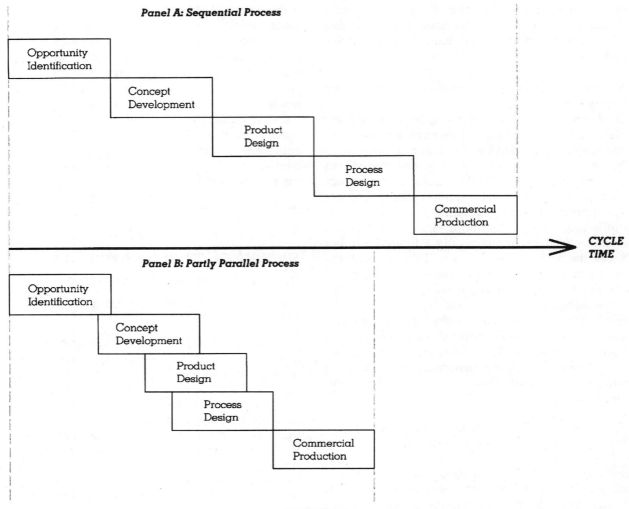

FIGURE 3
Sequential Versus Partly Parallel Process

erates between the product design and process design stages.[28]

To rectify this problem, and compress cycle time, the firm should use a partly parallel process.[29] As shown in panel B of Figure 3, sequential execution of the NPD stages is replaced by partly parallel execution. Process design, for example, should start long before product design is finalized, thereby establishing closer coordination between these different stages and minimizing the chance that R&D will design products difficult or costly to manufacture. This should eliminate the need for lost time between the product and process design stages. The cycle time should be compressed.

Strategic Imperative 7: Use executive champions
An executive champion is a senior member of the company with the power and authority to support a project. Research has indicated that the support of an executive champion can improve a project's chances for success in a number of ways.[30] An executive champion can facilitate the allocation of human and capital resources to the de-

velopment effort. This ensures that cycle time is not limited by resource constraints. An executive champion can stimulate communication and cooperation between the different functional groups involved in the development process. Given that interfunctional communication and cooperation is necessary to both compress cycle time and achieve a good fit between product attributes and customer requirements, the use of executive sponsors should improve the effectiveness of the NPD process.

Teams

There has been a great deal of consensus that using crossfunctional project teams should increase the likelihood of project success. Research in this area has examined the advantages and difficulties of using crossfunctional teams, including suppliers and customers on the project team, types of team structures, team leadership, and the constitution and management of teams.

Table 1

Key Characteristics of Different Types of Teams

Characteristics	Functional Team	Lightweight Team	Heavyweight Team	Autonomous Team
Project Manager	No	Yes	Yes	Yes
Power of Project Manager		Low	High	Very High
Primary Orientation of Team Members	Function	Function	Team	Team
Location of Team Members	Functions	Functions	Co-Located with Project Manager	Co-Located with Project Manager
Evaluation of Team Members	Functional Heads	Functional Heads	Project Manager and Functional Heads	Project Manager
Incentives Skewed Towards	Functional Performance	Functional Performance	Team and Functional Performance	Team Performance
Potential for Conflict between Team and Functions	Low	Low	Moderate	High
Degree of Crossfunctional Integration	Low	Moderate	High	High
Degree of Fit with Existing Organizational Practices	High	High	High	Moderate-Low
Appropriate For:	Not Appropriate	Derivative Projects	Platform Projects/ Breakthrough Projects	Breakthrough Projects

Strategic Imperative 8: Include a diverse range of functions in project teams

A lack of communication between the marketing, R&D, and manufacturing functions of a company can be extremely detrimental to the NPD process. Crossfunctional miscommunication leads to a poor fit between product attributes and customer requirements. R&D cannot design products that fit customer requirements without input from marketing. By working closely with R&D, manufacturing can ensure that R&D designs products relatively easy to manufacture. Ease of manufacturing can lower both unit costs and product defects, which translates into a lower final price and higher quality. Similarly, as we noted earlier, a lack of crossfunctional communication can lead to longer cycle times.

The use of crossfunctional product development teams should minimize miscommunication.[31] For instance, in Chrysler's vehicle deployment platform teams, team members are drawn from design, engineering, purchasing, manufacturing, product-planning, finance, and marketing. Teams with diverse backgrounds have several advantages, over less diverse teams.[32] Their variety provides a broader knowledge base and increases the "crossfertilization of ideas."[33] The variety allows the project to draw on more information sources.[34] By combining members of different functional areas into one project team, a wide variety of information sources can be ensured.

Strategic Imperative 9: Involve customers and suppliers in the development process

Many products fail to produce an economic return because they fail to meet customer requirements. Financial considerations often take precedence over marketing criteria. This may lead to the development of incremental product updates that closely fit existing business activities (for example, the firm may overemphasize the derivative projects shown in Figure 2).[35] The screening decision should focus instead on the new product's advantage and superiority to the consumer, and the growth of its target market.[36]

One way of improving the fit between a new product and customer requirements is to include customers in the NPD process. This may be accomplished by including the customer in the actual development team, or by designing initial product versions and then encouraging user extensions.[37] By exchanging information effectively with customers, the company helps maximize the product's fit with customer needs.

The logic behind involving customers in the NPD process also applies to involving suppliers. By tapping into the knowledge base of its suppliers, a firm expands its information resources. Suppliers may be members of the product team or consulted as an alliance partner. In either case, suppliers contribute ideas for product improvement or increased development efficiency. For instance, a supplier may suggest an alternative input (or configuration of inputs) that would lower cost. Additionally, by coordinating with suppliers, managers can help ensure that inputs arrive on time and that necessary changes can be made quickly.[38] Consistent with this argument, research has shown that many firms using supplier interaction are able to produce new products in less time, at a lower cost, and with higher quality.[39] For example, during Boeing's development of the 777, United employees (including engineers, pilots and flight attendants) worked closely with Boeing's engineers to ensure that the airplane was designed for maximum functionality and comfort. Boeing also included General Electric and other parts suppliers on the project team, so that the

Table 2

Tools Appropriate for Different Types of Projects

Tools	Appropriate for:			
	Basic R&D	Breakthrough Research	Platform Projects	Derivative Projects
Stage-Gate Process	X	X	XXX	XX
QFD-House of Quality		X	XXX	XX
Design for Manufacturing			XXX	XXX
Computer Aided Design	XXX	XXX	XXX	XXX
Computer Aided Manufacturing			XXX	XXX

engines and the body of the airplane could be simultaneously designed for maximum compatibility.

Strategic Imperative 10: Match team structure to project type

There are a number of different ways to structure teams: functional, lightweight, heavyweight and autonomous.[40] In a functional team, members from different functional divisions of the firm meet periodically to discuss the project. The team members are located together, their rewards are not tied to the performance of the project, and the team may be temporary. Functional teams also lack a project manager and dedicated liaison personnel between the different functions. There is a general lack of coordination and communication between the different functions involved in the product development process. As a consequence, the dangers of long cycle time and a lack of fit between customer requirements and product attributes become particularly acute.

Lightweight teams have both project managers and dedicated liaison personnel who facilitate communication and coordination among functions. In lightweight teams, the key resources remain under the control of their respective functional managers. Lightweight team members often spend no more than 25 percent of their time on a single project. Because of these characteristics, lightweight teams, are often unable to overcome interfunctional coordination and communication problems. Consequently, lightweight teams may not improve the success of the product development process. While the lightweight team has deficiencies, it may be appropriate for derivative projects (see Figure 2), where high levels of coordination and communication are not required.

Heavyweight teams also have project managers and dedicated liaison personnel. A critical distinction, however, is the power and influence of the project manager. Heavyweight project managers are senior managers with substantial organizational influence. They have the power to reassign people and reallocate resources, and they tend to devote most of their time to the project. Often the core group of people in a heavyweight team is dedicated full time to the project and physically located along with the heavyweight project manager. Nevertheless, within a heavyweight team the long-term career development of individual members continues to rest with their functional managers rather than the project manager. They are not assigned to the project team on a permanent basis and their functional heads still exert some control over them and participate in their performance evaluation. The heavyweight team is far more capable of breaking down interfunctional coordination and communication barriers, primarily because of the facilitating role of the project leader. Consequently, this type of team structure generally improves the performance of the NPD process, and would be appropriate for platform projects (see Figure 2).

The autonomous team also has a heavyweight team leader. The functional representatives are also formally removed from their functions, dedicated full time to the team, and located with other team members. A critical distinguishing feature of the autonomous team is that the project leader becomes the sole evaluator of the contributions made by individual team members. Also, autonomous teams are allowed to create their own policies and procedures, including their own reward systems, increasing the team members' commitment and involvement.[41] However, a problem with autonomous teams is that they can become too independent and get away from top management control. Moreover, once a project is complete it may prove difficult to fold the members of an autonomous team back into the organization since team members may have become accustomed to independence. Therefore, an autonomous team would be appropriate for breakthrough projects and some major platform projects. It is particularly appropriate when the existing routines and culture of the organization run counter to the objectives of the project, and the new project is likely to result in the development of a new business unit. Several of the business units of Quantum Corporation, a major disk drive manufacturer, were formed in this way. These business units are then integrated functionally in a matrix-like structure.

Table 1 summarizes a number of key dimensions across which the four teams vary. Note that the potential for conflict between the functions and the team, and particularly the project manager, rises as we move from

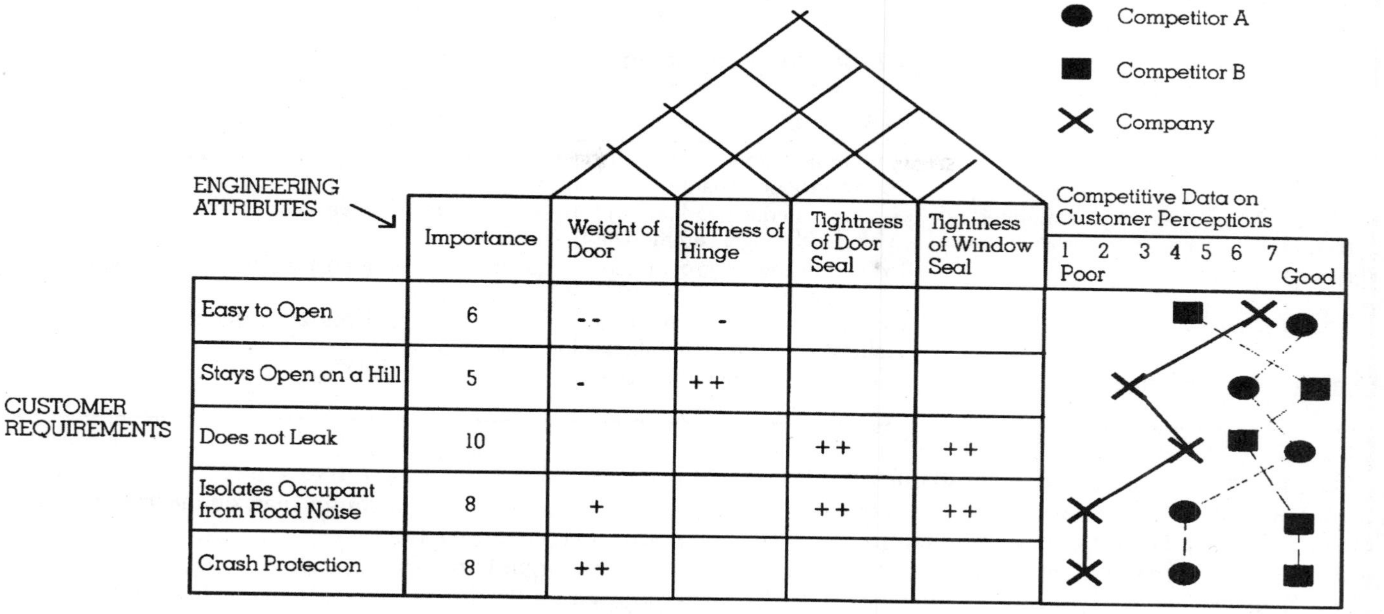

Competitor A
Competitor B
Company

FIGURE 4
House of Quality

CUSTOMER REQUIREMENTS	Importance	Weight of Door	Stiffness of Hinge	Tightness of Door Seal	Tightness of Window Seal
Easy to Open	6	- -	-		
Stays Open on a Hill	5	-	+ +		
Does not Leak	10			+ +	+ +
Isolates Occupant from Road Noise	8	+		+ +	+ +
Crash Protection	8	+ +			

functional teams to autonomous teams. This occurs because the independence of heavyweight and autonomous teams may mean that they pursue goals counter to the interests of the functions. It is the task of senior managers to keep such conflict in check.

Strategic Imperative 11: Match team leader attributes to type of team

An important factor determining the effectiveness of project teams, particularly of heavyweight and autonomous teams, is the kind of leadership skills exerted by the project manager.[42] Project managers in heavyweight and autonomous teams must have high status within the organization, act as concept champions for the team within the organization, be good at conflict resolution, have multidiscipline skills (i.e., must be able to talk the language of marketing, engineering, and manufacturing), and be able to exert influence on the engineering, manufacturing, and marketing functions.[43] Other things being equal, teams whose project managers are deficient on one or more of these dimensions will have a lower probability of being successful.

Strategic Imperative 12: Establish mission, charter, and contract book for the project team

To ensure that the project team has a clear focus and commitment to the development project, the team should be involved in the development of its mission. The team's mission should be encapsulated in a clear and explicit project charter, whose purpose is to articulate the broad performance objectives of the team. Once the team charter is established, core team members and senior managers must negotiate a contract book that defines in detail the basic plan to achieve the goal laid out

in the project charter. Typically, the contract book will estimate the resources that will be required, the development time schedule, and the results that will be achieved. It is common practice following negotiation and acceptance of this contract for all parties to sign the contract book as an indication of their commitment to honor the plan and achieve the results. Establishing a mission, charter, and contract book for the team not only increases the team's awareness and commitment to the project's objectives, but provides a tool for monitoring and evaluating the team's performance in meeting its objectives.

Tools

Some of the most prominent of these are Stage-Gate processes, QFD—House of Quality, Design for Manufacturing, and Computer Aided Design/Computer Aided Manufacturing. Using the available tools for improving NPD processes can greatly expedite the NPD process and maximize the product's fit with customer requirements. Table 2 summarizes the usefulness of each tool to different types of projects.

Strategic Imperative 13: Use appropriate tools to improve the new product development process

Stage-Gate Processes. The Stage-Gate process is a method of managing the new product development process to increase the probability of launching new products quickly and successfully.[44] The process provides a blueprint to move projects through the different stages of development: 1) idea generation, 2) preliminary investment, 3) business case preparation, 4) product development, 5) product testing, and 6) product introduction.

Table 3

Design Rules for Fabricated Assembly Products

Design Rule	Impact Upon Performance
Minimize the number of parts	Simplify assembly; reduce direct labor; reduce material handling and inventory costs; boost product quality.
Minimize the number of part numbers (use common parts across product family)	Reduce material handling and inventory costs; improve economies of scale (increase volume through commonalty).
Eliminate adjustments	Reduce assembly errors (increase quality); allow automation; increase capacity and throughput.
Eliminate fasteners	Simplify assembly (increase quality); reduce direct labor costs; reduce squeaks and rattles; improves durability; allows for automation.
Eliminate jigs and fixtures	Reduce line changeover costs; lower required investment.

The process is used by such companies as IBM, Procter & Gamble, 3M, General Motors and Corning. In fact, Corning has made the process mandatory for all information system development projects, and Corning managers believe that the process enables them to better estimate the potential payback of any project under consideration. They also report that the Stage-Gate process has reduced development time, allows identification of projects which should be killed, and increases the ratio of internally developed products that result in commer-

The house of quality makes the relationship between product attributes and customer requirements clear, focuses on design tradeoffs, highlights the competitive shortcomings of the company's existing products, and helps identify what steps need to be taken to improve them.

cial projects.[45] The Stage-Gate process is primarily used for research projects that are aimed at developing a specific commercial product, and is more likely to be used for major platform projects than derivative projects. It could also be used, however, to assess the resources or advantages to be gained through development of a basic R&D or breakthrough research project.

QFD—The House of Quality. QFD (originally developed in Japan[46]) is a conceptual organizing framework for enhancing communication and coordination between engineering, marketing, and manufacturing personnel. It does this by taking managers through an instructional problem solving process in a very structured fashion. Advocates of QFD maintain that one of its most valuable

characteristics is its positive effect on crossfunctional communication, and through that, on cycle time and the product/customer fit.[47]

The organizing framework for QFD is the concept known as the house of quality (see Figure 4), a matrix that maps customer requirements against product attributes. The starting point is to identify customer requirements. In the figure shown, market research has identified five attributes that customers want from a car door—that it be easy to open and close, that it stay open when the car is parked on a hill, that it does not leak in the rain, that it isolate the occupant from road noise, and that it afford some protection in side-on crashes.

The next step is to weight the requirements in terms of their relative importance from a customer's perspective. Once this has been done, the team needs to identify the engineering attributes that drive the performance of the product—in this case the car door. In the figure shown, four attributes are highlighted; the weight of the door, the stiffness of the door hinge (a stiff hinge helps the door stay open when parked on a hill), the tightness of the door seal, and the tightness of the window seal.

After identifying engineering attributes, the team fills in the body of the central matrix. Each cell in the matrix indicates the relationship between an engineering attribute and a customer requirement. This matrix should indicate both the direction and strength of the relationship. A fourth piece of information in the house of quality is contained in the roof of the house. The matrix here indicates the interaction between design parameters. Thus, the negative sign between door weight and hinge stiffness indicates that a heavy door reduces the stiffness of the hinge. The final piece of information in the house of quality is a summary of customer perceptions of the company's existing product compared with that of its competitors—in this case A and B.

The great strength of the house of quality is that it provides a common language and framework within which the members of a project team may fruitfully interact. The house of quality makes the relationship between product attributes and customer requirements clear, focuses on design tradeoffs, highlights the competitive shortcomings of the company's existing products, and helps identify what steps need to be taken to improve them.

Exploratory research has identified a number of project and implementation characteristics that distinguish successful attempts to apply QFD techniques from failed attempts.[48] QFD seems to work best for less complex product development projects, where QFD is seen as an investment that has the commitment of team members, where there is strong crossfunctional integration, where QFD is seen as a means of achieving an end, rather than a goal in its own right, and where the goals of the project stretch capabilities (note the fit with the concept of strategic intent discussed earlier). All of this would seem to suggest that QFD works best when used as a tool by a heavyweight project team pursuing a goal that is congruent with the strategic intent of the company, and when QFD is viewed for what it is—an aid to decision making rather than an end in itself.

Design For Manufacturing. To facilitate integration between engineering and manufacturing, and to bring issues of manufacturability into the design process as early as possible, many companies have implemented design for manufacturing methods (DFM). Like QFD, DFM represents nothing more than a way of structuring the NPD process. One way in which DFM finds expression is in the articulation of a number of design rules. A series of commonly used design rules are summarized in Table 3, along with their expected impact on performance.

As can be seen, the purpose of such design rules typically is to reduce costs and boost product quality by designing products that are easy to manufacture. This means reducing the number of parts in a product, eliminating any time-consuming adjustments that have to be made to the product during manufacturing, and eliminating as many fasteners as possible. The easier products are to manufacture, the fewer the assembly steps required, the higher labor productivity will be, and hence, the lower unit costs. Also, the easier products are to manufacture, the higher product quality tends to be.

The effect of adopting DFM rules can be dramatic. Taking manufacturing considerations into account at an early stage in the design process can compress cycle time. Also, because DFM tends to lower costs and increase product quality, DFM has a favorable impact on critical product attributes that customers normally require, such as high quality and an attractive price relative to the features of the product. When NCR used DFM techniques to redesign one of its electronic cash registers, it found it could reduce assembly time by 75 percent, reduce the parts required by 85 percent, utilize 65 percent fewer suppliers, and reduce direct labor time by 75 percent.[49]

Because DFM is oriented around improving the manufacturability of a product, it is more useful for platform and derivative projects than for basic R&D projects or breakthrough research.

Computer Aided Design/Computer Aided Manufacturing. Computer aided design (CAD) is another product development tool worthy of note. Rapid advances in computer technology have enabled the development of low priced and high powered graphics-based workstations. Using these workstations, it is now possible to achieve what at one time could only be done on a super-computer: construct a three-dimensional working image of a product or subassembly. The advantage of this technology is that prototypes can now be built and tested in virtual reality. The ability to quickly adjust prototype attributes by manipulating the 3-D model allows engineers to compare and contrast the characteristics of different variants of a product or subassembly. This can reduce cycle time and lower costs by reducing the need for physical model building. Visualization tools and 3-D software are used to allow nonengineering customers to see and make minor alterations to the design and materials. This has proven to be particularly valuable in architecture and construction.

By implementing machine-controlled processes as in computer aided manufacturing (CAM), manufacturing can operate faster, and accommodate more flexibility in the manufacturing process.[50] Computers can automate the change between different product variations, and allow for more variety and customization in the manufacturing process. Computer aided design is often used early in the development process, and may be implemented for basic R&D and breakthrough research projects, in addition to being used in the design of platform and derivative projects. Computer aided manufacturing is used in the later stages of those projects that become commercial projects, and therefore is more useful for improving platform and derivative projects.

Conclusion

Despite the rapidly increasing amount of attention that new product development has received over the last decade, the development project failure rate is still very high. Many companies develop interesting products—but only those firms that are effective in developing products that meet customer needs and efficient in allocating their development resources will succeed in the long run. Better new product development processes should translate into a higher completion rate of projects, more projects meeting their deadlines and budget requirements, and more new products meeting their sales objectives and earning a commercial return.

This article describes those strategies that have been shown to improve the process of new product development, and about which there is a great deal of consensus. This is not meant to imply that other, newly emerging processes will not also improve new product development processes. This is an area that is receiving a great deal of attention in both managerial and academic arenas. Just as innovation is rapidly producing new products from which we may choose, so too is the research into the NPD process producing new methods of configuring and managing development projects. Staying abreast of the work being done in this area is challenging. Being able to rapidly assimilate and implement strategies for maximizing the effectiveness of new product development may prove to be as important to a firm's competitiveness as the innovative products themselves.

Endnotes

[1] Booz, Allen, & Hamilton. 1982. *New products management for the 1980's.* Privately published research report. Mansfield, E. 1981. How economists see R&D, *Harvard Business Review,* November–December: 98–106. Page, A. L. 1991. PDMA's New product development practices survey: Performance and best practices, *PDMA 15th Annual International Conference,* Boston, MA, October 16.

[2] Qualls, W., 1981. Olshavsky, R. W., & Michaels, R. E. Shortening of the PLC—an empirical test, *Journal of Marketing,* 45: 76–80.

[3] Womack, J. P., Jones. D. T. & Boos, D. 1990. *The machine that changed the world.* New York: Rawson Associates.

[4] The automobile industry provides us with another example. In the mid 1960s the largest selling car in the US was the Chevrolet Impala. The platform on which it was based sold approximately 1.5 million units. In 1991 the largest selling car in the US was the Honda Accord, which sold about 400,000 units. Thus, in a market that is larger than it was in 1965, the volume per model has declined by a factor of four.

[5] Stalk, G. & Hout, T. M. 1990. *Competing against time.* New York: Free Press. Kessler, E. & Chakrabarti, A. 1996. Innovation Speed: A conceptual model of context, antecedents, and outcomes, *Academy of Management Review,* 21(4): 1143–1191.

[6] Note that brand loyalty may be important even in industries in which rapid technological change causes short product life cycles. In fact, when technological change is fast and the technology is complex, brand loyalty may reduce the uncertainty of customers who wish to stay on the technology frontier but who would be unable to adequately assess the quality of each successive technological generation.

[7] Lieberman, M. & Montgomery, D. 1988. First mover advantages: A survey, *Strategic Management Journal,* 9: 41–58.

[8] Abernathy, W. J. & Utterback, J. M. 1978. Patterns of industrial innovation, *Technology Review,* 80(7): 40–47.

[9] Schilling, M. A. 1998. Technological lock out: An integrative model of the economic and strategic factors driving success and failure. *Academy of Management Review,* 23; and, Arthur, W. B. 1994. *Increasing returns and path dependence in the economy.* Ann Arbor: The University of Michigan Press.

[10] Mahajan, V., Sharma, S. & Buzzell, R. 1993. Assessing the impact of competitive entry on market expansion and incumbent sales, *Journal of Marketing.* July: 39–52.

[11] Dhebar, A. 1996. Speeding high-tech producer, meet balking consumer, *Sloan Management Review.* Winter: 37–49.

[12] Crawford M. C. 1992. The hidden costs of accelerated product development, *Journal of Product Innovation Management,* September, 9(3): 188–200.

[13] Nijssen E. J., Arbouw, A. R. & Commandeur, H. R. 1995. Accelerating new product development: A preliminary empirical test of a hierarchy of implementation, *Journal of Product Innovation Management,* 12: 99–104, Schmenner, R. W. 1988. The merits of making things fast, *Sloan Management Review,* Fall: 11–17, Ali, A., Krapfel, B. & LaBahn, D. 1995. Product-innovativeness and entry strategy: Impact on cycle time and break-even time. *Journal of Product Innovation Management,* 12: 54–69; and, Bothwell, B. 1992. Successful industrial innovation: Critical factors for the 1990s, *R&D Management.* 22(3): 221–239.

[14] For example, Rothwell, R., Freeman, C., Horley, A., Jervis, P., Robertson, A. B. & Townsend, J. 1974. SAPPHO Updates—Project SAPPHO, PHASE II, *Research Policy.* 3: 258–291, Mansfield, E. 1981. How

economists see R&D, *Harvard Business Review,* November–December: 98–106; and, Zirger, B. J. & Maidique, M. A. 1990. A model of new product development: An empirical test, *Management Science,* 36: 867–883.

[15] Hamel, G. & Prahalad, C. K. 1991. Strategic Intent. *Harvard Business Review,* May–June: 63–76.

[16] Marino K. 1996. Developing consensus on firm competencies and capabilities, *Academy of Management Executive,* 10(3): 40–51.

[17] Wind, Y. & Mahajan, V. 1988. New product development process: A perspective for reexamination, *Journal of Product Innovation Management,* 5: 304–310.

[18] For an illustration, consider Intel's 486 microprocessor. This is a platform, but Intel also offers variations of the 486 platform along dimensions such as speed, cost, and performance, to appeal to different groups of consumers. These variations on the 486 theme (e.g. 486DX/30, 486SX/66) are derivative products.

[19] Teece, D. J. 1987. Profiting from technological innovation: Implications for integration, collaboration, licensing and public policy, *Research Policy,* 15: 285–305.

[20] Hamel, G., Doz, Y. L. & Prahalad, C. K. 1989. Collaborate with your competitors and win, *Harvard Business Review,* January–February: 133–139, Mitchell, W. & Singh, K. 1992. Incumbent's use of pre-entry alliances before expansion into new technical subfields of an industry, *Journal of Economic Behavior and Organization,* 18: 347-372, Shan, W. 1990. An empirical analysis of organizational strategies by entrepreneurial high-technology, *Strategic Management Journal,* 11: 129–39; and Pisano, G. P. 1990. The R&D boundaries of the firm: An empirical analysis, *Administrative Science Quarterly,* 35: 153–176.

[21] Rebello, K. 1996. Inside Microsoft, *Business Week,* July 15: 56–65.

[22] Hill, C. W. L. 1992. Strategies for exploiting technological innovations: When and when not to license, *Organization Science,* 3: 428–441, Shan, W. 1990. An empirical analysis of organizational strategies by entrepreneurial high-technology, *Strategic Management Journal,* 11: 129–39; and, Teece, D. J. 1987. Profiting from technological innovation: Implications for integration, collaboration, licensing and public policy, *Research Policy,* 15: 285–305.

[23] Williamson O. E. 1985. *The Economic Institutions of Capitalism,* New York: Free Press.

[24] Kogut B. 1991. Joint ventures and the option to expand and acquire, *Management Science,* 37(1): 19–33.

[25] Hurry D., Miller, A. T. & Bowman, E. H. 1992. Calls on high-technology: Japanese exploration of venture capital investments in the United States, *Strategic Management Journal,* Vol. 13: 85–101.

[26] Bowman, E. H. & Hurry, D. 1993. Strategy through the option lens: An integrated view of resource investments and the incremental-choice process, *Academy of Management Review,* Vol. 18: 760–782.

[27] Schilling, M. A. 1998. IBID.

[28] Griffin A. 1992. Evaluating QFD's use in US firms as a process for developing products, *Journal of Product Innovation Management,* 9:171–187; and, Kimzey, C. H. 1987. *Summary of the task force work shop on industrial based initiatives.* Washington DC: Office of the Assistant Secretary of Defense, Production and Logistics.

[29] De Meyer, A. & Van Hooland, B. 1990. The contribution of manufacturing to shortening design cycle times, *R&D Management,* 20(3): 229–239, Hayes, R., Wheelwright, S. G. & Clark, K. B. 1988. *Dynamic Manufacturing.* New York: The Free Press, Cooper, R. G. 1988. The new product process: A decision guide for managers, *Journal Marketing Management,* 3: 238–255; and, Takeuchi, H. & Nonaka, I. 1986. The new product development game, *Harvard Business Review,* 64: 137–146.

[30] Zirger, B. J. & Maidique, M. A. 1990. A model of new product development: An empirical test, *Management Science,* 36: 867–883, Rothwell, R., Freeman, C., Horley, A., Jervis, P., Robertson, A. B. & Townsend, J. 1974. SAPPHO Updates—Project SAPPHO, PHASE II, *Research Policy,* 3: 258–291, Rubenstein, A. H., Chakrabarti, A. K., O'Keffe, R. D., Souder, W. E. & Young, H. C. 1976. Factors influencing innovation success at the project level, *Research Management,* May: 15–20, Johne, F. A. & Snelson, P. A. 1989. Product development approaches in established firms, *Industrial Marketing Management.* 18: 113–124; and, Wind, Y. & Mahajan, V. 1988. New product development process: A perspective for reexamination, *Journal of Product Innovation Management,* 5: 304–310.

[31] Brown, S. & Eisenhardt, K. 1995. Product development: Past research, present findings, and future directions, *Academy of Management Review,* 20(2): 343–378.

[32] Rochford, L. & Rudelius, W. 1992. How involving more functional areas within a firm affects the new product process, *Journal of Product Innovation Management*, 9: 287–299.

[33] Kimberly, J. R. & Evanisko, M. 1981. Organizational Innovation: The influence of individual, organizational and contextual factors on hospital adoption of technological and administrative innovations, *Academy of Management Journal*, 24: 689–713, Damanpour, F. 1991. Organization innovation: A meta-analysis of effects of determinants and moderators, *Academy of Management Journal*, 34(3): 555–590; and, Aiken, M. & Hage, J. 1971. The organic organization and innovation. *Sociology*, 5: 63–82.

[34] Jervis, P. 1975. Innovation and technology transfer—the roles and characteristics of individuals, *IEEE Transaction on Engineering Management*, 22: 19–27; and, Miller, D. & Friesen, P. H. 1982. Innovation in conservative and entrepreneurial firms: Two models of strategic momentum, *Strategic Management Journal*, 3:1–25.

[35] Johne, F. A. & Snelson, P. A. 1988. Success factors in product innovation, *Journal of Product Innovation Management*, 5: 114–128; and, Gluck, F. W. & Foster, R. N. 1975. Managing technological change: A box of cigars for Brad, *Harvard Business Review*, 53: 139–150.

[36] Cooper, R. G. 1985. Selecting winning new product projects: Using the NewProd system, *Journal of Product Innovation Management*, 2: 34–44.

[37] Butler, J. E. 1988. Theories of technological innovation as useful tools for corporate strategy, *Strategic Management Journal*, 9: 15–29.

[38] Asmus, D. & Griffin, J. 1993. Harnessing the power of your suppliers, *McKinsey Quarterly*, Summer (3): 63–79; and Bonaccorsi, A. & Lipparini, A. 1994. *Journal of Product Innovation Management*, 11(2): 134–146.

[39] Birou, L. & Fawcett, S. 1994. Supplier involvement in new product development: A comparison of US and European practices, *Journal of Physical Distribution and Logistics Management*, 24(5): 4–15; and Ansari, A. & Modarress, B. 1994. Quality Function Deployment: The role of suppliers. *International Journal of Purchasing and Materials Management*, 30(4): 28-36.

[40] Wheelwright, S. C. & Clark, K. B. 1992. *Revolutionizing product development: Quantum leaps in speed, efficiency and quality*. New York: Free Press.

[41] Damanpour, F. 1991. Organization innovation: A metaanalysis of effects of determinants and moderators, *Academy of Management Journal*, 34(3): 555–590.

[42] Clark, K. B. & Wheelwright, S. C. 1993. *Managing new product and process development*. New York: Free Press, McDonough, E. F. & Barczak, G. 1991. Speeding up new product development: The effects of leadership style and source of technology, *Journal of Product Innovation Management* 8: 203–211; and, Barczak, G. & Wilemon, D. 1989. Leadership differences in new product development teams, *Journal of Production and Innovation Management*, 6: 259–267.

[43] Brown, S. & Eisenhardt, K. 1995. Product development: Past research, present findings, and future directions, *Academy of Management Review*, 20(2): 343–378.

[44] Cooper, R. & Kleinschmidt, E. J. 1991. New product processes at leading industrial firms, *Industrial-Marketing-Management*, May, 20(2): 137–148.

[45] LaPlante, A. & Alter, A. E. 1994. Corning, Inc: the stage-gate innovation process, *Computerworld*. 28(44): 81.

[46] The concept was pioneered in the early 1970s at Mitsubishi's Kobe shipyard. It was then picked up and refined by Toyota and its suppliers. Among other things, at Toyota the house of quality approach to new product development was credited with improving Toyota's rust prevention record from one of the worst in the world's automobile industry to one of the best.

[47] Clark, K. B. & Wheelwright, S. C. 1993. *Managing new product and process development*. New York: Free Press, Hauser, J. R. & Clausing, D. 1988. The house of quality, *Harvard Business Review*, May–June: 63–73, Griffin, A. 1992. Evaluating QFD's use in US firms as a process for developing products, *Journal of Product Innovation Management*, 9: 171–187; and, Griffin, A. & Hauser, J. R. 1992. Patterns of communication among marketing, engineering and manufacturing, *Management Science*, 38: 360–373.

[48] Griffin, A. 1992. Evaluating QFD's use in US firms as a process for developing products, *Journal of Product Innovation Management*, 9: 171–187.

[49] Clark, K. B. & Wheelwright, S. C. 1993. *Managing new product and process development*. New York: Free Press.

[50] Millson, M. R., Raj, S. P. & Wilemon, D. 1992. A survey of major approaches for accelerating new product development, *Journal of Product Innovation Management*, 9: 53–69.

About the Authors

Melissa A. Schilling is an assistant professor of management policy at the School of Management of Boston University. Professor Schilling received her PhD in strategic management from the University of Washington in 1997. She has published several articles in peer reviewed academic journals, including the *Academy of Management Review, Journal of Management History,* and *Public Productivity and Management Review.* Her current research interests include the strategic development and management of technology, stakeholder theory, and corporate governance.

Charles W. L. Hill is the Hughes M. Blake Endowed Professor of Strategic Management and International Business at the School of Business, University of Washington. Professor Hill received his PhD in industrial organization economics in 1983 from the University of Manchester's Institute of Science and Technology (UMIST) in Britain. He has published over 40 articles in peer reviewed academic journals, including the *Academy of Management Journal, Academy of Management Review, Academy of Management Executive, Strategic Management Journal,* and *Organization Science.* He has also published two best-selling college texts, one on strategic management and the other on international business.

Eli Goldratt's first novel,
The Goal, *shook up the factory floor.*
Will Critical Chain *do the same for projects?*

BRINGING DISCIPLINE
TO PROJECT MANAGEMENT

BY JEFFREY ELTON AND JUSTIN ROE

Critical Chain
Eliyahu M. Goldratt
Great Barrington, Mass.
The North River Press, 1997

How many projects in your organization have come in on time and on budget? If you are like most senior managers, the answer is likely none. And that despite using a plethora of project-management software tools, management processes, data management systems, team-training programs, and assorted "best practices." Every manager has an excuse for why a given project comes out poorly, but attempts to plan ahead to allow for unexpected problems rarely succeed.

Are these difficulties inescapable? One business thinker who says no is Eli Goldratt, a pioneer, if not the originator, of the *theory of constraints.* As introduced in his widely read novel *The Goal,* this theory provided a persuasive solution for factories struggling with production delays and low revenues. In his third novel, *Critical Chain,* Goldratt applies the framework to managing the development of new products and other projects.

Project management is a mature area that has systemic problems similar to many found in manufacturing processes, and the theory of constraints works well when dealing with individual projects. The book falls short, however, in explaining how companies can best manage a portfolio of projects, so senior managers need to supplement it with other advice. Still, its focus on constraints may be useful for dealing with one of the most difficult and pressing of management challenges: developing highly innovative new products.

Focusing on the Constraints

The theory of constraints explains how to boost the performance of any process that involves a series of interdependent steps. Instead of breaking the process down and improving the efficiency of each step, the theory has managers focus on the bottlenecks, or constraints, that keep the process from increasing its output. Once managers identify the bottlenecks, they widen them by making them more efficient—which often means

changing policies that may promote efficiency at other steps in the process but hamper effectiveness at the crucial bottlenecks. Next, they need to limit the volume of production coming from the nonbottleneck activities to the level the bottleneck can handle. Once the overall operation is as effective as it can be at a given capacity, managers can increase output by investing in extra capacity at the bottlenecks. These steps need to be repeated over time because constraints can emerge at other points in the process.

Of course, project management texts have long told managers to focus on constraints. For projects, the constraint is the *critical path,* the series of tasks that determines the minimum time needed for the project. No matter how quickly the other tasks are completed, the project cannot be finished any sooner unless the tasks on the critical path can be done faster. But Goldratt

Jeffrey Elton is a principal and Justin Roe a consultant at Integral, a management-consulting company based in Cambridge, Massachusetts.

Reprinted by permission of *Harvard Business Review,* March/April 1998, pp. 153-159. © 1998 by the President and Fellows of Harvard College; all rights reserved.

adds an important second constraint to this framework that managers often overlook: scarce resources needed by tasks not only on and off the critical path but by other projects. In the case of developing a new product, for example, a manager may schedule the differ-

Most managers tend to pay little attention to the needs of a project as a whole. Instead, they start off with a series of dysfunctional negotiations.

ent tasks according to the pace of the critical path but still face delays because the computer-assisted design machine needed for several of the tasks is bogged down with other jobs. The *critical chain* thus refers to a combination of the critical path and the scarce resources that together constitute the constraints that need to be managed.

To keep the critical chain flowing smoothly, the book advises managers to use safety buffers similar to the inventory buffers used in production lines to make sure that bottleneck machines always have material to work on. Because managers can't predict exactly when any task will be completed, they need to allow extra time for tasks that impinge directly on the critical path. By inserting a time buffer wherever the noncritical paths feed into the critical path, the tasks on the critical path will always have what they need to proceed. For the same reason, managers need to allow extra time for tasks not on the critical path that feed into the scarce resource. (No buffers are allowed within the critical path.) Once the buffers are in place, managers must tightly schedule the activities of the scarce resource to maximize its use. As the project proceeds, managers need to monitor closely the scarce resources and the expected completion times of tasks on the critical path.

Apart from warning managers about constrained resources, the book also adds

a useful discipline to what in reality is often a chaotic process. As the book describes, most managers tend to pay little attention to the needs of a project as a whole. Instead, they start off with a series of dysfunctional negotiations to get the project approved. Project managers pad their resource requirements to buy a margin of safety. At the same time, functional departments (such as information services) understate their resource requirements so their portion of the work can come in on budget. Then senior managers cut the overall requirements for the project and move deliverable dates up because they assume that estimates for time and resources are inflated.

Project managers generally create a project plan composed of all the interrelated activities of the project, one that ascribes responsibilities and estimates resource requirements. That project plan involves a *work-breakdown structure* that defines individual tasks and then aggregates them into a large plan. The plan is arranged so that items on the critical path can be completed in time to meet milestones. But managers typically make the plan in conjunction with their budget, and they design it to validate some core assumptions related to the project's fiscal requirements. In most organizations, the significance of the plan itself diminishes from that point forward. Project managers know that the plan is only advisory and suggestive of the project's true structure and requirements. They expect to manage the actual project in real time, relying on only a core group of team members and a set of resources for which they will constantly need to negotiate throughout the project's life. As a consequence, plans are almost always "wrong" in the sense that the resources used and the time actually taken to complete tasks rarely correspond to those projected in the original project plan.

To get a sense of how imperfectly this process works, imagine that we managed corporate finances as we do projects. Pro forma income statements would mix together expenses and revenues, results from one division would be inextricably intertwined with those of another, and the timing of specific events would be so unpredictable that cash flow projections would be little more than wall art.

The most successful organizations, fortunately, have begun to bring order to

this chaos. Project teams at those companies are placing particular emphasis on coordination and communication. Advances in project management soft-

Measurements should induce the parts to do what is good for the whole.

ware that can function over extranets are making such an approach possible. And in many industries, continual communication and coordination are becoming mandatory as the time allocated for project development shrinks dramatically, the members of the development team become geographically displaced, and the projects increasingly involve external partners and resources.

To this emerging discipline of coordination made possible through technology, Goldratt essentially adds a discipline for understanding what drives project performance and therefore what the focus of a project manager's attention should be. Goldratt does not discourage the use of plans, but he implicitly warns managers that elaborate plans should not distract them from focusing on constraints. By his analogy to production bottlenecks, he indicates to managers that most projects have only one essential constraint—and at most two—and that what they should be doing, therefore, is looking for and addressing this primary constraint.

Part of the discipline Goldratt offers involves the proper use of measurements. He reminds managers of two criteria: measurements should induce the parts to do what is good for the whole, and measurements should direct managers to those parts that need their attention. Many managers rely on milestones to monitor a project's progress (and individuals' performance), but that practice violates both of the above principles. Following the maxim, How you measure people is how they'll behave, the book points out that management by milestone motivates members of project teams and their managers to insert safety time before each milestone. Once safety time has been added to each task, various mechanisms arise that waste that time. So, Goldratt concludes, the fewer the milestones, the fewer the delays. We have found such dysfunctional behavior occurring when the milestones are set as artificial review points tied to the end of a development phase or task stream.

> **Project managers should stay focused on a few critical areas and not divide their attention among all of a project's tasks and resources.**

Goldratt weaves these lessons into the story of an executive M.B.A. class at a business school struggling with declining enrollment. The class's professor, who is himself battling to get tenure, is teaching a course in project management for which he seems woefully unprepared. Along the way, he hears about the theory of constraints, and he and his students feel their way through it by applying the theory to various problems that the students are having with their own projects at work. The novel displays a genuine understanding of the experiences of project managers across organizations in all industries.

As in *The Goal,* this fictional approach makes for easy reading. But while the factory setting in *The Goal* established a realistic context in which to develop and test the theory, *Critical Chain's* academic environment does not sufficiently bind together the various real-world vignettes. As a consequence, the reader is presented with hearsay evidence rather than given the opportunity to work through a full application of the theory during the course of the book.

The book is valuable to two main audiences: project managers and senior managers. Project managers and their teams will appreciate its main message: remain focused on a few critical areas and do not divide your attention among all of a project's tasks and resources.

Project phases do not matter, milestones are largely meaningless, and building large project plans out of streams of concurrent or sequential activities is not useful. Instead, the book suggests, we need to "design" a project in the same way we design a product. The project design needs to identify the potential sources of failure—critical-path tasks and critical resources—and then insert resource and work buffers to ensure maximum throughput.

The book addresses the concerns of senior managers in a brief discussion at its conclusion. Those managers need to know how to juggle a portfolio of projects, and the book's only advice on that subject is to make sure to allocate resources carefully across projects to minimize the constraints on the shared resources. But in our experience, managing project portfolios is far more com-

> **Many of the delays in individual projects arise from problems at the senior management level.**

plicated—and many of the delays in individual projects arise from problems at the senior management level rather than from mistakes made by project managers. The book is both accurate and useful in discussing the theory of constraints as it applies to individual projects, but it may not give senior managers enough insight to enable them to handle multiple projects. To attain substantial improvement there, senior managers will likely need to extend Goldratt's systematic perspective to the level of multiple, concurrent projects and add some elements that *Critical Chain* either ignores or gives short shrift.

Advice in this area is all the more important now, as the pace at which markets change in all industries quickens, the increased use of standard components and processes accelerates the rate of technological innovation, and expectations about customer service and product performance continue to rise. In response, companies are spending more time on projects and less

time on routine activities. The number of books and articles on project management, especially for developing new products, is burgeoning. Most major consulting firms have significant practices in this area, and the number of M.B.A. courses on this topic is increasing. Yet the success stories are few and often based on the same corporate examples, and the performance of project teams remains generally lackluster.

Managing Projects as a Portfolio

Focusing on individual projects allows Goldratt to give us useful and well-illustrated advice, but it does not allow him to examine some important drivers of project performance: namely, how well new initiatives align with strategy and how successfully an organization balances its overall capacity and capabilities with its portfolio of projects. Managers cannot isolate and control different projects as easily as they can handle different factory-production processes.

What senior managers need is the wider perspective of aggregate project planning, which Steven C. Wheelright and Kim B. Clark defined in "Creating Project Plans to Focus Product Development" (HBR March–April 1992). Too often, projects fall short of resources or lose direction because of a lack of agreement among senior business and functional managers. This misalignment of goals can lead executives to make a number of mistakes. They may slow a project down by failing to take necessary actions or by limiting the available resources. They may fail to kill a project (the "undead") in order to avoid disappointing another executive or project team. The net effect is that most organizations have too many projects relative to their available capacity, and those projects, when viewed as a set, only distantly resemble the company's strategic intent.

Even if the right projects are picked, the way the projects relate to one another, coupled with pressure to get the highest return from the investment in development, can easily lead to an excess demand on limited resources. And even when resources seem to be adequate, projects can still fall short because the company doesn't have adequate skills for some parts of the product development process. Rapidly shrinking product and technology cycles make it increasingly difficult for companies to excel at all aspects of a project, so many of them are allying with outsiders. Senior managers need to balance the requirements of their projects with their company's capabilities and those of their partners.

As a result, the progress of any individual project is limited by factors outside an individual manager's control. Goldratt would have presented a richer prescription for project management had

When the degree of change is great, managers need to approach projects differently.

he fully extended the theory of constraints to the portfolio level. He does so when he considers the issue of scheduling the resource bottleneck, but he does not address the issue of stagnation caused by running too many projects at the same time. Reducing the overall number of projects relieves constraints on common resources; companies can then give remaining projects the resources they need and stop managers from wasting their energy in negotiations aimed at overcoming the constraints.

Putting Flexibility Where It Counts

Goldratt's narrower focus, interestingly, may be ideal for certain kinds of new-product development. While many companies excel at understanding current customers' requirements and at integrating established technologies into their new products, they often do poorly when they tackle technologies that represent a fundamental change in a product's design or purpose—what Clayton Christensen called *discontinuous technologies* in *The Innovator's Dilemma* (Harvard Business School Press, 1997). When the degree of change involved is great, managers need to approach projects differently. Projects incorporating

discontinuous technologies involve much more risk and require managers to apply stringent and individualized criteria for determining how to proceed.

Because it focuses on eliminating constraints, which are necessarily unique in every project, the book does not show managers how to establish a detailed product-development process. But for projects involving discontinuous technology, the less managers try to lay out beforehand, the better. Projects incorporating discontinuous technologies by definition involve work outside a company's experience. In such cases, a detailed project plan would give managers a false sense of security, but if they pay attention to the constraints, they will be on their way to capturing and consistently managing the essential risks of their project. They need to rely on their intuitions about where the pressure points are likely to arise and focus on managing those sources of risk. The book's highly intuitive approach may help in this area. Nor can senior managers help the project managers much in such cases: discontinuous projects tend not to require the same kinds of resources that more conservative projects need.

Nevertheless, even innovative projects may require more structure than the book describes. Given the high degree of uncertainty involved, such projects usually need some milestones, not to act as arbitrary checkpoints but to serve as opportunities to reassess the project's viability. Fundamental to Goldratt's recommendation to eliminate milestones is the assumption that all projects that are begun should be completed. But in many industries, especially those in which most of the investment takes place at later stages of product development, companies may do well by starting many more projects than they expect to finish and then culling them along the way. And in some cases, milestones are not just self-imposed deadlines, they are hard stops. For instance, in the pharmaceutical and medical-products industry, the milestone may be the completion of a regulatory filing required for approval by the Federal Drug Administration, which must be obtained before the project can move forward. Between milestones, which are often years apart, managers can still run the projects by concentrating on the constraints.

The scheduling of milestones that mark the phases of a project may need to change, however. When it comes to products for the Internet and other fast-emerging technologies, customers' needs are

changing so rapidly that traditional, sequential product-development processes run the risk of generating products that are already obsolete by the time they are released. As Marco Iansiti and Alan MacCormack pointed out in "Developing Products on Internet Time" (HBR, September-October 1997), companies in those industries have responded by modifying the traditional sequential development process to allow changes in product design right up to the last possible moment. Their managers employ a rapidly iterative product-development process that involves successive rounds of customer feedback, development, and testing in order to integrate the latest knowledge of markets and technologies into their new products. Goldratt's flexible approach may be more easily applied to products that need to or can be frequently modified than to capital-intensive or mission-critical products, such as aircraft engines. For these latter products, milestones play a crucial role as checkpoints that guard against making changes that can cause great expense or may have possible catastrophic consequences.

Finding the Ultimate Constraint

Ultimately, the parallels between process and project management give way to a fundamental difference: process management seeks to eliminate variability, whereas project management must accept variability because each project is unique. That is especially true for new-product development, which involves taking a vague concept for a new service or

Project performance is often less a matter of understanding constraints and more a function of personal skills.

product that a particular market or customer segment will find valuable and turning it into an actual ongoing business proposition. Multiple individuals, functions, and increasingly even separate companies contribute to the concept's realization.

A significant weakness of *Critical Chain,* therefore, is that it leads us to believe that project management can be successfully accomplished largely through the same rational approach that works for production management. But projects involve much higher levels of uncertainty than processes do and depend much more on the contributions of individuals. For example, the book advises managers to work with the different individuals and functional departments involved in a project to set estimates for lead times so that they meet the needs of the critical chain. But anyone who has worked on a project, been a manager of key personnel on a project, or been a senior manager mediating a resource

conflict among a number of projects knows that it is a rare organizational culture indeed that is capable of such an impersonal, rational approach to setting lead times. Organizations with an open, team-oriented environment at all levels, that tie the way they compensate individuals and measure their performance to the realization of common goals, are the ones most capable of this form of collaborative management.

Essential to fostering the necessary collaboration are project managers who can handle the political, as well as the technical, aspects of their projects. But when we ask executives to give us the names of all the people in their companies who are qualified to serve as the manager for the next major project, we are fortunate to get a list of three. Project performance is often less a matter

of understanding the constraints of the project and more a function of the personal skills and capabilities of the potential leaders available. The skill to lead a team through unknowns depends not just on acquired but on inherent capabilities. Managers of product development projects also need unique leadership skills, such as the ability to perceive customers' future requirements before customers themselves can articulate those as-yet-unrealized needs. In our experience, the potential number of such leaders in almost all organizations is limited, usually fewer than ten. Critical Chain starts with a set of talented and driven project managers and assumes the resource constraints are inside the work of the project, not in its leadership. In truth, leadership may be the larger constraint.

Seven Keys to Better Forecasting

Mark A. Moon, John T. Mentzer, Carlo D. Smith, and Michael S. Garver

S ales forecasting is a management function that companies often fail to recognize as a key contributor to corporate success. From a top-line perspective, accurate sales forecasts allow a company to provide high levels of customer service. When demand can be predicted accurately, it can be met in a timely and efficient manner, keeping both channel partners and final customers satisfied. Accurate forecasts help a company avoid lost sales or stock-out situations, and prevent customers from going to competitors.

At the bottom line, the effect of accurate forecasts can be profound. Raw materials and component parts can be purchased much more cost-effectively when last minute, spot market purchases can be avoided. Such expenses can be eliminated by accurately forecasting production needs. Similarly, logistical services can be obtained at a much lower cost through long-term contracts rather than through spot market arrangements. However, these contracts can only work when demand can be predicted accurately. Perhaps most important, accurate forecasting can have a profound impact on a company's inventory levels. In a sense, inventory exists to provide a buffer for inaccurate forecasts. Thus, the more accurate the forecasts, the less inventory that needs to be carried, with all the well-understood cost savings that brings.

The ultimate effects of sales forecasting excellence can be dramatic. Mentzer and Schroeter (1993) describe how Brake Parts, Inc., a manufacturer of automotive aftermarket parts, improved its bottom line by $6 million per month after launching a company-wide effort to improve sales forecasting effectiveness. Nevertheless, firms often fail to recognize the importance of this critical management function. Our objective here is to take what we've learned about sales forecasting from working with hundreds of companies, and summarize that learning into seven key focus points (summarized in **Figure 1**) that will help any company improve its forecasting performance. Although no management function can be reduced to seven keys, or 70 keys for that matter, our hope is that the ideas presented here will inspire senior management to look closely at their own sales forecasting practices and recognize opportunities for improvement.

> *Excellence in sales forecasting can boost a firm's financial health and gratify customers and employees alike.*

Key #1: Understand What Forecasting Is, and What It Is Not

The first and perhaps most important key to better forecasting is a complete understanding of what it actually is and—of equal importance—what it is not. Sales forecasting is a management process, not a computer program. This distinction is important because it affects so many areas across an organization. Regardless of whether a company sells goods or services, it must have a clear picture of how many of those goods or services it can sell, in both the short and long terms. That way, it can plan to have an adequate supply to meet customer demand.

Reprinted from *Business Horizons*, September/October 1998, pp. 44-52. © 1998 by the Foundation for the School of Business at Indiana University. Used with permission.

Figure 1
The Seven Keys to Better Forecasting

Keys	Issues and Symptoms	Actions	Results
Understand what forecasting is and is not.	• Computer system as focus, rather than management processes and controls • Blurring of the distinction between forecasts, plans, and goals	• Establish forecasting group • Implement management control systems before selecting forecasting software • Derive plans from forecasts • Distinguish between forecasts and goals	• An environment in which forecasting is acknowledged as a critical business function • Accuracy emphasized and game-playing minimized
Forecast demand, plan supply.	• Shipment history as the basis for forecasting demand • "Too accurate" forecasts	• Identify sources of information • Build systems to capture key demand data	• Improved capital planning and customer service
Communicate, cooperate, collaborate.	• Duplication of forecasting effort • Mistrust of the "official" forecast • Little understanding of the impact throughout the firm	• Establish cross-functional approach to forecasting • Establish independent forecast group that sponsors cross-functional collaboration	• All relevant information used to generate forecasts • Forecasts trusted by users • Islands of analysis eliminated • More accurate and relevant forecasts
Eliminate islands of analysis.	• Mistrust and inadequate information leading different users to create their own forecasts	• Build a single "forecasting infrastructure" • Provide training for both users and developers of forecasts	• More accurate, relevant, and credible forecasts • Optimized investments in information/communication systems.
Use tools wisely.	• Relying solely on qualitative or quantitative methods • Cost/benefit of additional information	• Integrate quantitative and qualitative methods • Identify sources of improved accuracy and increased error • Provide instruction	• Process improvement in efficiency and effectiveness
Make it important.	• No accountability for poor forecasts • Developers not understanding how forecasts are used	• Training developers to understand implications of poor forecasts • Include forecast performance in individual performance plans and reward systems	• Developers taking forecasts seriously • A striving for accuracy • More accuracy and credibility
Measure, measure, measure.	• Not knowing if the firm is getting better • Accuracy not measured at relevant levels of aggregation • Inability to isolate sources of forecast error	• Establish multidimensional metrics • Incorporate multilevel measures • Measure accuracy whenever and wherever forecasts are adjusted	• Forecast performance can be included in individual performance plans • Sources of errors can be isolated and targeted for improvement • Greater confidence in forecast process

Forecasting is critical to a company's production or operations department. Adequate materials must be obtained at the lowest possible price; adequate production facilities must be provided at the lowest possible cost; adequate labor must be hired and trained at the lowest possible cost; and adequate logistics services must be used to avoid bottlenecks in moving products from producers to consumers. None of these fundamental business functions can be performed effectively without accurate sales forecasts.

Many companies consider the most important decisions about forecasting to revolve around the selection or development of computer software for preparing the forecasts. They have adopted the overly simplistic belief that "If we've got good software, we'll have good forecasting." Our research team, however, has observed numerous instances of sophisticated computer systems put into place, costing enormous amounts of time and money, that have failed to deliver accurate forecasts. This is because system implementation has not been accompanied by effective management to monitor and control the forecasting process.

One company we worked with has an excellent computer system with impressive capabilities of performing sophisticated statistical modeling of seasonality and other trends. However, the salespeople, who are the originators of the forecast, use none of these tools because they do not understand them and have no confidence in the numbers generated. As a result, their forecasts are based solely on qualitative factors and are often very inaccurate. A similar case is a technology-based company that has created another highly sophisticated forecasting tool, yet the salespeople continue to underforecast significantly because their forecasts have a direct effect on their sales quotas. Both of these examples show how some companies focus on forecasting *systems* rather than forecasting *management*.

On the other hand, some companies have been more successful in their efforts by recognizing the importance of forecasting as a management process. Some have organized independent groups or departments that are responsible for the entire forecasting process, both short- and long-term. One large chemical company has formed a forecasting group not associated with either marketing or production. It has ownership and accountability for all aspects of forecasting management, with responsibility not only for the systems used to forecast but also for the numbers themselves. The group accomplishes its mission in several ways: providing training in the methods and processes throughout the company; designing compensation systems that reward forecast accuracy; and facilitating communication among sales, marketing, finance, and production departments, thereby improving overall forecasting effectiveness. Recognizing the importance of forecasting, this firm has put an organization in place to manage the process, not just to choose and manage a system.

Another way in which companies confuse what forecasts are and what they are not is by failing to understand the relationship between forecasting, planning, and goal setting. A sales forecast should be viewed as an estimate of what future sales might be, given certain environmental conditions. A sales plan should be seen as a management decision or commitment to what the company will do during the planning period. A sales goal should be a target that everyone in the organization strives to attain and exceed.

Each of these numbers serves a different purpose. The primary purpose of the sales forecast is to help management formulate its sales plan and other related business plans—its commitment to future activity. The sales plan's purpose is to drive numerous tactical and strategic management decisions (raw material purchases, human resource planning, logistics planning, and so on), realistically factoring in the constraints of the firm's resources, procedures, and systems. The sales goal is primarily designed to provide motivation for people throughout the organization in meeting and exceeding corporate targets.

Whereas the sales forecast and the sales plan should be closely linked (the former should precede and influence the latter), the sales goal may be quite independent. The objective of those who receive a sales goal should be to beat that goal. It can be developed based on a sales forecast, plan, and motivation levels. However, because forecasters should strive for accuracy, it is not appropriate for a forecast to be confused with the firm's motivational strategy.

It is particularly problematic when sales forecasts and sales goals are intertwined, because this mixture

THE RESEARCH

The ideas presented in this article are drawn from a program of research that has spanned more than 15 years. **Phase 1** began in 1982 with a mail survey of 157 companies that explored the techniques they used to forecast. Ten years later, under the sponsorship of AT&T Network Systems, the survey was replicated and expanded in **Phase 2** to explore not only techniques but also the systems and management processes used by 208 companies. **Phase 3**, conducted between 1994 and 1996, was sponsored by a consortium of companies consisting of AT&T Network Systems, Andersen Consulting, Anheuser-Busch, and Pillsbury. It took the form of a benchmarking study that consisted of in-depth analysis of 20 companies: Anheuser-Busch, Becton-Dickinson, Coca-Cola, Colgate-Palmolive, Federal Express, Kimberly Clark, Lykes Pasco, Nabisco, JCPenney, Pillsbury, ProSource, Reckitt Colman, Red Lobster, RJR Tobacco, Sandoz, Schering Plough, Sysco, Tropicana, Warner Lambert, and Westwood Squibb. Finally, **Phase 4** has been conducted since 1996 and consists of a series of forecast audits. The forecasting practices of seven companies—Allied Signal, Du Pont Agricultural Products Canada, Eastman Chemical, Hershey Foods USA, Lucent Technologies, Michelin North America, and Union Pacific Railroad—have been studied so far in this phase and compared to those of the 20 benchmarked companies. The references to this research are listed at the end of this article.

In addition to these formal studies, the learning presented here is augmented by more than 20 years of experience in consulting with a large number of major corporations on their forecasting systems and processes. Our ideas are drawn from firsthand observation of what actually works in sales forecasting in companies, large and small, that sell products and services and that are manufacturers, distributors, or retailers.

"In one company, the production scheduling department was so distrustful of the forecasts developed by marketing that it completely ignored them and created a whole 'black market' forecasting system."

leads to considerable game playing, especially involving the sales force. If salespeople believe that long-term forecasts will affect the size of the next year's quota, they will be strongly motivated to underforecast, hoping to influence those quotas to be low and attainable. Alternatively, as one salesman at a parts supply company put it, "It would be suicide for me to submit a forecast that was under my targets." In both cases, because goals and forecasts are so intertwined, salespeople are motivated to "play games" with their forecasts. There is a built-in disincentive to strive for accuracy.

Some companies have expressed a reluctance to "manage to different numbers," suggesting that when the forecast and the goals differ, it creates confusion and lack of focus. The reaction to such perceived confusion is to develop inaccurate forecasts that can affect performance throughout the company. We believe the sales forecast and the sales goal must be distinct, because the behaviors they are meant to influence can conflict.

Key # 2: Forecast Demand, Plan Supply

One mistake many companies make is forecasting their ability to supply goods or services rather than actual customer demand. At the beginning of the forecast cycle, it is important to create predictions that are not constrained by the firm's capacity to produce. Consider the forecaster for a certain product who questions the company's sales force and learns they could sell 1,500 units per month. At the same time, current manufacturing capacity for that product is 1,000 units per month. If the forecaster takes that production capacity into account when creating initial forecasts, and predicts 1,000 units, there is no record of the unmet demand of 500 units per month, and the information on where to expand manufacturing capacity is lost.

This problem often occurs when historical shipments are used as the basis for generating forecasts. Forecasting shipments will only predict a company's previous ability to meet demand. Suppose demand

for a particular product in the past had been 10,000 units per month, but the supplier could only ship 7,500. Corporate history would show shipments at 7,500 units per month, thus causing this amount to be projected and produced again the following month. The result is twofold: the impression of an accurate forecasting system, but an actually recurring unfulfilled monthly demand of 2,500 units. Forecasting based on shipping history only leads a company to repeat its former mistakes of not satisfying customer demand. Predicting actual demand allows measurement of the disparity between demand and supply so it can be reduced in future periods through plans for capacity expansion.

Often the symptom of this key is the attitude, "We do a great job of forecasting. We are very accurate, always selling close to what we forecast." Notice in the previous example that the forecast accuracy would appear very good because both the forecast and the actual sales were 7,500 units each month. The key, however, is the failure to realize the 2,500 units in sales lost each month because of an inability to meet demand. In fact, the "true" demand forecasting accuracy was not 100 percent, but only 75 percent. Forecasting by shipments and obtaining accurate results are often symptomatic of chronic underforecasting of demand.

Unfortunately, determining actual customer demand is more difficult than predicting a company's ability to supply. Systems and processes are needed to capture this elusive demand that was not fulfilled. Mechanisms are needed to allow salespeople to provide valuable information about customers who would order more if they could. In addition, records of orders accepted but not filled in the period demanded adds to the demand versus supply level of information. Finally, such electronic data interchange (EDI) information as point-of-sale (POS) demand, retail inventory levels, and retailer forecasts are all valuable sources of information that help a company move toward demand forecasting.

Although it is more difficult, forecasting true demand will help a company make sensible, long-term decisions that can profoundly affect its market position. By identifying where capacity does not meet demand forecasts, the company has valuable information on where to expand capacity through capital planning. Such a long-term program of matching capacity planning to forecasts will reduce the incidence of chronic underforecasting and result in higher levels of customer satisfaction.

Key # 3: Communicate, Cooperate, Collaborate

Companies that forecast most effectively consider it critical to obtain input from people in different functional areas, each of whom contributes relevant information and insights that can improve overall accuracy. But employees are often unable or unwilling to work across functions to achieve high levels of forecasting performance. To do so requires a great deal of communication across department boundaries, and not all communicating is equal; some companies are simply better at it than others.

When it comes to cross-functional forecasting, we distinguish among three levels: communication, cooperation, and collaboration. Companies at lower levels of sophistication merely *communicate*. This can take the form of one-way reports, in which one department responsible for forecasting informs other functional areas of the results of its efforts. With *coordination*, representatives from different functional groups meet to discuss the forecast. Often, however, one area—usually the one that "owns" the forecast—will dominate the discussions and work to persuade the other functions to accept the forecast it has created.

Coordination is superior to one-way communication, because at least there is opportunity for some dialogue. But it does not promote as effective a forecasting process as when different constituencies in a company *collaborate*. Here, the views of each functional area receive equal consideration, and no one department dominates. Such collaboration is most likely to occur when management of the forecasting process resides in an independent department instead of being part of marketing, finance, logistics, or production. Each area, with its unique biases and agendas, can contribute equally to a true consensus forecast.

In several companies we have worked with, the functional area responsible for generating forecasts—usually marketing—makes little effort to obtain input from other affected areas, such as production planning, operations, or logistics. A number of negative consequences result. First, critical information about production lead times or capacity constraints are not taken into account when the forecast is finalized. Because this information is missing, forecast users have little trust in projections they did not help develop. This lack of trust leads to duplicated forecasting efforts. In one company, the production scheduling department was so distrustful of the forecasts developed by marketing that it completely ignored them and created a whole "black market" forecasting system. Had a consensus-based approach been used, such nonproductive duplication of efforts could have been avoided.

A further consequence of not working cross-functionally is a lack of understanding of the assumptions that go into forecasts, which leads to further distrust. In another company, a production scheduler would adjust the forecasts to take into account the seasonality she believed was present in the marketplace. However, she was not aware that the marketing department had already accounted for that

seasonality in the information they gave her. Had production planning been involved in a consensus-based forecasting process, the scheduler's adjustments—which skewed the forecasts—would not have been made.

It is most important in effective forecasting to establish a mechanism that brings people from multiple organizational areas together in a spirit of collaboration. Such a mechanism, often organized by an inde-

> *"The key is that both quantitative and qualitative tools are integral to effective sales forecasting."*

pendent forecasting group, ensures that all relevant information is considered before forecasts are created. One such mechanism is in place at a national consumer products firm, in which the forecasting group organizes and holds regularly scheduled, half-day meetings that bring together representatives from National Accounts (sales), product management (marketing), production planning, logistics, and finance. Each participant comes to the meeting prepared to discuss upcoming issues that will affect sales and demand over the forecast period. Formal minutes are kept to document the reasons for making adjustments. The end product is a consensus forecast, with numbers that its users have helped develop. Duplicate forecasting efforts are eliminated and all the parties can trust the final result: a more accurate and relevant forecast.

Key # 4: Eliminate Islands of Analysis

Islands of analysis are distinct areas within a firm that perform similar functions. Each area maintains a separate process, thereby performing redundant tasks and often having the same responsibilities. Because islands of analysis are often supported by independent computer systems (which often are not electronically linked to other systems within the firm), information contained within the different islands is not shared between them.

In our research, we have identified forecasting islands in logistics, production planning, finance, and marketing. They have usually emerged because of a lack of interfunctional collaboration between units, which leads to a lack of credibility associated with the forecast. Because the "official" forecast generated in a particular department may not be credible to forecast users, the latter often take steps to implement processes and systems to create their own forecast.

Islands of analysis are detrimental to corporate performance. Forecasts developed in this manner are often inaccurate and inconsistent. Because each area maintains its own forecasting process and often its own computer system, data—if shared at all—are shared only through manual transfers, which are prone to human errors. When completely separate systems are used, the assumptions that underlie the forecasts, such as pricing levels and marketing programs, tend to differ from one system to the next. Moreover, each area forecasts with a unique bias, making separate predictions inconsistent and unusable by other areas. Redundancies generated by separate systems cost the firm both money and valuable personnel time and energy. Employee frustration builds up, along with an overall lack of confidence in the forecasting process.

To solve this problem, management must devote attention to eliminating the factors that encourage the development of islands of analysis. Such a goal can be reached by establishing a single process supported by a "forecasting infrastructure." This process should consist of software that communicates seamlessly with other information systems in the firm. Appropriate tools should include a suite of statistical techniques, graphical programs, and an ability to capture and report performance metrics over time. Historical sales data can be accessed from a centrally maintained "data warehouse" that is electronically available to all functional areas and provides real-time data.

Once this forecasting infrastructure is in place, effective training aimed at a common understanding of the process and its system should be implemented for both users and developers. Employees should be trained to comprehend the overall process, each individual's role in the process, and the importance of accurate forecasting. They must be able to use the system effectively and efficiently.

Once islands of analysis are eliminated, the company can expect improved forecasting performance and significant cost savings. Forecasts will be more precise, more credible, and better able to meet the needs of various departments. When systems are electronically linked, the errors that result from manual data transfers can be avoided, and the necessary information can be accessible to all functional areas. From a cost perspective, a single forecasting process eliminates redundant efforts within the firm, thus saving valuable employee time and other resources. And because accuracy will be improved, all the well-documented cost savings in areas such as purchasing, inventory control, and logistics planning can be tracked and realized.

Key # 5: Use Tools Wisely

Many companies tend to rely solely on qualitative tools—the opinions of experienced managers and/or salespeople—to derive forecasts, ignoring such quantitative tools as regression and time-series analysis. Alternatively, many companies expect the application of quantitative tools, or the computer packages that make use of them, to "solve the forecasting problem." The key is that both quantitative and qualitative tools are integral to effective sales forecasting. To be effective, however, they must be understood and used wisely within the context of the firm's unique business environment. Without understanding where qualitative techniques, time series, and regression do and do not work effectively, it is impossible to analyze the costs and achieve the benefits of implementing new forecasting tools.

One common symptom of a failure to realize this key is the existence of detailed sales forecasting processes that, when examined, reveal the subjective judgments of managers or salespeople as the only input used in the forecast. In other words, the company has a quantitative sales forecasting process that supports only qualitative forecasts. It relies too much on the ability of experienced personnel to translate what they know into a forecast number, without taking into account the myriad of quantitative techniques and their ability to analyze patterns in the history of demand.

The opposite symptom is a sales forecasting process that performs intensive numerical analysis of demand history and the factors that relate statistically to changes in demand, but with no qualitative information on the nature of the market and what causes demand to change. The company depends too much on the ability of these techniques to determine estimates of future demand without taking experience into account.

A variation on these symptoms is relying on a "black box" forecasting system. This occurs when a company has a sales forecasting computer package, or "box," into which historical sales data are fed and the forecasts come out, but no one seems to know how it comes up with them, or even what techniques it uses. The company abrogates its responsibility by turning the important job of sales forecasting over to a computer package that nobody understands.

Using forecasting tools wisely requires knowing where each type of tool works well and where it does not, then putting together a process that uses the advantages of each in the unique context of the firm. Salespeople who do a poor job of turning their experience into an initial forecast may be good at taking an initial quantitative forecast and qualitatively adjusting it to improve overall accuracy. Time series models work well in companies that experience changing trends and seasonal patterns, but they are of no use in determining the relationship between demand and such external factors as price changes, economic activity, or marketing efforts by the company and its competitors. On the other hand, regression analysis is quite effective at assessing these relationships, but not very useful in forecasting changes in trend and seasonality.

To apply this key, a process should be implemented that uses time series to forecast trend and seasonality, regression analysis to forecast demand relationships with external factors, and qualitative input from salespeople, marketing, and general management to adjust these initial quantitative forecasts. This general recommendation must be refined for each individual company by finding the specific techniques that provide the most improved accuracy. Finally, key personnel involved in either the quantitative or the qualitative aspects of the forecasting process need training in using the techniques, determining where they work and do not work, and incorporating qualitative adjustments in the overall forecasting process.

Key # 6: Make It Important

What gets measured gets rewarded, and what gets rewarded gets done, say Mentzer and Bienstock (1998). This management truism is the driver behind our final two keys. Sales forecasting is often described by senior management as an important function. But although this assessment may be shared by individuals throughout the firm, few organizations institute policies and practices reinforcing the notion that forecasting is important for business success. There is often a gap between management's words and their actions. Companies frequently tell those who develop forecasts that "forecasting is important," but then fail to reward them for doing the job well or punish them for doing it poorly. Forecast users become frustrated by a perceived lack of interest and accountability for accuracy among forecasters. Such frustration often leads them to manipulate existing forecasts or, in the extreme case, develop islands of analysis that duplicate forecasting efforts and ignore valuable ideas.

One way to gauge how important forecasting is to a firm is to determine how familiar users and developers are with the entire process. Without such familiarity, individuals involved in forecasting throughout the firm have little appreciation of the impact of their inaccuracies and are therefore unlikely to spend the time and attention needed to do the job well. As a result, users perceive that forecasters are not taking the task seriously and thus discount the value of what they produce.

A number of actions can be taken to address this gap in forecasting importance. One way is to give all

> *"Salespeople, product managers, and other forecasters will see the importance of the task if salient rewards follow as a result of forecasting excellence."*

individuals involved adequate training. Forecast creators and users must know where and how forecasts are used throughout the firm. When forecasters become aware of all the downstream ramifications of sloppy work, the task takes on more relevance to them. Marketing and salespeople who typically are concerned about forecasting only at the product or product line level should understand that this does not provide the necessary detail for operations to plan stock-keeping unit (SKU) production or for logistics to make SKUL (by location) shipment plans. Similarly, forecast users should be more aware of the needs and capabilities of forecast developers.

Another action management can take is to incorporate forecasting performance measures into job performance evaluation criteria. Clearly, salespeople, product managers, and other forecasters will see the importance of the task if salient rewards follow as a result of forecasting excellence. Even senior managers become interested when the metrics of accuracy are worked into their personal performance evaluations and bonus plans.

But focusing on senior management is not enough. One company includes forecast accuracy as a meaningful part of the performance plans of its senior executives, but not of those on the "front line" who work with forecasts on a daily basis. The job has not been made to seem important to those who do it, with the effect that it is still not done very well.

This is particularly true of the people who are typically responsible for initial forecast input—the sales force. At nearly all the benchmark and audit companies, salespeople are critically important pieces of the forecasting puzzle. Yet in almost all cases, the ones who develop forecasts receive neither feedback on how well they forecast nor any type of reward for doing it well. Many agree with a salesman for a high-tech manufacturer, who said, "My job is to sell, not forecast." Similarly, product managers, who also provide critical input to the forecasting process at many companies, often consider forecasting an extra burden that takes them away from their "real jobs."

Key # 7: Measure, Measure, Measure

Obviously, before forecasters can be rewarded for excellence, a company must first develop systems for measuring performance, tools for providing feedback, and standards and targets for what constitutes forecasting excellence. Without the ability to effectively measure and track performance, there is little opportunity to identify whether changes in the development and application of forecasts are contributing to, or hindering, business success. This key may be intuitive for most business managers, yet our research has identified surprisingly few companies that systematically measure forecasting management performance. In cases where measures have been implemented, they are infrequently used for performance assessment or to identify opportunities for improvement.

A primary symptom indicating a lack of performance measurement can be gleaned from conversations with individuals involved in the forecasting process. Simply asking for a measure of forecasting accuracy typically elicits a response of "pretty good," "lousy," or other general descriptors. In some cases, the answer may include a number considered to be a measure of accuracy, such as "75 percent," or error, such as "25 percent." Further inquiry may indicate that the source of the measure is based on a general "feeling," estimate, or a second- or third-hand source of information, and the respondent is unsure of how such measures were calculated or what level of aggregation was used.

In cases where measures are collected and documented, there may still be insufficient detail or little realization as to how they can help identify opportunities for forecasting improvement. Generally we have found that even when accuracy has been measured over time, few individuals who contribute to forecast development review the history and can determine whether their performance has improved, remained constant, or deteriorated. This reflects a complacency toward performance measures when such measures are not used to evaluate a person's job performance, or do not provide support for identifying sources of forecasting error.

Effective measures evaluate accuracy at different levels of aggregation. Logistics operations are interested in forecast performance at the SKUL level; sales managers may be more interested in a forecast stated in dollars and at the territory or product line level of aggregation. Performance metrics should support these various units of measure as well as the aggregation of demand at different levels.

It is also important to track accuracy at each point at which forecasts may be adjusted. As an illustration, the forecasting task of the sales force of one company is to examine "machine-generated" forecasts for their customers and make adjustments. Those adjustments are then measured against actual sales to determine whether the salesperson's adjustment improved the forecast or not. Similarly, the product manager's job is to take the machine-generated forecast, which has been adjusted by the sales force, and make further adjustments based on a knowledge of market conditions or upcoming promotional events. Once again, these adjustments are measured against actual sales to determine whether they improved the forecast. In both cases, the salespeople and the product manager gain feedback that helps them improve their efforts.

Finally, companies should assess forecasting accuracy in terms of its impact on business performance. Accurate forecasts should not be an end in themselves, but rather a means to achieving the end, which is business success. Improvements in accuracy require expenditures of resources, both human and financial, and should be approached in a return-on-investment framework. For example, in a distribution environment, maintaining or improving customer service may be a worthy corporate objective. Investment in more accurate forecasts may be one way to achieve that objective. However, if the investment required to improve accuracy significantly is very high, then alternative approaches to improving customer service, such as carrying higher inventory levels, should be considered. The resulting strategy for improving customer service will then be based on sound business analysis.

Measuring and tracking accuracy will ultimately help build confidence in the forecasting process. As the users realize mechanisms are in place to identify and eliminate sources of error, they will probably use the primary forecast developed to support all operations in the company. Islands of analysis will begin to disappear, and the organization will be able to assess the financial return from forecasting management improvements.

As we work with companies, many of them come to realize what a profound impact these seven keys can have on their sales forecasting practices. As they improve those practices, they experience reductions in costs and increases in customer and employee satisfaction. Costs decline in inventory levels, raw materials, production, logistics, and transportation. Greater customer satisfaction accrues from more accurately anticipating demand and, subsequently, fulfilling that demand more often. Greater employee satisfaction comes from a more understandable process, easier information access and transfer, and explicit rewards tied to performance. But the first step any company must take before realizing these benefits is to recognize the importance of sales forecasting as a management function. With this recognition comes a willingness to commit the necessary resources to improving this critical process.

References

Kenneth B. Kahn and John T. Mentzer, "The Impact of Team-Based Forecasting," *Journal of Business Forecasting,* Summer 1994, pp. 18–21.

Kenneth B. Kahn and John T. Mentzer, "Forecasting in Consumer and Business Markets," *Journal of Business Forecasting,* Summer 1995, pp. 21–28.

John T. Mentzer and Carol C. Bienstock, *Sales Forecasting Management* (Thousand Oaks, CA: Sage Publications, 1998).

John T. Mentzer and James E. Cox, Jr., "A Model of the Determinants of Achieved Forecast Accuracy," *Journal of Business Logistics, 5,* 2 (1984a): 143-155.

John T. Mentzer and James E. Cox, Jr., "Familiarity, Application, and Performance of Sales Forecasting Techniques," *Journal of Forecasting, 3* (1984b): 27-36.

John T. Mentzer and Kenneth B. Kahn, "Forecasting Technique Familiarity, Satisfaction, Usage, and Application," *Journal of Forecasting, 14,* 5 (1995): 465-476.

John T. Mentzer and Kenneth B. Kahn, "The State of Sales Forecasting Systems in Corporate America," *Journal of Business Forecasting,* Spring 1997, pp. 6-13.

John T. Mentzer, Kenneth B. Kahn, and Carol C. Bienstock, "Sales Forecasting Benchmarking Study," Research Report No. 3560–ROI-1445-99-004-96, University of Tennessee, Knoxville, 1996.

John T. Mentzer and Jon Schroeter, "Multiple Forecasting System at Brake Parts, Inc.," *Journal of Business Forecasting,* Fall 1993, pp. 5-9.

Mark A. Moon is an assistant professor of marketing at the University of Tennessee, Knoxville, where **John T. Mentzer** holds the Harry J. and Vivienne R. Bruce Chair of Excellence in Business Policy and **Carlo D. Smith** is a research associate and doctoral candidate. **Michael S. Garver** is an assistant professor of marketing at Western Carolina University, Cullowhee, North Carolina.

TRANSPORTATION

AIRLINES MAY BE FLYING IN THE FACE OF REALITY

Big carriers are adding flights faster than demand can justify

In recent years, U.S. airline executives have been assuring investors that they've grown up. They keep insisting that the industry is now run by a more disciplined breed than the market-share-chasing, profit-decimating managers of yore.

Yeah, right. So that's why US Airways Group Inc. and United Airlines Inc. are bulking up flights a startling 53% at Washington's Dulles International Airport in the first half of this year. And that explains why U.S. carriers plan to beef up transatlantic capacity more than 10% in 1999, far outstripping the level of demand indicated by anticipated economic growth. All told, the industry expects to expand capacity by 5.6% this year, faster than the previous six years, says analyst Samuel C. Buttrick of PaineWebber Inc. Growth in 2000 should be close to 5% again. That's not massive compared with the 10% peak annual capacity growth in the '80s, but it's far faster than last year's 1.5% increase and 1997's 3.1%.

The inevitable result, predict a growing number of skeptics, will be too many seats chasing too few passengers—even taking into account rising estimates of U.S. growth, to around 3%, this year. Planes were more than 70% full on average in 1998. But analysts are bracing for more empty seats and a return to fare wars this year. Susan M. Donofrio of BT Alex. Brown Inc. figures net earnings for the 10 major carriers will fall 17% in 1999, to $4.4 billion, on 4% revenue growth. And that's assuming airlines can push through another fare increase, like the 2% to 4% hike adopted in late January, the first since September, 1997. "There is simply more capacity than is good for the long-term economics of the industry," says American Airlines CEO Donald J. Carty.

Airline analysts could see the buildup coming two years ago. But they didn't foresee the economic turmoil that would hurt demand in Asia and Latin America. Even at home, in the face of stronger-than-expected fourth-quarter economic growth and low fuel prices, the airlines posted flat revenue and falling

OVERBUILDING?			
Carriers are Aiming for More Expansion			
FORECASTS OF 1999 CAPACITY INCREASES			
	SYSTEMWIDE	DOMESTIC	INT'L
AMERICAN	4.0%	2.5%	7.4%
CONTINENTAL	8.6	4.0	17.5
DELTA	3.5	3.1	5.0
NORTHWEST	9.2	10.0	7.9
SOUTHWEST	11.4	11.4	—
UNITED	2.9	4.6	0.0
USAIRWAYS	7.8	7.3	12.2

DATA: PAINEWEBBER INC.

Reprinted with special permission from *Business Week*, February 22, 1999, p. 40. © 1999 by The McGraw-Hill Companies, Inc.

profits. One reason: Corporations have been curbing travel budgets and balking at sky-high business fares. And the carriers also face growing wage pressures. American pilots, for instance, staged a sickout in early February over wages and other contract issues, forcing the carrier to cancel more than 2,400 flights.

Predictably, each carrier with big expansion plans argues that its outsize goal makes strategic sense. Continental Airlines Inc., for one, says attempting an 8.6% increase in capacity this year, after last year's 10.6%, is justified because it underinvested in Newark, Cleveland, and Houston hubs during two bankruptcies. US Airways is expanding its Metrojet operation as a defense against Southwest Airlines Co. on the East Coast.

But, warns Carty, "if you have that mentality at four or five carriers, then it gets away from you." American has trimmed its growth plans from 6% to 4% for '99. And despite its buildup at Dulles, United's overall growth this year is expected to be a modest 2.9%, trimmed from 3.6%. "We are all concerned about industry capacity," says Rono Dutta, senior vice-president for planning at UAL Corp., United's parent.

FIRST TO BLINK. Competition on transatlantic routes may prove particularly intense. U.S. carriers have plans to boost capacity by 15% to 17% this summer. Some are re-routing planes from Asia, where demand remains slack. European carriers are expanding, too, which is likely to lead to deep discounts to fill empty seats in the peak travel season.

There is still time—not much—for airlines to scale back. Carriers start to promote summer flights to Europe in February and March. "If we don't see any [cutbacks] by mid-second quarter, we're stuck for this year," says Donofrio. And unless demand weakens considerably, some analysts believe the airlines won't feel the need to change course. After all, even the projected drop in earnings for 1999 makes this a good year by historical standards. But Carty argues that any missteps will badly wound the airlines' credibility on Wall Street.

Continental won't risk such a credibility gap, says President Gregory D. Brenneman. "If we see softness, we will stop the growth or even shrink the airline," he vows. "There's nothing sacred to us about the growth if we can't do it profitably." But for now, it looks as if Continental and others are waiting for someone else to blink first. The longer they wait, the better it looks for airline passengers—and the worse for airline profits.

By Wendy Zellner in Dallas, with bureau reports

Unit 5

Key Points to Consider

❖ How are the decisions presented in this unit interrelated?

❖ If a firm is seeking to build a new factory in the United States, how should it select a location?

❖ Which tools can aid a manager in logistics design?

 **Links**   **www.dushkin.com/online/**

These sites are annotated on pages 4 and 5.

Once a firm has identified its sales forecast and product design, it can turn its attention to other critical decisions in the operations/production area: capacity, location, logistics, and layout planning. These decisions are interrelated and require careful consideration.

Capacity planning involves an examination of the maximum output of a system in a given period. Economists recommend an analysis of short-run average cost curves for different levels of production. From these short-run average cost curves, a long-run average cost curve can be developed. The lowest point on the long-run average cost curve would indicate economies of scale and the most efficient quantity of production. Firms seek a high level of capacity utilization and face choices when capacity utilization is too low (selling equipment, subcontracting, reducing staffing) or when capacity utilization is too high (need for a subcontractor, expanding capacity, raising prices). In capacity planning, firms must also consider the seasonality of demand and attempt to level out production.

The location decision is important for both manufacturers and service organizations. Today firms have options to locate throughout the world. Most firms go through a sequence of deciding upon the country, deciding upon the region/community, and then an actual site decision. Factors such as proximity to markets, proximity to suppliers, labor productivity, exchange rates, costs, government incentives, and economic/political/social stability are among those that are considered.

The object of transportation planning is to have the right quantity of the right item, at the right place, at the right time, with minimum transportation cost. Various quantitative techniques have been developed to model transportation decisions. The major transportation techniques include the northwest-corner, the Vogel approximation, and the stepping-stone methods. These techniques aim at meeting customer requirements through minimal cost logistics. These techniques also permit analysis of situations where requirements exceed capacity or where requirements are below capacity.

The layout decision is also of great importance to a firm. Layout planning can aid with higher utilization of space, improved customer service, improved flow of information, materials, people, reduced time use, and reduced fatigue. The major types of layout are fixed-position, process-oriented, product-oriented, or hybrid. With a fixed-position layout, the customer or item worked on stays in one fixed place (dentist office or ship). With a process-oriented layout, machines and workers are grouped together by process performed (i.e. receiving, assembly, finishing, administrative offices). With a product-oriented layout there is a grouping around products or families of similar high volume or low variety. For many firms, a combination, or hybrid, approach is used for layout.

The articles in this unit present illustrations of company approaches to capacity, location, logistics, and layout planning. As the articles point out, these decisions are often interrelated.

Capacity, Location, Logistics, and Layout Planning

What Paris once was for New York's Seventh Avenue,
so is southern California for Detroit. They don't build many
cars in California, but it's where a lot of hot styling comes from.

Is it the sunshine?

By Kelly Barron

ERWIN LUI AND A TEAM of designers toiled for three months on a full-scale model of a quintessential American dining room, complete with a Colonial-style table, a hutch and a crystal chandelier. Lui then flew to Tokyo to set up the dining room in the design dome of Toyota Motor Corp.'s headquarters.

Lui works for Toyota's Calty Design Research center in Newport Beach, Calif. Did his bosses want the design as a model for their boardroom? Nothing of the kind. The year was 1982, and the Japanese car executives hadn't been able to come to terms with Americans' need for leg and elbow room. Seeing the good-size room filled with what to the Japanese looked like massive furniture opened their eyes. "It was pretty humorous," says Lui, 45, a California native with Chinese-born parents.

Lui, who played in a rock band and drove a cab before learning to style cars at Pasadena's Art Center College of Design, no longer has to explain U.S. lifestyles to his bosses, but he still serves as an interpreter of this country's faddish design preferences.

Lui managed the design team of Toyota's sporty new Solara coupe, styled by another Calty designer, Warren Cram. So central is Calty to Toyota's styling that nearly 50 of Toyota's Japanese designers have done three-year stints in southern California, moving on to create designs for Toyota mainstays such as the Camry.

What Paris once was to women's fashion, southern California has become to the motorcar. More than a dozen studios like Calty, in Ventura, Los Angeles, Orange and San Diego counties, are playing an ever-larger role in the design of cars destined to be manufactured elsewhere. Nissan recently turned over design authority for the North American market to Nissan Design International in La Jolla. The automaker's rather stodgy designs haven't been selling well in the U.S. lately. Jerry Hirshberg, president of N.D.I. and a former chief designer for General Motors' Buick division, wants to reverse course. He still mourns the fact that N.D.I.'s most radically designed car, called the Gobi—conceived as a multifunctional vehicle with a car-like cabin and a truck bed—was never produced. Now, says Hirshberg, "We're going to take some chances."

He takes FORBES behind a swooshing metal security door to one of his design studios. Inside is a full-scale clay model of a sport utility truck. The vehicle—reminiscent of the Gobi—has the cabin of a sport utility and a small truck bed. The bed can be expanded by folding down the rear compartment of the interior cabin. "This could go from sketch to market in record time," enthuses Hirshberg.

It's not only the Japanese who are tapping California taste. Ford's Lincoln Mercury division relocated its headquarters to Irvine, Calif. in July.

Today scarcely a car or truck is manufactured in southern California, except for the light trucks produced at a plant jointly run by Toyota and General Motors in Fremont. But when it comes to design and marketing, southern California is right in the heart of the car business. Roughly 200,000 Californians labor in car businesses. Jim Hall, vice president of industry analysis with the automotive consultancy AutoPacific, calls the southern part of the state "the car capital of the world." Graduates from the Pasadena Art Center College now head design departments at Ford, Chrysler, GM and BMW.

What makes southern California so special? To the locals in this car-dependent and car-obsessed region, passenger cars have long been as much a personality statement as transportation. (There's an old joke that when you ask a Californian who he is, he points to his automobile.)

California doesn't have a corner on automotive design. Chrysler's celebrated cab-forward designs were born in Auburn Hills, Mich. The current truck and sport utility vehicle craze was born in Detroit. Yet there is something about California that frees people from convention and encourages originality. The new Bee-

Reprinted by permission from *Forbes* magazine, September 21, 1998, pp. 123-124, 128. © 1998 by Forbes, Inc.

Detroit West

The wealth of new car introductions and a critical mass of designers in southern California are making the region an integral player in the auto industry.

1999 VOLKSWAGEN BEETLE▶

BMW Newbury Park, CA	Contributed to 3 Series sedan
Volvo Camarillo, CA	Contributed to Volvo S80 sedan
Volkswagen/Audi Simi Valley, CA	Designed the Beetle
Honda Torrance, CA	Designed Accord coupe, Acura Integra
Mitsubishi Cypress, CA	Designed Eclipse coupe
Samsung Huntington Beach, CA	Opened design studio in 1996
Hyundai Fountain Valley, CA	Contributed to Tiburon coupe

▲ **1999 TOYOTA PRIUS**
▼ **1999 NISSAN QUEST**

Toyota Newport Beach, CA	Designed Solara, Prius
Lincoln/Mercury Irvine, CA	Relocated headquarters and design studio in July 1998
Mazda Irvine, CA	Designed Miata convertible
Mercedes Irvine, CA	Contributed to M Class SUV
Kia Irvine, CA	Contributed to Sportage SUV
Chrysler Carlsbad, CA	Designed 300M sedan
Nissan La Jolla, CA	Designed Altima sedan, Quest

tle, luring shoppers into Volkswagen showrooms, was born not in Wolfsburg but in Simi Valley, Calif.

"Volkswagen of America is in business today because of the energy that comes out of this studio," boasts Simi Valley-based Freeman Thomas, chief designer for Volkswagen and a creator of the Beetle. Here's the story as Thomas tells it:

One February afternoon six years ago J. Mays, then a designer at Volkswagen and now vice president of design for Ford, drove down to Malibu for sushi with another designer, Peter Schreyer. VW was at a low ebb in the U.S., selling just 49,000 cars in the country in 1993; at the height of the original Beetle's popularity in 1970, it sold nearly 500,000. Peering over the Pacific and munching on raw fish, the pair batted around an idea: Why not bring back the Beetle?

Six months later Volkswagen designers were in Malibu, photographing a miniaturized model of the new Beetle on the beach to send to headquarters in Germany. It wasn't an easy sell, but Thomas says that the model looked so fresh filmed in the California sunlight that his bosses couldn't resist it.

Sitting around the pool at Mays' Malibu home after the all-day photo shoot, Thomas figured that the blue-green color of the water at night would be appealing backlighting for the Bug's instrument panel.

Thus did a vehicle designed originally as Hitler's "People's Car" end up being re-created 60 years later in California.

The state accounts for roughly 10% of the vehicles sold in the U.S. and at least a third of aftermarket specialty parts sold to dress up cars. For years, twenty-somethings in the

Los Angeles area have been customizing Honda Accords and Civics with fat tires, spoilers and brightly colored instrument panels. Honda designers in Torrance, Calif. took the bait when they redesigned the newest Accord coupe, lowering the roof line slightly, widening the headlights and integrating the rear bumper with the body for a sleeker look.

Has General Motors missed a cue? According to J.D. Power & Associates, the number one automaker's share in California has lagged behind its U.S. market share by roughly eight percentage points during the 1990s, a time when its national market share was also declining. Yet GM's Newbury Park, Calif. design studio fell victim more than two years ago to its cost-cutting campaign.

Penny-wise, pound-foolish?

Still a distant third in a rough-and-tumble business, Coors has a unique beer, but lacks market muscle.

No fizz in the profits

By Seth Lubove

ADOLPH COORS CO.'s annual distributor conventions used to be staid affairs. No longer. At last April's convention at the Grand Ole Opry in Nashville, President W. Leo Kiely III bounded onto the stage and jutted his substantial gut against the waist of his senior VP of sales, Carl Barnhill. Amidst hearty whoops and applause from the audience, the belly bumping was followed by a beer-soaked party that lasted into the wee hours.

Kiely has every reason to try to keep his distributors happy. He has been losing many of them. Through consolidation or defection, Coors has lost about 9% of its distributors in the past three years and now has only 600. Others are taking on two major brands, Coors and Miller, to fight the power of industry leader Anheuser-Busch.

Since Kiely left a division president job at Frito-Lay and arrived at Coors' headquarters in Golden, Colo. five years back, he has presided over a drastic change of atmosphere. Before, Kiely says, Coors may have been serious about its beer, but "we just weren't serious about making money."

FORBES interviewed Kiely in his open, wall-less office. Chief Executive Peter Coors, whose family owns all of the voting stock, is doing away with private offices because they stifle open exchange.

As Kiely and his managers readily admit, Coors (1997 revenues $1.8 billion) badly needs to change. It is a distant number three to Anheuser-Busch ($11 billion) and the Miller division of Philip Morris ($4.2 billion). Anheuser-Busch nets nearly 11 cents on the revenue dollar; Coors nets less than 4 cents. As number three, with a domestic market share of only 11%, it is subject to murderous pricing pressure at home while it badly lags in overseas expansion.

Pete Coors, a lean and taut mountain man of 51, says he has set no ambitious market share goals, but that he and Kiely are concentrating on improving profit margins. They still have their hands full there, despite just-announced worker buyouts. Consider Coors' perennial problem of incomplete and late deliveries to its distributors, a bad problem for a label that touts the freshness of its product. Until recently, Coors simply had not handled well its transition from selling a local, cult product mostly confined to the West into a national brand.

When Coors went national in the 1980s, it tried an ambitious logistics system that depended on 27 satellite warehouses that were supposed to get the beer closer to the wholesalers. Instead, the beer was often damaged, since it was being handled twice, and it took 20 days to get to a distributor rather than only 5 days if delivered directly from Golden. Often that meant either too little suds for a retailer to sell or too much to clear out before the expiration date.

By shutting down all but 12 of the warehouses and delivering more beer directly by truck, the company has improved delivery time while increasing its inventory turns to more than 11 per year, up from only 8 turns two years ago. (But Anheuser-Busch does more than 13 turns.) At the same time, Coors has been pushing more decision making into the field through eight "field business offices," each with its own profit-and-loss responsibility and authorization to match competitors' prices in local markets.

For too long Coors, basking in its regional popularity, neglected marketing and concentrated on product quality. "We didn't have a clue about how to sell beer," confesses Kiely. "If you're not as good at selling beer as brewing it, you won't survive." Kiely knows he can never outspend his larger rivals on advertising and promotion, so he concentrates his marketing bucks around big seasonal events, such as July 4 and Halloween, and uses innovative packaging as another vehicle to lure drinkers. Though the company makes only a handful of products, it uses some 600 different packages, including baseball-bat-shaped bottles—Coors Field is home to the Colorado Rockies—and holographic Coors Light labels.

Reprinted by permission from *Forbes* magazine, September 7, 1998, pp. 72-74. © 1998 by Forbes, Inc.

"If we can get the consumer to try our product, we've got a pretty good chance of keeping them," says William Weintraub, whom Kiely lured from Seagram's Tropicana unit to head Coors' marketing.

Having a somewhat unique product is clearly a major Coors strength. It uses the cold-filtered brewing process for nearly all of its products, compared with Miller and Anheuser-Busch, which mostly use heat pasteurization. The result is a beer that is clearer than water, since the process filters out yeast and other microorganisms that would otherwise continue fermenting after the beer is bottled. But it's not an inexpensive or easy method. The filter room itself, which the beer passes through before packaging, is like a scene out of Dickens, as workers sweat lifting heavy brass holders to change the hundreds of 15-pound cotton filters for each different brew.

The beer presumably tastes better, since it's supposed to stay cold all the way to your grocer's cooler. But that creates its own host of problems, including the challenge of packing slippery bottles and cans, wet

from their own condensation. To keep the cardboard cases from turning soggy, Coors has had to add an extra layer of coating to its packaging. Though the company has made improvements, South Carolina Coors distributor Byron Yahnis recalls steamy days when bottles of beer tumbled out of the bottoms of Coors' cardboard six-pack holders. Many retailers end up letting the beer get warm anyway in their warehouses or in the end-of-the-aisle displays that brewers covet.

As if boxing with Miller and Bud isn't enough to worry about, Coors remains something of a favorite target for interest groups on the left, unions and neoprohibitionists. Over the Internet, every bug-eyed advocate with access to a keyboard can revive all the old stories about the Coors family's political conservatism and funding for the Heritage Foundation and other right-of-center public policy groups. More recently, homosexual rights activists have been making anti-Coors noises. Despite the company's granting of benefits to same-sex couples and its vocal support of workplace "diver-

sity," the city council of heavily gay West Hollywood, Calif. recently rescinded an earlier commendation of the company after being pelted about the family's political orientation.

Pete Coors shrugs off the left's barbs with the weary indifference of a man who heard it all growing up under the shadow of his outspoken father and Coors vice chairman, Joseph, a member of President Reagan's "kitchen cabinet."

"They need a whipping post, and we have been one for a long time," he sighs.

So be it. What he is less able to live with is his company's industry-lagging profitability. Although Coors' stock more than doubled in 1997, it has been lackluster for most of the past decade. While year after year Anheuser nets close to 30% on shareholders' equity, Coors probably won't even do 10% this year. This is not a business where the number three spot is a comfortable position to be in—especially when you're competing against two of the world's smartest and toughest marketers.

Pulling Customers Closer Through Logistics Service

Theodore P. Stank, Patricia J. Daugherty, and Alexander E. Ellinger

Go beyond the basics. Meet your customers' needs with flexible processes that keep them buying and help create a competitive niche for your firm.

Marketers often describe their job as managing the proper mix of the "four Ps"—product, price, promotion, and place—to achieve strategic goals. In practice, however, they frequently emphasize the first three over the fourth. "Place," which includes the logistical processes involved in getting the right product to the right place at the right time, is too often regarded as a cost to be dealt with after demand has been created. It is rarely considered critical to business success. Rather, emphasis is placed on reducing logistics costs to the lowest level possible to maximize the profit potential of sales already on the books. Ideally, marketers should be exploiting logistics capabilities to increase customer satisfaction and maintain customer demand.

Research has found that purchasing managers for industrial customers deem place concerns as among the most important elements of the buying decision. **Figure 1** highlights a 1989 study by Lambert and Harrington that reported purchasing managers' perceptions of the relative importance of marketing mix elements. Six of the top nine variables influencing purchasing decisions were related to logistics and customer service.

Place, or logistics performance, is important to customers. And it will continue to be important as more industries reach maturity, necessitating "commodity"-type competition that forces marketers to seek alternative methods for differentiation. If product quality and features are seen as highly similar, a marketing strategy that focuses on something other than product, price, and promotions must be found to achieve

strategic goals. Logistics represents the service component of an augmented or value-added product that allows firms to focus not only on attracting new customers but on becoming closer to the ones they already have. It has emerged as a key differentiator in recent years as many firms have realized that competing on strong brands and a strong corporate image isn't enough; they must exploit logistical processes.

For many firms, logistical offerings are falling short of the performance mark set by customers. Byrne and Markham (1993) estimate that only 10 percent of companies are capable of totally satisfying their customers logistically. This finding is based on the responses of suppliers as to how well they meet customer-specified goals in five logistics service areas: damage-free receipt, invoice accuracy, order cycle time, order completeness, and speed of response to inquiries.

Our project was undertaken to provide a better understanding of how logistics can be used to provide enhanced customer value. Specifically, we examine the link between logistics service performance and customer satisfaction in two consumer goods industries.

Operational Effectiveness and Customer Closeness

Companies that recognize logistics service as a significant element in the buying process often respond by developing effectiveness in basic operational capabilities. This allows them to contribute value by performing such service elements better than any competitor. Total Quality Management, time-based competition, and benchmarking initiatives are frequently used to achieve the dual objectives of cutting waste from operations and ensuring customer satisfaction. Companies focusing on operational effectiveness seek to gain cost advantages over competitors. With such a focus, attaining internal performance goals and targeted operating standards (on-time delivery, shrinkage levels, fewer customer complaints, and so on) is an indicator of success.

Reprinted from *Business Horizons*, September/October 1998, pp. 74-80. © 1998 by the Foundation for the School of Business at Indiana University. Used with permission.

Improving operational effectiveness is highly desirable, and may be considered a building block toward gaining competitive advantage. Business success derived from a focus on operational effectiveness, however, is usually short-term at best. The managerial tools and techniques used are often easy to imitate, making performance differences gained from such programs difficult to sustain. A firm will only outperform its competitors if it can establish a preservable difference. Customizing service offerings that already demonstrate operational excellence allows a supplier to become an integral part of a customer's business.

Creating close customer relationships entails identifying long-term requirements, expectations, and preferences of current and potential customers and markets, as well as subsequent positioning for sustainable performance. A company that seeks to attain a competitive edge through customer closeness must be more dynamic with its customers, anticipating their expectations and measuring the extent to which it has satisfied their needs. Striving for such closeness, then, ensures that a firm will be focused on doing the things that create value for its customers.

Managers who pursue customer closeness must assess their firm's resources as they relate to customers' desires. By formally assessing its relative strengths, a company can deploy resources and capabilities to perfect customer-valued activities and services that competitors cannot match. Though few firms can successfully meet the needs of every potential customer or market segment, they can decide where to compete and where not to compete based on the fit between company strengths and customer needs. The success of customer closeness depends, therefore, on the level of knowledge a firm's managers possess regarding relative strengths as well as customers' needs and desires.

This discussion becomes particularly pertinent in marketplaces characterized by commodity-type competition. In such situations, product/service quality, features, and pricing converge toward a single industry standard. Achieving this standard through operational effectiveness becomes merely an entry requirement for competing. It does not differentiate a firm from its competitors. However, doing things customers really value provides an important differential. Firms that establish close relationships with customers provide heightened value by excelling in the areas customers consider important. These areas often center on logistical activities.

Logistics Capabilities

Logistics capabilities encompass the processes involved in fulfilling orders, such as customer service,

Figure 1
Summary of Most Important Variables Influencing Buyer's Decision Process

Description of Variable	Marketing Mix Component
Ability to meet promised delivery date	Logistics/customer service
Accuracy in filling orders	Logistics/customer service
Advance notice of shipping delays	Logistics/customer service
Action on customer service complaints	Logistics/customer service
Information on shipping dates	Logistics/customer service
Length of promised lead times for in-stock products	Logistics/customer service
Overall quality relative to price	Product
Competitiveness of price	Price
Prompt follow-up from sales force	Promotion

Source: Adapted from Sterling and Lambert (1987)

order cycle time, and responsiveness. Recently some firms have attempted to improve logistics capabilities to achieve business success. According to the Global Logistics Research Team at Michigan State University (1995), they do this by developing competencies that are "superior to competition in terms of satisfying customer expectations and requirements." World-class logistical competencies include:

- *positioning:* selecting strategic and structural approaches to guide logistical operations;
- *integration:* techniques used in achieving internal logistical operating excellence and developing external supply chain relationships;
- *agility:* a firm's ability to determine and respond quickly to changing requirements; and
- *measurement:* the degree to which a firm monitors internal and external operations.

"Hard-pressed to knock out competitors on quality or price," writes Henkoff (1994), "companies are trying to gain an edge through their ability to deliver the right stuff in the right amount at the right time." Reflecting the growing appreciation for logistics in the corporate world, Henkoff goes on to characterize logistics expertise as a hot competitive advantage. This is particularly true for the burgeoning adoption of service response logistics. For example, manufacturers and suppliers of commodity and convenience products for the retail grocery industry have developed innovative ways to compete in recent years based on distribution speed and agility. Crafting logistics service strategies to meet the specific requirements of customers can be a powerful form of differentiation. Today, logistics services provided for top customers are typically tailored to include the specific value-added dimensions desired.

Communication and computer technologies enable world-class logistical capabilities. The increased availability of affordable information at one's fingertips has allowed forward-thinking firms to develop flexible and responsive logistical service capabilities tailored to actual customer needs and desires rather than providing a generic solution based on aggregate market characteristics. Suppliers and customers can coordinate logistical activities and exchange goods and payments regardless of their geographic location. Electronic infrastructures enable goods, information, and funds to travel at the "speed of business."

A number of companies have risen above the crowd by making ordering and delivery faster, easier, or cheaper than their competitors. This requires an intimate and timely understanding of customers' needs and business characteristics, combined with the logistics capabilities to capitalize on that knowledge. Some computer manufacturers have used such knowledge to their advantage. Gateway and Dell have differentiated themselves with a build-to-order process based on direct custom ordering and delivery, rather than assembling and shipping to retail stores for purchase by end users. Their customers use a toll-free telephone number or the Internet to order, track, and pay for their customized computer configuration. The finished product is assembled and delivered directly to them within days. Consumers like the idea of an attentive, responsive marketer accessible 24 hours a day, seven days a week. Moreover, direct distribution based on actual customer demand guards against buildup of unpopular or outdated inventory.

In the highly volatile fashion industry, The Limited uses a quick-response logistics infrastructure to respond to market information culled from actual point-of-sale data by tracking up-to-the-minute consumer preferences. Premium air transportation is used for time-sensitive fashions to ensure immediate market availability, while basic articles of clothing (staples) are shipped by less costly means. The savings from reduced inventory levels make this a cost-effective solution. L.L. Bean has also gained a reputation for sensitivity and high-level customer service, relying on a similar logistics support structure to enable fast, responsive delivery.

Performance Implications

Successful logistics organizations engage in deliberate efforts to understand their customers' needs and expectations and be able to provide services to meet them efficiently. Firms that can leverage logistics in such a manner, particularly in industries with very homogeneous products, have more satisfied buyers.

Customer satisfaction is a critical performance outcome for service operations. It is believed to be one of the most viable means of gaining the loyalty of current customers. Anderson, Fornell, and Lehmann (1994) found that improvements in customer loyalty—the cognitive commitment by customers to continue purchasing over time—enhance such financial performance factors as market share and profitability growth.

Firms invest considerable time and effort in attracting new customers, but some of these expenditures could be conserved if a greater portion of the customer base remained loyal. Moreover, repeat customers may be less price-sensitive, providing the potential for greater profit margins and decreasing the risk of defection due to competitive price undercutting. Finally, repeat customers are more likely to purchase a greater volume and variety of products in any given transaction. Reichheld and Sasser (1990) estimate that companies can boost profits nearly 100 percent by retaining just 5 percent more of their customers.

LOGISTICS SERVICE: TWO PERSPECTIVES

We observed the impact of logistical service capabilities on customer satisfaction in two industries, personal products and food services. Independent surveys were conducted in each of the industries. Results, presented in **Figure 2,** provide an indication of the relative importance of logistics/distribution service elements within each industry. A few case histories of our findings are discussed below.

Personal Products Industry

Manufacturers of personal products face stiff competition as they try to gain preferred status with their grocery, drug, and mass merchandiser customers. Within the industry, logistics service is a primary differentiator and has received considerable attention in recent years. Interviews conducted with leading retailers of personal products revealed that logistics-related operational effectiveness and efficiencies are minimal requirements. These customers indicated that top vendors use elements of logistics positioning, integration, agility, and measurement to gain an edge over competitors.

Industry operational effectiveness issues reflect an emphasis on generic-type elements: fill rate, on-time delivery performance, and accuracy. Fill rate, the proportion of an order actually received, is a top priority. Most retailers track "orders shipped complete." With new policies aimed at dramatically reducing safety stock holdings, the retailers expect nothing less than complete shipments. And they expect them to arrive on time, usually within a pre-specified delivery window—say, between 1 and 2 p.m. on Thursday. Finally, they expect accuracy on the part of the vendor. In short, the new model of operational effectiveness can be termed the "perfect order" approach. The retailers expect the right product at the right time and place—with all supporting documentation accurate.

Industry standards of operational effectiveness don't reveal many surprises. Retail customers simply expect to receive what they order. However, our interviews with the retailers did uncover greater emphasis on making sure these threshold requirements are met. Retailers routinely and formally measure vendor performance on a wide range of service elements. Whereas in the past they might have relied on the vendors to track their own performance and make adjustments as necessary, this is no longer considered dynamic enough. Today they generate their own data on at least their top-tier vendors and, in turn, present each vendor with a scorecard. The implication is clear: Deficient areas must be improved to ensure a continued relationship. Top retailers aggressively manage relationships with their vendors.

Figure 2
Ranking of Importance of Logistics/Distribution Service Elements

Personal Products Industry	*Food Service Industry*
1. Fill rate	1. Delivery on due date
2. Orders shipped complete	2. Products delivered in good condition
3. Delivery on due date	3. Orders shipped complete
4. Communicating problems or changes	4. Responsiveness of distribution center personnel to requests
5. Invoice accuracy	5. Delivery when requested
6. Cycle time consistency	6. Ease of returning products
7. Cycle time length	7. Courtesy of distribution center personnel
8. Willingness to customize service	8. Best price
9. Frequency of deliveries	9. Driver courtesy
10. Use of preferred carriers	10. Good relationships using distribution center account representative
11. Use of advance ship notices	11. Good relationships using same driver for every delivery

During our interviews, the retailers were asked to develop a "wish list" or accounting of what they want from vendors. Their perspectives provide an indication of how vendors can go beyond the basics to create a closeness with retailers, thereby enhancing their competitive positioning. Many of the comments centered on communication. Top vendors, they say, keep in touch. As one retailer pointed out, there will always be glitches. But the top vendors are the ones who maintain contact and advise them of status, such as a late arrival or the need to substitute a product, so there are no surprises. Good communication also includes "better follow-up." A second retailer described the hands-on approach used by a top vendor, who assumed his firm's appropriate focus should be the entire supply chain—that is, all trading partners and service providers involved in the transaction. So he monitored the product until it was delivered to the retailer's distribution center, rather than just turning it over to the third-party carrier and hoping it arrived on time. Christopher (1994) likens this type of relationship among supply chain members to that of players on a football team as opposed to runners on a relay team.

Differentiation through communication requires a considerable commitment. One way to facilitate it is through system compatibility. The retailer/vendor information systems must easily be able to accommodate such things as routine exchange of purchase orders, point-of-sale data, advance ship notices (ASNs), and carrier tracing. With such connections, the trading partners can closely monitor and coordinate operations. Information is exchanged on a more free and open basis. Many of the retailers indicated they have entered into alliance-type programs with key vendors in which they share extensive information on scheduling and forecasting.

Another example of using logistics capabilities to gain closeness and improve competitive positioning is a focus on customizing offerings for specific custom-

ers. Our retailers cited numerous instances in which key vendors had developed specialized packs, custom displays, and unique pallet configurations in response to retailers' needs. These vendors were also able to ship to retail distribution centers, with products presorted and labeled for individual stores to accommodate cross-docking and reduce storage.

In general, the retailers described a two-tiered logistical program. Vendors start with the basics by providing comprehensive, high-quality delivery service—the right product at the right place at the right time. Basic service provides a foundation on which to build the relationship. Ideal vendors go beyond that to work closely with the retailers in fine-tuning and perfecting the delivery service to fit exact needs. They position themselves in the eyes of the retailers through customized logistical capabilities.

Food Service Industry

Competition in the prepared foods industry is intense. Fast-food restaurants must compete with more traditional food retail establishments in the battle for "stomach share." The fast-food environment requires rapid turnaround of inventory and continuous replenishment to ensure product freshness. Because space constraints at most fast-food restaurants preclude extensive storage capacity, food service distribution capabilities are critical to their success. A distribution company can differentiate by trimming costs through efficient operations and/or by providing customized service offerings.

In interviews conducted with food service customers, restaurant managers indicated that firms capable of providing high levels of basic distribution elements such as on-time delivery, order accuracy, and fill rate are required in addition to product quality and freshness. The managers noted, however, that several distribution elements that go beyond "core" capabilities distinguish the most valued food distributors. Companies that do "whatever it takes" to serve customers on their own terms earn the continuing business of fast-food restaurants. According to restaurant managers, preferred food service distributors provide frequent communications, make special deliveries in case of emergencies, possess the ability and willingness to "fix" problems, and can easily accommodate special requests.

We also conducted interviews with managers of food service firms–the vendors actually delivering products to the restaurants–identified as top performers by restaurant managers. They maintained that their business success starts and ends with the satisfaction and loyalty of their customers. They are willing to identify and provide the service levels necessary to satisfy customers over the long term. Such service often requires sharing sensitive cost and profitability information with customers to justify price increases that help cover heightened customer service levels–or to help customers understand why service levels cannot be raised.

The top service firms develop delivery systems and infrastructures that create added value for customers. Specifically, they are committed to using regular drivers on regular routes to facilitate customer/driver familiarity. They assign one marketing or sales representative or customer service staff person to each customer account to facilitate order taking and service failure response. And they establish communication channels for obtaining useful customer feedback. This includes meeting regularly with franchise presidents and monitoring customer satisfaction through a formalized approach that provides feedback for strategic and tactical planning.

Poorly regarded distributors exhibit deficiencies in non-core distribution capabilities, characterized by communication breakdowns, failure to provide advance notice of out-of-stock items and missed delivery times, inflexible response to special requests or service failures, and inconsistent service. They may have developed basic delivery capabilities, but they tend to miss the point regarding customer focus.

One restaurant manager told of a food service delivery made at lunchtime. The delivery truck blocked the restaurant parking lot and the manager could see potential diners pulling away because they could not enter the lot. When told of the problem, the driver expressed his need to proceed with his delivery so he could finish his route on time. The driver was ensuring that the food distribution firm performed well on logistical service alright–it just was the *wrong* service to satisfy the customer. The driver was working toward an inappropriate and myopic performance goal that totally ignored the supply chain "bottom line."

In a commodity-like business, service is the only way to create product differentiation," says James D. Robinson III, president of American Express. Robinson has captured the essence of the challenge facing many businesses today. Managers have little choice but to compete on service–often logistics or distribution service–to gain differentiation. Unfortunately, logistics traditionally has been viewed as a cost area. Many firms have not considered its appropriateness as a tool for creating market value, or recognized its potential for contributing to business success. But developing customer-oriented logistics offerings can be a sizable opportunity.

The research reported here supports the existence of a continuum of logistical capabilities, as depicted in **Figure 3**. At the least sophisticated level, a firm seeks merely to minimize logistics costs. Companies operating under this approach view logistics as an afterthought that must be accomplished after the primary thrust of creating demand has been realized. Because it must be done, the goal becomes one of doing it as cheaply as possible.

As firms realize that the delivery services in which their physical products are embedded represent significant elements in the buying process, they respond by developing effectiveness in basic operational logistics capabilities. This allows them to contribute value by performing these service elements–on-time delivery, order fill, and so on–better than any competitor. Processes such as benchmarking, time-based competition, and TQM facilitate this approach. These firms soon realize, however, that effectiveness in basic logistical categories is easily copied by competitors.

The relatively few firms that can differentiate themselves through customized logistical capabilities understand that sustainable advantage comes from the ability to tailor logistical offerings to the needs of each customer. Of course, operational effectiveness is a prerequisite of such an approach, but these firms go beyond the basics by developing a meaningful understanding of customers' needs supported by flexible processes that enable them to create customized solutions. Understanding can progress to an intimacy of customer operations in which firms actively seek customer closeness. They share information and use it to be more responsive to customers. Ultimately, this leads to partnering and alliance formation to solidify the relationship and sustain differential advantage.

How can managers realize the full potential to be gained by moving beyond basic logistical capabilities to enhance long-term corporate health? An obvious starting point is to inculcate a customer/marketing orientation among current and new employees. As clichéd as it sounds, business really does begin and end with the customers. So any service program should be developed around their input. Discover customer preferences. For logistics service, this would involve initially identifying core operational service elements. As detailed here, the minimum requirement for successfully competing is to provide high fill rates on time and accurately. Go back to Figures 1 and 2; they show the importance of specific logistics service elements from two perspectives. Figure 1 details the perceptions of purchasing managers–how important specific considerations are to them when making a purchase decision. Figure 2 provides industry-specific perspectives by comparing the relative importance of individual logistics service elements as reported by managers in the personal products and fast food industries.

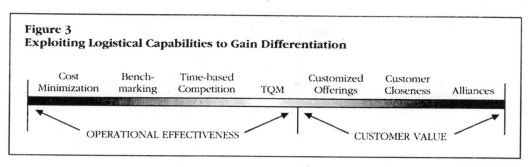

Figure 3
Exploiting Logistical Capabilities to Gain Differentiation

Cost Minimization — Benchmarking — Time-based Competition — TQM — Customized Offerings — Customer Closeness — Alliances

OPERATIONAL EFFECTIVENESS   CUSTOMER VALUE

Too many logistics service providers assume they know what customers want. Often the assumptions are based on marketing and sales department interpretations of customer needs rather than direct customer input. In reality, the customer often places far different relative values on individual service components than do the service providers. Even more important, customers' perceptions of service quality are often markedly different from those of the service providers. This usually happens because the two trading partners define key metrics differently. It is not uncommon for buyers to define on-time delivery based on a one- to two-hour delivery window, whereas sellers (in this case, the logistics service provider) use a broader interpretation of delivery to be made "on Tuesday." To ensure that service level goals are adequate and are being met, customer satisfaction levels should be routinely and formally measured. The goal is to create customer satisfaction–customers who are so happy with the service they receive that they aren't seriously tempted to defect. Once again, satisfied customers tend to be loyal customers.

Identifying core operational service elements is a minimum requirement for competing, but it certainly will not be enough to distinguish a service provider from the pack, or guarantee that customers will be loyal. *That* takes much more–going above and beyond standard service delivery. It requires customer closeness. Working with core service elements as a foundation, successful firms go on to build unique, customized service alliances with key customers. They "tweak" the basic service offering until it is just different enough to fit exactly what the customer needs.

Undoubtedly, this sounds much simpler than it is. The service provider is up against a multitude of chal-lenges, including a constantly changing business dynamic. What the customer wants today won't guarantee satisfaction in the future. Moreover, it is difficult to maintain momentum. Service providers work in an ongoing, neverending, unremitting environment. Embracing a "perfect order" philosophy, in which nothing less is acceptable, sounds good, but it's hard to pull off day in and day out. Hard–but worthwhile.

References

E.W. Anderson, C. Fornell, and D.R. Lehmann, "Customer Satisfaction, Market Share, and Profitability: Findings from Sweden," *Journal of Marketing,* July 1994, pp. 53–66.

R. Burns, "Capability Is Where the Action Is," *Logistics Information Management,* 7, 5 (1994): 58–60.

P.M. Byrne and W.J. Markham, "Global Logistics–Only 10% of Companies Satisfy Customers," *Transportation and Distribution,* June 1993, pp. 41–45.

M.J. Christopher, *Logistics and Supply Chain Management* (Burr Ridge, IL: Financial Times/Irwin Professional Publishing, 1994).

Global Logistics Research Team at Michigan State University, *World Class Logistics: The Challenge of Managing Continuous Change* (Oak Brook, IL: Council of Logistics Management, 1995).

R. Henkoff, "Delivering the Goods," *Fortune,* November 28, 1994, pp. 64–78.

D.M. Lambert and T.C. Harrington, "Establishing Customer Service Strategies Within the Marketing Mix: More Empirical Evidence," *Journal of Business Logistics,* 10, 2 (1989): 44–72.

MBNQA, *Application Guidelines,* (Milwaukee, WI: The Malcolm Baldrige National Quality Award Consortium, 1997).

M.E. Porter, "What Is Strategy?" *Harvard Business Review,* November-December 1996, pp. 61–78.

F.F. Reichheld and W.E. Sasser, "Zero Defections: Quality Comes to Services," *Harvard Business Review,* September-October 1990, pp. 105–111.

J.U. Sterling and D.M. Lambert, "Establishing Customer Service Strategies Within the Marketing Mix," *Journal of Business Logistics,* 8, 1 (1987): 1–31.

Theodore P. Stank is an assistant professor of marketing and supply chain management at Michigan State University, East Lansing, Michigan. **Patricia J. Daugherty** is the Siegfried Professor of Marketing at the University of Oklahoma in Norman, Oklahoma. **Alexander E. Ellinger** is an assistant professor of marketing at Villanova University, Villanova, Pennsylvania.

IMPROVING SHOP FLOOR OPERATIONS THROUGH PRODUCTION SEQUENCING AT EMC TECHNOLOGY

Why is it that even with advanced information technology and engineering resources, a vast majority of manufacturing organizations express dissatisfaction with the priority and capacity planning and control systems that drive the shop floor?

Since there is no standard method for planning and scheduling manufacturing, manufacturing professionals must evaluate the strengths and weaknesses of the various shop floor management system alternatives, and select the appropriate application of each in the factory.

At EMC Technology, Inc., management was able to meet the demands of its customers by employing production sequencing, a priority and capacity planning and control system that integrates the best of material requirements planning, kanban, finite scheduling, and demand-based flow techniques.

by Louis W. Joy, III and Francis Smith

EMC Technology, Inc., a manufacturer of radio frequency and microwave components for the commercial and military telecommunications markets for over thirty years, found itself in an enviable, but difficult, position. It was enjoying explosive growth among its direct customer base of sophisticated, world-class manufacturers. That extraordinary growth, however, strained EMC's business processes.

EMC's materials research planning (MRP) and kanban-driven shop floor management system was failing. With nearly 700 customer orders in the factory, manufacturing leadtimes extended beyond 12 weeks, and total customer leadtimes approached 20 weeks. In addition, it had become nearly impossible for EMC to provide customers with an accurate delivery schedule. Conflict and frustration between sales and operations created a less than harmonious work environment.

To relieve pressure, five of the plant's 45 multishift workcenters had been redesigned to cellular manufacturing for the high-volume, repetitive products. But this was only a small percentage of total manufacturing, and the balance of production was conducted in a complex, make-to-order job shop environment. In fact, almost every product was routed through outside operations located across the country.

Mike Marie, EMC's director of operations, recognized that action had to be taken to quickly rebuild the shop floor management system and support continued business

An APICS Fellow, Louis W. Joy, III is president of Manufacturing Excellence, Inc., in Newark, Delaware, and consults with manufacturing organizations in the areas of operations and human resource management. He is the author of *Frontline Teamwork* (McGraw-Hill/Irwin Professional Publishing) and numerous articles on the topics of teambuilding, constraints management, and shop floor management systems. Joy holds an MBA from Duke University and is an instrument-rated private pilot.

Francis Smith is the materials control manager of EMC Technology. Inc. in Cherry Hill, New Jersey, and the project leader for production sequencing implementation. He has been instrumental in managing the recent business success of the company. APICS certified, Smith holds a BA from Temple University.

From *National Productivity Review*, Spring 1998, pp. 19-28. © 1998 by John Wiley and Sons, Inc. Reprinted by permission.

growth. "It was obvious that an innovative and holistic factory management strategy was needed to regain the confidence of our customers," he said. The management team carefully evaluated shop floor management alternatives and chose to deploy production sequencing.

An integrative priority and capacity planning and control methodology, production sequencing, takes the best attributes of MRP, kanban, finite scheduling, and demand-based flow techniques and blends them into a single total shop floor management system. A simple no-software approach, production sequencing can be deployed to improve productivity, customer service, and leadtime in any discrete manufacturing environment, from make-to-order to make-to-stock, from complex job shop to repetitive flow. It comprises four elements: bill of routing analysis, bottleneck management, a sequenced master schedule, and innovative shop floor design.

BILL OF ROUTING ANALYSIS AT EMC

The bill of routing concept is based on the idea that even in the most complex job shop environments there are paths of material flow. This takes the concept of just-in-time workcells and extends the thinking beyond the ability to move equipment close together. While other well-established techniques for process analysis and diagramming are typically applied to single products or to product families, the bill of routing considers all products

in the factory. This single diagram, which depicts standardized routings for all products from workcenter to workcenter through a plant, enables workers to determine the source of material sent directly to each workcenter, and the destination of product sent from each workcenter. (A generic bill of routing is given in **Exhibit 1.**)

Creating an accurate bill of routing requires the participation and involvement of front-line supervisors and workers. It is often a time consuming and tedious process, requiring the analyst to sort through many opinions. No single individual completely understands the inner workings of the factory and only a collaborative fact-finding effort can yield the breadth and quality of information necessary. When complete, the bill of routing reveals:

Layout Flaws: The flowpath analysis promotes assembly-line or workcell layout. Consecutive flowpath workcenters should be located close together. In the example, it would be preferable if all four workcenters in flowpath #1 were in close proximity.

Organizational Design: Teams of workers should also be structured by flowpath. Supervisors assigned total flowpath responsibility can clearly focus on performance.

Clues to Process Improvement: The bill of routing identifies opportunities to streamline the steps in product manufacture.

Opportunities for Institutionalizing Assembly-Line Thinking: Even if workcells for consecutive processes cannot be physically next to each other, the production process can still be managed as though assembly lines connected the

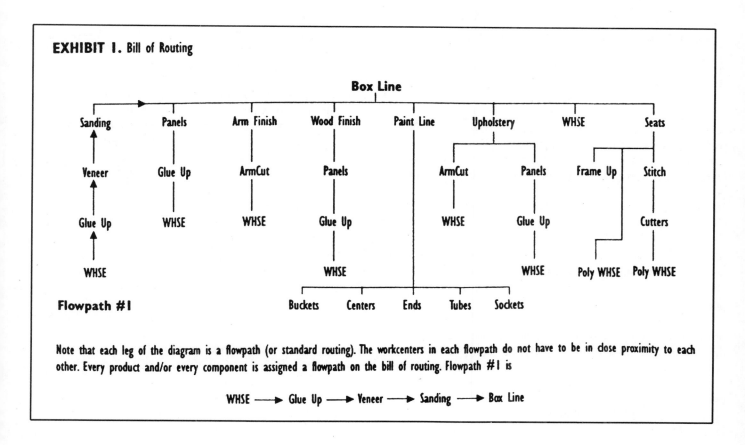

EXHIBIT 1. Bill of Routing

Note that each leg of the diagram is a flowpath (or standard routing). The workcenters in each flowpath do not have to be in close proximity to each other. Every product and/or every component is assigned a flowpath on the bill of routing. Flowpath #1 is

WHSE ⟶ Glue Up ⟶ Veneer ⟶ Sanding ⟶ Box Line

workcenters in each path. This assembly-line mindset provides significant new insight and solutions to solving production problems.

Pass-Through Design: To reduce the number of flowpaths in the factory, it is sometimes necessary to assign a standard routing to a product even though it may not be processed at every operation. While this incurs added material handling cost, the much greater benefit is that there are fewer paths and the priority of orders can be maintained. By using standard routings, it is easy to imagine that each path can be priority planned and managed as though it were an assembly-line process. Ensuring that every flowpath is driven by the same priority of orders is critically important when the product requires subassemblies to "mate" at various steps in the process.

The first step at EMC was to conduct a bill of routing analysis for all chip products. Frontline supervisors and workers began by fact finding and flowcharting product routings and comparing these results with the routing database. This exercise, which required several weeks to complete, resulted in a dramatic change in manufacturing strategy. The factory layout was streamlined, job assignments were redefined, and engineering solved recurring process problems that would otherwise blur the new vision of the factory.

> *The production sequencing system is designed to visually identify short-term bottlenecks and manage long-term bottlenecks.*

The bill of routing analysis revealed that a single flowpath could be created to support all chip products. The path was constructed so that all products would move in a single direction down the path, and would pass through operations that did not perform a process to the product. This reduced nearly 100 product routings to one and greatly simplified production sequencing system design.

Redefinition of jobs assigned each operator a single print station. Now each operator would perform a single task along the standard flowpath. This transition from a laboratory-style strategy to a high-volume assembly-line design dramatically increased throughput.

The clean room was re-engineered using sequencing principles. In the old system, the supervisor would prioritize queues and assign the next job to each print operator using MRP reports. Each print operator was responsible for processing all steps of a job. The clean room design was extended, creating a single path through the entire factory. This was accomplished without dramatically changing plant layout. EMC took a very complex factory and standardized

the product routings. Although most companies cannot deploy a single flowpath concept, quantum leaps in simplification can typically be made.

THE IMPORTANCE OF BOTTLENECK MANAGEMENT

To understand constraint management, it is important to know the difference between long- and short-term bottlenecks. A short-term bottleneck occurs when at any given time a resource is producing at the slowest rate, negatively affecting the flow through the plant. A long-term bottleneck occurs over an extended period of time when a highly utilized resource limits, or constrains, the output of the plant as it produces at a slower rate than other resources. For example, if, over the long term, all workcenters in the factory can produce 100 gallons per minute, except one that produces 60 gallons per minute, then the entire factory will only produce 60 gallons per minute. The long-term bottleneck determines plant capacity.

The production sequencing system is designed to visually identify short-term bottlenecks and manage long-term bottlenecks according to the master production schedule. Resolving short-term bottlenecks requires an immediate response to bring resources to workcenters that increase capacity. Increasing the capacity of long-term bottlenecks requires a combination of strategies. The long-term bottleneck must be the focus of worker training and productivity and quality improvement, and the target for capital expenditures.

The relationship between capacity constraint and manufacturing leadtime is revealed in the following example. Consider two separate flowpaths. Path 1 has a total of 500 customer orders, with 200 orders released to the shop floor, moving through the flowpath in sequence; 300 orders are in planning and waiting for release (**Exhibit 2**). Path 2 also has 500 customer orders, with 350 released to the shop floor, moving through the flowpath in sequence, and 150 orders waiting for release. Assume each order has the same work content, and both lines have the same capacity.

Analysis shows that the total customer leadtime is the same on both lines, and that the manufacturing leadtime is transparent to the customer. Assuming that the capacity of the bottleneck remains constant, reduced manufacturing leadtime has no impact on the speed and throughput of the lines. Bottleneck throughput determines the speed of the line and, therefore, the total customer leadtime.

This simple model also reveals that the benefit of work-in-process reduction is *greater planning flexibility*. It is far preferable to have as many orders as possible in planning so that there is a larger pool of orders from which the next order to be released can be selected. Changing the priority of orders already on the floor is a much more costly and disruptive process. Thus, production sequencing provides independent practical controls over both bottleneck capacity and work-in-process levels.

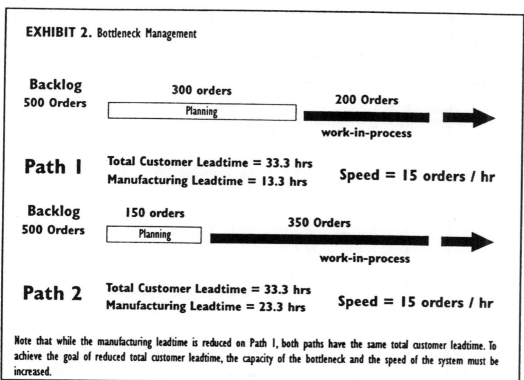

EXHIBIT 2. Bottleneck Management

Backlog 500 Orders — 300 orders — Planning — 200 Orders — work-in-process

Path 1
Total Customer Leadtime = 33.3 hrs
Manufacturing Leadtime = 13.3 hrs
Speed = 15 orders / hr

Backlog 500 Orders — 150 orders — Planning — 350 Orders — work-in-process

Path 2
Total Customer Leadtime = 33.3 hrs
Manufacturing Leadtime = 23.3 hrs
Speed = 15 orders / hr

Note that while the manufacturing leadtime is reduced on Path 1, both paths have the same total customer leadtime. To achieve the goal of reduced total customer leadtime, the capacity of the bottleneck and the speed of the system must be increased.

was at the expense of meeting customer dates. Initially, Mike Marie was skeptical about suboptimization of workcenters. Today, he has a new-found understanding of the strategy. "Suboptimization of workcenters has proven to be the key factor in systemwide gains in productivity and delivery performance," he notes. "We recognize that the MPS sequence *will* suboptimize some nonbottleneck workcenters. But the greater reward is satisfying customer delivery requirements." The philosophy at work here is simple: To achieve maximum total system performance, components of the system must be suboptimized or subordinate.

The FedEx system is an example of this philosophy.

DEVELOPING A SEQUENCED MASTER PRODUCTION SCHEDULE

The sequenced master production schedule is derived from the existing database of end items requirements. It is sorted by due date, and within each due date every order is sequenced. The master production schedule (MPS) format is presented in **Exhibit 3**. This single priority plan of orders is distributed across the entire factory. The due dates represent the completion date at the final operation.

Product moves in this sequence as though each flowpath were a workcell or an assembly line. Orders never skip ahead. This preserves the factorywide sequence of orders. Since the sequence of orders determines overall plant performance, the master scheduler must carefully consider and balance four primary factors in determining the final sequence: customer delivery requirements, capacity of the long-term bottleneck, plant productivity goals, and material availability. Whether the plant is make-to-stock or make-to-order, a complex job shop or designed into workcells, the sequenced MPS is a primary tool for minimizing traditional planning and scheduling system overhead. It drives the factory and puts the master scheduler in firm control of plant performance.

EMC's old order batching system scheduled to maximize productivity at each workcenter. This

EXHIBIT 3. Master Production Schedule

Customer	Sequence#	Product(s)	Quantity	Due Date
Alpha Co.	11	R B Y G	1	10/7
Bravo Inc.	12	B Y R G	2	10/7
Stock	13	G Y B	1	10/7
Stock	14	B Y R R	2	10/7
Spares	15	B B G	1	10/7
Charlie Inc.	16	R B	3	10/7
Bravo Inc.	17	Y Y Y	2	10/8
Echo Inc.	18	G	6	10/8
Foxtrot Co.	22	G B Y R R	1	10/8
Golf Co.	19	R Y Y B	1	10/8
Spares	20	Y Y B	1	10/9
Stock	21	B G G B	1	10/9
Hotel Inc.	23	R R Y G	2	10/9
India Co.	24	Y	3	10/10
Stock	25	G G	1	10/10
Juliet Inc.	26	B B R Y	1	10/10
Echo Co.	27	B Y G	1	10/10
Kilo Co.	28	G G Y	2	10/10

Note: Foxtrot Co. order was resequenced after release to the shop floor.

An overnight package destined for delivery across town may travel across the country. This apparent inefficiency maintains a simple set of sorting and transportation procedures, and maximizes the performance of the total FedEx system.

Most companies assign a single sequence number to their customer orders. Those that consume excessive bottleneck capacity are physically separated into two or more sequence numbers to ensure a steady rate of flow through the long-term bottleneck operation. Each sequence number travels through the system in a separate container with the sequence number displayed.

The EMC master scheduler is continually working to create a sequence of orders that satisfies the customer and the plant. Guidelines are established to balance production process tradeoffs. For example, no more than two jobs per day (within 15 sequence numbers) may require 100 percent final inspection. A daily morning meeting with front-line supervisors responsible for long-term bottleneck operations is conducted to finalize the next sequence of orders to enter the plant.

Mike Marie anticipated that "production sequencing would serve as a common platform for both sales and operations to schedule the shop floor." He points out, "Expediting ruled the old system. Our planners spent 80 percent of their time chasing customer orders. Today, the sales and planning teams drive the business. Analytical-effort is expended *before* the order is released to the factory."

THE BENEFITS OF A VISUAL SHOP FLOOR DESIGN

Enhanced performance results when *all* production is driven by a visual pull system with signals that authorize production and movement of material. Such a visual factory increases the accountability of all front-line personnel and motivates teams to meet system goals.

In the shop floor of a sequenced plant, a set of inbound and outbound squares (the quantity of each can vary) is assigned to each workcenter. The squares are usually painted or taped in close proximity and are empty and unnumbered. A sequence number is attached to the parts or components of each order, making a single line item in the MPS. All of the parts or components of an order (MPS line item) have the same sequence number. The parts move through the squares, from workcenter to workcenter, in the assigned flowpath. Only one sequence may reside in a square at any time. Each workcenter has a simple set of rules (**Exhibit 4**):

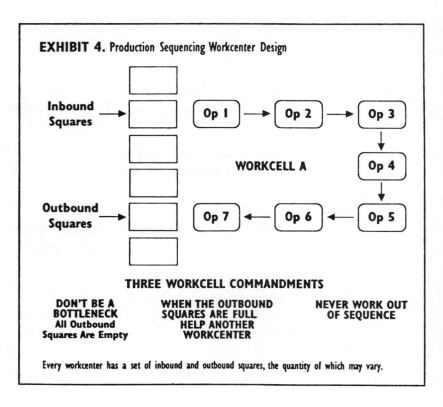

EXHIBIT 4. Production Sequencing Workcenter Design

Inbound Squares → Op 1 → Op 2 → Op 3 → Op 4 → Op 5 → Op 6 → Op 7

WORKCELL A

Outbound Squares →

THREE WORKCELL COMMANDMENTS

DON'T BE A BOTTLENECK
All Outbound Squares Are Empty

WHEN THE OUTBOUND SQUARES ARE FULL HELP ANOTHER WORKCENTER

NEVER WORK OUT OF SEQUENCE

Every workcenter has a set of inbound and outbound squares, the quantity of which may vary.

- Process orders from the inbound squares to the outbound squares in the sequence of the master schedule.
- The empty outbound square is the visual signal to produce.
- Process the next order only when an outbound square is empty.
- When the outbound squares are all full, stop producing, and seek other productive work.
- Make every effort to never let all of the outbound squares be empty.

The empty inbound square is the signal for the material handling system to move the parts for the next order from the feeding workcenter's outbound square into the open inbound square. Only the final operation receives an MPS with a completion date schedule. The MPS issued to all other workcenters has the due date information removed. These workcenters fill outbound squares in sequence. The pull system begins when the final operation empties its inbound squares (see **Exhibit 5**). This signals the material handlers to move the next sequence from the outbound squares of the feeding workcenters. Each workcenter reacts to fill the newly emptied outbound square.

By integrating the best features from several techniques, production sequencing creates a pull, using the squares as the visual signal, from the final operation all the way through the factory floor to the raw material stockroom.

The squares serve as a link, an invisible assembly line that connects all workcenters associated with the flowpath, even when workcenters are not in close proximity to each other. As all workcenters fill their outbound squares, parts will automatically "mate" at the appropriate inbound square. Expediting is dramatically reduced because each workcenter has all the required parts.

A workcenter is a short-term bottleneck when all the outbound squares are empty. This indicates a struggle to keep pace with the factory. The team response to add capacity includes shifting crosstrained workers, overtime, or moving equipment to increase output. When the problem causing the stockout of all outbound squares cannot be quickly resolved, the master schedule must be resequenced. The new master schedule is then issued to all workcenters in the plant, and the work-in-process is reorganized to reflect the new sequence of orders.

Performance in the sequenced plant is measured in two ways: how well the plant is meeting the MPS, and how often the MPS is resequenced. The first is a comparison of the MPS with actual completion dates; the second is a count of resequencing events. The primary goal is to meet the MPS. Worker teams conduct root cause analysis to eliminate the events that cause resequencing of orders released to the factory. Corrective measures are communicated plantwide and help institutionalize the value of meeting the master production schedule.

In designing its shop floor, EMC had to take work-in-process, training and documentation, outside operations, and performance measurement and data collection into consideration.

Work-in-Process. Upon completing its bill of routing, EMC had to locate and quantify inbound and outbound squares for each workcenter. The system was designed to achieve a three-week manufacturing leadtime. The formula for calculating the number of squares in the longest flowpath is: Manufacturing Leadtime (Days) = # Squares in the Longest Path / # Squares Completed/Day.

In the production sequenced factory there is a single manufacturing leadtime for all products. At EMC the system was designed to achieve a 15-day manufacturing

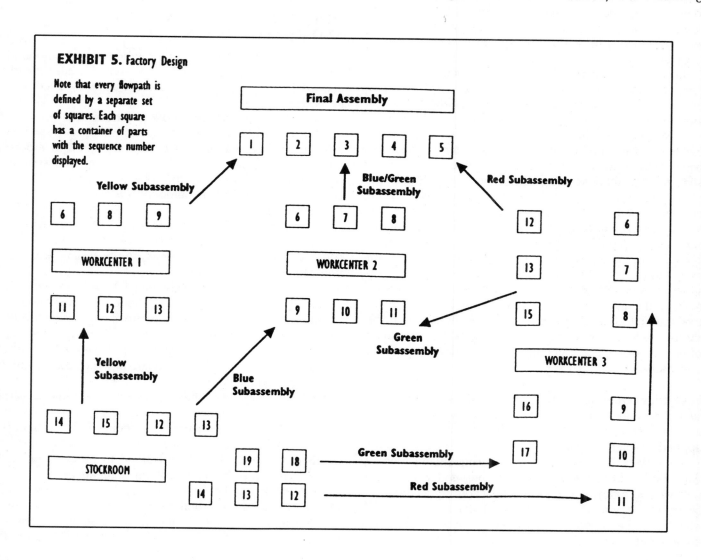

EXHIBIT 5. Factory Design

Note that every flowpath is defined by a separate set of squares. Each square has a container of parts with the sequence number displayed.

leadtime. With an estimated throughput of 15 orders per day, 225 squares would achieve the manufacturing leadtime goal. The number of inbound and outbound squares allocated to each workcenter would ensure a comfortable buffer of incoming parts for each workcenter. Square allocation was an initial estimate that was later refined.

> ## *Within six months after designing the system, EMC shipped its highest monthly volume of product.*

Training and Documentation. The entire frontline workforce participated in formal classroom training once the design of the shop floor was complete. There were also working sessions to finalize the system rulebook.

Mike Marie emphasized the need for upfront education of the workforce. "This was a vital component to a smooth transition," he said. "Resistance to this new way of working was reduced by investing time in our people and gaining their buy-in."

The trainers sought to not just teach system mechanics, but to initiate a change of the *value system* of frontline personnel. Frontline supervisors and workers came to realize that maintaining orders in sequence was more important than maximizing individual productivity. Each person learned to resist the urge to keep producing when his or her outbound squares were full. Individual responsibility extended to workcenters beyond the primary workcenter. The company continues to emphasize plant performance and the success of the business as the responsibility of all company members. A central component of the company's long-term vision is its extensive crosstraining effort to increase skills and flexibility at the short- and long-term bottleneck operations. "Crosstraining of our workforce is paramount to our continued success," said Marie.

Outside Operations. EMC's West Coast vendor presented an important management challenge, for sequencing required that this vendor adhere to the same rules applied to internal workcenters.

To address the issue, production sequencing training was conducted at the vendor site. The vendor agreed to receive and return daily shipments according to the MPS sequence. A virtual assembly line extended across the country to the vendor and returned to the next EMC operation with every order in its original position on the line.

The application of sequencing even simplified the administration of the vendor relationship. The past tension of expediting work through the vendor was relieved.

Performance Measurement and Data Collection. At EMC, the master schedule is distributed on hard copy to every workcenter in the plant. The final operation notes the date of actual completion for every order. A simple review of the MPS shows whether the plant is on or behind schedule.

The MPS is reviewed weekly to calculate a "nervousness index," which quantifies the extent of resequencing. Every workcenter maintains a logbook that records events that either jeopardize or cause the MPS to be resequenced, or result in all the outbound squares being empty. EMC uses these data to prioritize efforts to stamp out the root cause of resequencing and short-term bottlenecks. The performance results are tabulated, charted weekly, and displayed in the factory.

IMPLEMENTING THE NEW SYSTEM AND REAPING ITS BENEFITS

After 12 weeks of design effort, inbound and outbound squares were in place, frontline personnel were trained, and the initial MPS was ready. EMC was ready to convert to its new system.

Seven hundred orders of work-in-process had been deliberately reduced as much as possible during the weeks prior to implementation, but there were still 400 orders, and only 225 squares were designed into the new system. All orders were placed into the appropriate squares. Workcenters with inbound or outbound orders that exceeded the number of squares were stocked near the square. The old workcenter material requirements planning dispatch sheets were removed, and workcenters began to use the squares and the MPS as the new priority system. Production sequencing was born.

The MPS was initially sequenced based only on the position of orders in the factory. It required several weeks to fully drain the work-in-process to the planned levels. Orders not yet released and still in planning were sequenced using the MPS guidelines, and were released to the factory when the inbound square of the gateway workcenter opened.

Within six months after designing the system, EMC shipped its highest monthly volume of product—without adding resources. Production sequencing led to a *rebalance of resources* to both long- and short-term bottleneck operations. Frontline workers learned to move to operations suspected of being short-term bottlenecks.

The attack on the root causes of resequencing also boosted productivity. Frontline personnel at EMC explain that the added visibility of the square system is motivational. The initial MPS analysis showed that 44 percent of all orders had to be resequenced. Within a month resequencing was reduced to 11 percent of all orders. Root causes included quality and process problems, MPS sequence problems, vendor problems, and other typical root causes of expediting.

In the most recent month for which data are available, over 90 percent of the orders were completed within three working days of the promise date. This is a quantum leap improvement over the old system. Sales personnel know with great precision the sequence of order completion and can easily predict when an order will ship. This is a result of the assembly-line design of the system.

Manufacturing lead time has been reduced 75 percent, from 12 weeks to slightly over three weeks. This dramatic increase in planning flexibility provides the master scheduler the opportunity to work closely with sales to conduct a final prioritization of customer orders before release to the factory. Instead of managing 700 orders, the factory now has to handle only 225 orders, and the majority of the backlog remains in planning and can be easily prioritized.

Total customer leadtime has not yet been dramatically reduced. To accomplish this, there are plans to greatly expand the capacity of the long-term bottleneck operations. This will increase the throughput of the total system and reduce total customer leadtimes, assuming the rate of order receipt remains constant.

EMC will continue to refine and adjust its production sequencing system, paying particular attention to the long-term bottleneck operations so that the company can improve productivity, quality, and capacity. As Mike Marie noted, "The door to the 'hidden factory' has been opened. We now have a system to clear the continuous improvement path."

CHANGES IN PERFORMANCE MEASURES ON THE FACTORY FLOOR

ROBERT F. MARSH
School of Business Administration, University of Wisconsin-Milwaukee, Milwaukee, WI 53201

JACK R. MEREDITH
Babcock Grad. School of Management, Wake Forest University, Winston-Salem, NC 27109

As a management method, cellular manufacturing (CM) continues to gain acceptance. The reasons are obvious; CM reduces work-in-process (WIP) inventory levels and correspondingly reduces lead times. Not coincidentally, many companies have recently shifted focus to compete on time-based parameters, like lead time. Also, the Just-in-Time (JIT) management philosophy of reducing waste (and thus WIP) is naturally complemented by CM practices on the floor.

Essentially, CM involves finding repetitive procedures in an otherwise random set and then performing that work in a more efficient manner. In terms more congenial to manufacturing, it is moving some production from a job shop to a line process design, or moving down the diagonal in Hayes and Wheelwright's product/process matrix [2] to gain efficiency. Customization is sacrificed, but only for a portion of the work load. And for

many companies, the commitment to customization was never needed and was just another form of waste. Thus, CM often leads to lower costs and higher productivity than previously realized in job shops.

These two factors are the impetus for cells: lower costs and shorter lead times. If a company's management measures performance according to its objectives, cost and lead-time measures should be found in most cases of cell implementation. It might also be expected that data on these measures may have been kept prior to cells.

The objective of this study is to compare how management measures performance both before and after the move to cells. As the saying goes, "what gets measured gets done." On the other hand, in *The Goal* [1], we learn that activation and utilization are not synonymous. Therefore measuring something doesn't necessarily mean that it is important. This study also investigates what performance measures man-

From *Production and Inventory Management Journal*, First Quarter 1998, pp. 36-40. © 1998 by APICS, the American Production and Inventory Control Society. Reprinted by permission.

agement is evaluated on both before and after cells. Finally, we examine the relationships between measures and methods. For example, does the use of JIT correlate with measures of lead time or WIP levels?

METHODOLOGY

To answer these questions, a survey was designed and administered to managers from 42 companies, all but three from the Midwest. All companies were involved in metal machining and held Standard Industrial Classifications (SIC) beginning with 34 or 35. All had operated cells for at least one year. Table 1 shows the year CM started and Table 2 classifies the size of the 42 companies. Most of these firms had assembly operations in the same plant as fabrication, but most of the part fabrication took place in cells (as indicated in Table 3).

When possible, surveys were conducted in conjunction with a plant trip. This improved the reliability of the responses and even led to some data modifications. It was occasionally found that rater bias factored into questions concerning the application of current management techniques and collection of data. For example, most managers considered their firm to be an advocate of JIT, yet the preponderance of evidence (inventory) suggested otherwise. Further questioning usually resolved such issues. Elsewhere, managers would indicate quality was maintained using control charts. If the manager could not show evidence of charts, the measure was not counted.

Measures varied greatly from plant to plant and some of that variation was attributable to the specific product or process. Quality, for example, was sometimes measured as amount of scrap, percentage of good pieces, number of rework hours, customer satisfaction, etc. For simplicity, performance measures were categorized into nine different types: productivity, quality, inventory, lead time, preventive maintenance, schedule performance, utilization, cell completeness, and other costs. This classification sufficiently covered the data collected from the 42 companies without creating discrepancies in the assignment of measures to categories. Managers from two firms mentioned a safety-based measure but the authors did not consider this related to manufacturing performance. Although important, some form of safety measure is required of all companies. An argument can be made that WIP levels (inventory) and lead time are inversely related [4] and therefore one of these

TABLE 1: Beginning of Implementation

Year Cells Started	Percentage
1994	5
1993	5
1992	7
1991	5
1990	10
1989	21
1988	17
1987	5
1986	17
1985	7
Pre-1985	2

categories is redundant, but since the managerial objective differs, i.e., cost versus time, the categories were not merged.

PERFORMANCE MEASURES VERSUS PLANT DEMOGRAPHICS

As companies grew in their experience with cells, performance measures generally became more refined. It often occurred that many measures were kept to validate the conversion to cells but some fell out of date as time went on. Three of the most experienced cell users only tracked one performance measure. The size of the plant (small, medium, large) didn't correlate with the number of performance measures kept, although it did relate to the progress toward converting to cells. Production at all five of the small plants in this study was between 91% to 100% in cells, while almost half of the large plants had less than 50% of production in cells. More than half of the plants in the study indicated that conversion to cells was ongoing. There was no significant correlation between plant size, CM experience, or percent of production in cells and the type of performance measure.

TABLE 2: Plant Size

Size of Plant (sales)	Percentage
Small (less than $50 million in annual sales)	12
Medium (between $50 and $250 million)	57
Large (greater than $250 million)	31

TABLE 3: Production Completed in Cells

Portion of Production in Cells	Percentage of Plants
91%–100%	50
81%–90%	14
50%–80%	14
Under 50%	21

PERFORMANCE MEASURES BEFORE AND AFTER CM

The first observation from the comparison of before and after CM was that the number of performance measures increased after the conversion to cells, from an average of 2.7 to 4.3. Table 4 summarizes how performance was measured in these 42 plants before and after the implementation of cells. The greatest beneficiary of this increase was in the quality area, with inventory and lead time close behind. The tremendous improvement in these latter two areas after the conversion to cells was definitely related to their measures. In many companies, the tracking of lead time led to improvements in the marketing of products. The shorter and more stable lead times meant increased sales and decreased delinquencies. A few companies even dropped schedule performance measures in lieu of tracking lead time.

The most common inventory measure was the number of times inventory was turned each year. In many cases, JIT and CM were undertaken simultaneously and the reduced WIP was used to justify the conversion expense. Tracking WIP or turns then became a gauge of how well the conversion went and a tool for continuously improving the velocity of material throughout the plant.

Similar to the schedule performance and lead-time relationship, a drop in the use of productivity-based measures coincided with the increase in measuring turns. The managers indicated a preference for the latter because it more accurately assessed costs. Most of the productivity measures centered on direct labor, a much smaller portion of total costs than materials (5% to 15% versus 40% to 60%). These same managers also felt more in control of inventory levels than work-force levels.

The increase in quality-related performance measures is not as easily explainable. Many companies did adopt quality improvement programs in conjunction with CM, but many others already had the programs in place. Anecdotal evidence from managers' comments indicates that tools to collect data on quality have become more affordable and understandable in recent years. The underlying issue here is the fundamental change in how management treated performance data. Fully 79% of these 42 companies posted results for all employees to see. No definitive data was collected to determine how this has changed over time but many managers implied that posting was relatively new and growing. The message from virtually every new manufacturing improvement program included more worker involvement in the process. Along with that, support functions like accounting and management information systems are using tools like activity-based costing (ABC) and the personal computer to improve the reliability and accessibility of performance data. Openness in the workplace and the ability to compress volumes of data probably explain the increased emphasis on tracking quality performance.

The other changes in measures are understandable. Total preventive maintenance (TPM) programs are frequently adopted by CM and JIT users. The reduction in WIP means less buffer inventory so machines must keep running. Maintenance measures like time spent on PM and downtime show an understanding of TPM significance and a commitment to practice it. Utilization was only tracked by one company that extensively used computer numerically controlled (CNC) equipment, and they mentioned it might be abandoned in the future. Cell completeness was a meaningless measure before cells. Some of the "other costs" measures concerned setup time, depreciation, and budget performance.

TABLE 4: Measuring Operating Performance

Type of Measure	Before Cells (%)	After Cells (%)
Productivity measures	93	79
Quality measures	33	93
Inventory measures	24	74
Lead-time measures	31	64
Preventive maintenance	5	24
Schedule performance	81	71
Utilization	2	2
Cell completeness	0	5
Other costs	7	21

PERFORMANCE OF MANAGEMENT MEASURES

As indicated, there was a new openness among managers to share performance data with all employees, and this might be partially responsible for the increase in measures kept. But do all of these measures reflect what is actually important to the company? Are managers evaluated on the same performance criteria they measure? Indirectly, the question being asked is: Have company objectives changed since the adoption of CM? This assumes that objectives have been communicated throughout the company and management understands it must operationalize these objectives into performance measures for feedback purposes.

Productivity and schedule performance were the most common measures upon which managers said they were evaluated, with no other measure coming close (Table 5). Little has changed here over time because these same two categories finished first and second before CM; in fact, 52% of managers indicated their evaluation criteria did not change. Interestingly, many companies still consider the comparison of standard to actual labor times (usually referred to as "efficiency") as the most important indicator of improvement even though labor may only be 5% of the cost of goods sold. As noted before when tracking general manufacturing performance, there was a slight drop-off in the significance of productivity and schedule performance with the conversion to cells, replaced by an increase in quality, inventory, and lead-time measures. This increase can logically be attributed to the 48% of companies that did change their management evaluation measures and probably indicates a strategic

TABLE 5: Evaluation of Operations Managers

Type of Measure	Before Cells (%)	After Cells (%)
Productivity measures	93	79
Quality measures	26	43
Inventory measures	10	26
Lead-time measure	28	40
Preventive maintenance	0	10
Schedule performance	81	71
Utilization	0	0
Cell completeness	0	0
Other costs	5	10

change in direction facilitated by shorter lead times and better quality.

Comparing the "after implementation" columns of Tables 4 and 5 gives the impression that many of the performance measures being tracked are of little significance in either evaluating the managers or steering the company toward its objectives. Although productivity and schedule performance measures held steady, the other categories appear to be kept for show by many companies. Quality and inventory measures drop significantly when it comes to evaluating managers. So why are they even tracked? A few managers said the measures started as part of the conversion and justification of JIT or CM and were never abandoned. Also stated was, "The employees like to see how they are doing in these areas so we keep it (data collection) up as a motivational factor."

Another possible explanation for the divergence on quality is based upon Terry Hill's [3] description of *order qualifiers*, a competence that customers assume exists. In this case, all managers are assumed to be delivering quality. Managerial performance is thus differentiated on *order winners* like productivity and schedule measures.

Table 6 summarizes what percentage of the 42 companies in the sample are using some of the newer management methods. Seven such methods gaining acceptance in industry were studied: JIT, TPM, statistical quality control (SQC), setup reduction, concurrent engineering, work teams, and ABC. Self-directed work teams, used by 62% of the surveyed companies, were often responsible for the bulletin board's content, including the display of performance measures. Some managers gave the workers authority to collect data as long as they seemed relevant and were obtained at a reasonable expense. In two firms, work teams actually created a business plan containing a mission statement and planned objectives, so tracking performance became a matter of pride rather than a management manifesto.

MANAGEMENT METHODS AND PERFORMANCE MEASURES

There should be some correlation between management methods and performance measurement. To gauge the impact of these improvement programs on the manufacturing setting, a performance measure may be opera-

TABLE 6: Management Methods Currently in Use

Management Method	Plants Using (%)
Just-in-Time	71
Total Preventive Maintenance	64
Statistical or Total Quality Control	93
Setup Reduction	43
Concurrent Engineering or Design for Manufacture	48
Work Teams	62
Activity-Based Costing	29

tionalized. For example, tracking rework or warranty costs would be a natural measure of success in implementing SQC. And the correlation was perfect for the case of SQC and quality-related measures; all companies using SQC measured quality.

JIT success can be measured in a variety of ways including WIP levels, inventory turns, lead times, and worker productivity. Of the 30 companies claiming to be JIT, 27 used an inventory measure, 23 used a lead-time measure, and 28 used a productivity measure. TPM is claimed to be practiced by 27 firms, yet only ten of those 27 kept track of a measure like machine uptime or percentage of TPM completed. The success of TPM could show up indirectly from increased productivity or quality, but the implementation of TPM probably did not result in adding a measure in one of these categories. Some managers viewed TPM as a necessary burden for a JIT environment. Therefore justification of this policy didn't require additional proof.

Shorter setups could show up in productivity, inventory, or lead-times measures. Of the 18 firms practicing single minute exchange of die (SMED) or similar setup reduction methods, 17 also measured productivity, 15 measured inventory, and 17 measured lead times. Not all companies employed setup reduction to the same degree. Many would only look at setups to improve capacity at a bottleneck operation. Anecdotally, those companies using setup reduction appeared to be shifting to time-based objectives and it was very common for these same firms to be using concurrent engineering (17 out of 18). As ex-

pected, all but one of the 20 users of concurrent engineering also measured lead times.

Employee work teams of various levels of control were found in 26 of the companies including all but two of the firms with more than 90% of production in cells. Again, no direct measure of success can be attributed to teams, but productivity is the likely beneficiary with many secondary scenarios likely. Of these 26 companies, 24 measured productivity and all included at least one measure of performance. ABC was another method without logical correlation to one of the measure categories. This was also the method most difficult to verify. Nine of the 12 ABC users were classified as large companies. Based on the small number of firms using ABC, the significance of any relationships is difficult to determine.

CONCLUSIONS

Despite the moderate sample size of this research, enough evidence has been gathered at this time to suggest that performance measures in metal machining firms are increasing in number and variety. More emphasis has been placed on improving quality and lead-time performance since the adoption of cells. And posting performance results on the factory floor is now the rule rather than the exception, although this may be done more for worker motivation reasons than for measuring success toward corporate objectives. Managerial performance is still predominantly evaluated in terms of how well the plant achieves cost objectives and on-time deliveries. In other words, many items are measured for "show," but cost and schedule are tracked for "dough." This could, however, be changing in the future as a few managers indicated more significance is now being placed on quality and lead-time performance by their managers.

REFERENCES

1. Goldratt, E. M., and J. Cox. *The Goal.* 2nd rev. ed. New York: North River Press, 1992.
2. Hayes, R. H., and S. C. Wheelwright. "Link Manufacturing Process and Product Life Cycles." *Harvard Business Review* 57, no. 1 (1979): 133–144.
3. Hill, T. *Manufacturing Strategy: Text and Cases.* 2nd ed. Burr Ridge, IL: Richard D. Irwin, 1994.
4. Kekre, S. "Performance of a Manufacturing Cell with Increased Product Mix." *IIE Transactions* 19, no. 3 (1987): 320–339.

About the Authors—

ROBERT F. MARSH is an assistant professor of business at the University of Wisconsin—Milwaukee. He received his PhD in operations management from the University of Cincinnati. Prior to that he held positions at General Electric Aircraft Engines and Diebold. His recent articles have been published in Journal of Operations Management, International Journal of Technology Management, Omega, *and this journal. His research interests include cellular manufacturing, enterprise resource planning, and lead-time compression.*

JACK R. MEREDITH is professor of management and Broyhill Distinguished Scholar and Chair in Operations at the Babcock Graduate School of Management at Wake Forest University. He received his undergraduate degrees in engineering and mathematics from Oregon State University and his PhD and MBA from University of California, Berkeley. His current research interests are in the areas of research methodology and the strategic planning, justification, and implementation of advanced manufacturing technologies. His recent articles in these areas have been published in Decision Sciences, Management Science, Journal of Operations Management, Sloan Management Review, *and* Strategic Management Journal. *He has three textbooks that are currently popular for college classes:* The Management of Operations *(John Wiley & Sons),* Fundamentals of Management Science *(R. D. Irwin), and* Project Management *(John Wiley & Sons). He is the Editor-in-Chief of the* Journal of Operations Management, *an area editor for* Production and Operations Management, *was the founding editor of* Operations Management Review, *and was the production/operations management series editor for John Wiley & Sons, Inc.*

USING QUEUEING NETWORK MODELS TO SET LOT-SIZING POLICIES FOR PRINTED CIRCUIT BOARD ASSEMBLY OPERATIONS

MAGED M. DESSOUKY

Department of Industrial and Systems Engineering, University of Southern California, Los Angeles, CA 90089

The trend in today's manufacturing is to move towards a Just-in-Time (JIT) manufacturing environment. As outlined by numerous studies [11, 19, 23], successful implementation of JIT manufacturing principles may lead to reduced inventory costs, improved quality, and increased equipment utilization. A necessary requirement for successful implementation of JIT is the ability to run small lot sizes [5, 8, 17]. Numerous approaches have been developed to determine the appropriate lot size. For example, Hill and Raturi [9] propose an optimization model for determining the lot sizes, and Karmarkar et al. [12, 13] propose a queueing model.

Small lot sizes can reduce work-in-process (WIP) inventory and manufacturing lead time if the setup times are not much larger than the unit run times. A reduction in the lead time allows the manufacturer to respond quicker to new customer orders or any changes in demand and increases the likelihood of meeting the demand on time. Small lot sizes tend to reduce the WIP because a lot spends less time at a machining center, causing new arriving lots to wait less for the machines to become available. However, reducing the lot size too much can sometimes have the opposite effect by increasing WIP because machine utilization may increase significantly due to an increase in the setup times. Thus, the selection of an appropriate lot size needs to take the setup time into consideration. This consideration is especially important for automatic insertion machines used in printed circuit board (PCB) assembly where there is both a board and component setup time, and up to 35% of the theoretical assembly load of a PCB line is determined by the setup procedures [4].

Carlson, Yao, and Girouard [3] give an example where a PCB assembly manufacturer produced lots of 100 or more units because the setup time was on the order of three hours per production run. If the lot size is reduced to 5 boards, the setup time translates to around 36 minutes per board. Complicating the problem of determining the appropriate lot-sizing policy in PCB assembly is that the same line produces many different board types, each having its own unique setup time. These factors enhance the need for analytical tools to help determine how low the lot size can be without negatively impacting WIP.

In this article, a queueing network model is used to determine the lot size that minimizes WIP while considering setup time for a PCB assembly process. Although the focus of this article is on WIP reduction, not demand management, a reduction in the manufacturing lead time allows a manufacturer to respond faster to new customer orders, hence

From *Production and Inventory Management Journal,* Third Quarter 1998, pp. 38-42. © 1998 by APICS, the American Production and Inventory Control Society. Reprinted by permission.

increasing the likelihood of on-time delivery. Queueing network models represent the manufacturing process as a network of queues. Analytical formulas are developed to approximate steady-state performance measures of the manufacturing system such as average WIP, machine utilization, and average flow time (i.e., the average amount of time a part spends in the manufacturing process). The best lot size is determined by developing operating characteristic curves of the PCB assembly process. Operating characteristic curves of interest include WIP and machine utilization as a function of the lot size. We demonstrate our approach on a high product mix and medium production volume PCB assembly facility located on the West Coast.

A queueing network model is used rather than a simulation model because simulation may become tedious in the planning stage due to the numerous alternatives that need to be considered [22]. Suri [21] shows the robustness of analytical queueing network models for representation of real systems. The computation time required to solve a queueing network model is significantly less than the simulation run time, greatly facilitating the ability to consider numerous lot-sizing policies. Also, the queueing network models do not require any programming, making them simpler to develop than simulation models. Simulation also requires the analyst to have some knowledge in statistics.

Snowdon and Ammons [20] survey eight queueing network packages. Some of the queueing network software packages are public domain while others are commercially sold by a software vendor. MANUPLAN [16] is selected as the queueing software package because of its user-friendly interface, and it has been successfully used in the past in the design of PCB assembly lines. For example, Haider, Noller, and Robey [7] use MANUPLAN to help identify initial design alternatives for a PCB assembly facility at IBM. Other successful applications of MANUPLAN in the design of PCB assembly lines can be found in [1, 6].

PRINTED CIRCUIT BOARD ASSEMBLY PROCESS

The studied PCB assembly process is a high product mix and medium production volume facility. The product mix is approximately 300 board types and the daily production volume is around 600 boards. The assembly facility uses plated through hole (PTH) technology to insert components on a board. It is common to have both automatic and manual component insertions in PTH assembly lines. For an excellent review of the PTH process, the reader is referred to [14].

A diagram of the process flowchart of the studied PCB assembly facility is shown in Figure 1. The triangles represent inventory storage locations. This facility uses a mix of automatic and manual operations to insert components on a board. The boards and kits, where the components are stored, are withdrawn from inventory and are sent directly to the auto insertion process. There are two types of automatic insertion machines. One type is axial insertion using a variable center distance (VCD) machine. Sequencing is performed at this step to ensure the components are inserted on the board in the proper order. The other type of automatic insertion operation uses a dual in-line package (DIP) machine. The studied assembly facility has two VCD machines and one DIP machine. All board types do not necessarily have to be processed by both machine types. After the auto insertion process the boards and kits are stored in inventory. There is sufficient demand to justify maintaining a certain amount of inventory for each product type. Later, the boards and kits are withdrawn from inventory and put through a series of manual operations including loading and soldering. The last operation is a manual test and repair station. Since the boards go into inventory storage after the auto insertion process, the auto and manual processes are treated independently and modeled separately. In this article, the focus is on the auto insertion process since it comprises the majority of the setup time.

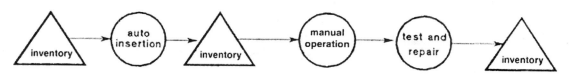

FIGURE 1: Printed circuit board assembly process flowchart

The total time to complete processing of a lot on an automatic insertion machine includes both a *setup time per lot* component and a *run time per board* component for each board in the lot. A setup is required whenever a changeover to a new product type is made. The setup time is incurred once at the beginning of processing of a new lot type. The setup time is independent of the lot size. The run time per board is incurred for each board in the lot.

Let S_{ik} be the setup time of board type i on machine type k ($k = 1$ refers to VCD and $k = 2$ refers to DIP). The setup time includes a fixed machine handling time and a time to prepare the components for insertion. The latter time is a function of the number of different component types to insert on the board. The setup time per lot of board type i at machine type k, S_{ik}, is

$$S_{ik} = a_k + m_k h_{ik}$$

where:

a_k = fixed prep time on machine k

h_{ik} = number of different component types to insert on board type i on machine k

m_k = component prep time on machine k.

Let B_{ik} be the run time per board of board type i on machine k. The run time includes a board handling time and a time to insert the components on the board. The latter time is a function of the number of components to insert on the board. Then, the run time per board type i at machine type k, B_{ik}, is

$$B_{ik} = fk + r_k P_{ik}$$

where:

f_k = board handling time on machine k

P_{ik} = number of components to insert on board type i on machine k

r_k = insertion time per component on machine k.

Let the total time to process a lot of type i on machine k be T_{ik}. Then, $T_{ik} = S_{ik} + q_i B_{ik}$, where q_i is the lot size. Note that the setup time is independent of the lot size.

Table 1 displays representative values for the setup and run times at both the VCD and DIP machines. The number of components inserted on a board (p_{ik} varied from a low of five to a high of 700 with the number of different types (h_{ik}) typically being two-thirds of that value.

MANUPLAN MODEL

MANUPLAN is a data-driven modeling tool. The input file contains data on board and machine characteristics. For each board type the demand rate, lot size, and route need to be specified. The route data contains the setup times and run times for each machine in the route. For each machine type, the capacity, the mean time between failure, and the mean repair time need to be specified.

The queue size in front of the machines is assumed to be unlimited, and the queue dispatching rule is first-come-first-serve (FCFS). Both the VCD and DIP machines are fairly reliable machines with 98% uptime. The material transfer in the auto insertion process is lot-for-lot. Since the material handling system is not capacity constrained and has negligible transfer time, the material handling system is not modeled.

The variability of the interarrival time of demand of each board type and the processing time in MANUPLAN are input as a percentage of the mean. Past experience in the facility has shown that the variability is typically 30% of the mean. The outputs of the MANUPLAN model are steady-state per-

TABLE 1: Representative Setup and Run Times in Minutes

Machine	Lot Setup Time(a_k)	Component Setup Time (m_k)	Board Prep Time (f_k)	Insertion Time (r_k)
VCD ($k = 1$)	7.5/lot	0	.25/board	.008/insertion
DIP ($k = 2$)	8.5/lot	1/component type	.25/board	.024/insertion

formance measures of the manufacturing system including machine utilization, average WIP, and average flow time at each machining center. If all the demand cannot be met within the planning horizon, the output of the MANUPLAN model is an error message indicating that the demand cannot be met with the current machine capacity. The Appendix provides an overview on how the performance measures such as average WIP and flow time are determined in MANUPLAN.

AN APPLICATION

In this section, we demonstrate the use of queuing network models to help set manufacturing policy for an automatic insertion process of a West Coast printed circuit board assembly facility. Currently, the lot size for each board type is based on past experience. The purpose of this study is to identify a new lot-sizing policy that reduces WIP and the manufacturing lead time over using the historical lot sizes.

Demand data over a six-month planning horizon is used to perform the analysis. The demand is based on market forecasts. It is assumed that there are 125 working days during the six months. The automatic insertion line operates in two shifts with each shift having 6.5 hours available for manufacturing.

Using the current lot sizes, we first validate the MANUPLAN model by comparing its output to actual values from the assembly process. With the current lot sizes, MANU-PLAN estimates the overall system WIP to be around 956 boards. This WIP includes boards in the queue and boards being processed, and is about 20% more than the levels experienced at the auto insertion process. To help identify the discrepancy between the results of the MANUPLAN model and the real system, a SLAM II simulation model [18] is developed to estimate the system performance measurements. Table 2 shows the machine utilization of each type and the average number of lots in the queue waiting for service.

The results show that the DIP machine is busy about 90% of the time while the VCD machine is busy only about 70% of the time. The percent busy time includes both the setup time and run time components of processing a lot. The DIP machine is heavily utilized because it spends about 35% of the time in the setup state while the VCD machine spends only about 8% of the time in the setup state.

TABLE 2: System Performance Measures

Machine Type	Percent Busy		Number in Queue	
	MANUPLAN	SLAM II	MANUPLAN	SLAM II
VCD	72.9	72.5	3.2	2.6
DIP	94.3	93.0	23.5	19.0

Due to high machine reliability, the machine utilization estimates from the MANUPLAN and simulation models are close to the static calculation. The estimates of the average number of lots in the queue differ by about 20% between the MANUPLAN and the simulation model. These results are consistent with the study by Huettner and Steudel [10], which showed that MANUPLAN tends to slightly overestimate the WIP levels. MANUPLAN is less accurate in estimating the WIP for the DIP machine in absolute terms because approximations for queueing networks are less accurate for heavily utilized machines [2]. Nevertheless, we are more concerned with making relative comparisons between different lot-sizing scenarios than with measuring the absolute value of the WIP. That is, typically one is not concerned with the absolute value of the WIP in determining the manufacturing strategy, but rather with how the WIP changes as a function of the strategy. Because MANUPLAN is data driven and solutions can be found quickly, a large number of scenarios can be compared in a small amount of computation time (roughly 30 CPU seconds per scenario on a Hewlett-Packard workstation).

Currently, each board type has a unique lot size and is set based on past experience. The lot sizes vary from a low of one board to a high of 747 boards. In order to move to more of a JIT environment, the PCB manufacturer wants to set a limit on the maximum lot size. In this manner, if any of the lot sizes based on historical experience are greater than the maximum limit, the lot size is reset to the maximum limit. Figure 2 plots the total average flow time in hours in the automatic insertion process as a function of the maximum lot-size limit. Setting a smaller limit reduces the overall average lot size and increases ma-

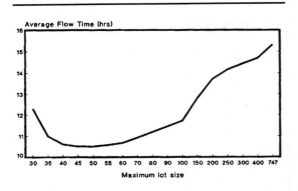

FIGURE 2: Average flow time vs. maximum lot size

chine utilization due to more setups. Figure 3 plots the equipment utilization as a function of the maximum lot-size limit. The results indicate that the best operating policy is a maximum lot size between 45 and 50. As the figure shows, bounding the lot size to a maximum of 50 reduces the average flow time (and subsequently the WIP) by 33%. A limit smaller than 45 increases the average flow time because the setup time starts to dominate. In fact, demand cannot be met with a limit smaller than 25 because the DIP machine utilization becomes greater than 100%. A limit greater than 50 increases the average flow time because a lot spends more time at a machining center due to the increased lot size, causing new arriving lots to wait more for the machines to become available.

The previous analysis helps determine an upper bound on the lot size. However, it still makes use of the historical lot-size values for

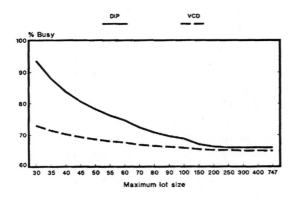

FIGURE 3: Machine utilization vs. maximum lot size

board types below the limit. The company is interested in setting an overall lot-sizing policy in terms of a universal number of lots. For example, if the number of lots to run is set to five, the lot size for a particular board type is simply the demand over the planning horizon divided by five rounded up to the nearest integer. Note that, as the number of lots increases, the lot size decreases. In Figure 4, we plot the WIP (in terms of individual boards) as a function of the number of lots policy. Setting the number of lots for each board type to five is equivalent to the current lot sizes in

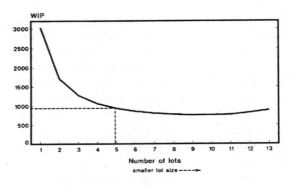

FIGURE 4: WIP vs. number of lots

terms of the resultant WIP because both lot-size policies yield a WIP level of around 950 boards. A number of lots policy of nine yields the smallest WIP levels of 756 boards which results in 21% less WIP than the current lot-size levels. Increasing the number of lots any further than nine will increase the WIP because the DIP machine incurs a lot of setups, causing high machine utilization.

CONCLUSION

As companies move towards a JIT environment, analytical tools are needed to guide factory managers on appropriate lot-sizing policies. Reducing the lot size too much may have a detrimental effect on WIP due to more setups. In this article, we demonstrate the use of queueing network models to develop operating characteristic curves on WIP for a studied PCB assembly process. The curves help identify appropriate lotsizing policies for WIP minimization. Historically, the facility sets the lot sizes based on past experience. The analysis using MANUPLAN shows that bounding the lot size to a maximum of 50 reduces the WIP by 32% with the same demand levels. The analysis also shows that the demand cannot be met with a bound smaller than 30 due to the frequent number of setups at this level, demonstrating that reducing the lot size will decrease the WIP up to a certain level. Future uses of MANUPLAN include determining an overall number of lots policy. Our initial analysis using the current demand levels shows that a policy of dividing the demand into nine production lots minimizes the WIP. Besides lowering inventory costs, reducing the WIP reduces the lead time which enables a manufacturer to be more responsive to new customer orders or any changes in demand.

Although the results are specific to the studied PCB assembly facility, the same type of analysis can be used to identify appropriate lot-sizing policies for other PCB assembly facilities. Previous to this study, the company had lot sizes, mentioned earlier, that varied between one and 747 boards. As a result of this study, the company set the maximum lot size to 50 for those products with lot sizes above this limit. Those products with lot sizes less than 50 were maintained at those figures. The advantage of using queueing network models for this type of analysis is that the models are simple to develop and many scenarios can be evaluated because of the fast computation time.

REFERENCES

1. Brown, E. "IBM Combines Rapid Modeling Technique and Simulation to Design PCB Factory-of-the-Future." *Industrial Engineering* 20 (1988): 23–36.
2. Buzacott, J. A., and J. G. Shanthikumar. *Stochastic Models of Manufacturing Systems.* Englewood Cliffs, NJ: Prentice-Hall, 1993.
3. Carlson, J. G., A, C. Yao, and W. F. Girouard. "The Role of Master Kits in Assembly Operations." *International Journal of Production Economics* 35 (1994): 253–258.
4. Feldmann, K., J. Franke, and A. Rothhaupt. "Optimization and Simulation of the Printed Circuit Assembly." *IEEE Transactions on Components, Packaging, and Manufacturing Technology—Part A* 17 (1994): 277–281.
5. Finch, B. I. "Japanese Management Techniques in Small Manufacturing Companies: A Strategy for Implementation." *Production and Inventory Management Journal* 27, no. 3 (1986): 30–38.
6. Garlid, S., C. Falkner, B. Fu, and R. Sun. "Evaluating Quality Strategies for CIM Systems." *Printed Circuit Assembly* (May 1988): 5–11.
7. Haider, S. W., D. G. Noller, and T. B. Robey. "Experiences with Analytic and Simulation Modeling for a Factory of the Future Project at IBM." In *Proceedings of the IEEE 1986 Winter Simulation Conference*, Piscataway, NJ, 1986: 641–648.
8. Handfield, R. "Distinguishing Features of Just-in-Time Systems in the Make-to-Order Assemble-to-Order Environment." *Decision Sciences* 24 (1993): 581–602.
9. Hill, A. V., and A. S. Raturi. "A Model for Determining Tactical Parameters for Materials Requirements Planning Systems." *Journal of the Operational Research Society* 43 (1992): 605–620.
10. Huettner, C. M., and H. J. Steudel. "Analysis of a Manufacturing System via Spreadsheet Analysis, Rapid Modelling, and Manufacturing Simulation." *International Journal of Production Research* 30 (1992): 1699–1714.
11. Im, J. H., and S. M. Lee. "Implementation of Just-in-Time Systems in U.S. Manufacturing Firms." *International Journal of Operations and Production Management* 9 (1989): 5–14.
12. Karmarkar, U. S., S. Kekre, and S. Kekre. "Lotsizing in Multi-item Multi-machine Job Shops." *IIE Transactions* 17(1985): 290– 298.
13. ———. "Multi-item Batch Heuristics for Minimization of Queueing Delays." *European Journal of Operational Research* 58 (1992): 99–111.
14. Kear, F. W. *Printed Circuit Assembly Manufacturing.* New York: Marcel Dekker, 1987.
15. Little, J. D. C. "A Proof of the Queueing Formula: L = SW." *Operations Research* 9 (1961): 383–387.
16. *MANUPLAN Users Manual.* Cambridge, MA: Network Dynamics, 1987.
17. Mehra, S., and R. A. Inman. "Determining the Critical Elements of Just-in-Time Implementation." *Decision Sciences* 23 (1992): 160–174.
18. Pritsker, A. A. B. *Introduction to Simulation and SLAM II.* New York: John Wiley & Sons, 1986.
19. Schonberger, R. J. *World Class Manufacturing: The Lessons of Simplicity Applied.* New York: The Free Press, 1986.

CHECKING IN UNDER MARRIOTT'S FIRST TEN PROGRAM

What can a hotel do to better serve its customers? One answer to that question, the Marriott Hotel Corporation discovered, was speed up the check-in procedure. In response to that finding, Marriott developed the First Ten program, which streamlines check-in so that waiting time is virtually eliminated. As outlined in this article, the program has not only improved operational efficiency, but also boosted customer satisfaction.

by Emily Knight and Gordon M. Amsler

You grab the last bag from the airport baggage claim conveyor and race to catch the shuttle to the hotel where you will be staying tonight. The rain is pouring down and the roads are congested with rush-hour traffic. You're about to doze off, when the van comes to a screeching halt; you have finally arrived at your hotel.

You head into the lobby where you expect to walk to the front counter, check in, and retire to your room for the evening. To your dismay, however, you see a long line formed in front of the registration desk, and the people in it don't look very happy. You notice that there are only two clerks working and that the express check-in desk is not staffed. Thirty minutes later, you have your keys and go to your room. But when you arrive, you discover that your request for nonsmoking accommodations had not been fulfilled.

Emily Knight is a service and marketing recruiter for Career Consulting, Inc., in Wayne, Pennsylvania. Previously, she was employed in the sales department of the Marriott resort described in this article. Gordon M. Amsler, Ph.D., is an assistant professor of management at Troy State University in Troy, Alabama. He teaches operations management at the undergraduate and graduate levels.

You go back to the first desk, where a clerk tells you that your request was noted but not guaranteed, and that all the rooms designated as nonsmoking were taken. With no energy left to fight, you go back to your room, hoping that someday you will come across a hotel that has your keys ready and room type requests confirmed when you arrive. Wouldn't it be great, you muse as you finally drift off to sleep, not to have to stop at the registration desk at all.

The Marriott Hotel Corporation has tested just such a hassle-free check-in procedure called First Ten. The concept behind the program's name is that guests ideally should be in their hotel rooms within the first ten minutes of their arrival.

COMPARING THE OLD SYSTEM WITH THE NEW

At a Marriott resort hotel in the southeast, the staff at the front desk in the lobby handle guest services and all check-in and check-out duties. The main piece of equipment used is the Property Management System (PMS), which holds all the data on each reservation for the hotel. This system records travelers' personal preferences, as well as credit card information, scheduled arrival, and departure dates. The mainframe computer for this system is located in the hotel's accounting department. Marriott's

From *National Productivity Review*, Autumn 1998, pp. 53-56. © 1998 by John Wiley and Sons, Inc. Reprinted by permission.

Automated Reservation Service for Hotel Accommodations, or MARSHA system, can be accessed by all company properties, other national reservations systems, travel agents, and car rental agencies. The mainframe for the MARSHA system is housed in Omaha, Nebraska. This reservation system is directly linked to PMS, and data are downloaded every three days. The current system has been used ever since the hotels were automated, twelve years ago.

Printed registration cards that provide a hard copy of all computer data are also used at the front desk, as are phones that connect to various hotel departments and guest rooms, credit card machines, and the mainframe for the in-room movie service.

The front desk is considered the heart of the hotel. Whenever there is a challenge or question, the front desk is the first place a guest calls. The individuals at this location are trained not only to be prompt on the computer but also to react quickly in any situation and to have the ability to provide excellent service at all times. The pay for this position often is higher than for other entry-level hotel positions because of the higher degree of stress and responsibility.

Sixteen people on average are employed at the front desk of the hotel. They work varying schedules and receive training for one week on Marriott's Computer Based Training program (CBT) before they are allowed to interact with guests. There are three managers who also interact on the front line. One director oversees the entire operation and handles the administrative duties. During slow times when there are no more than fifty check-ins and fifty check-outs during a shift, the front desk is staffed by two to three clerks and one manager. When a large group is checking in, as many as six clerks and two to three managers are available. These clerks function both as guest service representatives and front office associates.

Before the First Ten process was implemented, the check-in process at the hotel involved these steps:

- The guest arrives at the hotel and, if there is no line, steps up to the counter to be assisted. If there is a line, the guest joins a queue formed within strategically placed stanchions. The guest presents his or her name and/or confirmation number. The clerk pulls the reservation up on the computer and puts it into "I" status, which means "In-house." The clerk then pulls the registration card and has the guest sign it, verifying the arrival date, departure date, rate, address, and method of payment.
- The clerk swipes the credit card, prints a manual copy of the receipt for the guest to sign, selects a room, and enters it into the system, checking for any special request codes and guarantees.
- The clerk makes card keys in a computerized key system, hands them to the guest and directs the guest toward his or her room, or to the bell stand. Not taking into consideration any questions the guest may

have or problems that might arise, this process takes on average four and one-half minutes (**Exhibit 1**).

Under the First Ten check-in system:

- The guest arrives at the hotel and is met by a guest service agent.
- The guest is escorted into the lobby, with the guest service agent carrying bags. The agent pulls the guest's registration card from a large card rack in the center lobby area.
- The agent verifies the information, hands keys to the guest, and escorts the guest to his or her room. If changes need to be made to the guest's account, the agent escorts the guest to the counter where changes can be entered directly into the PMS. This entire process takes less than two minutes, not including the time spent walking to the room. The process is completed by one person. The bell stand, guest service, front office, and switchboard operations are combined into one team, thus ensuring a faster check-in for all guests (**Exhibit 2**).

THE IMPACT ON OPERATIONS MANAGEMENT

When analyzing the First Ten program's impact on hotel operations management, several factors must be considered:

Capacity—The capacity of a work center depends on its ability to process units of work per unit of time. At the original front desk, no more than five people could check in at a time because of the fixed number of computers available. With the First Ten process, check-in is limited only by the number of guest service agents you have on the floor at one time. These agents can easily determine what time guests will be arriving because this information is solicited when the original reservation is placed into MARSHA. Staffing and effective scheduling are crucial in First Ten.

Setup time is also an important factor in determining the capacity of a system; with the original system, setup is not necessary, because all data are already within the computer. With First Ten, however, there is a tremendous amount of preregistration work—time that must be used to complete registration cards, pre-key guest rooms, verify credit card information, and select rooms according to guaranteed characteristics. This setup time, however, can be spent during off-peak hours, especially on the graveyard shift, when people do not work to full capacity.

Analyzing the true capacity for the hotel's front desk is difficult to break down into time spent with each guest. Under both systems, check-ins will have varying capacity requirements, because some individuals may require more time when checking in if they have questions or if there is a breakdown in the system. This is especially true under the original front desk operation, where there is a high

EXHIBIT 1. Original Process Check-In Flow

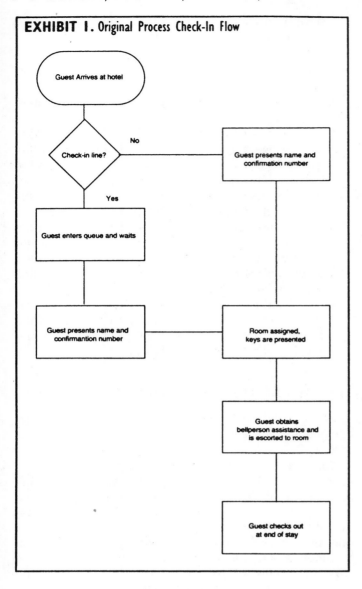

EXHIBIT 2. First Ten Process Check-In Flow

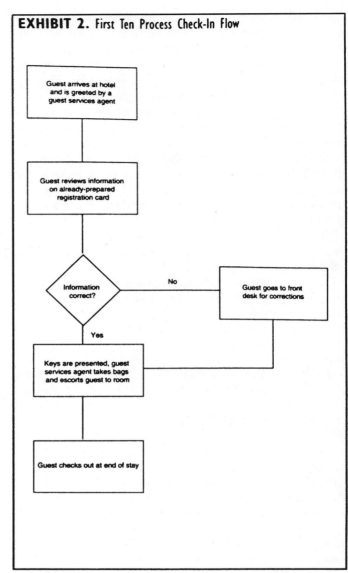

degree of variety leading to high complexity, which, in turn, makes the exact capacity of the entire process difficult to determine.

Queues—Under the old system, when every front desk was being used, a line would form in the center of the lobby. No sign was posted to let guests know that this was the process; nevertheless guests would intuit that they should form a line within the stanchions and advance through this line until reaching an available clerk. This meant that all individuals waited for the guests in front of them to finish checking in before they could begin their own check-in procedure.

With the new system, the lobby has neither queue nor stanchions. There is instead a guest services representative who watches the lobby and several guest service agents who complete everything from bag delivery to key selection. This saves guests valuable time; they no longer feel that they are waiting in an endless line. The clerks at the front desk are there only to cash checks, answer phones,

and make any changes to rooms; there may be only one individual at the desk. The back office may have several agents preparing the documents for the next business day and putting the guests who check in during the day into "I" status.

Bottleneck—With the old system, bottlenecks frequently occurred. An arriving guest who was originally only fifth in line might be required to wait an extraordinarily long time for even a simple request, if those guests being served first had several questions about their reservations.

With First Ten, each person is brought into the lobby by a guest service agent and presented his or her keys; that same agent takes the bags up to the guest's room. With one individual completing all steps at check-in, arriving guests don't have to wait for the guests in front of them to finish. The check-in takes as long as the guest would like, depending on any questions or immediate requests, or as long as it takes to walk to the guest room.

Scheduling of hotel staff is determined by each particular day's arrival schedule, to ensure that there is always a guest services agent available to meet any arriving guests.

Time standards—As previously discussed, the old system, on average, took about four and one-half minutes to complete if there were no changes. The new system has cut that time in half, allowing less than two minutes for the actual selection of the room and presentation of keys. Guest service agents now complete the work of selecting a room behind the scenes, during down times. The initial reservation now is more detailed when it enters the MAR-SHA system; it allows smoking or nonsmoking preferences, choice of credit card for final payment, arrival and departure dates, and bedding size preferences to be recorded. Accuracy here is vital and the quality of the information must be the best available. The agents at the hotel use this information from their PMS terminals to select an appropriate room for each individual.

Cycle and Throughput Time—For both the old and the new systems, the cycle starts when the guest enters the hotel and ends when he or she leaves. This cycle includes the initial check-in, as well as any time the guest spends at the desk while in-house, to the time of check-out. The cycle for this process happens the same way for each person that stays on the property. Once the guests check into the system, they must subsequently check out. This cycle allows for immediate "double checks" to see who is in what room and to see whether any one person stayed over the allotted time established in the reservation process.

With the implementation of the new system, the cycle has stayed relatively the same. The throughput time has remained the same as in the first system, which still depends on the length of stay the guest has established. The time for a particular job or unit to pass through an operating unit is the basic definition of throughput, so this will stay the same for either system when evaluating the entire system process.

COMPETITIVE CONSIDERATIONS

All performance evaluations of an operating unit should be driven by the overall goals of the firm. In some environments, customer service is, if not most important, at least considered in a different light. For any hotel faced with increasing competition, this remains true. Many surveys of individuals frequenting hotels emphasize the importance of a hassle-free check-in process with a minimum amount of time spent at the desk. This was the main reason why the Marriott Corporation developed the First Ten system.

The current check-in system has decreased the amount of time a guest waits for a room and the number of errors stemming from having to quickly enter data when a individual arrives on the property. In evaluating the First Ten system, Marriott discovered that efficiency, capacity, and guest satisfaction increased.

Before the implementation of First Ten, two of every ten individuals had difficulties with their check-in process. Under the new system, the number is down to one. This is a dramatic improvement, for the new system added capacity and increased speed while improving the accuracy of each transaction. Such results have not gone unnoticed. Since the implementation of First Ten three competitors have adopted very similar hassle-free processes.

The hotel used in the pilot program has formally adopted it, and many other Marriott Properties are making the necessary changes to switch to First Ten. In a couple of years, this process may be added to the list of Standard Operating Procedures for all Marriot-run hotels, for it supports Marriott's mission statement of providing 100 percent guest satisfaction 100 percent of the time.

Unit 6

Key Points to Consider

❖ Should a firm place a high value and concern on shortage cost or should the firm assume that it is of little or no consequence?

❖ What is so different about supply-chain management compared to how firms have always gone about supplier and distributor relations?

❖ What role have computers played in making supply-chain management easier?

 **Links**   www.dushkin.com/online/

These sites are annotated on pages 4 and 5.

Inventory and supply-chain management is very important for a firm. Inventories are found in raw materials, work-in-process, and finished goods. Inventories allow for meeting anticipated demand. The objective of inventory management is to satisfy customer requirements and to minimize total inventory cost. Inventory decisions rely upon an accurate sales forecast as an input and consideration of existing inventories, scheduled receipts, and production schedules. Inventory management is linked to both the MPS (Master Production Schedule) and MRP (Material Requirements Planning). Inventory management examines both dependent demand and independent demand. Dependent demand is the demand for raw materials, parts, and component items. Independent demand is the demand for finished goods.

Firms must analyze their inventory costs and determine the optimal reorder quantity. The major inventory costs are holding, reorder, and shortage costs. Holding costs are the costs associated with storing inventory and are measured in terms of the cost to keep one unit of inventory in storage for a year. The reorder costs are the costs associated with preparing and reordering inventory, and this is usually measured in terms of the cost per reorder. Shortage costs are the cost of having stock-out and not being able to satisfy customer requests for an

item. Shortage costs are more intangible and tie in to the firm's marketing philosophy about maintaining adequate quantities to provide customer service. The EOQ (economic order quantity) formula examines the holding and reorder cost to determine the optimal reorder quantity. The formula needs as an input facts on annual demand, the reorder cost, and the holding cost. The EOQ quantity will minimize total inventory costs by balancing the holding and reorder costs. The EOQ formula assumes level demand throughout the year, ignores price breaks from quantity discounts, and ignores shortage costs.

Supply-chain management involves a coordination of suppliers, manufacturers, and distributors to increase efficiency and effectiveness for all parties. From the earlier technique of EDI (Electronic Data Interchange), firms now utilize intranets to coordinate information flow through the supply chain. This new focus on coordinated management has received a great deal of attention by companies. This unit presents articles that review the historical roots of supply-chain management, that explain the details of how to successfully implement supply-chain management, and that offer case illustrations. As firms become more global, with both global suppliers and global distribution points to customers, there is a greater need to properly manage the supply chain.

Inventory and Supply-Chain Management

AN EXAMINATION OF INVENTORY TURNOVER IN THE *FORTUNE* 500 INDUSTRIAL COMPANIES

ROGER C. VERGIN, PHD
Department of Management, Penn State University, Malvern, PA 19355

Faced with formidable foreign and domestic competition, American corporations have pursued many paths to reducing costs in recent times. They have downsized and outsized to reduce personnel costs. They have undertaken mergers and acquisitions to achieve increased economies of scale. Manufacturing firms have sought to reduce costs and improve competitive advantage by improving quality, reducing lead times, automating operations and a host of other improvements. As part of the improvement process in manufacturing firms, a major shift has occurred in how inventories are viewed. It was once common to maintain large inventories in order to smooth manufacturing system imbalances such as variations in demand and production rates, quality deviations and transportation uncertainties. In more recent times, the dysfunctional role that inventories play in masking production problems has been increasingly recognized. This recognition was stimulated by the success of Just-in-Time (JIT) production in the Japanese automobile industry beginning in the 1970s. The JIT system was recognized as improving efficiency by shortening production cycles, reducing setup times and costs, reducing floor space requirements and improving quality, with the major emphasis placed on reducing raw material, work-in-process (WIP) and finished goods inventories.

Anecdotal evidence suggests inventory reductions as large as 80% to 90% in American firms from using JIT. For example, Harley Davidson, Inc., implemented JIT and reported an inventory turnover increase from 4 times per year in 1981 to 30 times by 1990 [4]. The OPW Division of Dover reported increasing turnover from 3.5 in 1983 to 32 in 1988 by adopting JIT [8].

In addition to JIT, American firms have emphasized improvements in supply chain management, materials requirements planning, throughput time and computer-aided manufacturing, which all include inventory reduction among their main objectives.

What has been the result of this emphasis on inventory? Has there been widespread reduction in inventories in American firms? Have inventory changes affected competitiveness and profit?

If there has been extensive successful implementation of inventory reducing programs in the United States in recent times, rather than merely isolated cases which are widely reported, then an aggregate measure of inventory on a broad scale, such as companywide inventory turnover ratios, should reveal that success. This study analyzes trends in the turnover ratios of the *Fortune* 500 largest industrial corporations in the United States for the years 1986 through 1995. The purpose of the research was to determine if there have been significant changes in inventory turnover ratios and how turnover patterns varied by factors such as industry, size of firm, and the effectiveness of previous inventory management. In addition, the effect of inventory changes on earnings was examined.

Comparisons were made by using time-series analyses of inventory turnover ratios for the years 1986 through 1995, calculated by using yearly cost of goods sold, as obtained from the corporation profit and loss statement, and year-end inventory, as obtained from the balance sheet. Data were obtained from *Compact Disclosure Guide to Public Company Information* [3], a database containing information from the 10K filings submitted to the Securities and Exchange Commission by publicly held corporations. Companies were obtained from the 1994 list of the *Fortune* 500 Largest U.S. Industrial Corporations. Over 95% were manufacturing firms, with the balance in wholesaling, mining, and oil and gas

From *Production and Inventory Management Journal*, First Quarter 1998, pp. 51-56. © 1998 by APICS, the American Production and Inventory Control Society. Reprinted by permission.

extraction. Inventories constitute a major portion of total assets for all the firms, and effective management of inventory is important in determining their competitive success. The 1994 list was the last produced by *Fortune*. In 1995, *Fortune*'s list became the 1,000 largest corporations, including those in service industries, for which inventory management is often only incidentally important.

For some firms, a once-a-year measurement may not provide an accurate picture of average inventory because of factors such as seasonality, year-end inventory reduction to "dress-up" financial statements, etc. However, any such patterns in a corporation are likely to persist from year to year, so year-end inventory levels should be reflective of real changes. There was no attempt to uncover or adjust for changes in accounting and reporting procedures of individual companies. No account was taken for acquisition, divestitures, or other major corporate adjustments. Many such events certainly occurred. However, this is a look at broad trends in inventories, and the complexities involved in factoring out such corporate changes are prohibitive.

Complete information was found on 427 of the 500 companies. The others were eliminated because they were not in existence as public enterprises over the full ten-year period or because they did not report cost of goods as a separate item.

COMPUTATION PROCEDURES

For the *Fortune* 500 industrial companies, inventory turnover ratios (ITRs) increased for eight consecutive years before a drop in 1995, for a total improvement of 14.71% over nine years (Table 1). Of the 427 companies, 286 (67%) improved inventory turnover, while 141 (33%) had lower turnover ratios. Also, 164 increased turnover by more than 25%, while 52 had turnover decrease by more than 25%. An

---

Inventory Turnover Ratio:

$$ITR = \frac{\text{Annual Cost of Goods Sold}}{\text{Year-end Aggregate Inventory}}$$

% Change in Inventory Turnover Ratio in Year n:

$$\Delta ITR_n = \frac{(ITR_n - ITR_{n-1})}{ITR_{n-1}} \times 100$$

% Change in Inventory Turnover Ratio from 1986 to 1995:

$$\Delta ITR_{1986-1995} = \frac{(ITR_{1995} - ITR_{1986})}{ITR_{1986}} \times 100$$

---

analysis of variance was run to determine if the improvements in turnover rates were statistically significant. The resulting *F* statistic was significant at the .037 level. Thus, it can be concluded that there was an increase in inventory turnover during the 1986–1995 period. [See "Inventory Turnover Ratio box for computations.]

DIFFERENCES BY PRIMARY STANDARD INDUSTRIAL CODE

There is a large difference in inventory turnover ratios by industry. For example, the newspaper publishers in the *Fortune* 500 make products with one-day shelf life and uniformly have high turnover ratios that average about 40. By contrast, distillers of alcoholic spirits must age some of their products for several years to acquire full value, and have turnover ratios below 2. To confirm there is a real difference in ITRs by industry, an analysis of variance was run and the resulting *F* statistic was significant at .0001.

It may not be obvious, however, if improvement in turnover ratios over the 1986–1995 period varied by industry. If JIT and other inventory reducing programs are more applicable to some industries than others, a difference in improvements in inventory turn-

TABLE 1: Results for All 427 Companies

Year	ITRn	ΔITRn
1986	6.29	n.a.
1987	6.34	0.64%
1988	6.44	1.71%
1989	6.67	3.53%
1990	6.97	4.46%
1991	7.02	0.79%
1992	7.22	2.83%
1993	7.34	1.66%
1994	7.44	1.34%
1995	7.22	-2.89%
1986–1995		14.71%

over ratios by industry might be expected. Therefore, investigation was made of the Δ ITRs differences by industry.

Segmentation was done by primary Standard Industrial Code (SIC) number at the major industrial group level, that is, by the first two digits of the four-digit code. There were 21 categories that varied from three companies to 59 companies. Table 2 shows the result of the analysis. Changes

TABLE 2: Inventory Turnover Ratios by SIC Primary Code

SIC	Firms	Code Description	ITR_{1986}	ITR_{1995}	% Chg.
13	11	Oil and Gas Extraction	9.6	13.8	44%
35	59	Industrial Machinery & Computers	4.5	6.3	40%
30	8	Rubber and Misc. Plastic Products	5.1	7.0	38%
34	12	Fabricated Metal Products	3.7	5.1	35%
25	9	Furniture and Fixtures	7.5	10.1	35%
37	36	Transportation Equipment	6.0	7.8	30%
39	5	Miscellaneous Manufacturing Industries	5.5	6.6	21%
36	28	Electronic & Other Electrical Equipment	4.2	5.0	20%
27	18	Printing and Publishing	14.6	17.2	18%
50–51	12	Wholesale Trade	6.4	7.5	18%
38	26	Instruments and Related Products	4.1	4.7	14%
26	30	Paper and Allied Products	6.9	7.7	11%
33	23	Primary Metal Industries	5.3	5.8	9%
10	3	Metal Mining	5.0	5.5	8%
28	52	Chemicals and Allied Products	4.2	4.5	7%
32	10	Stone, Clay, and Glass Products	6.8	7.3	7%
29	25	Petroleum and Coal Products	11.3	11.8	5%
21	3	Tobacco Products	1.9	1.9	-3%
23	9	Apparel & Textile Products	3.6	3.5	-5%
20	42	Food and Kindred Products	9.0	8.1	-11%
22	6	Textile Mill Products	5.9	5.2	-12%
Total	427		6.3	7.2	15%

in inventory turnover ratios ranged from 44% for the oil and gas extraction industry to minus 12% for the textile mill products industry. An analysis of variance was run and the resulting F statistic was significant at the .010 level, demonstrating that there was a real difference in improvement rates by industry. While results by industry are mixed, there seemed to be a tendency for ITRs to improve more for firms making industrial products compared to firms making consumer products. All four categories that showed decreases were in the food and clothing industries.

DIFFERENCES BY SIZE OF COMPANY

Since turnover ratios and improvement in turnover ratios were found to vary by industry, it is also conceivable they might vary by size of firm. Perhaps, for example, larger firms might benefit from greater economies of scale. Alternatively, smaller firms might have been more aggressive in improving inventory management.

To determine if there were significant differences in ITRs by size of firm or differences

in Δ ITRs by size of firm, regression analyses were run using all 427 companies. The 1995

TABLE 3: Companies by _Fortune_ 500 Rank

FORTUNE #	ITR_{1986}	ITR_{1995}	$\Delta ITR_{1986-1995}$	n
1–100	6.37	7.61	19.5%	92
101–200	6.87	7.49	9.0%	91
201–300	6.84	7.80	14.0%	84
301–400	5.22	6.76	29.5%	80
401–500	6.02	6.31	4.8%	80

turnover ratio was regressed against company rank in the _Fortune_ 500. The resulting equation is $ITR_{1995} = 8.21 - .0040 \times$ _Fortune_ rank. The t statistic for the slope being different than 0 was −2.08, which is significant at the .038 level. The negative slope suggests that the firms with the higher _Fortune_ rank number (the smaller firms) had lower turnover ratios. Alternatively, the larger firms turned inventory over more frequently.

The improvement in the inventory turnover (Δ $ITR_{1986-1995}$) was also regressed against company rank in the _Fortune_ 500. The t statistic for the slope of the resulting equation being different than 0 was .68, which is not significant with a *p* value of .499. To demonstrate the above relationships, the companies are shown by *Fortune* 500 rank in Table 3.

Even though there was a statistically significant relationship between the size of the firm and the magnitude of the 1995 inventory turnover ratios, it can be seen from the discontinuities in Table 3 that firm size does not appear to be a dominant factor. The figures also show that there was no apparent general relationship between the size of the firm and the amount of improvement in turnover from 1986 to 1995.

DIFFERENCES BY PREVIOUS INVENTORY MANAGEMENT EFFICIENCY

When corporations find they are unable to meet the competitive forces in the marketplace, they have an extra incentive to improve. While ITRs are certainly dependent on many factors such as industry, type of organization (manufacturer, wholesaler, etc.) and so on, it seems reasonable to assert that turnover ratios are related to the effectiveness of inventory management and that firms with better inventory management will, in general, have larger ITRs. If that assertion is true, then the firms with the smaller 1986 ITRs had a greater need to improve their inventory management. Analysis was done to see if such firms were more effective in improving inventory turnover.

A regression analysis was run using all 427 companies to determine if there were significant differences in Δ ITRs by initial ITRs. Improvement over the period 1986–1995 was regressed against the turnover ratio in 1986. The resulting equation is $\Delta \text{ITR}_{1986-1995} = .553 - .038 \times \text{ITR}_{1986}$. The *t* statistic for the regression slope being different than 0 was −5.32, which is significant at the <.0001 level. The negative slope suggests that the firms with the lower initial turnover ratios were the most successful in improving inventory turnover.

To illustrate this differing improvement as a function of beginning inventory turnover ratio, the companies were classified by the magnitude of their 1986 ITRs. Four categories with approximately equal numbers of companies were established, as shown in Table 4.

This classification confirms that the firms with the lowest ITRs in 1986 were able to achieve the greatest improvement over the next decade. Although ITRs increased in all catego-

ries, the firms with 1986 ITRs below 3.50 achieved an average improvement of 55.8%, while firms in the highest bracket of 1986 ITRs achieved an average improvement of only .8%. Although the firms with the lowest initial ITRs improved the most on a percentage basis, they still trailed on an absolute basis.

EFFECT OF IMPROVEMENT IN INVENTORY TURNOVER ON EARNINGS

Organizations that embrace new concepts for reducing inventories may focus on short-term improvements in direct inventory measures. In doing so, there is a danger of ignoring second-order effects. For example, inventories may decrease at the cost of adversely affecting a company's long-term competitiveness. While inventory improvements are important, adoption of performance improvement programs such as JIT must yield long-run benefits that improve a company's competitive success and financial health. While many articles document how reducing inventory levels improves operation performance by reducing consumption of resources such as floor space, there is little systematic evidence that operational improvements affect financial performance [10]. Unless freed resources are profitably redeployed, there may be little financial benefit to the firm.

The financial effect is difficult to isolate since JIT and other programs typically take many years to fully implement, and countless other changes are occurring at the same time. Two recent studies looked at the effect of implementing JIT on earnings with mixed results. Huson and Nanda [6] identified 55 firms that applied JIT between 1980 and 1990 and compared their operating results to averages of other firms in the same SIC code. They found that inventory turnover improved by 23.7% for the firms adopting JIT compared to only 7.7% for nonimplementing firms. However, earnings per share decreased by 24.6% for the adopting firms compared to decreasing by 13.9% for nonadopting firms. Balakrishnan et al. [1] paired 46 firms that had publicly disclosed adopting JIT production during the 1985–1989 period with 46 control firms matched on industry, customer concentration, and size. While tests revealed no differences in inventory utilization prior to JIT adoption, treatment firms reported markedly superior utilization of inventory after adopting

JIT production. However, earnings on both treatment firms and control firms declined over the study period due to other economic factors. More importantly, the decline reported by treatment firms was not significantly different from that reported by control firms.

For the Fortune 500 firms in this study, an attempt was made to measure the relationship of improvements in inventory turnover ratios with corporate earnings. A regression was run with the $\Delta ITR_{1986-1995}$ values as the independent variable and the annual growth rate of earnings per share of common stock from 1986–1995 as reported in Fortune as the dependent variable. Since Fortune did not report earnings on all companies, the sample size was reduced from 427 to 330. The resulting equation was: % Annual Growth in Earnings = .2725 - .0016 $\Delta ITR_{1986-1995}$. The negative slope

TABLE 4: Companies Classified by ITRs

ITR_{1986} Range	Ave.ITR_{1986}	Ave.ITR_{1995}	$\Delta ITR_{1986-1995}$	n
<3.50	2.49	3.88	55.8%	114
3.50–4.99	4.18	5.28	26.3%	110
5.00–7.49	5.96	6.45	8.2%	97
7.50–higher	12.79	12.89	0.8%	106

suggests that companies with greater improvement in inventory turnover ratios tended to have lower rates of growth of earnings. However, the t statistic for the slope being different than 0 was - .69, which is not significant with a p value of .488. Thus, it cannot be concluded that increased inventory turnover affected profits on the basis of this evidence.

TURNOVER IN SELECTED COMPANIES CITED AS APPLYING JIT

In an earlier study, Billesbach and Hayen [2] identified 28 companies that had implemented JIT and compared their inventory turnover ratios for the period 1977–1979 to the period 1987–1989 and found that 25 had increased inventory turnover rates over that ten-year span. Twenty-two of the 28 companies from that study were among the 1994 Fortune 500 companies included in this study. Seventeen of those 22 increased their turnover ratios for the 1986–1995 period. The average

ITR for all 22 companies increased from 4.72 to 6.09 for an average $\Delta ITR_{1986-1995}$ of 28.9%, which is more than double the 13.9% average $\Delta ITR_{1986-1995}$ for the remaining 405 companies of this study. It is often noted that JIT is a process that can take more than a decade to fully implement. While there is some overlap in the time periods of the two studies, the results here suggest that most of the companies of the Billesbach and Hayen study were continuing to benefit through a second decade from their JIT efforts.

DISCUSSION

Inventory levels in large national and multinational corporations vary because of a multitude of organizational, economic, and financial factors. Still, any measurable major change or trend toward increased inventory turnover is congruent with the well-documented efforts of industrial organizations, such as JIT, supply chain management, lean production, etc., to implement operating policies that reduce inventories. Examination of the ITRs of the Fortune 500 largest industrial corporations in the United States during the period of 1986–1995 indicates that ITRs have increased by an average of 14.7%.

This improvement, however, falls far short of the anecdotal examples of dramatic inventory management improvement found in the literature. That suggests that many such quoted figures are for isolated operations in the large organization, and total company inventories have been reduced much less. For example, the earlier cited article [4] reported that Harley Davidson Inc. increased ITR from 4 in 1981 to 30 in 1990. Yet, the company financial statements show ITR at 5.78 in 1990 and show it going from 5.58 in 1986 to 7.00 in 1995. While this is an impressive increase of 25.4%, it falls far short of the cited improvement. This suggests that the dramatic improvements that may occasionally be achieved in one production process may not be achievable throughout an organization.

While there was improvement in inventory turnover for the Fortune 500 industrial corporations over the 1986–1995 decade, it averaged only about 1.5% per year. This seems less than the typical observer of operations management might have suspected, given the attention that inventory reduction has received over that time.

One cannot attribute all of the improvement to programs such as JIT, lean production, etc. For example, oil and gas extraction, which was the industry which had the greatest improvement in inventory turnover (Table 2), has not been noted for applying JIT. Prices of oil and gas products change frequently. The increased inventory turnover may be misleading, since the improvement might have been due more to changing product values than to changing physical stocks.

There are also cases where increased attention to managing inventory has led to larger manufacturer inventories. For example, the grocery industry has been implementing major changes in supply chain management through a process called *continuous replenishment* in which the manufacturers monitor and manage the retailers' inventories for them. While this has resulted in substantially reduced inventories and fewer stockouts for retailers, those improvements have come at the expense of shifting some of the storage burden to the manufacturers [9]. The food and kindred products manufacturers in this study showed a reduction in inventory turnover of −11%.

This study, as others before it, failed to find a direct link of improved inventory turnover to profits. Finding such a link may continue to prove illusive. Manufacturers of consumer products other than foods are also increasingly using electronic data interchange to monitor and manage retailers' inventories. Those manufacturers leading these efforts are increasing their competitive advantage and capturing larger market share [9]. While this may lead to greater profits, it sometimes comes at the expense of carrying relatively larger inventories.

REFERENCES

1. Balakrishnan, R., T. Linsmeier, and M. Venkatachalam. "Financial Benefits from JIT Adoption: Effects of Customer Concentration and Cost Structure." *The Accounting Review* 71, no. 2 (1996): 183–205.
2. Billesbach, T., and R. Hayen. "Long-Term Impact of Just-in-Time on Inventory Performance Measures." *Production and Inventory Management Journal* 35, no. 1 (1994): 62–67.
3. *Compact Disclosure Guide to Public Company Information.* Bethesda, MD: Disclosure Incorporated, 1986–1995.
4. Cooper, B. "Just-in-Time System Acted More Like Domino Theory during Harley Strike." *The Business Journal-Milwaukee* 8, no. 22 (1991): 4–9.
5. Fry, T. "Manufacturing Performance and Cost Accounting." *Production and Inventory Management Journal* 33, no. 3 (1992): 30–35.
6. Huson, M., and D. Nanda. "The Impact of Just-in-Time Manufacturing on Firm Performance in the U.S." *Journal of Operations Management* 12 (1995): 297–310.
7. Norris, D., R. Swanson, and Y. Chu. "Just-in-Time Production Systems: A Survey of Managers." *Production and Inventory Management Journal* 35, no. 2 (1994): 63–66.
8. Orth, D., R. Hubil, and D. Korzan. "Analysis of a JIT Implementation at Dover Corporation." *Production and Inventory Management Journal* 31, no. 3 (1990): 34–36.
9. Vergin, R., and K. Barr. "Continuous Replenishment: Progress in the Grocery Industry." Penn State University, unpublished manuscript, 1997.
10. Young, S., and F. Selto. "New Manufacturing Practices and Cost Management: A Review of the Literature and Directions for Future Research." *Journal of Accounting Literature* 10 (1991): 265–298.

About the Author—

ROGER C. VERGIN, PhD, is professor of business administration at Penn State University at the Great Valley Graduate Center, where he served as director of the Master of Management program from 1990–1995. He earned his PhD from the University of Minnesota and was formerly a professor at the University of California at Berkeley, the University of Washington, and Simon Fraser University. He has published in Management Science, Journal of Industrial Engineering, Financial Management Journal, California Management Review, *and* Journal of Investing. *Outside the academic arena, he is the author of a 1997 book titled* Brando with His Guard Down, *which resulted from a stint as Marlon Brando's business manager in the 1970s.*

THE ULTIMATE GOAL

BALANCING
Inventory &
Service Levels

The act of juggling inventory and service levels is difficult because of the inherent contradiction between the two in the contemporary marketplace—shorter product life cycles make it costly to stock finished goods and spare parts, yet customers demand rapid response after placing an order.

By Rob Cunningham

COMPANIES THAT ARE ADDRESSING THE PROBLEM ARE SHOWING that it can be done. In only six months, PC ServiceSource planners reduced on-hand inventory by 12 days while simultaneously increasing customer service levels by more than 10 percent. Xerox increased service levels and reduced inventory while handling 200,000–300,000 transactions daily across 74 countries. Cisco Systems kept its inventory flat and service levels strong across 8,500 part numbers while growing at 80 percent a year. AlliedSignal substantially reduced active inventory while simultaneously realizing significant increases in fill rates, thereby leading to better customer service.

Planners are now using new business practices and a new breed of information systems to rapidly forecast, plan and allocate materials across worldwide supply chains to balance inventory cost and service levels so they can satisfy their customers while maintaining profitability. They are working at single, integrated desktop screens to view and manipulate the myriad elements of their inventory strategy; enabling their corporations to deliver custom-configured products on time without excessive inventory.

Communication Between Field and Planning

ONE OF THE MOST IMPORTANT THINGS that can help planners balance inventory and service levels is to establish better lines of communication between the planners making the decisions of what to build or buy and the people in the field. Sales and marketing personnel need to communicate back to the planning organization, at a detailed level, what is going on with the company's products.

Very often, people in the field may know that most of a company's customers are moving away from a particular model of a finished good. But because they don't quickly filter that information back to planning, the company will end up with too much product, especially if the finished good has a long lead time. Even worse is the situation of the service planner, who doesn't find out until even later that there is an insufficient installed base to support the forecast for future demand.

Today's supply chain planning systems can search out these patterns and warn companies earlier in the product cycle. It all boils down to information—the number one ingredient that helps planners reduce inventory while improving service. And information, at its core, is valid data.

Most companies think they either don't have the budget to track certain data elements to gain the necessary information, or they believe the departments that need to be involved won't cooperate. While companies understand they need to invest in new processes and systems to help balance inventory and service levels, they often don't re-

From *APICS—The Performance Advantage*, August 1998, pp. 42-44, 46. © 1998 by APICS, the American Production and Inventory Control Society. Reprinted by permission.

The ability to balance inventory and service levels increasingly distinguishes successful companies from marginal ones. With compressed life cycles, managing the "end life" of a product is particularly critical. Insufficient inventory means the customer will go to a competitor; too much stock runs the risk of obsolescence and a charge on the books for product that cannot be sold. With today's thin margins, this can wipe out profits on what originally might have been a successful product launch. During the manufacturing renaissance of the past 20 years, manufacturers have generated tremendous operational efficiencies in the areas of engineering and manufacturing. The next frontier to be tackled —through better practices and software tools—is inventory planning to simultaneously reduce stocks and working capital while improving customer service.

alize that they need cleaner and better fuel—information—to run these new high-powered systems.

One of the most important pieces of information that is required is accurate, on-hand balances. That would seem obvious, but it's still a big problem in industry. Another critical piece of information is actual demand, especially if you're going to do statistical forecasting and safety-stock analysis.

Actual demand is not what a company shipped—it's what a customer ordered. For example, suppose you received 10 orders for a particular product each week during a three-week period when you don't have inventory available. When inventory shows up the third week, you ship 30 products. Many companies enter that demand as 30 in the third week. This fouls up the statistical engine of an inventory planning system, because it looks like an erratic part, not one that customers have been ordering on a regular basis.

Tracking Cancellations

ANOTHER WAY COMPANIES CAN IMPROVE the balance between inventory and service levels is by tracking cancellations. Companies need to understand why a customer canceled an order. A lot of companies automatically back out cancellations from demand. But if the customer called and canceled because you didn't have the product and someone else did, you don't want to remove that item from your demand counter or you won't have it available the next time the customer calls.

Another crucial issue in balancing inventory and service levels involves multiple warehouses and the failure to track the source of actual demand. If a company's Portland, Ore., warehouse doesn't have inventory to ship to a customer, they may call the Dayton, Ohio, warehouse to have it shipped. In this case, demand is often recorded at the Dayton facility. This information is then fed to an inventory planning system, which sees demand in Dayton and none in Portland. So it keeps scheduling for inventory to be built and stocked in Dayton.

Another important issue involves scheduled orders. Companies often get an order from a customer in advance, with the indicated ship date somewhere out in the future. Many companies record that demand in the week they enter the order. They don't have a mechanism for telling the planner that the new order actually matches the forecast for, say, week six, and the order has been placed and locked in.

From a planning perspective, this information is especially helpful for low-volume, high-dollar items. These are situations where you know you're going to sell one item in the next 12 weeks, but you're not really sure in which of those 12 weeks you're going to sell it. Companies without a sophisticated time-phase capability in their planning systems will ship the item to the warehouse in week one and let it sit on the shelf until the actual shipment date. This artificially inflates inventory cost because you're car-

Inventory planning systems must be **linked** to other corporate **information systems** to **gather** the information they need to help planners **balance** inventory and service levels.

rying the part for those extra weeks and not taking advantage of information you already have but are not feeding into the system properly.

Linking Planning to Other Information Systems

INVENTORY PLANNING SYSTEMS must be linked to other corporate information systems to gather the information they need to help planners balance inventory and service levels. For example, information on cancellations can be fed directly from call centers. It would really help inventory planners if companies created a process or code in the call center system to indicate if an order has been canceled and why. This information can then be sorted into categories and fed to the planning system to analyze the details.

Customer order information will be fed into inventory planning systems from the order entry-processing module within an enterprise resource planning system. On-hand balance information typically comes from inventory control systems. Inventory counts will come from warehousing systems that track stock and in-transit material.

Purchasing is another system that needs to be tightly linked with inventory planning. Many companies have "dirty" purchase order books, with as much as a third of their inventory recorded as vendor due dates that might be as much as a year old. This means that the vendor was never going to ship the product or has already shipped it and nobody closed the order.

This kind of incorrect information will really skew the exception messages the planner is getting. If you're a planner with 100,000 items to plan and you're trying to do exception-based planning, you need systems that can sort through data and present intelligent exceptions. In this case, the system will tell you not to buy more, but rather, expedite more. The planner may then call up the vendor and find out the items were shipped a year ago and have been in on-hand balance for 12 months. If you don't go in and clean up these and other systems before you turn on a planning system, the system will do nothing but provide you mistakes, albeit extremely fast.

Another way to realize improvements in the balance between inventory and service levels is vendor management. Companies need to tell vendors what dock to show up at on what day, and give them a one-hour time slot during which their trailer needs to be there and unloading or you will make it circle the block or send it back at their cost.

Often, companies cut orders for the next several months and give a vendor information to phase the deliveries. If the vendor happens to have all the inventory on the shelf, the vendor may ship all the orders as if they're one order. This may improve your service levels, but at the expense of inflated inventory. A lot of companies simply have not worked out with their vendors all the arrangements involved such that when they provide an order in advance, they also provide a specific window during which that order should be shipped. All the planning in the world to balance inventory and service levels will not be successful if you go ahead and let your receiving dock receive inventory prematurely from a vendor.

Planning at the Desktop

PLANNERS FOCUSED ON BALANCING inventory and service levels should be presented daily, at their desktop, with a work queue from the planning system that includes a prioritized analysis of the items that need to be attended to immediately. This queue will include all the information a planner needs from multiple information systems, presented in a single, integrated desktop, and built around exception messaging and drill-down and "what-if" modeling capabilities.

As companies have fewer and fewer planners handling more and more items, it becomes increasingly important that the system do a lot of the upfront analysis. The work queue must be very robust in terms of how many conditions it checks for. It should look not only for simple conditions like stockout and back orders, but also for more sophisticated situations like inaccurate forecasts or projected problems.

At the beginning of the day, the first thing planners will typically do is work on service-level problems. They'll look at anything with a back order or stockout. They'll check their e-mail and voice mails to find out what the problems are.

In addition to addressing service-level problems, it's also important that planners look for a chance to cancel orders and reduce what's coming in. A lot of companies miss a great opportunity here. Their planners are so geared to go after service-level issues that they spend the bulk of their time expediting, not "de-expediting."

If you can uncover, for example, that you have a 1,000 items on order and haven't sold any in a couple of months, you might be able to go in and cancel the order. Companies need to understand that if they don't look a little further out into the future, they'll always be fighting fires, not preventing them.

A planner working with a good inventory planning system as he or she moves down the queue, will not only find back orders and stockouts, but also parts where they need to buy more inside or outside of lead time. They will also find parts where the system is telling them that they need to push out the order or cancel it all together because demand hasn't materialized to match the forecast.

Flexibility

FLEXIBILITY IS ALSO AN IMPORTANT consideration for a planning system that will help you balance inventory and service levels. As a planner, you want a system that will allow you to set up rules differently for different sets of items. For example, if you've got inexpensive items that are important to stock for service-level reasons, they keep people happy and they cost you almost nothing; you want to bias the planning algorithms for those parts towards service levels.

You also want a system that will let you identify the items that represent the core of your business. The classic rule is that 20 percent of the parts cover 80 percent of the business. In our experience, however, the rule is more like 5 percent of the parts account for 95 percent of the dollar value of demand. Even if that 5 percent only represents 200 items, it's important that planners focus on them, even at the expense of the other 3,800 items that might be only 5 percent of the business in dollar value. If you can just plan five of those 200 core parts better, it will pay for every bit of excess inventory you create by not giving the same amount of attention to the other 3,800 parts.

This points to a critical problem in industry—people have the wrong mix of inventory. A company may say the industry standard is 12 turns a year and that it's doing 12 turns a year, but its service level is not where the company wants it to be. The reason for that is that the company is probably looking at its inventory in aggregate and has not done the detailed analysis. Companies will find that they can buy a lot of service level and customer satisfaction if they focus on specific parts.

Companies also need to set flexible thresholds for inventory and service levels. You want the ability to tell the planning system that, for example, the ideal plan for this item or group of items is an investment of $1 million in inventory and a 95 percent service level, but the system can float between $1.2 million investment and $800,000 as long as the service-level percentage stays at plus or minus two points. If you don't let the system set up these thresholds, it will bring your planners huge numbers of messages every day that they can't act upon and will think are meaningless.

For example, you do not want the system putting in the planner's work queue an item that is set for 1,000 pieces of safety stock if you're down to 999 and the rest of the plan is fine. The planner is going to look at that and say, "I'm not even going to bother with that." But they have already spent the time bringing up the part and processing it.

When this happens, planners begin to ignore review reasons or turn them off. By this point, a company has invested a lot of money in buying a system, cleaning up its information and training its planners; but because it failed to properly tune the system, the planning group loses confidence in it and everyone goes back to their spreadsheets.

You need a system that really lets you tune and tweak so your planners can adjust the work queue to the business environment they're in. For example, you want a system that incorporates more than one type of safety stock strategy; it should be able to configure safety stock strategies differently to different items. Some items you never want to stock, some items you never want to stockout. You also want to be able to configure the system differently to incorporate different forecasting methods. Some products may have 15-year life cycles, others may have a one-year life cycle. Even in one-year life cycle products, components within those products will often last a lot longer than that one-year period.

You also need a system that will allow you to blend statistics and human intuition. If you go on purely statistical forecasting for items at the beginning of their life cycle, that usually works fine; but at the end of the life cycle, you need the ability to blend planner and marketer intuition with the statistics.

Playing with the Numbers

ALSO CRITICAL FOR BALANCING inventory and service levels is the ability to play with numbers to come up with new scenarios. Whenever you're putting together your hardware requirements, include within them sufficient processing power to support a full-size clone of your database. This will allow you to take a "snapshot" of your database for modeling new scenarios. Most systems allow planners to model at the item level, online. But if you're looking at radical changes—for example, restructuring inventory flows between five warehouses—you'll want to do that off-line on a separate database.

The ability to perform a "what-if" analysis to rationalize a distribution network is where more and more companies are realizing savings and improving the relationship between inventory and service levels. For example, at one company, the vast majority of items were only used in one or two outlying warehouses. The problem this company discovered was that these items were being received into the main warehouse and then distributed out to the satellite warehouses, resulting in a 50 percent increase in lead time.

The company used its modeling database to create different location hierarchies and assign parts with distribution flows that were more appropriate to the demand pattern. This, in turn, enabled the company to cut 50 percent of the projected safety stock needed to achieve the same service level. There was no change to service level or overall manufacturing lead time—the company just improved the way it was routing the component within its own network and was able to reduce safety stocks.

Rob Cunningham is product manager at LPA Software Inc., Fairport, N.Y., where his responsibilities have included implementing supply chain planning software at customer sites.

Just-in-time manufacturing

Christine A. Swanson and William M. Lankford

State University of West Georgia, Carrollton, Georgia, USA

Introduction

William J. Stevenson, in *Production/Operations Management*, defines the term just-in-time manufacturing as "a repetitive production system in which processing and movement of material and goods occurs just as they are needed, usually in small batches" (Stevenson, 1996). However, just-in-time (JIT) is more than an inventory system. JIT manufacturing is a philosophy by which an organization seeks continually to improve its products and processes by eliminating waste (Ptak, 1997). Since one purpose of JIT manufacturing is to reduce any waste and inefficiencies that do not add value to a product, it should come as no surprise that the JIT approach was developed in Japan—a country with scarce resources and space limitations. Organizations wanting to use the JIT approach to manufacturing must have several building blocks in place. These building blocks were first established in the early 1950s by T. Ohno, former Executive Vice President of Toyota Motor Company (Ansari and Modarress, 1990). The building blocks include:

- company-wide commitment;
- proper materials at the right time;
- supplier relationships;
- quality;
- personnel.

The JIT manufacturing approach can give organizations the necessary benefits required to survive, and perhaps even prosper, in an economy with increasingly scarce resources.

From *Business Process Management Journal*, Vol. 4, No. 4, 1998, pp. 333-341. © 1998 by Christine A. Swanson and William M. Lankford. Reprinted by permission.

Company-wide commitment

Proper planning before implementation of a JIT manufacturing system is essential and begins with a commitment from top management. Knowledge of key items such as the cost of converting to a JIT system, how long the conversion will take, and expected results can aid upper management's decision to support the JIT endeavor. Additionally a financial commitment is necessary during the early stages of development and implementation of JIT manufacturing. Without the commitment of upper management, the JIT manufacturing plans for an organization will not get off the ground (Galhenage, 1997).

Besides the commitment of top management, the implementation of JIT requires support from all facets of an organization. This support takes the form of dedication and trust to ensure that all parties meet the required production schedules. If one party fails to meet their schedule, the entire JIT system can crumble. Everyone in the organization must believe in and strive to meet JIT's ultimate goal—continuous improvement and the elimination of waste.

All personnel in an organization must be committed to the JIT system for the operation to be successful. With commitment and cooperation from employees on the production line and all other employees up to top management, the organization has the first, and possibly most crucial, building block necessary for the implementation and operation of the JIT manufacturing process.

Effective implementation of JIT requires a substantial and continuing effort on the part of management to educate the employees about the techniques of JIT production (Browne, 1995). Education and training of employees at all levels is a large investment in time and money, which sometimes keeps firms from instituting a JIT production strategy. JIT implementation needs the support of management (Shannon, 1993).

Another requirement for successful JIT implementation is properly functioning and maintained equipment, that produce products that are perfect every time. Total productive maintenance is a system that is used in JIT to ensure machines and tools needed to make quality products are available. This maintenance team has the responsibility of preventing breakdowns on the production line. The operator using the machine does most repairs (Willis, 1992). These maintenance activities include keeping the equipment clean and always in good working order, so they will not break down.

Producing a quality product in any organization is the goal of JIT systems. One of the results of JIT systems is the elimination of waste or non value-adding activities; this contributes to quality. The difficult task in achieving quality is achieving the level of quality that the customers require. To be able to give customers the quality they require the company must be committed to a continuous quality improvement program (Sinnamon, 1993).

Proper materials at the right time

With the JIT manufacturing system, materials are purchased in small quantities delivered frequently just before they are needed for production. By ordering small batches that are consumed almost as soon as they arrive, an organization can utilize space for production purposes that they would normally hold for "just-in-case" inventory management. Additionally, the costs of a capital outlay for the "just-in-case" ordering mentality, when combined with the costs associated with holding large amounts of inventory, are in most cases higher than the freight costs and smaller discounts associated with the smaller lot size purchases. According to A. Ansari, "Ford Motor Company estimates that every dollar's worth of parts carried in inventory costs the company 26 cents, mainly in interest and insurance" (Ansari and Modarress, 1990). The JIT manufacturing process eliminates wasted space and tied-up capital that can be allocated to alternative uses to improve the overall success of the organization (Ptak, 1997).

In addition to ordering smaller batches of materials at the proper time, successful JIT organizations should keep the following requirements in mind:

Overall requirements for proper materials at the right time

• an acceptable level of quality;

• on-time delivery schedule;

• reasonable cost (Galhenage, 1997).

Supplier relationships

Besides smaller lot orders, the JIT philosophy mandates a reduction in the number of suppliers. The impact of this reduction is that the quality of the relationship between buyers and suppliers improves as these material "partners" work closely together. Moreover, better communications occur because important changes in order specifics only need to be communicated to a few suppliers. Yet another benefit of reducing the number of suppliers is the reduction in paper work. An organization will reap many benefits in terms of costs and time savings by reducing the number of suppliers and improving relationships with these valued partners in the JIT manufacturing process.

Companies with just in time production systems depend on suppliers to deliver quality goods on time. Just in time purchasing is a concept that coordinates delivery of materials just as they are needed for production. Suppliers must deliver goods as frequently as required. Suppliers must make numerous deliveries each day in the exact quantity specified. Because of frequent deliveries, central receiving areas and warehouses are not needed. Generally materials are delivered straight to the area of the production process. Suppliers also have the burden of inspecting goods before shipping them out. If goods are damaged or defective, the company's whole production line could be shut down. Companies must build relationships with suppliers. The company and the supplier both benefit from just in time systems. The company benefits because of reduced cost. The supplier benefits by long-term business relationships with companies as long as they continue to supply quality products on time.

The traditional perspective sees the purchaser-supplier relationship as both parties competing with each other for profit margin. Purchasers want the lowest cost per unit, while suppliers want the highest cost per unit. However, the JIT approach presents a very different perspective on the relationship. The JIT purchaser-supplier relationship is one of a partnership-in-profit creation.

The JIT relationship is another cornerstone of the whole JIT philosophy. In this partnership, the emphasis of the purchaser is to develop a close cooperative relationship with a relatively small number of carefully selected suppliers, with a long-term partnership in mind (Leavy, 1994). This type of relationship fosters a high degree of interdependence between purchaser and supplier. It also promotes significant cooperation, which can help the profitability of each. The purchaser must produce a closer coordination with schedules, promote cooperation on process and product improvements, and foster a joint action on cost reduction measures to reduce their inventory investment and improve profit margins, while increasing the overall levels of quality and service of the suppliers.

The cooperative relationship, on the supplier's side, insulates them from the full force of competition in the supply segment of the market chain. This is particularly noticeable when the supplier is committed to only one, or at most, a few purchasers. The buyer, on the other hand, can benefit from the non-investment and low risks of this "vertical integration." The following list from Brian Leavy contains the main features of the JIT relationship:

- Buyers and suppliers become partners;
- It is a win-win game for both parties.
- Primary focus is profit-margin gain for both and equal sharing of the rewards.

Communication linkage

In this win-win environment, communication is an essential ingredient for developing successful purchaser-supplier relations. New or enchanted communication patterns being practiced include:

- more freely exchanged cost, schedule, and quality control information;
- the elimination of purchase orders for each shipment;
- involving suppliers in the development of design specifications;
- the formation of joint task forces to resolve concerns;
- the use of supplier and manufacturer plant visits;
- the use of electronic data interchange (EDI).

The above list is from the *International Journal of Purchasing & Materials Management* (Richeson *et al.*, 1995). By opening the channels of communication, companies foster the development of trust between the purchaser and its supplier, thereby facilitating openness in the exchange of information.

An effective relationship between a purchaser and a supplier depends not only on the type of communication but more importantly on the effectiveness of each partner's communication. In a JIT environment this dimension is critical; it reflects the trust and commitment of the two partners to achieve mutual goals.

Schedule and delivery performance are seen as the most important reasons for communication. The combined communication efforts of JIT relationships have a greater impact on improving delivery performance. The emphasis, therefore, should be in improving communication on operational and informational linkages concerning the managing of schedule and delivery performance.

Quality

Quality is an integral part of a JIT program. Rather than assessing quality control at the final inspection of completed items, the quality control staff is concerned with the prevention rather than the detection of defects. By changing the role of the quality control (QC) staff, many organizations can reduce the number of QC members and assign the traditional responsibilities of QC to production departments. The remaining QC staff members work closely with production workers, teaching them techniques in statistical quality control (SQC) so they may identify and resolve minor quality problems. Quality control staff also trains suppliers in SQC so they can use these techniques to improve their products (Ansari and Modarress, 1990).

While SQC is a commonly used statistical quality tool, many other tools are available to assist in the quality control area including frequency charts, scatter graphs, and Pareto charts. In addition to the above mentioned SQC process, the Pareto chart is also an excellent tool for several reasons. The charts are easy to construct as well as flexible in their application. The chart formulation is based on the premise that 20 percent of the quality control occurrences account for 80 percent of the total value of the occurrences (Duncan, 1988).

The quality component of the JIT system cannot be overlooked. JIT allows immediate feedback to the production line so that when defects occur problems are detected and remedied easily. Moreover, only a few items in the production process are adversely affected. The traditional manufacturing system can delay the quality inspection process for days or even weeks. By the time QC detects a defect, production has manufactured and stored many problem parts in finished goods inventory. The cost of quality with the JIT system is much lower than the wait-and-see system of traditional manufacturing. Several types of costs related to specific quality problems and solutions are shown in Table I.

The result is that with continuous refinement in the quality process an organization utilizing JIT

manufacturing will see far greater cost savings by implementing these quality steps.

Quality at the source

One of the most important issues of just-in-time is quality. Just-in-time companies should follow the concept of quality at the source, or doing it right the first time throughout all areas of the organization. Just-in-time can only be successful in a company that is already producing quality goods. The traditional approach, known as after-the-fact assessment, is to produce a product and then inspect it. There are three steps to be accomplished to successfully transition from after-the-fact inspection to reaching the goal of before-the-fact error prevention. The first is defining requirements. The company must accept the definition of quality by meeting requirements rather than adding on unnecessary costly components. A question arises, "Can these products be produced to always meet requirements?" If this step is accomplished, quality is well within reach.

The second step is to get the manufacturing process under control. The operator needs to be his or her own inspector and to participate in data gathering to identify problems. The operator is the key to quality within his or her production operation. The third process is to keep the process under control. The operator needs to keep the process working the right way. A fail-safe design figures how to make the process easy to do correctly, or difficult to do incorrectly. This inspection would detect a defect before the process

Table I.

Quality problems and solutions

| *Quality problems* | |
Internal failure costs	External failure costs
Scrap	Complaint adjustment
Rework	Returned material
Retest	Warranty charges
Downtime	Allowances or discounts
Yield loss	
Disposition	

| *Quality solutions* | |
Appraisal costs	Prevention costs
Incoming material inspection	Planning activity
Inspection and test	Preventive maintenance
Test equipment maintenance	Quality reporting
Resource consumption	Training
	Process control

Source: Duncan (1988)

begins or during the process. A light or a buzzer would alert the operator that a defect is made. This would help the company cut back on waste, and reduce the production of unacceptable or inferior products.

Uniform plant load

A uniform plant load has two ideas: cycle time and frequency of production. Cycle time deals with the rate of production, and level loading deals with the frequency of production. Cycle time with just-in-time is the measure of the rate of requirements. This is usually measured by the rate of sales. Instead of producing what the machine is capable of producing, a company should preferably produce only to the demand that is needed. The cycle time should be implemented with the last operation in mind; with the last operation being the need of the consumer, and then going backwards through the master schedule.

The second part of a uniform plant load is producing the product at the right frequency or level loading. The main idea with level loading is that the product must be produced as frequently as the customer has the need for it. The goal is to produce smaller and smaller amounts with more setups, but without additional setup costs. Finding ways to reduce setup time, and then reinvest the time saved into more frequent setups should do this.

The most important benefits of level loading are that it lays the groundwork for balance by producing the product smoothly and predictably. A company can also learn curve improvements by producing that item every day. The employee gets in the rhythm of the production without production activities changing daily. Another benefit of level loading is increased mix flexibility. If a consumer changes their purchase, a company is more able to successfully fill their order reflecting the order modifications. Lead times will also be reduced with level loading. If a product was produced once a month previously, and now it is produced daily, the consumer will receive the product sooner. By meeting customers' demand in a timely fashion they will have more repeat customers and increase the total number of customers.

The last benefit of level loading is quality improvement. It is a fact that the faster the setup times the better the setup. In addition the more repeatable the process is the more consistent the product will be.

Controlling system

In the just-in-time operation, the controlling system begins with the operator. The operator can use the statistic process control, which involves self-inspection and gathering data about the process. The statistic process control sets up control limits for the process to perform within guidelines. This system shows how the process is performing and calls for corrective actions when defects appear. The corrective action is taken before many defects appear. In the traditional operation, several batches may be produced before a defect has been detected.

Personnel
Another important building block in the JIT process is an organization's personnel. Workers are considered assets to an organization utilizing JIT manufacturing and are given more latitude with authority to make decisions. However, the workers are also expected to perform a more varied role within the company because they are cross-trained to perform several different functions, allowing flexibility in reducing bottlenecks as well as substituting for absent coworkers (Stevenson, 1996). The workers in a JIT facility are considered experts in the processes they perform and hence become an important part of the JIT team.

While production workers are given greater authority and responsibility within the JIT organization, upper management is also affected. These managers are expected to use leadership and management skills rather than being a "boss" or "supervisor". Communication among the ranks is encouraged and helps foster a positive attitude about the interpersonal relations within the organization (Stevenson, 1996).

The overall message for personnel in the JIT manufacturing environment is one of management by consensus. Often the production line workers have the most appropriate suggestions for improving the manufacturing process since they are actively involved in day-to-day operations. Compared to the traditional manufacturing environment, which traditionally practices "management by edict", the JIT philosophy prescribes involving the workforce in all aspects of manufacturing decisions (Neumann and Jaouen, 1986; Walleigh, 1986).

There must be total employee involvement, including both management and production employees. Employees' involvement cannot be stressed enough. A production operator should be a part of the quality inspection process because they work the closest with the machines that are producing the items. If there is a problem with

Figure 1.
JIT versus typical inventory systems

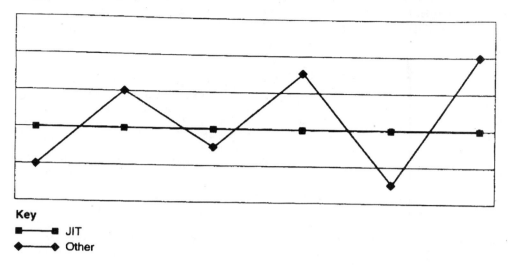

Key

■——■ JIT

◆——◆ Other

the machine, the operator of that machine would be the best one to understand the problem and be able to help in the process to achieve a better quality product. Production employees' involvement also helps to build better employee relations. If an employee feels that they are respected and their opinions are valued, they will be more receptive to changes in production schedules, work schedules, and new production techniques. Therefore, with production employees being involved, better quality products will result.

Management's involvement with a JIT production system reqiures that they take a step back and allow production employees to take on some of the responsibilities themselves. Management has to become more of an overseer of the operation, instead of decision maker. A good way to describe their role is to say they are coaches. They must stand on the side lines, only being allowed to advise and observe.

With the JIT system, the corporation runs more like a team than a traditional boss/employee relationship. Everyone's input is vital and necessary. Only if all of the people in the total production operation are allowed to have a voice can a just-in-time system work.

Along with everyone having a voice, everyone must have adequate training. Training must be in several areas. For example quality: even with a shared definition and a shared attitude of quality, training is required to assure that every employee has a complete understanding of what a quality product is.

Another area where training will be needed is in maintenance. All employees will require basic knowledge of the maintenance required for fixing

minor problems with the machines. This will dramatically decrease downtime. The employees may even do some preventive maintenance. Problem solving is another form of training that will be beneficial to employees. If all employees are able to work as a team to solve problems in production, they will take on a sense of pride and be more conscious of the products they are producing. Training in problem solving also forces unity among employees and management. They must work as a team to solve problems with production and among themselves. Once this training has been performed, the result will be a multi-skilled work force that provides depth in the workplace.

Conclusion

Figure 1 illustrates the relationship between the JIT manufacturing process and a typical inventory system. The JIT system runs smoothly with no peaks or valleys. The typical inventory system, on the other hand, is fraught with peaks and valleys that represent costs to the organization in the form of inventory holding costs, back order and stock-out costs, overtime and idle time labor costs, and waste of materials and space.

The beauty of the JIT manufacturing process is that the entire operation is continually improved upon and is not static but rather dynamic in nature. The process is not thought of as a short-term investment but rather a long-term philosophy of company management that yields many benefits. As previously discussed, several items are key "building blocks" to the JIT manufacturing process. These blocks include the commitment of all employees in the organization, having the proper materials at the right time, supplier relationships, quality aspects and personnel considerations. As demonstrated by the Japanese since the early 1950s, the JIT manufacturing process allows an organization to make use of scarce resources and eliminate waste in the search for the elusive profit dollar. By implementing the JIT manufacturing process, organizations in the global marketplace can prosper in the face of scarce resources as the Japanese have since the early 1950s.

References

Ansari, A. and Modarress, B. (1990), *Just-in-Time Purchasing*, The Free Press, New York, NY.

Browne.J. (1995), "Forecasting demand for services", *Industrial Engineering*, February, pp. 16–17.

Duncan, W.L. (1988), *Just-in-Time Manufacturing*, Society of Manufacturing Engineers, Dearborn, MI.

Gaihenage, G. *et al.* (1997), "Just-in-time manufacturing". Internet address: http://rolf.ece.curtin.edu.au/~clive/jit/jit.htm. 1997.

Leavy, B. (1994), "Two strategic perspectives on the buyer-supplier relationship", *Production and Inventory Management Journal*, 2nd Quarter, pp. 47–51.

Neumann, B.R. and Jaouen, P.R. (1986), "Kanban, ZIPS, and cost accounting: a case study", *Journal of Accountancy*, August, pp. 132–41.

Ptak, C. (1987), *MRP and Beyond: A Toolbox for Integrating People and Systems*, Irwin, Chicago, IL.

Richson, L., Lackey, C.W. and Starner, J.W. (1995), "JIT purchasing: analyzing survey results", *International Journal of Purchasing and Materials Management*, November/December, pp. 21–8.

Shannon, P. (1993), "Push/pull manufacturing simulation: a hands-on training experience", *Production and Inventory Management Journal*, 1st Quarter, pp. 13–17.

Sinnamon, G. (1993), "Just-in-time schedules for the small make to order shop", *Canadian Journal of Administrative Sciences*, December, pp. 340–51.

Stevenson, W.J. (1996), *Production/Operations Management*, Irwin, Chicago, IL.

Walleigh, R.C. (1986), "Getting things done: what's your excuse for not using JIT?", *Harvard Business Review*, March–April, pp. 38–54.

Willis, H.T. (1992), "Supplier certification: concepts and techniques", *Logistics Information Management*, Vol. 5, No. 1, pp. 32–8.

JIT IMPLEMENTATION: A CASE STUDY

DIXIT GARG
O. N. KAUL
Department of Mechanical Engineering, Regional Engineering College, Kurukshetra-136119, India

S. G. DESHMUKH
Department of Mechanical Engineering, Indian Institute of Technology, New Delhi-100016, India

Since the seminal work by Schonberger [11] in the early 1980s, many studies [1, 2, 8, 9, 13] in the United States, Italy, Korea, and the United Kingdom have indicated that an industry can grow and become competitive by a successful JIT implementation. The industries adopting JIT have achieved benefits such as fast response to engineering changes, improved worker and equipment efficiency, increased flexibility, less scrap, reduced production lead times and space requirement, increased quality and productivity, and inventory reduction at every stage. JIT can be summarized as a set of processes and techniques to eliminate waste and achieve excellence in an organization.

Though there is certainly an awareness of JIT in Indian companies, only a few have implemented it, while others are making serious efforts towards its implementation. The results of a Delphi study and a survey have indicated [5, 10] that the major problems in JIT implementation are: a general resistance to change and to adopt innovations, lack of cooperation of middle management, little motivation for workers, poor quality of incoming materials, lack of trained suppliers and employees, unreliable communication and trans-

portation systems, and poor performance measurements systems. The scope of JIT implementation in India is fair. Small companies are more optimistic than large and medium-sized companies about JIT implementation. However, worker motivation and literacy need to be addressed for a successful implementation of JIT. Table 1 gives a comparative overview of the problems of implementing JIT in developed countries and in India.

In this article we present a case study of an Indian tractor assembly industry which has benefited significantly by JIT implementation. The objective of the case study is to give useful insights into a JIT implementation from a practitioner's viewpoint.

PROFILE OF THE COMPANY

The company, XYZ Ltd., is located near Delhi. (For technical reasons, the name of the company is concealed.) It has an annual turnover of more than Rs. 3,000 million (one U.S. dollar = Rs. 40). In collaboration with a Japanese company, it assembles tractors at an annual rate of 24,000 units, in three models of 24, 30, and 35 horsepower (HP). It intends to manufacture

From *Production and Inventory Management Journal*, Third Quarter 1998, pp. 26-31. © 1998 by APICS, the American Production and Inventory Control Society. Reprinted by permission.

TABLE 1: Comparative Overview of Problems in JIT Implementation

Parameter	Developed Countries	India
Literacy level	Very high	Low
Language	One language	Many (regional & local)
Religion	Mostly homogeneous	Heterogeneous, represented by different religions & sects
Level of bureaucracy	Minimal	Very high, with emphasis on paperwork
Legal system	Streamlined	Time-consuming
Level of infrastructure	Very good (excellent transportation & communication facilities)	Fair (still in developing stage)
Level of advanced technology	Very high	Moderate
Computer literacy	Very high	Fair

two more models of 42 and 50 HP in the coming years. The company employs 800 personnel, including a purchasing staff of 70, of which 20 are executives. The company utilizes the total employee involvement (TEI) concept (one of the JIT elements) and considers the technique to have been successful. There is some obsolete machinery, but it is achieving reasonably good results which are improving due to better management (mainly because of Japanese total quality management (TQM) and Just-in-Time (JIT) systems). Several managers of the company have reported that they have free access to top management and, also, that top management contacts them frequently. They have a good communication and information flow with other departments. The general profile of the company under study is summarized in Table 2.

RESEARCH METHODOLOGY

In the beginning, two questionnaires were prepared and sent to managers of the plant. The objective of these questionnaires was to gain insight into JIT implementation. The responses were analyzed, and were then followed up by several plant visits, structural interviews, and meetings with managers from different departments (including training, purchasing, quality assurance, production and project) and shop-floor personnel.

IMPLEMENTATION

The customer is the driving force for the company. When the company started implementing JIT in the mid 1980s, sales of tractors were around 12,000 units. The company undertook many measures to improve, such as: more advertising; improving quality in design and manufacturing,

as per feedback from the customers; better service to customers; even helping farmers to get loans. Initially, the company received discouraging results in almost all areas for several years, but management was confident about the ultimate success of their program.

After a few years, everything was streamlined and management began achieving significant results. Records of the company indicate that significant visible improvements in the cylinder head line, internal liner, control housing, hydraulic line, transmission line and final tractor assembly line were observed through JIT implementation. These results have been summarized in Tables 3 through 6. Significant benefits were achieved by reductions in inventory, material movement, space, manpower, work in process and lead time; and increases in productivity, linearity, and quality. The key steps of JIT implementation were: extensive training of the employees on

TABLE 2: General Profile of Company

Type of company	Automobile
Type of layout	Product oriented
Annual capacity	24,000 units
Total number of employees	800
Products being manufactured	Tractors
Number of suppliers	300
Number of purchasing staff	70
Number of purchasing executives	20
Fraction of outside purchased parts to total parts	0.65 to 0.70
Fraction of purchased material cost to total cost	0.70 to 0.72
Number of purchased parts	1,380
Number of parts purchased from single sources	800 (58%)
Percent of parts received directly on shop floor	79%

TABLE 3: Benefits of JIT Implementation

Parameters	Cylinder Head Line		Internal Liner		Control Housing	
	Old	New	Old	New	Old	New
Inventory	250	75	176	43	400	86
Material movement (meter)	88	24	33	10		
Space	150	100	60	35	206	155
Production per shift	40	55	40	55	40	55
Manpower: Direct	16	12	8	4	32	22
Indirect	4	0.5	4	2	4	4
Straight pass (%)	22	84	91	98		
Lead time (min.)	2,000	1,000	1,800	300	4,592	815
Value-added time (min.)	116	81	41	41	82	65
Non-value-added time (min.)	1,884	908	1,758	258	4,500	520

pull concepts, identification of key performance parameters, assessing current performance on the above parameters, new layouts based on U-shaped cells (wherever applicable), standardization of operations, a maintenance plan for each machine, housekeeping, visual control, and multiskill training.

Before implementing JIT principles, tractor parts were manufactured and assembled at different sites located at distant places. Since tractors came from different locations, customer complaints and product failures could rarely be tracked to their cause. With different parts coming from different plants and the assembly operations being carried out at all plants, it was difficult to assess the stage and place of manufacture at which the fault occurred. Under the new plan, the existing manufacturing setup was reorganized by making each site specialized in a particular field. For example, the plant near Delhi was assigned to assemble tractors. Another plant, at a distance of 70 km, was responsible for the manufacture of engines. As a result of the new

manufacturing plan, certain benefits were achieved: clarity of operations, accountability of operations, and specialization of operations, leading to better results.

Purchasing System

The Indian legal system makes the use of purchase orders, bills and many such papers a compulsion in any buying arrangement. Although paperless purchasing is not feasible at present, the purchasing personnel are making every effort to reduce unnecessary paperwork. Documents from the purchasing department have revealed that purchasing agreements now developed at the company have provisions for: quality—zero-defects; quantity—flexibility; long-term

TABLE 4: Benefits of JIT in New Hydraulic Line

Indicators	Before	After
Space (sq. m)	280	140
Manpower	15	7
Productivity (MMU)*	140	75
Work in process	9	5
Dust	Uncontrolled	Controlled

* MMU = Man minutes per unit

TABLE 5: Benefits of JIT in Transmission Line

Indicators	Before	After
Lead time (hours)	96	6
Productivity (MDU)*	1.2	0.5
Linearity (%)	40	90
Quality: Straight pass (%)	50	97
Demerits (per gear box)	NA	0.1
Work in process (units)	200	20
Space (sq. m)	500	320
No. of kaizens (per month)	NA	1.3
No. of product design-related problems resolved	NA	15
No. of helpers	15	Nil
Material movement (min.)	700	300

* MDU = Man days per unit

TABLE 6: Benefits of JIT in Tractor Line

Indicators	Before	After
Lead time (min.)	480	200
Productivity (MMU)*	320	135
Linearity (%)	60	87
Quality: Straight pass (%)	NA	28.35
Demerits	NA	0.88
Work in process	100	40
Space (sq. m)	1,400	770
No. of kaizens	NA	35
No. of product design-related problem resolved	NA	8
No. of helpers	90	Nil
Material movement (min.)	120	50
Inventory components	75	6

* MDU = Man days per unit

agreement; lead time reduction; and on-time delivery. About 300 suppliers are delivering 1,200 parts, excluding engines which are supplied by another unit in the company. In the plant near Delhi, 60% of the suppliers, comprising 80% of value generated, are located nearby. Many of these companies are delivering materials daily to the point of use. The security staff is informed well in advance concerning the parts allowed to enter the company. Seventy-nine percent of the parts (by number) are received directly on the shop floor. The parts being supplied directly on the shop floor are mostly of proprietary, hardware, barstock, and semiproprietary type. Proprietary-type parts are those in which design and manufacturing is completely left to the buyer. These parts include some sheet metals, castings and forgings. Monthly rejection rates from the suppliers are determined, and feedback is conveyed to them for corrective action. The performance of a supplier is determined on the basis of how much time the tractor as-

sembly line had to be stopped because of a lack of their parts. Reasons might be: materials not delivered on time, or poor quality of delivered materials.

The supplier performance rating is also based on other parameters such as systems, aggressiveness and progressiveness, proximity, delivery performance, breadth and depth of management, performance of inventory, financial status, product quality, physical layout, administrative talent, engineering talent, and service. The relative importance of these parameters varies from supplier to supplier depending upon the parts being supplied by it.

The process of supplier selection is also being standardized with the aim of reducing the number of suppliers. The factors on which suppliers are being selected are: proximity to manufacturing facility, quality, technology, feasibility, capacity limits, financial strength, ability to build long-term relationship, readiness to adopt TQM and JIT, delivery performance, and response to change. The relative importance of these parameters varies from supplier to supplier for logistical reasons. In the selection process, a committee consisting of managers from the materials and quality assurance departments assesses the supplier's performance.

The company's policy dictates that suppliers should deliver materials strictly per given specifications. The company's supplier certification managers are helping to solve the perceived problems of suppliers. They also visit suppliers' plants, if necessary. Interaction programs between suppliers' and the company's managers are organized. An annual conference between the company and its suppliers is also held.

An analysis of the questionnaires indicates that the company is obtaining good results from JIT attributes such as multiskilled workers, standard containers, etc. The company is also obtaining good results from most of the identified JIT purchasing attributes [11]. The company is using fewer suppliers, more long-

TABLE 7: Financial and Other Indicators of Company

Particulars	1990–91	1991–92	1992–93	1993–94	1994–95	1995–96
Tractors sold (units)	20,030	20,537	20,579	17,656	18,159	21,085
Sales turnover (Rs. mil.)*	1,846	2,166	2,531	2,384	2,836	3,170
Profit (Rs. mil.)*	150	148	125	77	107	134.8
Market share (%)	14.49	13.67	14.33	12.79	11.06	11.03

* One U.S. dollar = Rs. 40 approx.

term contracts, increased volume to suppliers, quality circles, increased customer support, mutual trust and cooperative relationships, and increased information sharing. The company is also using continuous improvement, more frequent deliveries, elimination of receiving inspection, and is receiving fairer prices. Freight consolidation, contract carriers, and supplier involvement in design were not deemed important from the company's point of view. It can also be seen that outcome attributes, in general, are being given maximum importance, followed by supplier, joint buyer-supplier and buyer actions.

ADDITIONAL CHALLENGES

Based on the extensive interactions with people during the JIT implementation, the two main problems faced by the company were: human problems and system problems.

Human Problems

When the company started the JIT implementation, the aim was for a flow type of production where there is no need for helpers. The trade unions felt that such a program would render many helpers jobless. When the workers saw that they would be asked to do more work, they refused to attend the training programs. A team of trade union leaders, along with management representatives, were sent to visit plants in Japan which were following JIT practices. It was explained to the trade union leaders that the aim of such practices was to reduce fatigue, which would lead to work simplification and job satisfaction. Once the trade union leaders were convinced, they had no problems in convincing their fellow workers of the benefits of JIT. The need for extensive training and education was felt by top management and, accordingly, training sessions for various employees were arranged.

System Problems

The initial system problems were, in fact, a manifestation of earlier problems related to quality. When the authority to stop the lines was given to the workers, frequent line stoppages occurred due to quality, material and manpower problems. It was found that about 30% to 40% of the time lost daily was due to line stoppages. Therefore, problems causing the loss were identified and rectified to achieve

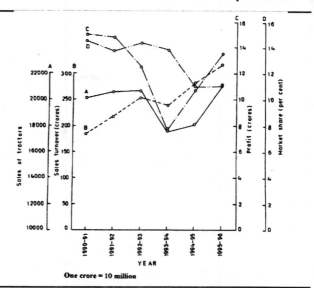

FIGURE 1: Performance indicators of the company

future benefits. The advantage was that the customers received only quality products.

COMPANY AND MARKET

Table 7 and Figure 1 illustrate financial and other indicators during the last six years. Both sales of tractors and annual turnover increased in the first three years. Then there was a sharp decline during 1993–94, after which sales again started moving upward. Market share of the company was unfortunately showing a downward trend. Profit of the company first decreased sharply during the first four years; then profits increased in the last two years. The company has achieved a 40.85% market share in 21 to 30 HP tractors and is the leader in this market segment; but it has only a 3.63% market share in the 31 to 40 HP tractor market segment. Kumaresh [7] pointed out that since the company manufactures mainly 25 HP tractors, it has been most adversely affected by a government policy of increasing the subsidy for tractors of more than 30 HP and decreasing the same subsidy for smaller tractors. As a result of this government policy, the cost differential between low and high HP tractors has decreased. That is why customer focus is shifting toward higher HP tractors. It is indicated that the growth rate of 31 to 40 HP tractors is 55% against a growth rate of 22% for 21 to 30 HP tractors during the last five years. New multinational players are also likely to enter the tractor market shortly [7].

FUTURE STRATEGY OF THE COMPANY

In view of the decreasing market share in the last years and the expected entry of new players, the company will have to increase its competitiveness. The company is likely to increase the annual capacity of its plant near Delhi to 36,000 tractors from its present capacity of 24,000 units. It has begun the planning of its new plant near Bhopal, with the collaboration of a Japanese company. The company is likely to utilize part of its capacity for higher HP tractors in view of their increasing demand. It intends to modernize its plants in a phased manner. The company will focus on single sourcing, and is likely to prepare database software classifying the suppliers based upon their type; for example, component/non-component location, supplier or processor. It has also been reported that the company plans to export 15% of its output in the coming years.

SUMMARY AND CONCLUSIONS

While a number of U.S. companies have implemented JIT, only a few Indian companies have as yet been able to implement this system. Some of the problems being faced by Indian companies, such as general resistance to change and adopting innovations, convincing employees and their unions, poor quality of incoming materials, and performance measurements, were also faced by U.S. companies when they started implementing JIT. Some other problems being faced by Indian companies, such as little motivation for workers, unreliable network and transportation systems, and lack of cooperation of middle management, were not reported to be faced by U.S. companies.

In describing how JIT was implemented in an Indian tractor company, it was found that most of the JIT purchasing and supplier evaluation criteria attributes were given strong emphasis. The supplier program within the company is achieving continuously good results. It has been determined that the company has significantly benefited in many areas by JIT implementation. In a wide sense, it can be said that the company is sustaining its competitiveness in the tractor market by applying JIT, total quality management, and total employee involvement. JIT purchasing has contributed significantly in helping the company achieve competitiveness in the marketplace.

In general, it is our recommendation that Indian companies should seriously consider and implement JIT, perhaps in a phased manner, in order to achieve and sustain competitiveness in today's highly dynamic environment. The JIT elements which are easiest to implement and give significant benefits in the Indian context may be identified, and attention may be focused on these. Efforts must also be concentrated to overcome problems in the Indian environment, especially on training and education. This is significant given the fact that the literacy level of employees at the shop-floor level is very low.

References

1. Ahmed, N. U., E. A. Tunc, and Montagno. "A Comparative Study of U.S. Manufacturing Firms at Various Stages of Just-in-Time Implementation." *International Journal of Production Research* 29, no. 4 (1991): 787–802.
2. Bartezzaghi, E., F. Turco, and G. Spina. "The Impact of the Just-in-Time Approach on Production System Performance: A Survey of Italian Industry." *International Journal of Operations and Production Management* 12, no. 1(1992): 5–17.
3. Billesbach, T. J. "A Study of the Implementation of Just-in-Time in the United States." *Production and Inventory Management Journal* 32, no. 3 (1991):1–4.
4. Crawford, K. M., J. H. Blackstone, and J. F. Cox. "A Study of JIT Implementation and Operating Problems." *International Journal of Production Research* 26, no. 9 (1988): 1561–1568.
5. Garg, D., S. C. Deshmukh, and O. N. Kaul. "Critical Analysis in JIT Purchasing in Indian Context." *Productivity* 37, no. 2 (1996): 271–277.
6. Golhar, D. Y., C. L. Stamm, and W. P. Smith. "JIT Implementation in Small Manufacturing Firms." *Production and Inventory Management Journal* 31, no. 2 (1990): 44–48.
7. Kumaresh, T. V. "Good for the Long Haul." *The Economic Times* (November 18, 1996).
8. Lee, C. Y. "The Adoption of Japanese Manufacturing Management Techniques in Korean Manufacturing Industry." *International Journal of Operations and Production Management* 12, no. 1 (1993): 66–81.
9. Payne, T. E. "Acme Manufacturing: A Case Study in JIT Implementation." *Production and Inventory Management Journal* 34, no. 2 (1993): 82–86.
10. Prem, V., S. Mitral, and K. Tyagi. "Implementation of JIT in Indian Environment: A Delphi Study." *Productivity* 34, no. 2 (1993): 251–256.
11. Schonberger, R. J. *Japanese Manufacturing Techniques: Nine Hidden Lessons in Simplicity.* New York: The Free Press, 1982.
12. Stamm, C. L., and D. Y. Golhar. "JIT Purchasing: Attribute Classification and Literature Review." *International Journal of Production Planning and Control* 4, no. 3 (1993): 273–282.
13. Voss, C. A., and S. J. Robinson. "Application of Just-in-Time Manufacturing Techniques in United Kingdom." *International Journal of Operations and Production Management* 7, no. 4 (1987): 46–52.

About the Authors—

DIXIT GARG is presently serving as a lecturer in the Mechanical Engineering Department, Regional Engineering College, Kurukshetra, India. His areas of interest are JIT, TQM, and production planning. He has published papers in national journals, conferences and seminars.

O. N. KAUL is presently a professor in the Mechanical Engineering Department, Regional Engineering College, Kurukshetra. He earlier served as a principal in the Regional Engineering Colleges, Srinagar and Kurukshetra. His areas of interest are machine design, vibration control, diagnostic maintenance and JIT. He has published papers in Archives of Mechanics, Proceedings of Canadian Congress of Applied Mechanics, Technische Mechanik, *and* ISTAM.

S. G. DESHMUKH is an associate professor in the Mechanical Engineering Department, IIT New Delhi, India. Previously he was an associate professor in the School of Management, IIT, Mumbai. His areas of interest are JIT, simulation and modeling, and multi-attribute decision making. He has published in IJPR, IJOPM, IJPE, JORS, PPC, Productivity, *and* Industrial Engineering.

TAILORED JUST-IN-TIME AND MRP SYSTEMS IN CARPET MANUFACTURING

Z. KEVIN WENG, PHD

School of Business, University of Wisconsin–Madison, Madison, WI 53706

A great deal of attention has been focused in the literature on Just-in-Time (JIT) manufacturing since the last decade [1, 2, 3, 4, 8, 9, 10]. It is typical that JIT is applied and studied when the entire production process moves to JIT [6]. The purpose of this article is to show how, under certain circumstances, JIT can be applied to low-tech industries and can be used alongside a traditional MRP system. Of course, JIT in this form is a variation of the classical JIT manufacturing techniques [4, 6].

This article is a description of how a carpet manufacturer met standard orders within 24 hours by tailoring its JIT manufacturing techniques. In particular, the following managerial questions are addressed. How can a company compete on time with both customized and standard products? How can "mass customization" be achieved by managing standard products with JIT and customized products with MRP in one production facility?

PRODUCT, MANUFACTURING PROCESSES AND PROBLEMS

The firm under consideration for this new manufacturing process is a producer of high-end carpet tiles. Carpet tiles with a hard backing are installed much like traditional hard surface tiles. The company was the recent winner of the Malcolm Baldrige Outstanding Quality Award and is well known in the carpet industry for its capability to quickly respond to the market by developing new high-quality products. Along with quality, customer service is another selling point of the firm. Specifically, the firm was the first one to install "Quick Response," which guarantees shipment of products the following week. However, recent developments and competition in the carpet industry have led to some carpet manufacturers promising shipment of broadloom carpet in 24 hours. Note that while broadloom is not the same product as carpet tiles, its lower prices make it a competing product.

Two product lines are offered by this company. One line, representing approximately 65% of current total sales, is a series of standardized products called "standards," that sell through catalogs. The other line, representing approximately 35% of current total sales, provides customized products called "specials," in which new base colors and/or patterns are specified by customers and checked by the company's designers. While the fabrication of the products is identical for both product lines, the dyeing processes are different since special colors and/or designs are utilized for specials. Accordingly, a considerably higher markup is applied to specials due to the special attention given to these products and their customers during the whole production process.

The existing process encompasses two facilities located several miles apart. Materials are transferred between the two facilities several times a day. The company's marketing

From *Production and Inventory Management Journal*, First Quarter 1998, pp. 46-50. © 1998 by APICS, the American Production and Inventory Control Society. Reprinted by permission.

department receives incoming orders and establishes due dates (see Figure 1). The average (total) manufacturing lead time is one week, or five working days. A traditional MRP system is employed to determine due dates and reorder quantities for raw materials. Basic raw materials are the same, and dye shades are made by combining a small number of primary colors.

The production flow and process are illustrated in Figure 2. The specific process can be characterized as follows. First, dyes are prepared to color the yarn that will be used for the base of the carpet tile. The yarn is then dyed. The dyed yarn is then either tufted or bonded into a broadloom form of carpet. Ordinary carpet would then be backed with a flexible backing. However, carpet tiles are given a hard backing instead. After the broadloom form of the carpet has been backed, it is then cut into squares (18" × 18"). For the standards product line, customers can choose between plain base carpet and geometric or a commonly designed carpet pattern. Specials are often made of standard base colors with special logos or colors dyed on the carpet tile. Products are then ready to ship after the dying process is completed.

A big part of the process involves setups and changeovers between the two product

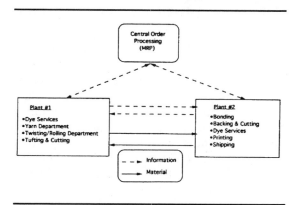

FIGURE 1: Business layout/information and material flow

lines. In the last stage of the production process (tile pattern), patterns are dyed in what is called a colorway. A colorway is a set of five different dyes. The dyeing machines can produce any pattern using the current five dyes that are loaded on the machine. When products call for a different set of colors, a changeover must be made. The changeover takes approximately 45 minutes. When producing standards, production can start immediately after a changeover. When producing

specials, a "strike" is required before production can begin after a changeover. A strike is a trial run of one yard of the product to test the shade of the dye and the detail of the pattern. A strike takes approximately 30 minutes. When the strike is off-shade, adjustments must be made on the machinery or the dye and then another strike must be run. When specials are run, it takes an average of 2.5 strikes before production can begin. Thus, an average changeover for specials takes two or more hours while an average changeover for standards takes only 45 minutes.

In the first process, yarn dyeing, a similar process occurs. The greige yarn is dyed a single color. In order to fulfill an order for a base, often two or three colors of yarn are combined in the twisting department. Thus, two or three vats must often be used in order to complete one order. Standards are again much easier to produce. The colors of standards are well established and do not require trial dyeing before the actual yarn dyeing can begin. Like in the tile pattern area, changeover for standards dyes are much quicker than specials. In both the yarn dyeing and pattern dyeing departments, standards dyes are also easier to make since the formulas have been well defined over a long period of time. The most frequently used standards dyes are made in large 500 and 1,000-gallon containers and are maintained at all times.

Efforts have been made to reduce both the lot sizes and lead times in the production process. Lot sizes have been reduced to the point where they currently equal the order size plus 5% for specials and 500 yards or more for standards. Manufacturing lead times are fairly consistent between production processes due to the company's low off-quality and smaller batch sizes resulting in less queueing time. It was also observed that work-in-process (WIP) spends the majority of its time in queue rather than actually in production.

JIT PHILOSOPHY APPLIED TO STANDARDIZED PRODUCTS

From the discussion in the previous sections, one can see that the line of standards seems to be an ideal candidate for consideration of JIT manufacturing. For the implementation of JIT to be successful, it is required that very few changes be made in the products themselves [3, 4, 6]. This implies that a firm must already have high-quality production

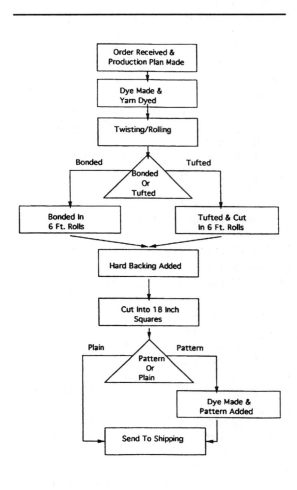

FIGURE 2: Current process flow

tomed to producing them with quick change-overs. The standards product lines are also well established in the marketplace and demand for them has remained steady for quite some time. For every point that can be made in favor of producing standards by JIT techniques, a counterargument can be made concerning specials that would make it impossible to manufacture them using JIT. For this reason a process must be established that allows standards to be produced using JIT and allow specials to be produced the same way they are currently being produced.

The production of carpet tiles, like most other textile products, utilizes multiple, slow-paced, and low-capital equipment. From the yarn dyeing though the pattern printing, this is a valid statement. The only process that is completed on only one machine is the backing process. The backing process, however, can change carpet shade and change from tufted to bonded instantaneously. The use of multiple machinery in each department will make it possible to dedicate machinery to the production of standards or specials and thus produce standards using JIT procedures and specials using the traditional MRP system.

THE NEW PRODUCTION PROCESS

Under the new system, raw materials are ordered using the existing procedures that utilize a reorder point. Since the raw materials are the same for both standards and specials and are used in the same proportion, this works efficiently without increasing the number of stockouts. The new system requires additional planning personnel to handle the standards orders. JIT manufacturing simplifies the production planning process so only one additional planner is necessary. Reduced work loads for specials production planners free up their time to help plan for the production of standards. Very few changes are needed in the com-

processes, steady demand, quick changeovers, short lead times, and low variability in the production process. In this company, efforts over many years have led to high-quality processes with low variation. The standards product lines are already established and require few changeovers per day for production. The standards product lines have been produced for years, and operators are accus-

TABLE 1: Production Information for Standards Products

Department	Number of Machines	Standards Production Rate	Standards Changeover Time	Machines Needed To Produce 250 Yd/Hr
Yarn Dying	10 Vats	200 Yd/Hr	1 Hr	5 Vats
Yarn Rolling/Twisting	2 Rollers	400 Yd/Hr	.5 Hr	1 Roller
Tufting & Splicing	12 Tufting Machines	25 Yd/Hr	.5 Hr	6 Tufting
Bonding	8 Bonding Machines	40 Yd/Hr	.5 Hr	4 Bonding
Backing	1 Machine	530 Yd/Hr	0 Hr	Shared
Cutting	2 Cutters	450 Yd/Hr	.5 Hr	1 Cutter
Tile Pattern	2 Printers	250 Yd/Hr	1 Hr	1 Printer

pany's computerized production planning system since the JIT production process is self-regulating. The new planning personnel are responsible for ensuring that the daily, and often hourly, production plans are met in each department to ensure smooth-flowing production. This often requires working closely with those in charge of producing specials so that resources can be shared when needed. The lines between standards and specials should not be drawn stringently, but should be loose so that as demand for one type of product fluctuates, resources can be shared between the two production types.

The production of the standards products is done on machinery dedicated to them. One may recall that currently demand is split almost 65/35 between standards and specials. However, when looking at time to produce, standards require considerably less time. Thus, the split between standards and specials for machinery requirements is approximately 50/50 (see Table 1). The machinery that is dedicated to standards can be used for specials and vice versa when the current demand alters greatly from this 50/50 split. This flexibility is the key to the success of the newly established JIT production system. During some days, demand for standards is greater than what can be produced on the dedicated machinery. When this happens the other machinery, which has more flexibility in meeting its due dates, can be used for the production of standards. This should actually happen very rarely. Most often the opposite will occur, in that standards equipment will be used to help meet specials delivery due dates when the daily standards production has been met.

It should be pointed out that this new production system is not able to function as a typical JIT *pull* system. The reason for this is that the flexibility in the standards product line is established during its first and last processes. For this reason the system's individual departments cannot pull from each of their preceding processes like a typical JIT system. Instead, information needs to be shared between the first dyeing process and the last dyeing process/base order fulfillment. Working in this way, as an order begins in the last processes, work to replace the base inventory can begin in the first process. From the perspective of customer demand determining the work load, this can be viewed as JIT. Furthermore, the existing rule of 500-yard batches was changed for standards to match the size of customer orders exactly. Using these procedures requires WIP to be carried in substantial amounts to buffer the formation processes and the final dyeing and order fulfillment processes.

When this new production system was first installed, we recommended that a one-day inventory be carried between the formation processes and the final fulfillment processes for each base product. As the production system began to become refined and any problems that occurred were fixed, this quantity has been reduced greatly. After the new system had been fully implemented for a short time, we recommended that these levels be reduced to 12 hours' worth of WIP for common base patterns and fewer hours' worth of WIP for less popular base patterns. This represents a substantial reduction in total WIP from the previous production system which, at all times, had five full days of WIP on hand.

The installation of this JIT system was a gradual adjustment. Changes in the manufacturing process dictated the correct lot sizes and WIP inventory that should be carried. It was safe to discontinue WIP buffers between every process except the last pattern dyeing process. Lot sizes initially continued to be 500 yards or greater. However, these were quickly reduced or increased to exactly equal the periods' demand requirements for each base product. In the beginning, production periods were one day. That is, orders received today should be planned for tomorrow so that the first yarn dyeing process can set its day's production plan knowing what the final production process, tile pattern, is going to produce. As the new production process came on line, this one-period-per-day production was increased to two production periods a day. In this way, every 12 hours the first process, yarn dyeing, will know what the final process, tile pattern, is going to produce and can establish a 12-hour production plan. The remaining processes between yarn dying and tile pattern are captive to the production rates established by tile pattern. As a result, demand pulls inventory from base stock to tile pattern and sets the replenishment production in motion. The items will be replenished in 12 hours, just in time for demand to pull from them again.

RESULTS AND INSIGHTS

The obvious benefit to this new production system is the ability to gain market share by meeting orders for standards products in 24 hours. The current facilities have ample available space if capacity expansion becomes necessary in the long run. Since the majority of the textile machines being used are low-capital and easy-to-install items, capacity expansion is not a future concern. Even if there are no increases in market share, this new production system will allow the firm to maintain its current market share by meeting its competitor's new quick delivery programs in broadloom carpet. No other competitors producing carpet tiles are currently offering this type of quick response. One-time start-up costs were required for adjustments in the MRP system and the development of new system requirements; however, these were minimal. Savings that were realized in this new production process came from reductions in WIP inventory, based on a 12% annual holding cost. Calculations of these expenses and savings are summarized in Table 2.

While these annual savings are not very significant, cost savings are not the driving force behind the tailored application of JIT manufacturing techniques. This was and still is seen as a way to further meet customers' desires and thus improve the firm's overall profitability. Quick response as a key manufacturing strategy [5, 7] will continue to be emphasized in the carpet industry. The development of a production system of this type allows this firm to stay on the cutting edge of technology in the carpet market. Over time, ad-ditional savings can be realized in this system as lead times, lot sizes, and WIP are further reduced.

One area in which this firm is currently focused is in-depth research into the production flow. The production rates of each department are currently balanced. However, the exact timing between departments, and total production time from dyeing to receiving the tile into WIP inventory, would need to be investigated. The total production time should be targeted somewhere between 8 and 12 hours.

ACKNOWLEDGMENT

The author would like to thank Derik Davis, executive manager of a carpet manufacturer in Georgia, for his assistance in developing the ideas and data presented in this article. The author is also grateful to Scott Armstrong and Kathy Rye for their helpful comments on earlier versions of this article.

REFERENCES

1. Coleman, B. J., and M. R. Vaghefi. "Heijunka (?): A Key to the Toyota Production System." *Production and Inventory Management Journal* 35, no. 4 (1994): 31–35.
2. Merrills, R. "How Northern Telecom Competes on Time." *Harvard Business Review* 67, no. 4 (1989): 108–114.
3. Mishina, K. "Toyota Motor Manufacturing, USA., Inc." HBS Case N1-693-019, 1992.
4. Monden, Y. *Toyota Production System.* Norcross, GA: Institute of Industrial Engineers, 1983.
5. Peters, T. J. *Liberation Management: Necessary Disorganization for the Nanosecond Nineties.* New York: Ballantine, 1994.
6. Schniederjans, M. *Topics in Just-in-Time Management.* Boston, MA: Allyn and Bacon, 1993.
7. Stalk, G., Jr. "Time—the Next Source of Competitive Advantage." *Harvard Business Review* 66, no. 4 (1988): 41–51.
8. Webster, S., and Z. K. Weng. "Improving Repetitive Manufacturing Systems: Analysis and Insights." University of Wisconsin–Madison School of Business, 1996.
9. Weng, Z. K. "Manufacturing Lead Times, System Utilization Rates and Lead Time-Related Demand." *European Journal of Operational Research* 89, no. 2 (1996): 259–268.
10. Womack, J., D. Jones, and D. Roos. *The Machine that Changed the World.* New York: Harper Perennial, 1991.

TABLE 2: Cost/Savings of New Production System

One-Time Start-Up Expense	
Adjustment to existing production planning system	$100,000
Annual Operating Expense/(Savings)	
Adjustments	
Planning personnel salary	$50,000
Reduction in standards WIP (reduction of 52,000 yards)	$124,800
Net Expense/(Savings)	$74,800

About the Author—

Z. KEVIN WENG, PhD, is a faculty member at the University of Wisconsin–Madison School of Business. He received his PhD. in operations management from Purdue University Krannert Graduate School of Management. His current research interests center on global supply-chain coordination and management, robust manufacturing and distribution system design and improvement, and competitive lead-time management. His work has appeared in Management Science, IIE Transactions, Naval Research Logistics, European Journal of Operational Research, and International Journal of Production Research.

IMPLEMENTING JIT/MRP IN A PCB MANUFACTURER

KIT-FAI PUN
KWAI-SANG CHIN, PHD
Department of Manufacturing Engineering, City University of Hong Kong, Tat Chee Avenue, Hong Kong

K. H. WONG
Mica-AVA Industrial Ltd., Tai Po Industrial Estate, New Territories, Hong Kong

Facing the escalating costs of material, land, equipment, and labor, coupled with increasing customer demand for reduced price, more product variety, reduced order quantity, and shorter delivery lead time, manufacturing companies must equip themselves aggressively and seek new ways for continuous improvement, growth and survival. Various modern manufacturing technologies, systems, and accompanied programs have been promoted in industry to enhance operational efficiency and global manufacturing competitiveness. Just-in-Time (JIT) manufacturing and material requirements planning (MRP) are two notable methodologies. Adoption of these methodologies may necessitate changes in the overall production system, in the structure as well as the vision of an organization. Probably, those organizations with the ability to achieve a higher flexibility and adaptability in these changes will have a better chance of success. In light of this, we will describe the implementation of a JIT/MRP system in the production system of a multinational printed circuit board (PCB) manufacturing company.

INTEGRATING JIT AND MRP

The JIT approach levels the production load by eliminating waste in the production processes and by providing the right part at the right place at the right time; whereas MRP stresses the completion of shop-floor orders on schedule and the assurance of proper operation of production lines [6, 10, 11, 14]. There have been numerous reported cases of successful implementations of both ap-

proaches [2, 4, 7, 9, 10–14]; however, they still have weaknesses. For instance, JIT may lack the forward visibility of future material requirements and it takes time to achieve results. MRP suffers from a lack of a system vision and is incapable of efficiently solving excessive inventory problems [6, 10, 11, 14]. Therefore, integrating JIT and MRP may be a possible answer.

Nowadays, many manufacturing companies are operating in a hybrid manufacturing setting (i.e., a mix of intermittent and repetitive production) where the use of an MRP or a JIT system solely is not feasible. Since MRP-push and JIT-pull practices are synergistic, elements of both can cooperate with each other in an integrated platform [1, 6, 10]. The authors have advocated an integrated JIT/MRP approach in an attempt to deal with such hybrid environments. The approach primarily focuses on selected improvement areas, striving to preserve the MRP components in the original production system, as long as they do not violate the JIT philosophy. This allows the JIT components to be effectively injected into the master production schedule (MPS) and shop-floor control. The simplicity of the JIT control can reduce the complexity of executing the MRP programs in accordance with the constraints of lead times and reorder levels [6, 8, 10].

COMPANY BACKGROUND

MAVA is a subsidiary of a multinational group of companies. It has a PCB factory in Hong Kong, and operates two joint-venture plants simultaneously in mainland China.

From *Production and Inventory Management Journal*, First Quarter 1998, pp. 10-16. © 1998 by APICS, the American Production and Inventory Control Society. Reprinted by permission.

These plants manufacture copper-laminated boards and multilayer raw materials (called the prepreg) for use in the PCB industry in Europe, the USA, China and other Asia-Pacific Rim countries. In MAVA, a conventional push-type MRP system has been used for years. Monthly master production schedules would be produced in line with the sales forecasts, orders and inventory records. Raw materials would be pushed into the production line as planned. Production priorities would be determined by means of backward loading using fixed capacity calculations; and orders of the same products would be grouped into a large production batch to minimize setup costs. Such a system relied largely on the availability and accuracy of the shop-floor data, and any data errors and mistakes would deteriorate the operational efficiency and productivity. Moreover, MAVA has been facing difficulties in responding to any dynamic operation situations (e.g., material delays, order changes). Consequently, excessive inventories in raw materials, work-in-process (WIP), and finished goods would always result.

In early 1995, a task force was instituted by the management to tackle these deep-rooted production problems of the company. The possibility of adopting an integrated JIT/MRP production system was studied, and technical aspects of the system were analyzed. The final recommendation was that the new system would use MRP as the framework for capacity planning, with JIT components injected into the master production scheduling and shop-floor control. Moreover, the JIT philosophy of striving for continuous improvement in all areas of production would be employed.

DEVELOPMENT OF INTEGRATED JIT/MRP SYSTEM

The task force has diligently examined its corporate objectives, organizational resources and constraints (both external and internal), current problems and potential improvement areas. A critical diagnosis of both JIT and MRP elements has also been carried out. It was found that the MRP-push elements (e.g., materials, capacity, and business planning) could bring the sales forecasts into detailed production schedules and material requirements, while JIT-pull elements (e.g., mixed-model scheduling, single sourcing, and kanban system) could be injected to tackle the dynamic inventory problems and improve the efficiency of the system. Figure 1 illustrates an analytical examination of MAVA's production system, problematic situations and potential improvement areas.

The skeleton of a proposed JIT/MRP system was built upon the results of the analytical examination. As shown in Figure 2, the annual business plan would provide information concerning the markets and product mix

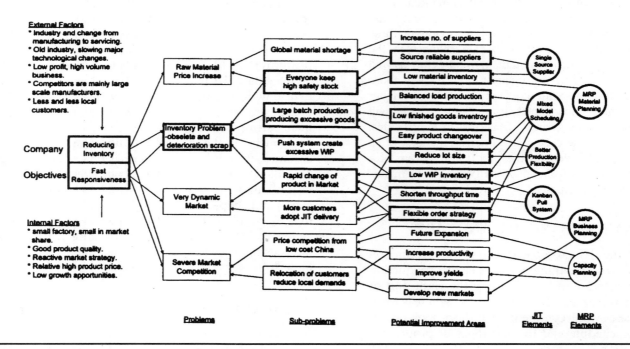

FIGURE 1: MAVA's production system

of the company, and also project annual sales and material forecasts, which would be used for long-term order arrangements with suppliers. Based on the business plan, quarterly aggregate production plans would be determined, and the physical and financial resources would be identified to help formulate the sales and production programs for the company. For instance, the issue of quarterly purchasing orders, the portfolio of product mix, and the allocation of resources would be determined. Incorporating the philosophy of the JIT approach, the master production plan would then detail all production requirements. Moreover, mixed-model scheduling and load balancing would be used in line with market forecasts, orders on hand, and roughcut capacity planning of the company. All scheduling and loading information would be put into an MRP program for the release of materials and orders, as well as for shop-floor control.

THE IMPLEMENTATION MODEL

The implementation of the integrated JIT/MRP system went though four distinct stages: prerequisites, preparation, system implementation, and evaluation. The duration of the overall implementation project was 14 months. Figure 3 depicts the logic flow of the system implementation.

In the prerequisites stage, a self-assessment of the production system was conducted to objectively diagnose its strengths, weaknesses, opportunities and threats. Figure 4 presents a summary of the assessment. MAVA obtained a total score of 23, which fell into class D under the classification category of the Fisher test [3]. Although the result was not encouraging, it helped the company to identify potential improvement areas as well as JIT elements in quality management, production process, master planning, factory flow, purchasing, education and training, and data integrity. Since striving for new JIT/MRP practice required strong management commitment and support, a steering committee was then formed. The committee provided management leadership and took strategic initiatives for the new system implementation. Three collaborative working groups were formed under the guidelines of the steering committee. First was the mixed-model scheduling group which was composed of the production and material control (PMC) manager as leader, and production planners, shop-floor

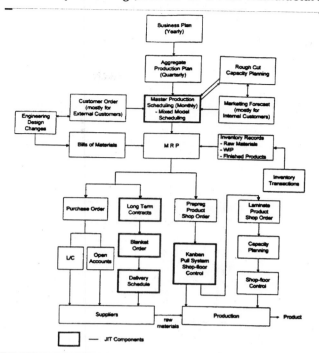

FIGURE 2: Proposed JIT/MRP system

supervisors, and sales coordinators as members. Second was the kanban system group which consisted of the production manager as leader, and production planners and shop-floor supervisors as members. Third was the procurement group which consisted of the purchasing manager as leader, and procurement officers and PMC controllers as members. The most challenging task was to consolidate mutual understanding and set common goals among staff members toward the new system implementation. Therefore, there have been several internal and external speeches and workshops conducted to eliminate the diversity among staff members and promote a cross-functional commitment toward the new system. With the joint efforts of the steering committee and the working groups, the prerequisites stage has built a nurturing ground for the implementation of the core JIT/MRP programs and tasks. Detailed schedules of the system implementation, together with the required organizational resources, were then determined.

The preparation stage has two elements: JIT concept training and system stability building. A JIT training program was tailored for employees of different hierarchies to drive the new system implementation. There were three tiers of education and training programs. The first tier was a series of seminars

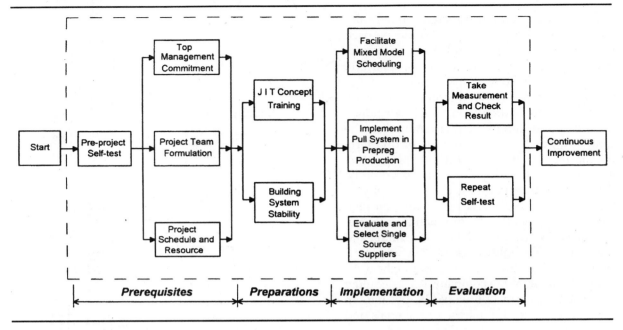

FIGURE 3: JIT/MRP system implementation

for senior managers, aimed at explaining the concepts and benefits of JIT and promoting the new JIT/MRP system. The structure and schedule of the system implementation were also addressed. The second tier was in-house training (with the aid of video materials), which was intended to bring the JIT concepts and the philosophy of JIT/MRP integration to all employees. The goal and schedule of the implementation project were also explained. The third tier was intensive in-house training for the working group members, which was designed to equip them with the JIT/MRP strategies, techniques and skills to implement the new system across the company. These training programs have facilitated proactive changes among employees and also stabilized the implementation of the new system in the company. There have been several improvement programs (such as preventive maintenance, JIT quality management and changeover time reductions) proactively initiated in the company during the preparation stage.

The mixed-model scheduling approach, the kanban control system and JIT purchasing practices have been the three building blocks of the implementation stage. Mixed-model scheduling was introduced to formulate monthly master production plans. According to the sales forecast and process characteristics, the company's product mix was segregated into four main categories. Scheduling rules were set to reduce the maximum daily products for each particular product type or model. The daily

unitary production schedule was then determined for the mixture of the product models. In other words, more product varieties could be handled in daily production (the average number of models produced per day increased from 4.3 to 6.5). With the reduction of changeover time in the production process and an increase in the flexibility of the sales delivery schedule, mixed-model scheduling improved the quick response to customers, especially for urgent orders. In conjunction with mixed-model scheduling, the kanban system was employed to improve the efficiency of shop-floor control by eliminating unnecessary WIP and shortening throughput time in prepreg production. Moreover, JIT purchasing practices were adopted to consolidate the raw materials and parts into groups, as well as the supplier base. With careful selection of single-source suppliers, a JIT supplier partnership plan was initiated.

In the final evaluation stage, the performance of the new JIT/MRP system was assessed and compared against the predetermined standards and performance indexes of the company. The measured results would then be elaborated to verify the viability of the system.

EVALUATION OF IMPLEMENTATION RESULTS

The new JIT/MRP system was implemented according to its development plan in 1995/96. This was an ongoing implementation and involved all main functional areas in MAVA. Its progress was monitored monthly in the early phases and bimonthly afterwards. The overall performance would be measured and the system audited every six months. A considerable number of problems were tackled by the collaborative efforts of the management, the steering committee and the working groups. Table 1 shows the major problems encountered and the solutions proposed for the new system implementation.

The JIT/MRP system was proved feasible and practical. The improvements in efficiency and productivity have been recorded as a result of the mixed-model scheduling, kanban control, and JIT purchasing practices. When compared with the past performance indexes of the company, measurable improvements were achieved and summarized as follows:

- Inventory levels were reduced by 20% in WIP with the kanban system, and by 25% in final product inventory with mixed-model scheduling.
- Obsolete scrap per month was reduced by 38%, as realized in the latest scrap analysis.

JIT Self Tests Results for Mica-Ava

Item	No. of Question	No. of Yes
Quality Management	9	7
Production Process	11	3
Master Planning	6	4
Factory Flow	9	1
Purchasing	7	0
Education and people	9	4
Data Integrity	7	4
Results	10	0
Total	68	23 → Class D

Individual Rating Scheme - Repetitive

Use this rating scheme if only one individual is being tested.

Score		
Class A	57 to 68	Well implemented! Don't quit now!
Class B	45 to 56	Some missing elements! Check which items are answered "no" and begin analysis. Prioritize items by cost-benefit then by shortest time to implement.
Class C	32 to 44	Half way there! There are a number of major procedural problems to be solved. More training may be needed. Do not let perceived benefits from JIT slow your attention to process flows and WIP reductions. Investigate support groups.
Class D	20 to 31	**You are making some headway! Considerable change to the flows and planning processes will be difficult to overcome. Management support may be lacking or misunderstood. Training in both applications and concepts are an absolute necessity. Support groups will be having real trouble adjusting.**
	Below 19	This could be any company. Many of the basic activities for JIT are also necessary for any well-operating firm. The JIT philosophy will require a refocusing of old planning habits, quality control disciplines, demand management data accuracy, and manufacturing process changes.

FIGURE 4: Self-assessment

TABLE 1: Summary of Encountered Problems

Step	Encountered Problem	Solution
Pre-project Self Test:	No major problem.	—
Project Prerequisites:		
(a) Top Management Commitment	No major problem.	—
(b) Project Team Formulation	Some invited members were reluctant to participate.	Replaced the member with his senior subordinate.
(c) Project Scheduling and Resources	No major problem.	
Project Preparation:		
(a) JIT Concept Education	High absenteeism of some members during training.	Spent much time to explain, discuss and convince these members on the project, some even have to use directives from their superiors. More expediting was required and the situation become better in the later stage.
(b) Building System Stability	Assigned project jobs always finished late in the early stage of the product implementation.	
Model Implementation:		
(a) Mixed-Model Scheduling in Master Production Planning	(1) Productivity decreased and scrap increased due to too much product changeover.	(1) Engineers modified and improved the machines and processes such that it returned to normal.
	(2) Increased usage of indirect materials in the beginning.	(2) In long term, the usage was lowered as the total finished good inventory was decreased.

(continued)

TABLE 1: *(Continued)*

Step	Encountered Problem	Solution
	(3) For overseas large orders, the benefits of mixed-model scheduling were not significant.	(3) After analysis, the team was convinced that inventory is always a waste and the mixed-model scheduling was still helpful in this case.
	(4) Some methods to reduce changeover time were too costly.	(4) Pressure exerted on the manufacturing engineers to improve. Eventually feasible methods with normal cost are developed.
	(5) Serious interruption of production in the early stage of running the new scheduling method.	(5) Solicit strong management support and seek cooperation from the supporting departments.
	(6) Large amount of JIT (urgent by small) orders come at the end of this stage	(6) After implementing the mixed-model scheduling, the factor was well prepared for such orders and not many problems found.
	(7) Misunderstanding on project goal by marketing staffs. They just concentrated on the benefits of reduced lead time and make every orders as JIT orders.	(7) Explain to them the production constraints and JIT orders are luxurious and costly. Also discussed raising the product price of the JIT orders.
(b) Kanban System in Shop Floor Control	(1) One process needed a sudden increase in WIP in every month to sustain continuous production in subsequent processes.	(1) Special kanban cards added to account for the sudden increase. Removal of these cards by the MRP control afterwards.
	(2) Usual transfer size between the processes was large and required a lot of kanban cards if each card maintained the basic unit of one.	(2) Kanban cards with multiples of the basic unit are used. Several cards are combined to represent the actual quantity.
(c) JIT Purchasing—single source reliable suppliers	(1) Some materials are not possible to have only a single source.	(1) Dual sources or multiple sources are allowed as long as these are a minority of the total material purchased.
	(2) Some purchasing officers still wanted to maintain multiple source and develop partnership with all. These suppliers sometimes did not honor their own commitments as there is always backup from other suppliers.	(2) They found that it is difficult and time-consuming to develop partnerships with so many suppliers. Eventually they are convinced that single source is the solution.
	(3) Many distant suppliers were invited to develop as partnership suppliers in the beginning but their response time did not meet our requirement.	(3) More and more distant suppliers are replaced by local and vicinal suppliers for delivery lead-time reduction.

- Setup and changeover times were reduced by 33% to 75% on various items.
- Throughput time was reduced by 43%.
- Supplier lead time was reduced by 30% as more local sources were appointed.

Furthermore, promising feedback was reported from product design and development in eliminating design waste; from manufacturing accounting in simplifying cost tracking; and from marketing in better technical support and

TABLE 2: Fisher Test Results

Item	No. of Questions	No. of Yes
Quality Management	9	8
Product Process	11	8
Master Planning	6	6
Factory Flow	9	6
Purchasing	7	2
Education and People	9	8
Data Integrity	7	5
Result	10	5
Total	68	48

servicing. Another Fisher JIT test was conducted, and its results are given in Table 2. This score was 48 which fell into Class B, compared to the score of 23 in Class D at the prerequisites stage of the system. implementation, showing a significant improvement after JIT/MRP implementation.

CONCLUSION

MRP deals with establishing an ideal system for inventory control and production capacity arrangement, whereas JIT emphasises the philosophy of waste elimination and continuous improvement. It is advantageous to integrate the dynamic features of JIT into the discipline of MRP to close the loop between the shop floor and the medium- and long-term planning processes. The integration could also drive continuous improvements in production planning and control systems. The case study presented in this article is a demonstration of a successful experience in adopting the integrated JIT/MRP concepts in a multinational manufacturing company.

REFERENCES

1. Bockerstette, J. A., and R. L. Shell. *Time Based Manufacturing.* New York: McGraw-Hill, 1993.
2. Bowson, D. J. "A Decade of Just-in-Time Experience." *Proceedings of the 33rd APICS International Conference,* New Orleans, LA (October 8–12, 1990): 332–333.
3. Fisher, D. "The Just-in-Time Self-Test," *Proceedings of the 33rd APICS International Conference, New Orleans, LA* (October 8–12, 1990): 272–275.
4. Griffith, W. E., and S. F. Tuscher. "Time-Phased JIT: The MRP Path to JIT." *Proceedings of the 32nd APICS International Conference,* Orlando, FL (1989): 601–603.
5. Hobbs, O. K. "Application of JIT Techniques in A Discrete Batch Job Shop." *Production and Inventory Management Journal* 35, no. 1 (1994): 43–47.
6. Mejabi, O., and G. S. Wasserman. "Basic Concepts of JIT Modelling." *International Journal of Production Research* 30, no. 1 (1992): 141–149.
7. Miller, I. G. "Supporting JIT Manufacturing with a JIT Organization." *Manufacturing Systems* (September 1990): 24–30.
8. Oden, H. W., C. A. Langenwalter, and R. A. Lucier. *Handbook of Material and Capacity Requirements Planning.* New York: McGraw-Hill, 1993: 270–282.
9. O'Grady, P. J. *Putting the Just-in-Time Philosophy into Practice: A Strategy for Production Managers.* London: Kogan Page, 1988: 32–51, 80–101.
10. Przybyla, K. "JIT Scheduling with the MRP II Production Environment." *Proceedings of the 33rd APICS International Conference,* New Orleans, LA (October 8–12, 1990): 322–327.
11. Schniederjans, M. J. *Topics in Just-in-Time Management.* Boston, MA: Allyn & Bacon, 1993: 24–154.
12. Sohal, A. S., and O. Naylor. "Implementation of JIT in a Small Manufacturing Firm." *Production and Inventory Management Journal* 33, no. 1 (1992): 20–25.
13. Vora, J. A., J. V. Saraph, and D. L. Petersen. "JIT Implementation Practices." *Production and Inventory Management Journal* 31, no. 3 (1990): 57–59.
14. Wasco, W. C., R. E. Stonehocker, and L. H. Feldman. "Success with JIT and MRP II in a Service Organization." *Production and Inventory Management Journal* 32, no. 4 (1991): 15–21.

About the Authors—

KIT-FAI PUN is a lecturer in the Department of Manufacturing Engineering and Engineering Management at the City University of Hong Kong. Before joining the teaching profession he worked in industry as an operations executive, researcher and engineer. He has also provided consultancy and in-house training services to companies in Hong Kong and Mainland China. Mr. Pun is a member of the Society of Manufacturing Engineers, ASQ, and IIE (USA), and the Hong Kong Society for Quality and Hong Kong Computer Society.

KWAI SANG CHIN, PhD, is an assistant professor in the Department of Manufacturing Engineering and Engineering Management, City University of Hong Kong. Before joining the university, Dr. Chin had more than ten years of experience in the manufacturing industry. He is a Charter Engineer in the UK and a Registered Professional Engineer in Hong Kong. Dr. Chin is a senior member of IIE and the Society of Manufacturing Engineers (USA). He is currently the Hon. Secretary of the Hong Kong Society for Quality. His current research interests are future product development strategies, quality management strategies beyond ISO 9000 for Hong Kong and China, and the use of expert systems technology in product design.

K. H. WONG is the Director of Engineering of the Meadville Group and the Operations Manager of Mica-AVA (F.E.) Industrial Limited. He has worked in the assembly, PCB and laminate businesses for more than 17 years, in the areas of production, PMC, quality control, purchasing, maintenance and engineering.

FUNDAMENTAL GROUNDING

The Critical Importance of

MASTER PRODUCTION SCHEDULING

Why MPS is one of the most CRITICAL POINTS needed to be addressed in order for MANUFACTURING COMPANIES to execute the CONCEPTS involved in the hottest trend SWEEPING THE INDUSTRY.

BY STEVE WILSON, CPIM, and CHUCK DAVENPORT

THERE ARE ANY NUMBER OF IDEAS FLOATING AROUND THE BUSINESS world that espouse the virtues and possibilities of supply chain management (SCM). However, each of these definitions describes a top layer of information interaction. For any initiative using these philosophies to succeed, there must be an underlying infrastructure of capability in manufacturing supply and demand planning. Therefore, the critical link to success in a supply chain initiative, no matter what the level of information interaction, is the ability to plan and schedule production at each link in the chain so that the entire supply chain is synchronized. This link is the master production schedule.

Manufacturing Control Supporting SCM

THERE ARE MANY new technological developments that are adding to management's excitement over actual or potential SCM arrangements: the advance of client/server technology; the expanding use of electronic commerce; enterprise resource planning (ERP) software utilizing real-time data; and advanced planning and scheduling applications balancing and optimizing supply and demand across the supply chain. After spending all this money on technology, CIOs see supply chain improvements as one of the primary payoffs and sources of competitive advantage.

It is indeed a fact that through technology investments, manufacturing companies are now not only better accessing real-time data to make internal decisions, but also are sharing this information across the enterprise among customers, suppliers and distributors. Information sharing of this type has essentially created any number of opportunities under the guise of SCM (see Figure 1).

Certainly critical to effective supply chain management alliances is timely, complete and correct data and information upon which to make decisions. But you must remember, technology is no panacea. It is a new and improved—and expensive—tool that you still must learn to use properly in order to make better decisions. But how do you know what decisions to make? For what customers? For what products? And when, how much and across what locations? Underneath the hood in any successful SCM arrangement is discipline in master scheduling skills and processes, ensuring that capacity, inventory and productive assets will be used and cost effective in serving and leveraging your SCM business relationships.

Master scheduling is defined by APICS as "the process where the anticipated build schedule is reviewed and adjustments are made to the master production schedule (MPS) to ensure inventory levels and customer service goals are maintained and proper capacity and material planning occurs." In an SCM environment, this process and its resulting MPS now involves your suppliers, distributors and customers. Your SCM partner's inventory, material plans, capacity schedule and order information is now information available to the master schedule to develop a more integrated picture of demand and supply. This insight allows the master scheduler to make better MPS decisions to optimize the entire supply chain and execute SCM.

So what are these decisions that need to be made to execute SCM? Given that the master scheduling role is to ensure customer service and balance demand with supply and stable production, Figure 2 provides an example of decisions that would need to be made through the master schedule in response to supply chain information. All of

From *APICS—The Performance Advantage*, October 1998, pp. 40-43. © 1998 by APICS, the American Production and Inventory Control Society. Reprinted by permission.

these decisions, and the range of potential consequences, are vital to servicing a SCM partner.

Critical to their success, SCM arrangements require effective sharing of information. But the larger question is: What do you now do with all this newfound information? For a manufacturing company, that responsibility falls primarily to the master scheduling process. Master scheduling is the fundamental manufacturing control process that allows you to leverage information to carry out supply chain planning and focuses management on optimizing operations—not just on expediting orders. Only with the kind of discipline and prioritization possible through the planning decisions made in developing a master schedule can a company anticipate and effectively balance customer service with supply chain costs and a stable, balanced production.

Where Has Master Scheduling Been?

MASTER SCHEDULING is not new. But in the dynamic world of SCM, it is changing—and becoming more critical. A robust master scheduling process is or should be a part of any disciplined operation and a standard part of a company's manufacturing control system. However, a master schedule in the more demanding SCM world must do more than just calculate finite loads and run MRP to generate dependent demand. The days are gone when the master scheduler could run weekly MRP/DRP batch applications and hide the inaccuracies and errors behind inventory or excess capacity. Inventory is low, capacity is short, and the range of events that can happen across a manufacturer's supply chain makes the manufacturer's master schedule the fulcrum for its entire supply chain.

A master scheduler in a lean, SCM environment where customers are demanding responsiveness and flexibility does not have the time or inventory to react slowly to orders or bottlenecks. Managing the master schedule and capacity requires dynamic responses to demand and supply events. Fortunately, with advances in computer processing power and the functionality existent in advanced planning systems, planning cycles have been cut and planning parameters can be changed as the environment dictates—not just in arbitrary weekly buckets. In SCM environments there is simply no longer the buffer and

slack that can hide slow decision-making and static master scheduling.

The following scenario illustrates the new MPS role where planners can—and must—react quickly to events throughout the supply chain:

Reduced productivity due to poor raw material quality in the most recent lot, and a series of unplanned maintenance downtime is impacting the week's manufacturing schedule. In addition, higher sales than forecasted for two key VMI customers generated a new set of replenishment orders this morning. Also, additional transportation capacity is available due to unanticipated back haul routes. Using APS (advanced planning and scheduling) applications, the planner must develop a new plan by evaluating a number of schedule and customer service alternatives. Instead of relying on the week's now outdated MRP run or running a full replan—or worse yet, just telling the people in the plant to figure it out and do the best they can, and not taking advantage of reduced transportation costs—the master scheduler in the SCM world must now react to these events. An event-driven master schedule must take event information available and in very short planning cycles evaluate the impact on resource availability, raw ma-

FIGURE 1: THE EVOLUTION OF SUPPLY CHAIN MANAGEMENT CONCEPTS

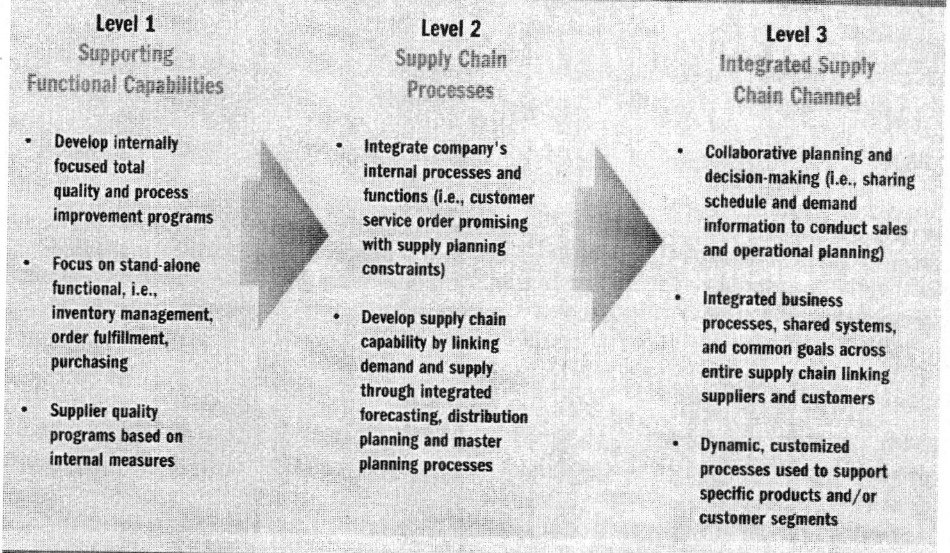

FIGURE 2: MASTER PLANNING

CASE STUDY: THE POTENTIAL FOR PROBLEMS WITHOUT PROPER MPS

A manufacturing organization serving the retail grocery industry had a definite lack of MPS planning skills and a broken process for making MPS decisions. Its master schedule was essentially a finite load calculation, calculating open orders against manufacturing capacity at each of its plants. The lack of master scheduling taking place seemed at first a mild nuisance that the organization coped with well enough in times of excess capacity. But as capacity tightened in several of its plants and the industry began indicating interest in additional services in the name of supply chain management, the lack of good master scheduling became a direct cause for increasing customer service failures, high supply chain costs and a distinct competitive disadvantage.

Management and the process participants were quick to point to poor data and poor IT tools as the source of their problems; but as is often the case, there were process issues masquerading as systems issues.

Following are the characteristics of the company's master scheduling process:

• No process orientation or understanding of cause and effect throughout the process on customer service, capacity and plant scheduling.
• No established process roles and unclear responsibilities between customer service reps, sales reps, master scheduler, plant schedulers and shift supervisors. The different functions affecting the process had limited process perspective on the upstream and downstream activities.
• Inconsistent framework and criteria used for making decisions. Decisions made with insufficient information.
• Process relied on informal cross-functional interaction and limited flow of information.

The company's MPS policies also had the following problems:

• Lack of finite scheduling overloaded the MPS. This was the root cause for erosion of the process and high customer service failure rates.
• No business rules or use of time fences associated with the master schedule to stabilize production schedules.
• MPS was not linked with sales planning exercises or customer service reps order profiles, or integrated with plant scheduling systems.
• No systematic inventory practices and no formal guidelines within the MPS to support order promising and the order fulfillment process.
• Inconsistent tracking of inventory performance.
• No alignment of customer service guidelines, inventory practices and MPS time zone policies.

This lack of discipline in planning operations in an increasingly tight capacity situation created havoc across the company's manufacturing plants, resulting in a high number of expedited orders, stock outs and customer service failures. In addition, bad manufacturing controls kept them from having any confidence in inventory and manufacturing capacity numbers, therefore resulting in no integrity—or confidence—in their ability to make MPS decisions.

Because of all these shortcomings, most order decisions were relegated to the shop floor. This meant that important decisions such as what orders to run, what orders to move out and what stocks to replenish (essentially what customers to serve!) were being made, in some cases, by the shift supervisor who had just gotten off the phone with an irate sales rep. Thus, the company was in no position to promote and pursue SCM arrangements. Nonetheless, marketing and sales reps were in the marketplace developing a customer service strategy based on value-added SCM principles, such as vendor managed inventory and continuous replenishment of a variety of retail supply items.

This is just an example of how a company's operation and its supply chain capabilities did not match its avowed sales strategy. The fact is, their operational shortcomings and ineffective master scheduling processes prevented them from aggressively pursuing SCM opportunities with their key customers in the retail industry.

"They haven't proved they can manage our inventory turnover in these items better than we can," said one customer.

"We just can't be cost effective with our current operations," said one of the company's logistics managers. Therefore, the great potential for customer penetration and increased market share in a mature, commodity industry was lost.

terial availability, order priorities and distribution inventories to develop a superior recommendation that supports the entire supply chain.

These are obviously important decisions. For a manufacturing company living in an SCM world, they must be the right decisions. They also are the source for your company's ability to demonstrate the kind of SCM responsiveness that can differentiate it from its competitors.

Taking Strategy Towards Execution

SCM AS A STRATEGY is important. As discussed earlier, SCM concepts are well established in the marketplace, and manufacturing senior executives need to understand the business opportunity and competitive advantages associated with SCM relationships. After years of focusing on manufacturing costs, executives are now recognizing the supply chain as the primary cost lever and competitive differentiator in many industry environments. In fact, as SCM evolves and expands, manufacturing companies will not compete solely on their product, but on the basis of their supply chain—how it collaborates and integrates with suppliers, distributors and customers to achieve its marketing and customer service strategies.

But when defining supply chain vision and direction, as with the concepts of reengineering and Six-Sigma quality, the topics are easily discussed and make good fodder for business conferences—but how many companies actually follow through and execute? Consumer retail is at the forefront in deploying SCM, but studies suggest that only about 20 percent of retailers have turned over their replenishment programs to vendors. The reason: A majority of customers did not believe that vendors could adequately support their continuous replenishment requirements.

So it comes back again to your people and the execution of business processes through management, systems, technology and skills. The execution process for a manufacturing company—promoting its ability to support and enable SCM business relationships—must also include an integrated master scheduling process using real-time data to make order promising, replenishment and capacity planning decisions.

Focus on Master Scheduling

ORGANIZATIONS GOING down this path should be very aware of what it takes. ERP transaction systems can provide data and information, but they must be incorporated into your processes to be an effective decision support tool. And don't forget that within a few short years there will be few, if any, of your major competitors without this kind of IT capability. It will be the companies that have leveraged technology to improve their master scheduling process and shorten their planning cycles—not just new systems and reliable data—that will be the industry leaders in SCM. They will be the companies that best plan and utilize their manufacturing, distribution and inventory re-

sources to create competitive advantage in their supply chain capabilities.

So as you hear SCM discussed, proposed or expanded in your company, take account of how your master scheduling process works and how it acts as a decision support tool. Look at how it utilizes distribution and customer data; how it is used to broker customer service and plant scheduling; and how the master schedule supports order promising and the ability to optimize supply and demand decisions throughout your supply chain operations.

In many industries and for many companies, the SCM opportunity is well documented; for others it represents new opportunities and great potential. But execution and, more specifically, a robust master scheduling process remains the critical success factor. Don't simply confuse your new investment in an ERP system and running MRP with execution. Execution in the SCM environment depends on your company's ability to control its operation through the master scheduling function—the process, people, data and decision support tools that allow organizations to implement and meet the high expectations in their important SCM initiatives.

Steve Wilson, CPIM, is a manager with Pittiglio, Rabin Todd & McGrath, Inc. Chuck Davenport is a senior consultant with Deloitte & Touche.

Does Your SUPPLY CHAIN System Measure Up?

By Christopher D. Gray, CFPIM

**Find out by following these guidelines
for creating your own supply chain scorecard.**

IN THE LAST FIVE YEARS, companies have been installing new computer systems at an unprecedented rate. Faced with increasing competitive pressure, the specter of the "millennium bug," and promises of enterprise-wide visibility, huge numbers of companies have replaced their old systems and software. In the area of supply chain management alone, many large corporations have invested sums ranging from $30 million to $200 million. And the business press reports several failed implementation projects that cost more than $100 million.

No wonder so many CEOs are asking some hard questions. They want to know how effective their new systems are, whether there are specific problems that need correcting, and how their systems' performance stacks up, both against other companies' and against objective standards.

To answer such questions, you need a supply chain scorecard. A well-balanced scorecard would normally cover four areas:

1. Reliability. Is the supply chain process reliable and capable? Have variability and volatility been removed from the process? Are the individual elements (equipment, transport, process yields) reliable?

2. Simplicity. Is there as much streamlining as possible in the systems, the physical organization and distances associated with the lines of supply, the manufacturing and transfer lot sizes, the equipment setups, and so on? Many times, firms don't get the desired, or even predictable performance, because the processes and systems are too complex.

3. Coordination of activities. Are the sourcing, manufacturing, inter-plant, and distribution activities operating in lockstep? Can everyone everywhere in the supply chain reliably answer the question, "What do we need next, and when?" Is schedule conformance high?

4. Overall velocity of the supply chain and the productivity of the key resources. Do the supply chain processes support fast and nimble response, or is making a change like turning the Titanic? Is the productivity of inventory, transportation, and equipment increasing or decreasing?

You can find a set of performance measurements for some key supply chain elements (No. 3 above) at my company's Web site, www.gray research.com. We developed what we call the "Supply Chain Vital Signs" based on experience in implementing and operating effective supply chain systems. The vital signs cover processes such as customer-order promising, performance to schedule, and data quality—the ones most affected by new system and software implementations.

From *APICS—The Performance Advantage*, January 1999, pp. 56-57. © 1999 by APICS, the American Production and Inventory Control Society. Reprinted by permission.

Creating your own program

LET'S SAY you want to implement a measurement program in your own company to assess a new system's impact on your supply chain. You should plan to tailor it in four areas:

1. Pick the appropriate measurement. Generally speaking, you'll need to choose methods appropriate to the way you operate. For example, the correct on-time measurement depends on whether you operate to a schedule or to a visual signal (kanban).

2. Establish the scope of the supply chain you'll measure. Are you checking one site or several? Customer delivery performance for a single plant assesses deliveries to that plant's immediate customers. In a multi-site situation, customer delivery performance measures deliveries to the "ultimate customer," and the site-to-site performance is measured by interplant metrics.

3. Determine minimums and objectives. Minimums are industry standards. Objectives are your company's internal goals, which are normally higher than minimums. For example, 95 percent on-time delivery against

the master production schedule represents the bare minimum for claiming good MPS performance—even though the objective in your company is probably 100 percent.

4. Establish reasonable tolerances. Tolerances recognize acceptable ranges in performance (e.g., plus-or-minus one day on delivery) or limitations in your ability to measure because of equipment issues, system capabilities, or human ability (plus-or-minus 3 percent on inventory count). You can use rules of thumb when you start establishing your tolerances and then grow more precise later.

If you decide to use something similar to the Supply Chain Vital Signs when creating your own measurements, such vital signs would normally exist as an upper tier of a larger assessment program. As Lynch and Cross point out in their excellent book, *Measure Up!*, measurements must be tiered and linked. Otherwise you end up with levers that are disconnected from the process and that fail to influence what is truly important to your company and its strategy.

A program's lower tiers should include additional diagnostic measure-

ments you can use to chase problems back to their real causes.

Once you can trace performance problems back to their root causes, make sure you have an action plan to eliminate them. Many times the difference between systems that are competitive weapons and ones that are "more for show than go" is how effectively you can use the systems to take corrective action.

By implementing these concepts across the key elements of your supply chain, you get a comprehensive and quantitative performance measurement system. However, as you adapt the measurements to your own needs, the system should give you the ability to trace problems back to root causes as well as a framework for additional company performance measurements.

Christopher D. Gray, CFPIM, is president of Gray Research, which provides consultative services on software selection and implementation for supply chain management, MRP II and DRP. Gray can be reached by calling 603/778-9211, or by visiting his Web site at www.grayresearch.com.

Unit Selections

Key Points to Consider

❖ How has information technology had an impact upon the job of an operations/production manager?

❖ Why are some consumers hesitant to use the Internet for electronic shopping? Why are some firms slow to establish their presence on the World Wide Web?

❖ What are the possible positive and negative consequences for consumers from mergers in the automotive industry?

 **Links** **www.dushkin.com/online/**

These sites are annotated on pages 4 and 5.

The field of operations and production management has evolved over time and continues to evolve today. There are emerging trends that require careful examination by firms and managers. This unit examines three emerging trends: use of information technology, concern for the environment, and globalization of business.

The first few articles examine the growth of information technology, and the growth of the Internet and electronic commerce. Illustrations are provided showing the results that companies obtain from their Web sites. The articles discuss the impact that information technology has today on supply-chain management and forecasts for the future.

There has been growing concern by manufacturers for environmental management. Green marketing and ISO 14000 provide evidence of how managers must incorporate environmental planning into their firms. The article by William Ruch reviews three decades of progress on productivity, quality, and impact on the environment.

The final articles examine globalization of business. The articles examine the consolidation taking place in automobile manufacturing via mergers among the major world producers of automobiles.

In looking at the future of operations and production management, one can develop either a pessimistic scenario or an optimistic one. The pessimist could argue that current theories and concepts for managing are applicable for manufacturers and that they are inadequate for managing services and information based firms. The pessimistic view would see the challenges as too great for managers and think that American firms will face major difficulties competing on a global basis. The optimistic scenario is that newer managerial concepts have emerged and have proven to be successful. This scenario holds that firms that are flexible in adapting to new market demands by remaining customer-focused should do well. Technology provides managers with new tools to support their decision making. American firms through their own competitive advantages and strategic alliances with other global firms should not fear their future in a global market.

Emerging Trends in Operations and Production Management

AUTOS

GM: MODULAR PLANTS WON'T BE A SNAP

What works for rivals in Brazil may not for the U.S. giant

Auto executives have a dream. They envision a super-efficient factory where premade chunks of a car roll in to be bolted together into a finished vehicle by a handful of assembly-line workers, the way a child snaps together Lego blocks. The result: spectacular sav-

ings on capital investment, payroll, and per-vehicle costs.

The dream, or at least some attempt to reach it, is slowly nearing reality. So far, low-volume versions have appeared, mainly in emerging markets like Brazil, where Volkswagen, Chrysler, Ford, and GM are

jumping in, or for niche products like Mercedes-Benz's tiny SMART car in France. General Motors Corp.'s first modular plant, the cutting-edge Blue Macaw factory in Brazil, will open next spring. But GM, in a plan called Project Yellowstone, also intends to roll out several more such

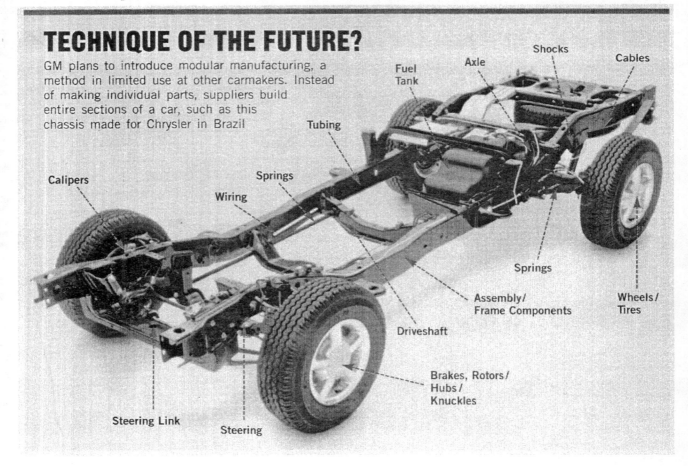

TECHNIQUE OF THE FUTURE?

GM plans to introduce modular manufacturing, a method in limited use at other carmakers. Instead of making individual parts, suppliers build entire sections of a car, such as this chassis made for Chrysler in Brazil

Calipers

Wiring

Springs

Tubing

Fuel Tank

Axle

Shocks

Cables

Springs

Assembly/ Frame Components

Wheels/ Tires

Driveshaft

Brakes, Rotors/ Hubs/ Knuckles

Steering Link

Steering

Reprinted with special permission from *Business Week*, November 9, 1998, pp. 168, 172. © 1998 by The McGraw-Hill Companies, Inc.

plants over the next few years to replace inefficient plants in the U.S. Rust Belt.

GM's effort will be the most ambitious test of the futuristic factory. No other carmaker plans to go modular in so many plants. Ford Motor Co. and Chrysler Corp. won't risk a falling-out with their workforces in the U.S., where the United Auto Workers (UAW) is sure to oppose shifting thousands of jobs to lower-wage, often nonunion suppliers. Critics warn that the whole idea of modular assembly is overblown and unlikely to achieve big savings. But if GM can pull it off, carmakers around the globe will likely rush to follow suit. Suppliers can "come up with better solutions [than GM's] and take costs out with smart designs," says GM President G. Richard Wagoner Jr., who adds that GM will decide in early 1999 which vehicles Yellowstone will make first. One likely candidate, say analysts, is the Chevrolet Cavalier, now built at aging plants in Lordstown, Ohio, and Lansing, Mich.

Modular assembly is, at heart, an extension of outsourcing, the common practice of buying parts from outside suppliers. For years, auto makers have been shifting away from producing most of a car's 5,000 components by contracting parts, or even groups of them, to suppliers. The module approach goes further, handing off engineering and production responsibility for entire chunks of the car, such as the chassis or interior. Suppliers design a module, making some of its hundreds of parts and subcontracting others. They set up plants next to—or even inside—the auto maker's and deliver modules right to the assembly line, where carmaker employees bolt them together.

The idea looks great on paper. Suppliers shoulder more risk and investment, allowing auto makers to cut the size of an assembly plant by two-thirds. A carmaker can slash its workforce and capital investment in new plants—often $1 billion a pop—by half. It also can slice its engineering and testing budget. Auto makers say such cost-sharing is essential. "It is impossible for any auto company to have all the resources in-house to do all of the R&D and technology investment needed today," says Chrysler Chairman Robert J. Eaton.

DESPERATE. Advocates say the result can be more efficient designs with fewer parts. "It's easier to handle complexity if you break [cars] into modules and enlist your suppliers," says Daimler Benz marketing chief Dieter Zetsche. Adds Mike Laisure, vice-president for modules at auto parts maker Dana Corp.: "We can get the job done quicker."

For GM, modular's appeal is particularly strong; the auto giant desperately needs the promised savings for its small cars, on which analysts estimate GM loses at least $1,000 each. GM's Wagoner says small cars and compact pickups are likely modular candidates.

But the pitfalls are many. For one, the idea won't please GM's union workers, with whom relations still are frayed after crippling strikes. While GM says it will shrink staff by attrition, the UAW won't like outsourcing thousands of jobs.

GM is pressing ahead anyway. Small-car chief Mark Hogan, who launched the Blue Macaw project and is spearheading Yellowstone, says he discussed GM's plans with Richard Shoemaker, head of the UAW's GM unit, on Oct. 14. "We're going to have to find some middle ground," was all Hogan would say afterward. The UAW declined comment. UAW officials may seize on a possible silver lining, though: the chance to recruit lower-wage supplier workers, who will work side-by-side with higher-paid union ones. "That's a perfect opportunity" for UAW recruiters, says Wayne State University labor historian Steve Babson.

Chrysler and Ford, whose plants already are efficient, don't feel the urgency to follow GM. They already have modular operations or plans in Brazil: Chrysler opened a $315 million modular truck plant there this summer, and Ford's Project Amazon aims to build a Brazilian car plant by 2001. But neither plans a modular U.S. plant. "You can't lay people off and pay somebody else to do" the work, says Chrysler's Eaton.

BUILDING THE MODULAR CAR

Here's how auto executives hope to boost efficiency:

SUPPLIERS

Help design whole sections of a new vehicle, such as the chassis and interior, striving for simplicity and greater efficiency; suppliers also do engineering, assembly, and testing of modules.

SUB-SUPPLIERS

Provide hundreds of individual parts and are accountable to the suppliers.

EMPLOYEES

The suppliers' workers are stationed near or even in the carmaker's assembly plant. Carmaker employees work mainly on bolting together the finished chunks to complete the car.

COSTS

The auto maker cuts its R&D budget and engineering staff, has a shorter assembly line, and can employ half the number of workers. It can halve the $1 billion typical cost of building a new plant.

Supplier relations could be another stumbling block for GM. Modular assembly requires auto makers to work closely with key suppliers. But General Motors still hasn't mended all the rifts created in the early 1990s by the heavy-handed cost-cutting tactics of then-purchasing czar José Ignacio López de Arriortúa. GM's Hogan says its supplier relations are improving but concedes they still aren't perfect.

Naysayers of modular note Daimler's rocky experiment with the SMART minicar. Earlier this year, the German auto maker launched its micro-car in a joint venture with SMH, the Swiss maker of Swatch watches, in a plant in eastern France. Quality problems were rife, delaying the car's introduction by six months. "We had to learn that what makes sense in theory has headaches in real life," says Daimler's Zetsche. Although he says modular assembly now works well for the $9,200 SMART car, Daimler doesn't want to entrust suppliers with big pieces of its more complex Mercedes luxury sedans.

EXTRA VALUE. Some critics see the module concept as little more than a shell game. "All it does is shift labor from one facility to another, without reducing the labor involved," says ING Baring Furmam Selz auto analyst Maryann Keller. The only real gain comes if suppliers can build parts better than the carmakers. If not, they'll try to recoup by raising prices. Japanese auto makers are leery in part for this reason. With modules, "Toyota's labor cost is just transferred to suppliers, which has no meaning for cutting costs," says Toyota spokesman Koki Konishi.

GM is betting that the module approach can wring big efficiencies out of its U.S. factories. But rocky relations with suppliers and blue-collar workers make the difficult job of turning an untested dream into reality even tougher.

By Kathleen Kerwin in Detroit, with bureau reports

ELECTRONICS MANUFACTURING

A WELL-INTEGRATED IT APPROACH

BY BRUCE REINHART, CPIM

"What-if" scenario modeling, the **ubiquitous** best-practices tool and **first choice** of accountants and R&D groups in **virtually every** business, is **winning over** new proponents in the manufacturing planning and **scheduling arenas.** What prevented **more frequent** use of modeling for manufacturing/planning sooner were **the simple,** but **sizable tasks** of pumping information into the system and front-ending the data with a **practical user interface.**

MAKING SUPPLY CHAIN PLANNING an everyday tool in the company's enterprise resource planning (ERP) system is one of those things that manufacturing planners at the Kimball Electronics Group (KEG) had as a priority on their radar scope. Specifically, they envisioned supply chain integration affording a critically needed ability to quickly validate customers' delivery schedules and understand how subsequent change orders would affect delivery. Yet, while early attempts proved problematic, the company remained watchful for the new elements that brought integration of supply chain tools and what-if modeling within range.

Thirty years ago, KEG'S product line featured electronic keyboard instruments. Today, the product line is vastly different and far more diverse. From three facilities—based in Jasper, Ind.; Burbank, Calif.; and Renosa, Mexico—KEG produces a range of complex electronic components including circuit boards, multi-chip modules and semiconductor components that are shipped worldwide. KEG also

contracts services to customers in the automotive, defense, aerospace, telecommunications, data communication, computer and medical industries.

At the Jasper facility, a single order alone can comprise over 300 components, and at any given time there may be 500 open orders in various stages of production. While the complexity of the individual products has obviously increased, so have manufacturing standards (KEG achieved QS9000 registration for its automotive customer base), complicating ERP and supply chain solutions.

In such dynamic environments, the industry relies heavily on information systems simply for survival. For example, it's not unusual for a top-50 customer with a current order for 20,000 circuit boards to decide one week before production is scheduled that the order must be doubled. On top of this, a minor configuration change must be made to these additional boards. In these cases, KEG also must be able to quickly confirm the feasibility of the change order and describe the impact on the initial de-

From *APICS—The Performance Advantage,* October 1998, pp. 26-28. © 1998 by APICS, the American Production and Inventory Control Society. Reprinted by permission.

> Cost INCREASES, SHIPMENT schedules and other IMPACTS NEED TO be reported, timely and ACCURATELY, IN ORDER to keep that CUSTOMER. Not LONG ago, performing ALL THESE FUNCTIONS would have SEEMED unreasonable, but IT HAS SINCE BECOME a part of EVERYDAY manufacturing.

livery date. Cost increases, shipment schedules and other impacts need to be reported, timely and accurately, in order to keep that customer. Not long ago, performing all these functions would have seemed unreasonable, but it has since become a part of everyday manufacturing.

At KEG, we turned to the current generation of MRP II and supply chain planning software to handle increasing flexibility while supporting product quality standards. Our current system, which has evolved over the past four years, addresses inevitable, yet unforeseen and potentially disruptive changes to production schedules.

Higher customer expectations

DEVELOPING AN IT SYSTEM capable of addressing change order requests, along with the ability to answer the numerous questions that accompany such change orders, has enhanced our overall competitiveness. Meeting expectations hinges upon the ability to diagnose exactly what is happening on the shop floor at any given moment, along with the ability to determine how change orders alter the current production schedule. In short, an electronic manufacturing service requires applications to enable what-if scenario modeling for open orders and for accurately predicting the outcomes.

KEG's legacy system centered around IBM's COPICS MRP application, which the company had been running for some 20 years. It was a loosely integrated system which had grown with the addition of numerous in-house programs. The system had been customized with our own scripts for performing such tasks as order entry, master scheduling and shipping.

Initial use of what-if simulations at KEG began in 1992 with the creation of two separate instances of the MRP application on the mainframe for testing the impact of change orders. It was a cumbersome process, however. For each what-if scenario, it was necessary to refresh the test system with production data, return to the test system and enter customer changes to simulate the new scenario. Since this was a batch MRP system, the simulation could not be run until evening. KEG's service representatives

needed at least 24 hours before they'd have preliminary feedback for a customer. Material planners, too, needed three to five days to process test data, in addition to their production MRP, in order to spot any problems that might arise on their end.

That slow turn-around time kills lucrative contracting relationships. Improving upon this picture required a dramatically transformed and improved IT solution.

Opening the Door

KEG WAS PLANNING TO UPGRADE to a new MRP II system in the early 1990s, but with constant pressure from change orders, the company's supply chain capability needed to be implemented immediately. Since KEG had already purchased i2 Technology's Rhythm software for scheduling shop floor operations, the company elected to leverage whatever capabilities were possible from the existing MRP system by interfacing it with Rhythm's supply chain components.

Despite very distinct architectures of these systems (COPICS and Rhythm), interfacing was relatively straightforward since the software interfaces needed only to extract data.

This early experience proved a good foundation for a subsequent upgrade to the current MRP II system based on the CIIM application from Avalon Software (integrated with Rhythm). The new MRP II application runs on one HP 9000 Model K450 server that was configured, or sized, to meet users' response time demands with dual processors. Several additional servers were added to the network, ranging from the HP Model E- to K-Servers for network, application, and Oracle database support, as well as several HP 9000 workstations that support CAD applications. Platform standardization is aimed at minimizing administration and support costs.

Besides the standard reports that the supply chain component provides, KEG users extract manufacturing and supply chain data files and download these to off-the-shelf applications—Microsoft Excel and Access as well as Impromptu for ad hoc reporting. In this fashion, the planning system was made easy to use and provides immediate access to data

> ... PERSONNEL can easily create AD HOC REPORTS CONTAINING basic information WITHIN MINUTES AFTER KEYING in the SPECIFICS of a CHANGE ORDER. Customers can also be PRESENTED with the NUMBERS INVOLVED in their RESPECTIVE CHANGE ORDERS.

for a variety of plant processes. This includes the order fulfillment group, master scheduler, production planners and material planners for assessing the impact of customer change order requests.

Integrated Supply Chain Planning Tools

THE FIRST SUPPLY CHAIN planning interfaces established a positive trend for KEG'S other IT environments. We are planning to implement similar systems in our facilities at Burbank and Renosa. Currently, MRP II systems at the three facilities stand alone from each other. However, while the respective MRP II systems are autonomous, there is an exchange of information and mutual support among the three sites. (Kimball International, our parent company, provides the wide area network which connects the corporation's U.S. and Mexico locations via T1 frame relay links.)

At the KEG Jasper facilities, the payoffs from the MRP II system were seen immediately. Our ability to respond more rapidly to virtually any customer request has increased dramatically. For one, personnel can easily create ad hoc reports containing basic information within minutes after keying in the specifics of a change order. Customers can also be presented with the numbers involved in their respective change orders.

Other payoffs of this IT solution include: reduction of stress on the shop floor (and everywhere else in the company) with such abilities as extracting daily runtimes and improving throughput significantly; in the warehouse, inventory has been cut by 59 percent; and KEG sales have doubled.

Bruce Reinhart, CPIM, is the materials manager for the Kimball Electronics Group.

The "E" Transformation

Are You Ready For the
E-SUPPLY CHAIN?

The Internet has become the fastest accepted communications medium ever, with 50 million people connected in five years. It took radio 38 years to reach that milestone and 13 years for television. Obviously, a technological groundswell like this is bound to affect every facet of our lives—personal and business. In this article, we will explore the impact the Net will have on one of today's most pressing business initiatives—how we manage the supply chain.

BY JIM TURCOTTE, CPIM, BOB SILVERI, C.P.M., AND TOM JOBSON

Undoubtedly, you have already heard about e-business. E-business can be described as the business transformation that occurs by exploiting the benefits of enterprise integration and global network connectivity. Think of e-business as the umbrella for any business process implemented using network technology. Under this umbrella fall many types of business processes including e-commerce, which is the transactional business process of selling and buying via the Net.

The type of e-business we want to focus on is aptly called e-supply chain. It refers to the management of the supply chain using Internet technologies. Currently, this is a tall order, but the concepts are sound and the technologies are proven. Most of us have used Internet technology to surf the Net, send e-mail to a friend or even do a little shopping. In fact 80 percent of businesses use the Web today, although less than 7 percent use it in support of supply chain management. So, while the technology is readily available and the applications are very pervasive, the use of the Net for supply chain management remains in its infancy.

The Net comes in Three flavors

BEFORE GOING ANY FURTHER, an explanation is required for the three types of "nets" that are used to support e-supply chain operations. (see Figure 1). Think of these as various types of information highways used to connect different parts of the supply chain. Each of these information highways is used for different reasons

From *APIC—The Performance Advantage*, August 1998, pp. 56-59. © 1998 by APICS, the American Production and Inventory Control Society. Reprinted by permission.

and therefore tend to support different business processes within the supply chain.

An intranet is an internal net that is normally used within the boundaries of a company. It may stretch across many manufacturing sites or even countries for that matter. Much of the data found in an intranet environment is considered sensitive, and therefore access is usually limited to people within the company. Companies are linking their ERP systems, or at least making information available from their ERP systems, to the intranet. Intranets are protected from outside access by a "firewall."

BUSINESS NETWORK VARIATIONS

FIREWALL
Company "A" Intranet
FIREWALL
Company "B" Intranet
SECURED LINK
Company A & B
SHARED DATA EXTRANET
INTERNET BACKBONE
PUBLIC ACCESS INTERNET
Figure 1

Think of an extranet as an external intranet shared by two or more companies. Each participating company moves certain data outside of its private intranet to the extranet, making the data available only to the companies sharing the extranet. An example of this use would be providing inventory data to your supplier to help support an automatic replenishment process.

Last but not least, is the Internet with which we are most familiar. This form is open to the general public. The Internet tends to be used more for e-commerce today, but has some emerging uses in supply chain management, such as advertising surplus inventory to outside brokers. In summary, think of the intranet as a private net, an extranet as a shared net and the Internet as a public net.

Making the Link!

By now, you are wondering how an e-supply chain might operate. Let's start by creating a simple e-supply chain example (see Figure 2). Imagine that you are a toothpaste manufacturing company called TastyPaste. Not just any toothpaste, but the new flavored types that all the kids want. Yes, you have 99 flavors from bubble gum to apple-flavored toothpaste. You sell it to 250 retail chains throughout the world, which translates to thousands of retail stores and millions of consumers. You purchase the flavor additives, tubes and other materials from 50 suppliers. The question is: Given the complexity of this supply-demand environment, how can you manage the supply chain to achieve the right balance of customer responsiveness and low inventory levels with an aggressive cycle time.

Now imagine for a moment that TastyPaste's direct customers, the retail chains, have provided access to their inventory data through a shared data extranet. As consumer purchases occur, the data is fed to the retail chain's ERP system. The retail chain then moves the updated demand data to the extranet. At this time, the critical data is automatically fed to the TastyPaste ERP system. This system runs and makes the appropriate quantity and schedule adjustments. The key output is copied to the extranet set up between TastyPaste and its 50 suppliers. This data might include updated inventory snapshots as well as updated, forecasted demands and orders for additives, etc. Based on the data the suppliers see in the extranet, they automatically replenish TastyPaste's inventory and adjust their own ERP gross requirements to meet demands. The end result is the real-time update of demands from the consumer to the raw material suppliers.

The TastyPaste company has created what amounts to a seamless environment that stretches from customers right through to suppliers. Customer demand flows to those

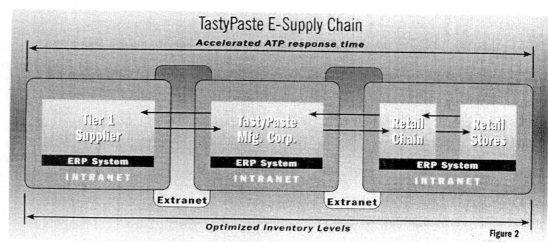

TastyPaste E-Supply Chain
Accelerated ATP response time

Tier 1 Supplier | TastyPaste Mfg. Corp. | Retail Chain | Retail Stores
ERP System | ERP System | ERP System
INTRANET | INTRANET | INTRANET

Extranet | Extranet

Optimized Inventory Levels
Figure 2

who need it, when they need it. And this supply chain capability is not limited to a single tier of customer or supplier, but can extend to multiple tiers of both. The bottom line is that they have created an integrated enterprise through the global connectivity of the Net.

The Benefits

So JUST HOW DOES e-supply chain benefit us? The objectives of any company are to reduce costs, reduce cycle time and grow revenue. E-supply chain supports these objectives by doing everything from improving the effectiveness of customer- supplier relationships to enabling faster customer response. Let's take a closer look at some of these below.

Companies are finding that enterprise integration is leading to a new level of supplier-customer working relationships never before imagined. Customers can literally check on their order status through access to a joint extranet, or a supplier can have access to your inventory levels in order to know when to replenish your stock. Data is able to move more easily and quickly between the links; but more importantly, the sharing of data is taking place like never before.

This is leading to significant business advantages for members of the supply chain. While strong relationships might have been considered an intangible item in earlier times, it is not so today. World-class competitiveness demands a closer relationship with our supply chain partners and the building of "value-based" relationships.

The benefits of reduced cycle time are a different matter, for they provide measurable, competitive advantages of both cost and performance. When we talk cycle time here, we are talking about the time it takes to react to a new demand statement from our customers. The quicker we can move critical data through the pipeline, the quicker we can react and hence, deliver the end product to our customer. We all know this leads to improved customer satisfaction and promotes a fertile environment for revenue growth.

Information Technology Implications

As DISCUSSED in the earlier example, Net technologies can dramatically extend the value of supply chain management systems. This is accomplished by shrinking the cycle time in the movement of information up and down the supply chain. However, there are other positive features of using the net.

One of the benefits IT (information technology) folks especially like is the ability of the Net to support the thin client paradigm. Basically, the less software we need on the client workstation, the "thinner" the client becomes. Since the net is a server-centric environment, we can keep the majority of the software on the server and less on the client. A user (client) can access his key applications/data through a browser such as Netscape.

COMPANIES ARE FINDING that enterprise integration is leading to a new level of supplier-customer working relationships never before imagined.

Why do we care about how thin a client is? Two key reasons. One is that it's easier to upgrade a few centralized servers to a new software release than it is to upgrade several hundred widely dispersed client workstations. Second, the thinner the client, the less computing power required, reducing capital spending and ongoing maintenance costs for companies moving to Net-based technologies. In fact, some companies have moved to what is known as an NC (network computer), which is the equivalent of a stripped down personal computer optimized for Net use.

Another big IT expense-related benefit is the ease of installation and low costs of connectivity. This is where the net really enables enterprise integration. If you are a new supplier joining a supply chain, one of the requirements may be that you connect to an extranet. All you would need are three items. An NC system as previously noted, an ISP connection (Internet service provider) and a Web browser. This ease of connectivity also makes it easier for your own employees to access critical data while traveling. In fact, a sales person can have the ability to view the latest available-to-promise (ATP) data to make commitments and place orders while in a customer's office. The order is then fed directly to the sales person's company ERP system and immediately scheduled. In addition, transportation software is even being linked to ERP systems to allow

WHAT IS JAVA?
Developed in 1995 by SUN Microsystems, JAVA is an object-oriented programming language. This characteristic enables software engineers to achieve high levels of application productivity by virtue of the reusability of the code. Significant applications written in JAVA have been developed for the Internet and make use of the language's inherent capability to work on multiple software platforms. All major software product developers today have significant efforts in place writing JAVA-based versions of their platform products. Further, the advent of JAVA-compatible browsers is enabling the end-user to experience the same look and feel for all company applications written in JAVA which reside on its intranet. The combination of all these advantages is thrusting JAVA into a leading role in the development of e-commerce applications.

for the delivery information to be supplied along with the delivery date. The customer ends up placing a real-time order, is given a real-time delivery commitment, and is even told how it will ship—all done in the customer's office.

FOR AN E-SUPPLY CHAIN TO BE SUCCESSFUL,
you need to undergo both business process and technological transformations in order to maximize the benefits.

Application software direction

A SURE SIGN that Internet applications are being taken seriously is the massive amount of R&D dollars being spent. Key areas of expenditure include the development of software, hardware and services to support e-business by all the major software developers. More specific to e-supply chain are the moves of software industry heavyweights to make their applications Web-enabled. Major ERP providers, as well as major supply chain management players have comparable efforts. Many other companies, developing products from transportation logistics software to ERP tools, are racing to make their products Web-enabled.

On the technology side, one of the most promising avenues of Internet application software development is the explosive growth of the JAVA programming language. This is allowing companies to develop software that is portable across different operating system platforms and has high reuse capability (see sidebar). These benefits are particularly important as companies reengineer their applications for e-business opportunities.

Key items

WHILE WE TALKED A LOT ABOUT how great the Net will be when moving forward with e-supply chain uses, there are, however, a few items you need to be aware of. First and foremost, for an e-supply chain to be successful, you need to undergo both business process and technological transformations in order to maximize the benefits.

The other major items are security, scalability, integration and reliability. None of these are insurmountable, one just needs to address them to avoid problems. Security speaks for itself. No company wants sensitive data to get into the wrong hands or be corrupted. A properly set up intranet or extranet can be quite secure with today's technology. Scalability allows for long-term growth as well as seasonal spikes. The last thing a major retailer wants is for the system to get bogged down during the holidays when high net traffic is likely. Integration is the ability to use many of a company's existing applications together with future applications. A company's challenge is to migrate smoothly from its legacy systems to an e-supply chain environment. And finally there is reliability. Make sure you build a network that is robust and has sufficient redundancy, especially if you are talking about running mission-critical applications.

The Net of It All

IT'S NO LONGER A QUESTION of whether the e-supply chain is going to occur, it's now a question of when you will operate in an e-supply chain mode. While the "e" in e-supply chain stands for "electronic," it can also stand for "evolving," because that is what we are doing in the area of supply chain management. We are engaged in a continuous, business process and technological evolution!

Jim Turcotte, CPIM, has been with IBM for 17 years and is currently involved with advanced planning and scheduling tool development at IBM Corp. Logistics. Robert A. Silveri, C.P.M., is a consultant with Analysts International Corp. Tom Jobson is a senior IT architect at IBM.

Digital denim

After three years of hemming and hawing, Levi Strauss began selling on-line last month. Why the hesitation?

By Luisa Kroll

LAST MONTH, 125 YEARS AFTER it began selling blue jeans out of a San Francisco warehouse, Levi Strauss & Co. began peddling jeans from a virtual warehouse. It launched on-line stores for its Levi's and Dockers brands, stocking more than 120 items in 3,000 variations.

These Web sites are cool: A "Fit Calculator" suggests the best sizes; a "Changing Room" mixes and matches tops and bottoms to show how they look together; a "Style Finder" uses "filtering technology" to recommend rags based on your taste for music, fashion and lifestyle.

It's a custom fit—the question is, what took so long? After all, Levi first opened a Web site three years ago—an eternity in cyberspace—but without a sales window. Eddie Bauer has been selling clothes on-line since 1995; The Gap started a year ago. And Levi could use a boost: Its market share has shrunk 14 points, to 16.9%, since 1990, says researcher Tactical Retail Monitor, New York.

But going on-line is a lot harder than it looks, and Levi's struggle offers lessons for all marketers pondering a foray into cyberspace.

Levi had abundant reasons to proceed warily. Retail stores provide virtually all Levi's $7 billion a year in sales and may resent the jeansmaker going into competition against them. "It's a bit of a touchy spot," says a Levi executive. "We don't want to be perceived as arrogant."

For similar reasons, rival VF Corp., which owns Lee and Wrangler jeans, straddles the fence even more than Levi does. It plans to sell on-line—but only obscure brands such as Healthtex, a line of kids' clothing. Other famous brands won't go even that far.

"As a matter of policy, we have thrown our lot in with department stores," says Albert Shapiro, marketing vice president at apparel maker Liz Claiborne Inc. "We don't want to compete with our retailers."

Levi's first flirtation in cyberspace came in 1994 at the urging of Janie Ligon, who had just relocated from the U.S. to London to run Levi's U.K. business. When the company first balked, she threatened to open a Levi Web site of her own. By the summer of 1994 a committee was working on it. In late 1995 the first Levi's site was up and running.

That first effort was self-consciously hip, a place to hang, chat and read about graffiti "art" and South African street styles. Everything, in other words, but what consumers really wanted, which was to buy some jeans. No wonder it didn't click.

"We weren't very focused. We wanted to put something up and learn along the way," says Jay Thomas, director of digital marketing for the Levi's brand.

The company spent the next three years trying face-lifts, experimenting with on-line soap operas and blurbs about cool kids, to no avail. Web visitors didn't want to be entertained by Levi—they wanted to buy pants.

Frustrated customers zapped thousands of e-mails asking where they could buy and why they couldn't do it on-line. "Get a clue," one on-liner flamed. "My patience is close to expiration," another warned. "I want to buy direct!!!" pleaded a third.

As it dawned on the company that the Web might offer a new sales channel, the sales staff was telling big retail chains they weren't to sell Levi's or Dockers on-line themselves. In spring 1997 Levi formed another task force—simply to study on-line sales. A short time later the team's goal was clearer: It named itself SOTI—Selling on the Internet.

The project accelerated late last year after Gordon Shank, then president of Levi's Americas unit and now Levi's chief marketing officer, visited a customer-service center and heard the frustration firsthand. Customers couldn't find what they wanted or even place orders over the phone.

He quickly fixed those problems, then turned to the Internet. By January he had sold Levi's brass on a test of on-line sales in Canada, and in 60 days the virtual store was open for business.

Reprinted by permission from *Forbes* magazine, December 28, 1998, pp. 102-103. © 1998 by Forbes, Inc.

Warring wallets

WHAT'S THE WORST PART of shopping on-line? Filling out those cumbersome forms when you want to buy with a single click. Bill Gross wants to make it easier.

The founder of the Pasadena, Calif.-based Internet incubator company idealab!, Gross hopes to solve this problem with an electronic wallet, a Web-shopping device that holds your name, address and credit card information. The idealab! company eWallet crunched for six months to launch in time for Christmas.

Here's how it works: PC users download free software at eWallet.com and fill in a template based on research from 10,000 Web sites. An eWallet icon then pops up on a user's Windows screen and stays there. To buy on-line, click the wallet, select a credit card icon and drag it onto the site. eWallet fills in the forms instantly.

"It's a very simple and elegant solution to a tricky problem," says Nicole Vanderbilt, an analyst with Jupiter Communications. Which is why Gross faces plenty of competition from such heavyweights as America Online, Yahoo! and Excite.

Their wallets, however, are usable only at selected Web outlets, while Gross maintains his can be whipped out anywhere. "Nobody's had a broad consumer application like this," he says. He hopes to make money by charging credit card companies for occupying the best default spot in each wallet.

Time and trial will tell whether shoppers bite. Using eWallet entails its own hassle: downloading a program, something that isn't required by Quick Checkout, AOL's wallet, which also rolled out last month and works at 35 merchants.

Says AOL e-commerce Vice President Wendy Brown: "There's a limit to how much choice you put in front of a consumer. The merchants you see should be well-known brands." But Gross is betting Web shoppers want the wider reach he hopes to deliver.

—ANN MARSH

Retailers in Canada had been given the soft sell. Local director Shelley Nandkeolyar met with the biggest accounts to explain that this was simply an experiment that would help everyone sell more product. "We presented it as a wonderful opportunity to learn about the customer," he says.

Just a month later Levi decided to get cracking in the U.S. and threw more than 50 people at the project. About half worked on the site itself. The other half worked on the back end, crunching computer code to build systems for order-processing, distribution and inventory flow and to integrate a new Web site tracking system with the existing ones.

Levi's U.S. sales force didn't hear of the on-line invasion until a month before the launch. And while Levi plotted to compete against the stores by going on-line, it continues to forbid them from doing the same. So you can buy Lee jeans at jcpenney.com and Calvins at macy.com—but to buy Levi's from these retailers you must visit their real-world stores.

Levi says it must retain control of its own image. Its major retailers, including Sears, Federated and Kohls, are too polite to say whether they find this unfair or unwise. JC Penney notes only that it has 4,300 suppliers—and Levi is the only one to impose such a ban.

Critics say the approach is shortsighted and thoughtless. "What [Levi] is doing is stupid-dot-com," says Angela Kapp, an on-line vice president at Estée Lauder, which just opened clinique.com on the Web. "You must always remember who brought you to the dance." Estée sells Clinique on-line and helps its retailers do the same.

The folks at Levi may offer a sop to the stores: It would like to emblazon Levi's banners on the retailers' own Web sites and pay them a commission when their customers buy new duds at the jeansmaker's sites. But that may not happen for another year, Levi's Shank says.

For now Levi's executives won't reveal any numbers, but say they are pleased with the new Web stores' results. They meet daily to track the traffic and pore over sales numbers. In the first two weeks, on-line sales exceeded the volume at one of the company's flagship Levi's-only stores.

Jay Thomas, Levi's digital-brand czar, says moving onto the Web "is a monumental task in terms of investment and time. It's easy to underestimate." But he makes no apologies for how the company handled the retail partners that helped build the brand. "It wasn't about them," he says flatly. "It was about the customer."

THREE DECADES OF PROGRESS: PRODUCTIVITY, QUALITY, ENVIRONMENT

Over the past two decades, organizational progress has been defined by the revolutionary productivity and quality movements. So what can organizations expect to face as they embark on the new millennium? In this article, the author predicts that the next decade will focus on environmental management systems and offers guidelines for dealing with the critical issues, challenges, and opportunities that ultimately will arise.

by William A. Ruch

If 1975 to 1985 was the decade of productivity, and 1985 to 1995 was the decade of quality, will 1995 to 2005 be the decade of the environment? Many believe that is the case, and they can make a very strong argument. The rapid development and implementation of ISO 14000 on the heels of ISO 9000, the burgeoning legislation dealing with environmental regulations, and the increasing number of articles in academic and professional publications dealing with environmental issues and organizational responses to those concerns are just a few of the signs.

If the "quality revolution" began in Asia—Japan in particular—is there an "environmental revolution" beginning in Europe—particularly in Germany? Germany has the most far-reaching and stringent regulations on pollution control and recycling of any country in the world. If those regulations were imposed on U.S. businesses, it would indeed create a revolution in organizational policies, practices, and culture.

Those who argue that the environmental revolution decade is inevitable cite the many characteristics it shares with the productivity and quality movements that preceded it. But there are those who say the path to the future is not a linear extension of the productivity- and quality-related events of the past two decades. No one can predict the future with perfect accuracy, but if organi-

zations are to be prepared for future battles, their leaders should study history as well as the present. Only then can they make intelligent predictions about the strategies, tactics, and weapons that may be needed to survive.

THE DECADE OF PRODUCTIVITY: 1975 TO 1985

In the mid-seventies many a plant manager proclaimed, "We had to increase productivity so we started working overtime." But those managers eventually realized that there was a difference between productivity and production. Productivity during overtime hours can go up, down, or remain the same, depending on the measures (labor, capital, material, energy, or total productivity), how they were defined, the measurement systems being used, and any organizational assumptions that accompanied them. During the decade of productivity, organizations learned that:

- Productivity always refers to outputs over inputs.
- Productivity can be partial (labor, capital, materials, or energy), multifactor (some combination of these), or total (all of these).
- Productivity increases come not from working harder or faster, but from working smarter.

A member of the *National Productivity Review* editorial advisory board, William A. Ruch is a professor of operations management at Arizona State University in Tempe, where he has conducted research and taught productivity and quality for over 30 years. He participated in the early development of the Malcolm Baldrige National Quality Award and served for three years as an examiner. He is a fellow in the World Academy of Productivity Sciences.

From *National Productivity Review*, Winter 1998, pp. 13-20. © 1998 by John Wiley and Sons, Inc. Reprinted by permission.

- A productivity increase does not mean that some workers have to be laid off.
- Productivity can be increased by adding more inputs if the result is a more than proportional increase in outputs. This is managed growth. (Actually, the productivity ratio can be increased five ways, depending on the direction and relative strength of the change in outputs and inputs; six ways if you include increases in the quality of outputs.)
- Productivity at the individual level, the plant level, and the national economy level are not additive; they may be different concepts with different measures.
- White collar or knowledge worker productivity was (and to a great extent still is) an uncharted frontier because it is so difficult to define and measure.

This was the decade that saw C. Jackson Grayson establish the American Productivity Center (whose name would be changed in the next decade) in Houston, Texas, under a different model than the productivity centers in Asia and Europe. Thousands of articles and hundreds of books were published on productivity, and *National Productivity Review* was established to devote every article of every issue to the understanding and improvement of organizational and national productivity. Countless hours of managerial training were devoted (within some organizations in "Productivity Colleges") to spread the new knowledge of managing productivity to all employees.

By the end of the decade, however, attention shifted to the downside of productivity improvement: productivity improvement efforts that failed, measurement systems that did not work, workers that were laid off as a result of productivity improvement changes in processes, and automation being carried to extremes to maximize worker productivity. Eventually the debate cooled and the knowledge base of productivity became assimilated into standard organizational practice.

THE DECADE OF QUALITY: 1985 TO 1995

In the early 1980s, American industry became painfully aware of the threat of Japanese competition, starting in basic industries like steel and progressing through automobiles, electronics, and others. The primary basis for the competitive edge was product quality, and American managers struggled to determine how the Deming method had transformed a country known for producing "cheap junk" into a major competitive threat to all industries.

Up to this time, American managers defined quality as percentage defects, and they were pleased that they had dropped simple inspection methods for the use of statistical quality control techniques. Enlightened firms had quality assurance programs, but few managers had heard of or read anything by Deming, Juran, Feigenbaum, or Crosby. In 1980, NBC aired the white paper "If Japan Can, Why Can't We?" and some mark that date as the dawn of the quality revolution.

In 1983, a White House conference on productivity included a section on quality. The participants, including executives, consultants, academics, and government officials, discussed the possibility of a national quality award similar to the Deming Prize in Japan. Fast forward to 1987, through the thousands of hours of discussion by hundreds of devoted individuals, and the result is the Malcolm Baldrige National Quality Award. Interestingly, the American Productivity Center played a major role in the development of the Baldrige Award program, along with the National Institute for Standards and Technology and the American Society for Quality Control (whose name also would change).

But it would take some time for a true understanding of the term "quality" to develop. A vice president of one of the nation's largest retailing firms, who declined to participate in the White House conference quality section, voiced a common misconception of the time when he said, "You don't understand. We are a retailing firm; we don't manufacture anything. Therefore, we have nothing to do with quality."

This decade eventually saw a virtual explosion of knowledge, including models, approaches, tools, and techniques, that proposed an entirely new way of looking at quality within an organization's processes. The definition of quality expanded from percent defects to customer satisfaction and then to customer delight. The scope of quality improvement efforts reached beyond manufacturing to services, government, and virtually every form of organized activity. Articles, books, and training programs increased exponentially over the previous decade. Quality Colleges replaced Productivity Colleges. Cadres of executives went on pilgrimages to Japan and everyone began benchmarking everyone else. Deming and Juran were practically canonized; Crosby, Feigenbaum, and other quality gurus were revered as prophets.

The incentive for quality improvement clearly came from foreign competition, and one of the key factors in the vast changes in American organizations was the de-

---

This decade eventually saw a virtual explosion of knowledge, including models, approaches, tools, and techniques, that proposed an entirely new way of looking at quality within an organization's processes.

---

velopment and dissemination of the Baldrige Award. Few firms have won the award, but thousands of organizations now have guidance from the Baldrige model: the core values, the criteria, and the evaluation process to diagnose their quality shortcomings and develop a plan for quality improvement. For the first time, the model made it possible to judge the quality of an entire organization (not just its products and processes) and make comparisons across industries and even across sectors.

The American Productivity Center (APC) became the

EXHIBIT 1. Models and Standards for Quality and the Environment

QUALITY	ENVIRONMENT
BALDRIGE AWARD Model Core Values Criteria Evaluation Process "Ideal Quality Management Systems and Results"	
ISO 9000 Systems Standards Procedures "Minimum Quality Responsibility"	ISO 14000 Systems Standards Procedures "Minimum Environmental Responsibility"

American Productivity and Quality Center (APQC). Later, the American Society for Quality Control (ASQC) dropped the last word from its name and became ASQ. Other terminology changes abounded. Benchmarking, quality function deployment, process capability, design for quality, seven quality tools, Baldrige 4.0, customer delight, process maps, ISO 9000, Shingo system, continuous improvement, pokayoke, kaizen, jidoka, PCDA cycle, and, of course, TQM became part of the common lexicon.

Once again, the downside began to emerge toward the end of the revolution. Debates flourished over the relative merits of the Baldrige versus the ISO 9000 approaches. Applications for the Baldrige Award declined and many organizational programs for quality improvement waned as firms focused on more pressing problems. Statements like "TQM is dead" were heard more frequently. In fact, organizations had internalized and institutionalized quality values and approaches so that what had been considered revolutionary five years earlier was now common practice. The spotlight was beginning to move to another issue.

THE DECADE OF THE ENVIRONMENT: 1995 TO 2005

Have organizations entered the decade that will focus on environmental issues? Will they follow the same paths of development? What have they learned in the last two decades that will enable them to predict the challenges ahead and deal with them proactively and effectively?

Predictors to support the contention that environmental issues constitute the next major wave in organizational changes are many. They include:

- Increased regulation concerning environmental interactions, such as the use of hazardous materials and waste disposal. As strong as this trend is in the United States, it is even stronger in Europe.
- Increased levels of activity by environmental advocacy groups in the United States and throughout the world.
- Increases in the number of articles in the popular press and in the academic and professional journals dealing with environmental issues and organizational reactions.
- Increased incidents of leading organizations with proactive environmental programs producing positive results in environmental quality, as well as increased performance by the organization.
- Increases in models, approaches, and techniques for planning and implementing environmental quality programs. Primary among these is ISO 14000.

As seen in the previous decades, here, too, there is a certain level of naïveté regarding the issues to be confronted. For example, an economist with the World Bank, explaining why the United States should export toxic wastes to Third World countries, said, "I've always thought that underpopulated countries in Africa are vastly underpolluted."

Let's look at the similarities and differences between the productivity and quality movements in the last two decades and try to predict whether similar trends will occur in the proposed environmental decade.

Currently, many equate environmental concerns only with pollution control and, perhaps, hazardous waste disposal.

An Expanding Definition—Productivity, once defined as "units per hour," expanded into a concept that encompassed all factors of production and all levels: the individual worker, the plant, the organization, and the economy (although organizations are still working on the links to try to make it additive). Quality began as "percentage defects" but quickly expanded to "meeting or exceeding customer expectations," and its scope broadened to include all organizational activities from product development to customer use. It also expanded to include all industries and sectors.

Currently, many equate environmental concerns only with pollution control and, perhaps, hazardous waste disposal. That definition is being quickly, if not systematically, expanded to include any interaction with the environment that has any discernible effect. The definition will expand to include all environmental impacts associated with the design of products or services, design of processes, raw materials used, control of production, emissions, waste disposal, storage, transportation, and final disposal of the product. It will also encompass tangential activities, such as personnel policies related to car-pooling, telecommuting, and virtual teams.

At a minimum, environmental considerations include:

- Depletion of natural resources
- Use and conservation of renewable resources
- Reduction or elimination of pollution—air, water, soil, noise, odor, and aesthetic pollution
- Adverse effects on the environment (such as dams diverting streams, or converting forest, desert, or wetlands to agricultural, commercial, or residential use)
- Creating waste (hazardous or not) that adds to landfills, sewage, or special disposal sites.

If an executive from a retail firm says his company doesn't affect the environment because it doesn't manufacture anything, one can point to the company's 40-acre asphalt parking lot, which affects local weather patterns, and its enormous use of energy for heating and cooling. Likewise, government agencies cannot be left out of the environmental picture. For example, the contracting policies of the Department of Transportation for highway construction should contain proactive environmental considerations.

Environmental Measurement and Evaluation—An organization can achieve only what it can measure. As **Exhibit 1** illustrates, ISO 9000 and the Baldrige Award help evaluate quality efforts and results. ISO 9000 provides the "floor"—that is, the baseline requirements for competing on quality in international markets. Baldrige provides the "ceiling"—that is, the ideal that defines a world-class quality organization. ISO 14000 defines the systems and controls that must be in place if the organization is to be environmentally responsible. But the upper right quadrant is vacant at present.

This is not to suggest the development of a Baldrige-type environmental award program. But just as Baldrige provided a set of core values that an organization could use to assess its organizationwide quality efforts, some system is needed to establish a set of core values for an environmentally-conscious organization, a definition of world-class environmental responsibility, and a set of criteria by which organizations can evaluate their environmental management efforts and results. A way to compare organizations is needed, so the leaders can be rewarded and help others with specific plans for improvement. Would the criteria be a simple re-write of the Baldrige materials, substituting the word "environment" for the word "quality"? Preliminary research indicates that there would be some overlap, but the two sets of criteria would

not be the same. Additional research and development are needed to formulate the new set of environmental values.

Environmental Strategies—Although many organizational quality strategies can be identified, the basic strategies are inspection, statistical quality control, and total quality management. Similarly, the following three basic strategies will come into play during the environmental decade:

1. *Compliance.* Most organizations today view compliance with environmental regulations as a necessary evil and a cost of doing business. If they meet all federal, state, and local guidelines and restrictions, no more is required. One organization, when asked if it did anything proactive in environmental actions, responded: "Yes, we are very proactive in trying to determine what the new regulations will be so we can remain in compliance."

2. *Proactive.* Some firms are beginning to go beyond the regulations and implement changes that are more environmentally friendly. Some do it for publicity and public relations, some from a sense of corporate responsibility and citizenship, and some see the possibility of tangible benefits from the changes. McDonald's eliminated Styrofoam packaging in favor of paper and cardboard, not because it was required, but because the company felt it was the right thing to do.

3. *Profit-Motivated.* Anecdotal stories are beginning to emerge of process or product changes instigated by a concern for environmental issues, but resulting in a great cost saving for the organization. Motorola, for example, sought to reduce the use of a hazardous fluid it used to clean integrated circuits in the final manufacturing step. After studying the process and going through several iterations of finding less toxic cleaning agents, the company discovered a way to alter the process upstream to eliminate the need for the cleaning step altogether. The result was not only the elimination of the hazardous material, but a substantial cost savings and profit boost for this product. As more of these examples emerge, there could well be the publication of a book called "Environment Is Free."

Models, Approaches, and Tools—Undoubtedly, many new approaches to environmental management will emerge in the future, but many of the models used in productivity and quality improvement may serve well with minor modifications. Let's look at a few examples:

1. *Benchmarking.* This has been an important tool in quality improvement, so why not in environmental management? If organizations can identify others that have world-class environmental products and pro-

cesses, they can employ the same benchmarking methodology to obtain and spread that knowledge.

2. *Continuous Improvement.* This has been a byword in the quality revolution and could be in the environmental decade. Organizations can continuously strive to reduce hazardous material use, recycle more materials and products, reduce pollution, reduce depletion of nonrenewable resources, conserve renewable resources, and lessen their ecological impact. Perhaps some executive will say: "Environmental management is a race without a finish line."

3. *Corporate Quality Culture.* This umbrella term covers everything from top management support to specific techniques used to improve product and process quality. If organizations are to develop a corporate environmental culture, they have to include top management support; environmental policies in the organization mission statement; assurance that all employees are trained in environmental management and understand their responsibilities; a pervasive attitude toward prevention, rather than correction; control mechanisms to assure that environmental goals are being met; and so on. Most of the changes spurred by the quality movement have a counterpart in environmental management.

A LOOK AT THE DIFFERENCES

In spite of the similarities outlined above, many argue that environmental management is structurally and fundamentally different from productivity and quality management. The differences most frequently cited are:

1. *Motivation.* Productivity improvement is profit motivated. Greater productivity leads to higher margins and only those inside the firm know how the benefits from productivity are to be distributed: higher profits, larger dividends, lower prices, or reinvestment. Quality, on the other hand, is customer motivated. Quality is a competitive factor that is often obvious and important to the customer (unlike productivity). Only if the customer is satisfied does the organization succeed.

   But neither those inside the organization nor the customer is keenly motivated by environmental variables. Although many citizens are active in movements to improve the environmental performance of organizations, it is not yet clear whether the average customer will make a purchase decision based on environmental responsibility, especially if it means a trade-off with price or quality. How many new customers did McDonald's gain by eliminating Styrofoam packaging? How many customers did Exxon lose because of the Valdez incident and the way the firm responded to it?

2. *Government Regulations.* Very few regulations affect productivity improvement programs, but quality im-

provement efforts are bordered by product liability laws, as well as those affecting warranties, fraudulent labeling and advertising, and fair credit reporting. Environmental issues are fraught with government regulations at the federal, state, and local levels. Given this maze of regulatory requirements, it is not surprising that the predominant organizational environmental strategy at present is compliance.

3. *Stakeholders.* Productivity improvement has few stakeholders. Quality, on the other hand, includes customers, employees, stockholders, and suppliers as stakeholders who affect and are affected by changes

---

Quality, on the other hand, is customer motivated. Quality is a competitive factor that is often obvious and important to the customer (unlike productivity).

---

in the quality of the organization's products and processes. Quality is transaction-based. That is, if a customer buys, say, an Amana refrigerator, he or she is concerned with the quality of the product and that will affect the purchase decision. The customer purchasing the Amana is not concerned or affected by the quality of a Kenmore, GE, or other competing product.

But that is not the case with environmental issues. If Kenmore or GE uses processes that adversely affect the environment, if they fail to properly handle hazardous materials, or if they produce products that pollute the environment, everyone is affected, regardless of whether they are customers. In the environmental sphere, every human being is a stakeholder in every organization. The environment is a closed, interdependent system; it is affected by every organization in its realm and it affects every inhabitant within it.

AN ENVIRONMENTAL CLASSIFICATION SYSTEM FOR ORGANIZATIONS

If the premise that every organization affects the environment in some way is true, then it also can be argued that the impact differs considerably across the spectrum of organization types. An educational institution, for example, would appear to have minor impacts on the environment, yet commuting students, faculty, and staff pollute the air; science labs may use hazardous materials; thousands of tons of waste (mostly paper) may be created; and even landscaping (or the lack thereof) will affect the environment. Although some conscientious institutions have excellent environmental programs, many universities and high schools could develop better environmental poli- .

EXHIBIT 2. An Environmental Classification of Organizations

		RISK TO THE ENVIRONMENT		
		Low	**Moderate**	**High**
INTERACTION WITH THE ENVIRONMENT	Low	Financial Institutions Software Development Educational Insitutions	Research Laboratories Pharmaceutical Manufacturing Machine Shops	Nuclear Power Plants Biogenetics Ammunition Manufacturing
	Moderate	Food Processing (dry goods) Printing (books, newspapers) Trucking Companies	Automobile Manufactguring Electronics Manufactguring Highway Construction	Chemical Processing Steel Mills Oil Refining
	High	Fishing Hydroelectric Power Landscaping	Agriculture Forest Products Mining	Off-Shore Oil Drilling Waste Disposal Pest Extermination

cies if they had the motivation to do so and an understanding of what steps to take.

Certainly, schools, financial institutions, retailers, and accounting firms would not be lumped in the same category with oil drilling companies, chemical processors, and nuclear power plants. But what are the categories? According to what dimensions should they be separated? Existing categories, such as SIC codes or types of manufacturing and service processes, offer little help, for they may not relate directly to environmental variables.

Exhibit 2 offers a typology based on two variables: the degree of interaction with the environment and the degree of risk to the environment. The degree of interaction refers to how the organization's normal operations disturb the natural ecology. Interaction does not necessarily mean adverse effects; it simply means that the organization "touches" the environment in some way.

The degree of risk is independent of the degree of interaction. Risk refers to the chance that the normal operations of the organization could have significant adverse effects on the environment. For example, a hydroelectric generating plant will have a high degree of interaction with the environment through a dam that controls water flow. The dam will create a lake upstream and make some downstream changes to the natural ecology of the area. The risk of a major adverse effect, however, is limited to the possibility of a dam break—a small probability that could possibly result in a small effect, depending on the location of the dam. Compare this to the risk of a nuclear power plant. Although the probability of a failure is relatively small, the effect of a meltdown would be a major disaster to a large area and all the living things within it for a substantial period of time.

Exhibit 2 displays these two presumably independent dimensions on three levels and provides illustrations of specific organizations for each of the nine categories. Research is needed to determine whether the types of firms listed are in the correct category. Moreover, the possibility

of variations within each grouping must be addressed, as a specific firm might demonstrate that its environmental policies, controls, and results qualify it to move to the left or upward in the matrix. For example, a city delivery service that uses alternative fuel vehicles could be considered both less interactive and less of a risk to the environment than a service that relies on traditional fuel.

Different categories in this typology would lead organizations to develop policies and approaches for environmental management similar to those in the same category, but different from those in categories across boundaries. It would give firms direction for benchmarking partners and it might even give legislators guidance in writing constructive regulations based on the type of firm and the challenges faced by organizations in a given category.

KEY QUESTIONS ON THE ROAD AHEAD

If real progress is to be made in the environmental arena, several key questions must be addressed.

1. Is environmental quality compatible with performance quality? Are the two strategies contradictory, complementary, competitive, or synergistic? Must there always be tradeoffs between environmental goals and goals for productivity, quality, and profitability? It was once said that higher quality could only be achieved by sacrificing productivity and profit. Now organizations know that improved quality generally leads to higher levels of productivity by eliminating rework and product waste, leading to better financial performance through higher sales, lower costs, better margins, and satisfied customers. The common opinion today is that environmental controls lead to reduced performance results, but some experiences have shown that environmental programs can pay dividends.

2. Can environmental quality be redefined to include more than just pollution control? If so, organizations can then deal with environmental issues in a more systematic, comprehensive way across the spectrum of organization types. Just as they learned to include quality considerations at all stages of business activity, they can include environmental variables throughout the organization as they design products and processes, select suppliers, develop employee policies, control operations, and deal with post-production activities, such as transportation, storage, delivery, and retrieval (reverse logistics) and recycling of used products.

3. Can incentives for proactive environmental strategies be developed? It is doubtful that customers or citizen advocacy groups can or will put enough pressure on organizations to incite significant changes. Increased restrictive legislation is an incentive only to comply; it is unlikely to create positive motivation. The most promise lies in revising existing accounting and performance measurement systems to reflect the realistic costs and benefits of environmental actions in the short and long run. Just as Feigenbaum and Crosby alerted managers to the costs of quality, organizational leaders need an explanation of the costs and risks associated with environmental concerns. Some firms involved in Superfund clean-up projects are getting a fundamental lesson in environmental costs.

4. Can organizations be creative, innovative, and forward-looking? Can more organizations be like the company that now leases carpet instead of selling it so that at the end of its useful life it goes back to the manufacturer to be recycled? If the German recycling regulations find their way into U.S. law, American companies will have many challenges and opportunities to change their old way of doing business.

5. Can organizations find a unifying discipline of environmental consciousness? Much of the progress in organizational quality programs can be traced to the teachings of Deming and Juran and the many who followed them. The environment has had such advocates as Rachel Carson, Jacques Cousteau, and E.F. Schumacher, but their experiences are too far removed from hard-nosed business operations to be of direct help. Al Gore's book, *Earth in the Balance,* is a start, but it probably won't be as influential as Juran's volumes were on quality management. The environmental counterpart to Deming has not yet emerged.

6. Can business leaders develop the strategies that are needed to create environmentally friendly, sustainable organizations? Can the models, approaches, tools, and techniques employed for quality and other efforts be adapted to develop effective environmental programs? Can new methods be created to deal with the unique aspects of environmental management? The simple answer is, Yes, they can. The relevant question is, Will they?

No organization is independent of the environment. Yet each does differ in its effect upon, interaction with, and

---

No organization is independent of the environment.

---

risk posed to the environment. The actions of every organization affect everyone in a closed interdependent ecosystem; therefore, every human being is a stakeholder in every organization—and the stakes are higher than just business success or failure. In this context, "survival" takes on a more ominous meaning.

If a label is needed for the coming era, it can be ECE: Environmentally Conscious Enterprise. Manufacturing, service, government, and not-for-profit organizations that are environmentally conscious must address appropriate environmental concerns in strategies and operating decisions. Such Environmentally Conscious Enterprises:

- Cannot be merely altruistic; they also must be economically motivated so profit-making firms will buy into the concept.
- Cannot be legislated except at the most basic levels. Doing otherwise would be far too complex.
- Must be long-term and broad in scope. The ecosystem does not respond well to short-term local efforts.
- Must be interorganizational to avoid sub-optimization and conflicting objectives.

ECEs will develop core values, criteria for evaluation, and measurement systems for control. This, in turn, will lead to environmental awareness by all members of the organization, and will foster the development of goals and monitoring of progress toward their accomplishment. In other words, ECEs will develop proactive environmental management systems that will eventually become standard business practice.

Environmental management presents many challenges and opportunities. During the next decade, the potential rewards that come with a new way of thinking and operating are great, while the penalties for not being environmentally responsible include irreversible harm not only to the economic system but also to the very quality of life.

Here's how the world auto industry will likely shake out: New economies of scale beef up the big boys, which gobble up less efficient parochial players. So who will be left?

THE GLOBAL
SIX

It was a whirlwind first week on the job for Ford Motor Co.'s new CEO, Jacques Nasser. It began Sunday, Jan. 3, with rumors swirling in snowbound Detroit that cash-flush Ford was about to gobble up one of the world's big auto makers. By Tuesday morning, reporters were calling Nasser at home at 6 a.m. to inquire about a tantalizing but erroneous French radio report that Ford was taking over Honda Motor Co. "By Tuesday evening, we were supposed to be acquiring BMW, Honda, Volvo, Nissan—and there was someone else that I can't remember," quips Nasser.

By week's end, Nasser's every move was being scrutinized for hints as to how he might spend Ford's staggering $23 billion in cash. When he called a press conference for Friday evening's black-tie gala at the Detroit auto show, speculation was rife that he would announce a mega-deal to rival last November's $35 billion DaimlerChrysler merger. "I'm not sure if I should be speaking to you in German, Swedish, or Japa-

nese, the way the rumors have been flying," Nasser told a packed audience of Detroit swells. "I'm really pleased we're so popular." Nasser's only news was that Ford was bringing the Three Tenors to Detroit this summer. No big deal—yet.

But the green flag is flying for motor merger mania, and a dramatic shakeout is at hand. The top players are awash in cash and eager to buy, while the weakest are drowning in debt and glutted with factory capacity: The industry can make 20 million more cars and trucks a year than it sells, while global auto sales could hit a cyclical downturn within three years. What's more, consumers are demanding lower prices and more high-tech gizmos on their cars, forcing carmakers to squeeze costs. The result: Only a quarter of the world's 40 auto makers are profitable. "You're going to see a much more consolidated industry within the next five years," says Schroder & Co. analyst John Casesa. "The faster the global economy turns down, the faster it will happen."

Speeding the auto industry down the road to megamergers is a group of hard-driving bosses with expansive egos and big appetites for acquisition. Volkswagen's Ferdinand Piëch has snapped up European boutique players Rolls Royce and Lamborghini and is believed to have eyes for BMW. Denials aside, Ford's Nasser has at least investigated acquiring Honda and Volvo, and wouldn't mind picking off BMW, too.

MATING DANCE. Toyota's President Hiroshi Okuda, a black belt in judo, is particularly aggressive for a Japanese business leader and has started picking up bargains among Japan's struggling second-tier auto makers. And DaimlerChrysler Co-Chairman Jürgen Schrempp, having engineered a big German-American merger, now says he might be interested in hooking up with Japan's troubled No. 2 carmaker, Nissan. "Who knows, eh?" a smiling Schrempp said, following a Jan. 10 speech in Detroit. "We do not exclude the possibility of equity participation" in Nissan's car business.

Reprinted with special permission from *Business Week*, January 25, 1999, pp. 68-70, 72. © 1999 by The McGraw-Hill Companies, Inc.

Insiders expect the giants to pick up healthy, small brands in Europe, as well as bargains in Asia

He's already talking to Nissan about its heavy-truck business, and a deal could happen by the end of January.

This automotive mating dance is being triggered by cost pressures and cutthroat pricing on top of the overcapacity problem. "The industry lately has been a giant cotillion, with everybody looking for the best partner," says DaimlerChrysler Co-Chairman Robert J. Eaton, who predicts a big European deal this winter, although not involving his company. "Companies will have to rethink their ability to survive alone," he says.

Indeed, it was the stunning merger of Daimler-Benz and Chrysler Corp. that changed the rules of the road. The two prosperous companies saw that by combining they would have a better chance of growing in each other's home markets as well as in Asia. To make it in the high-cost, tech-intense global auto business, carmakers need vast resources and reach. And old national identities are becoming obsolete in a brave new auto world where size matters above all. "The industry landscape will need to change," says Nasser. "For global players to be really competitive, their sales volumes will have to be over 5 million a year." Predicts Toyota's Okuda: "In the next century, there will be only five or six auto makers."

Who will make it into the elite five-million-plus club? So far, only General Motors Corp. and Ford make that mark. But others are knocking on the door. Many industry leaders believe it will only take a decade for the world's 40 auto makers to collapse into the Global Big Six. To be sure, the shakeout will occur in stages, with profitable players such as Porsche or national champions like Renault holding out the longest. But by 2010, the thinking goes, each major auto market will be left with two large home-based companies— GM and Ford in the U.S., Daimler-Chrysler and Volkswagen in Europe, and Toyota and Honda in Japan. Players such as Nissan or Volvo may keep their brand names but won't be running the show.

As the industry reshapes itself, insiders expect the giants to head in two directions: They will seek out healthy but small brands in Europe, while picking up distressed merchandise in Asia. For the top companies, the goal is to establish an all-encompassing global footprint. No auto maker in the world has that now. The Americans and Europeans are mostly minor players in Asia, while the Japanese need a stronger presence in Europe. "The key is finding the right partner, who has complementary products, geography, and a similar philosophy," says auto consultant Christopher Cedergren of Nextrend Inc. in Thousand Oaks, Calif.

Volvo could be the next company to be scooped up. It put itself in play on Jan. 6 by hiring J. P. Morgan to shop its car business. Fiat admits it's talking to Volvo; analysts say the two Europeans could make a good fit. Fiat would gain access to the luxury trade and the U.S. market, while Volvo, which sells less than 400,000 cars a year, would broaden its small base. Fiat needs a boost. With car sales down in its big markets, Italy and Brazil, the Italian company's auto division lost $38 million in the third quarter of 1998, vs. earnings of $245 million the year before.

But even a Fiat-Volvo combination might not be strong enough to survive longer-term, analysts say. Eventually, smaller players would need a big brother. Ford insiders say they are talking to Volvo, too, but they scoff at the $6 billion price tag Volvo's bankers are suggesting. Says one Ford insider: "Their car business is worth $3.5 billion, tops."

ASIAN SALES. Alongside Volvo, Nissan tops the list of rumored takeover targets these days. Japan's once mighty No. 2 player is on the brink because sales have plunged, thanks to lackluster models and economic distress in Japan. Nissan has been playing catch-up to Toyota and

---

GENERAL MOTORS

1998 EARNINGS $2.8 billion*
1998 REVENUE $140 billion
WORLDWIDE VEHICLE SALES
 7.5 million
CASH $16.6 billion
STRATEGY GM is getting its own house in order. But it has found time to take a 49% stake in Japan's Isuzu and a 10% stake in Suzuki. Some speculate GM will rescue South Korea's Daewoo.

FORD MOTOR

1998 EARNINGS $6.7 billion
1998 REVENUE $118 billion
WORLDWIDE VEHICLE SALES
 6.8 million
CASH $23 billion
STRATEGY With a mountain of cash to spend, Ford is the hottest suitor on the global automotive scene. Predicted targets: Volvo, Honda, BMW.

DAIMLERCHRYSLER

1998 EARNINGS $6.47 billion**
1998 REVENUE $147.3 billion**
WORLDWIDE VEHICLE SALES
 4 million
CASH $25 billion
STRATEGY By merging, Daimler-Benz and Chrysler have created a global powerhouse. But it needs a presence in Asia and is already talking to Nissan about a deal.

*Includes one-time charges for restructuring
**Estimates of Daimler-Benz and Chrysler combined results.

Honda since the mid-1980s and now is so debilitated it can no longer afford the same level of investments as its competitors. The auto maker is expected to lose as much as $626 million for the fiscal year ending in March, and is burdened with $22 billion in debt. Rivals says Nissan could be had for about $30 billion.

Nissan's neighbor, Mitsubishi Motors Corp., is in even worse shape. Struggling with $18.5 billion in debt, a bland product line, and recession in its home market, Mitsubishi, like Nissan, needs a white knight. Mitsubishi Motors President Katsuhiko Kawasoe admits he's talking to potential foreign partners, although he declines to discuss them. All the big global players are seen as prospective suitors for Mitsubishi. Daimler-Chrysler heads the list because Chrysler once had a 24% stake in the company and still buys from it.

Others likely to fall quickly include the remaining smaller players in Asia. GM recently increased its sake in Isuzu from 37.5% to 49% and took a bigger chunk of Suzuki—up from 3.3% to 10%. In Korea, meanwhile, Ford attempted to acquire bankrupt Kia Motors Corp. last year but was outbid by Hyundai Motor Co. Now, Hyundai, which piled Kia's $8 billion in debt on top of its own imposing $6.6 billion, is looking to launch discussions with foreign partners. But Ford isn't interested in bailing out Hyundai. "We're not going to do that," comments Henry D. G. Wallace, Ford's group vice-president for Asia-Pacific operations.

FORCES BEHIND THE RACE TO MERGE

OVERCAPACITY More than 20 million units of manufacturing overcapacity, plus downward pressure on prices are forcing auto makers to slash costs and swallow rivals.

TECHNOLOGY Auto giants want to amortize heavy research and development investment in new high-tech features over a greater number of cars.

CASH The industry's biggest players have more than $100 billion in cash for deals, while smaller, less profitable players are seeking suitors. Europeans and Americans also have lofty share prices that allow them to swallow up smaller companies.

CULTURE Nationalism is declining in Europe as the new single currency spurs companies to compete, while in Asia economic crisis is compelling companies to consider foreign partnerships as never before.

DATA: BUSINESS WEEK

Over time, the biggest predators in Asia are likely to be Japanese giants. With $23 billion in cash, Toyota has as much money to spend as Ford. For now, the company is preoccupied with restructuring at home. It is considering creating a holding company that would make it far easier to streamline its vast operations—as well as merge with other auto makers. Toyota already owns stakes in Daihatsu and Hino.

While Honda lacks Toyota's cash, it is blessed with strong growth—particularly in the U.S., where its 1998 sales topped 1 million vehicles for the first time ever. To make it into the Big Six, Honda needs to double its worldwide sales. Japan's No. 3 auto maker wants to go it alone. But with strong

profits, the company is positioned to chart an independent future.

Compared to Asian players, Europe's smaller auto makers are likely to hold on more fiercely to their independence. So while the industry remake may be just as profound, the drama is not likely to unfold overnight. That's partly because of government stakes in companies such as Renault, and the opposition to job cutbacks that could accompany mergers. "You would have to see Europe facing economic recession or crisis before it merges volume-car manufacturers," says John Lawson, auto analyst at Salomon Smith Barney in London.

Indeed, analysts believe Fiat can prolong its independence if it can ac-

VOLKSWAGEN

1998 EARNINGS $1.3 billion
1998 REVENUE $75 billion
WORLDWIDE VEHICLE SALES 4.58 million
CASH $12.4 billion
STRATEGY VW has already acquired Rolls Royce, Bugatti, and Lamborghini. Hard-driving Piëch is often rumored to be eyeing BMW and Volvo, which itself is in talks with Fiat.

TOYOTA MOTOR

1998 EARNINGS $4 billion
1998 REVENUE $106 billion
WORLDWIDE VEHICLE SALES 4.45 million
CASH $23 billion
STRATEGY Toyota wants to strengthen its hold on Japanese auto maker Daihatsu Motor, truckmaker Hino Motors, and affiliated parts suppliers like Denso.

HONDA MOTOR

1998 EARNINGS $2.4 billion
1998 REVENUE $54 billion
WORLDWIDE VEHICLE SALES 2.34 million
CASH $3 billion
STRATEGY Honda must grow bigger if it is to make it into the Big Six. Honda insists it wants to go it alone. But joining forces with luxury carmaker BMW could result in a dream team.

DATA: MERRILL LYNCH & CO., SCHRODER & CO., SALOMON SMITH BARNEY, J.P. MORGAN, WASSERSTEIN PERLLA, COMPANY REPORTS

quire Volvo without taking on too much debt. And Renault is developing breakthrough products such as the Mégane Scenic compact minivan, which was a hot seller in Western Europe in 1998. CEO Louis Schweitzer aims to double Renault's sales over the next decade—a goal that could allow it to survive on its own.

TARGET: BMW. But a reckoning in Europe could be not far down the road. The emergence of a single currency is changing the rules of competition. Under European Union plans to liberalize its markets, foreign auto makers will gain unfettered access to Europe at yearend. An expected onslaught of Japanese competition could highlight the inefficiencies of Europe's smaller players. "Europe will become a battleground," predicts Furman Selz auto analyst Maryann Keller. "The Japanese are getting themselves ready to do in Europe what they did in the United States." Eventually, many observers believe, the battle will force Europe's smaller players to succumb.

The juiciest European target for the likes of Volkswagen or Ford would be BMW. The profitable brand would help these mass marketers move upscale. BMW made $624 million last year, but sells only 1.2 million cars worldwide. The Munich maker of luxury sedans is struggling to profit from its $1.3 billion acquisition of Britain's Rover Group Ltd. in 1994. Since then, the German company has invested $3.5 billion in Rover. Now, it must decide between investing the billions needed to develop a new line of front-wheel-drive cars for Rover, or seeking a partner to help.

Such a partnership—perhaps with Ford—could open the door to acquisition, but only if the Quandt family, which owns 47% of BMW, would give way to new ownership. For now, there's no sign of that. On Jan. 11, Heinrich Heitmann, BMW's North America chairman, declared in Detroit that his company will still be standing alone in five years.

But going it alone will get more expensive. The biggest wheels in the auto industry have already begun playing by the costly new rules. Advances in computer-aided design now allow them to develop vastly different models from one basic chassis. Consider three of Ford's newest models—the sexy $45,000 Jaguar S-type luxury car, the $30,000 Lincoln LS sedan, and the retro, reinvented Ford Thunderbird, which is expected to sell for $35,000. Each is built off the same roughly $3 billion platform, code-named DEW98, but they couldn't look more different. Thanks to breakthroughs in manufacturing technology, hot models race to market in 14½ months—one-third of what it took a few years ago.

For the strongest and richest auto makers, these are giddy times. Amid the feeding frenzy of rumors at the Detroit auto show, Ford's Nasser couldn't help but sound like a man intent on building a global empire. "We already have a Japanese brand and two very British brands," said the Lebanese-born Nasser, who was raised in Australia and speaks four languages. "We've got the ability to absorb and really be quite comfortable with a lot of different cultures." No doubt. But the question is: Who will Ford, and the industry's other big wheels, absorb next?

By Keith Naughton with Karen Lowry Miller and Joann Muller in Detroit, Emily Thornton in Tokyo, Gail Edmondson in Paris, and bureau reports

FIRST:

THE AUTOMAKERS:

More Mergers. Dumb Idea.

BY ALEX TAYLOR III

Remember *The Reckoning,* David Halberstam's weighty 1986 bestseller that celebrated the success of Nissan and other Japanese automakers? Halberstam attributed their rise to cultural spirit, fierce domestic competition, and a "demonic need for excellence." In retrospect, he should have added cheap money, closed markets, and a rigged economy. Despite all those advantages, however, Nissan has

repeatedly faltered, losing money year after year and accumulating $24 billion in debt. Now the company has essentially put itself up for sale by saying it will accept a capital infusion from a foreign automaker. It identified its preferred partners as Ford Motor, DaimlerChrysler, and France's Renault.

Nissan may have stumbled before, but its timing here is impeccable. The global auto industry has become in- fected with a virulent case of merger madness in the wake of the linkup between Daimler-Benz and Chrysler last year. Everyone is worried that the con-

solidation predicted for 20 years has finally begun, and no one wants to be left behind. Ford CEO Jacques Nasser says he's interested in buying another automaker as long as the price is right, while Daimler-Chrysler chairman Robert Eaton predicts that two major European auto companies will join forces "in the next 90 days." In addition to Nissan and its suitors, Honda, BMW, Fiat, and Volvo have been the subject of merger rumors.

It all sounds plausible. Other industries—oil, banking, telecommunications—are consolidating, and autos would merely be accelerating a process that began 65 years ago. But on second look, the urge to merge looks more hysterical than rational. "I do not think there is any logical, economic, or strategic reason why only five to ten giant automakers need to survive in the world," says Takahiro Fujimoto, an economics professor at Tokyo University and a member of MIT's International Motor Vehicle Program.

Nissan is a case in point. At first glance, it makes an attractive partner because it provides an opening into the growth markets of mainland Asia. But putting a Japanese company together with a Western one would create a welter of cultural and linguistic problems that could make hash of any attempt at cooperation. Even after installing its own top executive team, Ford has needed several years to straighten out Mazda, and Nissan would be a much harder case. It is larger, older, more bureaucratic, and infinitely more complex, with dozens

Reprinted from the February 15, 1999, issue of *Fortune*, pp. 26-27, by special permission. © 1999 by Time, Inc.

of subsidiaries whose finances are intertwined with the parent company's.

Four arguments are usually put forth to justify the industry's supposedly inevitable consolidation into (pick a number) six, eight, or ten global megacompanies. Let's take them one at a time:

"There are too many companies": DaimlerChrysler's Eaton likes to observe that of the 40 auto companies in the world today, only about ten make money and perhaps just half of those earn back their cost of capital. Are all those companies needed? Probably not. If the U.S. has three automakers, why does Japan need nine? But auto companies

THE AUTO INDUSTRY HAS GONE ON MERGER BINGES BEFORE, AND THEY'VE ENDED BADLY.

are like cockroaches: they are hard to kill. Nobody wants to buy the weak ones, especially because many of them are in even worse straits than their annual reports suggest. Remember, national governments coddle carmakers because they provide jobs and reflect civic pride. You'll recall how the U.S. government guaranteed a $1.5 billion loan for Chrysler in 1980. Logically, France can't support both Renault and Peugeot/Citroen, two automakers whose product ranges and markets overlap, but they are important sources of employment, and France's government isn't about to let them fail.

"Merging can cure overcapacity": Excess production capability has become the industry's bogeyman, the all-purpose explanation for skimpy profit margins. But overcapacity has been a fact of life in the auto industry for decades. Except for unusual periods such as immediately after World War II, capacity has always exceeded utilization because auto companies want to meet demand during peak periods. Excess capacity has remained relatively steady at about 25% of total production capability, and mergers don't always reduce it; they often only put it under one roof instead of two.

"Size means success": Adding volume through mergers is a good way to spread research and engineering costs, but it ignores the advantages of agility and focus. Honda and BMW are only a fraction of General Motors' size, but that hasn't prevented them from handily outperforming the General for the past 20 years. Put two lumbering companies together, and you get one that runs worse, not better.

"Global equals growth": Despite their financial collapse, markets in Asia and Latin America are considered the Holy Grail because they contain millions of new customers. But there are other ways to reach those markets besides buying a local producer. Fiat has a strong presence in Latin America, while Mitsubishi is powerful in southeast Asia. By working out joint production and distribution agreements, the two companies could deploy their complementary strengths without the nuisance of a full-fledged merger.

The auto industry went on a merger binge in the late 1980s, with unhappy results. Saab has been a consistent money-loser since GM bought a half interest, and Jaguar cost Ford some $5 billion before it turned profitable. Chrysler bought and then sold Lamborghini and Maserati in quick succession.

This time the companies are bigger, but the prospects are no more promising, with one exception: Sweden's Volvo. Smaller even than BMW, it has neither the technical resources nor the brand power to remain successful for the long term. Ford is a frequently mentioned suitor, but the two companies overlap geographically and Volvo adds little to Ford's brand portfolio. A more likely partner is Italy's Fiat, which could benefit from Volvo's strength in northern Europe and the U.S. Something appears to be in the wind: According to the latest reports, both Ford and Fiat have made bids for Volvo. One question they'll have to answer: Can Swedes work better with Italians or Americans?

THE NUMBERS

The FORTUNE Business Confidence Index

Despite Brazil's recent woes, the FORTUNE Business Confidence Index rose for the third month in a row, hitting 124 in mid-January. This is well above the low of 67 last October, although it's still far from the index's year-ago level of 152. Mirroring Fed Chairman Alan Greenspan's recent comments that the economy performed "in an outstanding manner" through year-end, chief financial officers appear more confident about growth, despite the dim prospects for any further interest-rate cuts. Some 61% of CFOs said they were confident about the economic situation for the next couple of years.

Regarding their own businesses, 74% of CFOs said business is good or very good. Still, four out of ten CFOs remain cautious in such business policies as capital budgeting and advertising, with only 28% saying that they are aggressive.

– Lenore Schiff

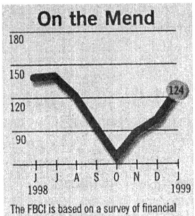

On the Mend

The FBCI is based on a survey of financial executives at FORTUNE 1,000 companies. The index is compiled from responses to a series of questions about business conditions.

AE Article Review Form

We encourage you to photocopy and use this page as a tool to assess how the articles in **Annual Editions** expand on the information in your textbook. By reflecting on the articles you will gain enhanced text information. You can also access this useful form on a product's book support Web site at ***http://www.dushkin.com/ online/.***

NAME: _____ DATE: _____

TITLE AND NUMBER OF ARTICLE: _____

BRIEFLY STATE THE MAIN IDEA OF THIS ARTICLE: _____

LIST THREE IMPORTANT FACTS THAT THE AUTHOR USES TO SUPPORT THE MAIN IDEA:

WHAT INFORMATION OR IDEAS DISCUSSED IN THIS ARTICLE ARE ALSO DISCUSSED IN YOUR TEXTBOOK OR OTHER READINGS THAT YOU HAVE DONE? LIST THE TEXTBOOK CHAPTERS AND PAGE NUMBERS:

LIST ANY EXAMPLES OF BIAS OR FAULTY REASONING THAT YOU FOUND IN THE ARTICLE:

LIST ANY NEW TERMS/CONCEPTS THAT WERE DISCUSSED IN THE ARTICLE, AND WRITE A SHORT DEFINITION:

ANNUAL EDITIONS revisions depend on two major opinion sources: one is our Advisory Board, listed in the front of this volume, which works with us in scanning the thousands of articles published in the public press each year; the other is you—the person actually using the book. Please help us and the users of the next edition by completing the prepaid article rating form on this page and returning it to us. Thank you for your help!

ANNUAL EDITIONS: Production and Operations Management 00/01

ARTICLE RATING FORM

Here is an opportunity for you to have direct input into the next revision of this volume. We would like you to rate each of the 45 articles listed below, using the following scale:

1. Excellent: should definitely be retained
2. Above average: should probably be retained
3. Below average: should probably be deleted
4. Poor: should definitely be deleted

Your ratings will play a vital part in the next revision. So please mail this prepaid form to us just as soon as you complete it. Thanks for your help!

RATING   **ARTICLE**

1. An Empirical Assessment of the Production/Operations Manager's Job
2. Reengineer or Perish
3. The Perceived Impact of the Benchmarking Process on Organizational Effectiveness
4. Putting Commitment to Work through Short-Cycle Kaizen
5. Rally of the Dolls: It Worked for Toyota. Can It Work for Toys?
6. Fly, Damn It, Fly
7. Evolution of the Quality Profession
8. Fool Proof Service: Poka-Yoke
9. A Conversation with Joseph Juran
10. One More Time: Eight Things You Should Remember about Quality
11. ISO 9000 Myth and Reality: A Reasonable Approach to ISO 9000
12. Whatever Happened to TQM? Or, How a Good Strategy Got a Bad Reputation
13. Critical Implementation Issues in Total Quality Management
14. Relying on the Power of People at Saturn
15. The Million-Dollar Suggestion Box
16. Tellers Who Hustle
17. How Mirage Resorts Sifted 75,000 Applicants to Hire 9,600 in 24 Weeks
18. The Legal Limitations to Self-Directed Work Teams in Production Planning and Control
19. How Great Machines Are Born
20. Managing the New Product Development Process: Strategic Imperatives
21. Bringing Discipline to Project Management
22. Seven Keys to Better Forecasting

RATING   **ARTICLE**

23. Airlines May Be Flying in the Face of Reality
24. Is It the Sunshine?
25. No Fizz in the Profits
26. Pulling Customers Closer through Logistics Service
27. Improving Shop Floor Operations through Production Sequencing at EMC Technology
28. Changes in Performance Measures on the Factory Floor
29. Using Queueing Network Models to Set Lot-Sizing Policies for Printed Circuit Board Assembly Operations
30. Checking In Under Marriott's First Ten Program
31. An Examination of Inventory Turnover in the Fortune 500 Industrial Companies
32. The Ultimate Goal: Balancing Inventory & Service Levels
33. Just-In-Time Manufacturing
34. JIT Implementation: A Case Study
35. Tailored Just-In-Time and MRP Systems in Carpet Manufacturing
36. Implementing JIT/MRP in a PCB Manufacturer
37. The Critical Importance of Master Production Scheduling
38. Does Your Supply Chain System Measure Up?
39. GM: Modular Plants Won't Be a Snap
40. Electronics Manufacturing: A Well-Integrated IT Approach
41. Are You Ready for the E-Supply Chain?
42. Digital Denim
43. Three Decades of Progress: Productivity, Quality, Environment
44. The Global Six
45. The Automakers: More Mergers. Dumb Idea

(Continued on next page)

We Want Your Advice

**ANNUAL EDITIONS: PRODUCTION AND OPERATIONS
MANAGEMENT 00/01**

NO POSTAGE
NECESSARY
IF MAILED
IN THE
UNITED STATES

BUSINESS REPLY MAIL
FIRST-CLASS MAIL PERMIT NO. 84 GUILFORD CT

POSTAGE WILL BE PAID BY ADDRESSEE

**Dushkin/McGraw-Hill
Sluice Dock
Guilford, CT 06437-9989**

ABOUT YOU

Name _____ Date _____

Are you a teacher? ☐ A student? ☐
Your school's name _____

Department _____

Address _____ City _____ State _____ Zip _____

School telephone # _____

YOUR COMMENTS ARE IMPORTANT TO US!

Please fill in the following information:
For which course did you use this book?
_____

Did you use a text with this *ANNUAL EDITION*? ☐ yes ☐ no
What was the title of the text?
_____

What are your general reactions to the *Annual Editions* concept?
_____

Have you read any particular articles recently that you think should be included in the next edition?
_____

Are there any articles you feel should be replaced in the next edition? Why?
_____

Are there any World Wide Web sites you feel should be included in the next edition? Please annotate.
_____

May we contact you for editorial input? ☐ yes ☐ no
May we quote your comments? ☐ yes ☐ no
_____